WITHDRAWN

Green Lantern

THE SINESTRO CORPS WAR
volume two

Geoff Johns   Dave Gibbons   Peter J. Tomasi
Writers

Patrick Gleason   Angel Unzueta   Ivan Reis   Pascal Alixe
Dustin Nguyen   Jamal Igle   Ethan Van Sciver
Pencillers

Prentis Rollins   Drew Geraci   Vicente Cifuentes   Oclair Albert
Julio Ferreira   Rodney Ramos   Rob Hunter   Marlo Alquiza
Jerry Ordway   Rod Reis   Derek Fridolfs   Tom Nguyen
Drew Geraci   Dan Davis   Rebecca Buchman
Inkers

Guy Major   Moose Baumann   Rod Reis   David Curiel   JD Smith
Colorists

Phil Balsman   Rob Leigh   Steve Wands   Nick J. Napolitano
Letterers

DC COMICS

Dan DiDio Senior VP-Executive Editor
Eddie Berganza Editor-original series
Adam Schlagman Assistant Editor-original series
Bob Joy Editor-collected edition
Robbin Brosterman Senior Art Director
Paul Levitz President & Publisher
Georg Brewer VP-Design & DC Direct Creative
Richard Bruning Senior VP-Creative Director
Patrick Caldon Executive VP-Finance & Operations
Chris Caramalis VP-Finance
John Cunningham VP-Marketing
Terri Cunningham VP-Managing Editor
Alison Gill VP-Manufacturing
David Hyde VP-Publicity
Hank Kanalz VP-General Manager, WildStorm
Jim Lee Editorial Director-WildStorm
Paula Lowitt Senior VP-Business & Legal Affairs
MaryEllen McLaughlin VP-Advertising & Custom Publishing
John Nee Senior VP-Business Development
Gregory Noveck Senior VP-Creative Affairs
Sue Pohja VP-Book Trade Sales
Steve Rotterdam Senior VP-Sales & Marketing
Cheryl Rubin Senior VP-Brand Management
Jeff Trojan VP-Business Development, DC Direct
Bob Wayne VP-Sales

Cover art by Ivan Reis, Oclair Albert and Moose Baumann.

GREEN LANTERN: THE SINESTRO CORPS WAR
Volume 2

DC Comics, 1700 Broadway, New York, NY 10019
A Warner Bros. Entertainment Company
Printed by Quad/Graphics, Dubuque, IA. USA. 12/01/2010
Fourth Printing.

ISBN: 978-1-4012-2036-5

SUSTAINABLE FORESTRY INITIATIVE

Certified Chain of Custody
Promoting Sustainable
Forest Management

www.sfiprogram.org

THE STORY SO FAR...

Once hailed as the greatest of the Green Lanterns, Sinestro was expelled from the ranks of this intergalactic police force when his pupil Hal Jordan discovered how he kept his space sector in line: with fear. Sinestro has waged war against the Green Lantern Corps and its founders, the Guardians of the Universe, ever since—but it is no longer a one-man war.

On the antimatter-universe planet of Qward, Sinestro creates thousands of yellow power rings like his own, powered by fear just as the Green Lanterns' rings are fueled by willpower. They are wielded by the universe's most frightening beings, and together this Sinestro Corps will create a new universal order of absolute obedience—and abject terror.

When one of these rings is captured by former Green Lantern Kyle Rayner—now host to the awesome power of Ion—it escapes and kidnaps him, bringing him to the Sinestro Corps's headquarters on Qward.

Meanwhile, on the planet Oa the Lanterns' home base is ambushed by Sinestro's forces. They free the Lanterns' most dangerous prisoners: the indestructible man-machine Cyborg-Superman, grandmaster of the relentless robotic Manhunters; the insane alternate-universe Kryptonian Superman-Prime; and the ancient fear entity Parallax. Dozens of Green Lanterns are slain in the process.

On Qward, Sinestro reveals to Kyle that the source of his Ion powers is itself a living entity, an embodiment of willpower akin to Parallax. After removing Ion from within Kyle, Sinestro tells the Earthling that his mother's death was in fact murder at the hands of Despotellis, a sentient virus and member of the Sinestro Corps. Paralyzed with fear, Kyle falls prey to Parallax, which takes possession of him as it once did Hal Jordan.

Sinestro, Parallax, Superman-Prime and Cyborg-Superman together take their place as heralds of their secret Guardian: The Anti-Monitor, a terrifying being who once destroyed the Multiverse and, now reborn with the Multiverse's recent re-creation, seeks to feed upon all of existence once more.

The Sinestro Corps then attacks Mogo, the sentient planet who guides the Green Lanterns' power rings to new recruits. Their main weapons against Mogo are the living city Ranx and the telepathic suicide-bombers the Children of the White Lobe.

While the majority of the Green Lanterns, led by drill sergeant Kilowog and maverick rookie Sodam Yat, defend Mogo, a small contingent of Lost Lanterns—Corpsmen attacked by Hal Jordan during his Parallax possession—head to Qward to rescue Ion. Reluctantly joining forces with Jordan, they free both the Ion entity and captured Lanterns John Stewart and Guy Gardner—but not before losing beloved comrades to the new Parallax and the Anti-Monitor.

Jordan, Stewart and Gardner flee to Earth to seek reinforcements from the Justice League of America, while the Lost Lanterns escort Ion back to Oa—the center of the universe—which they believe will be the Sinestro Corps's main point of attack.

In the council of the Guardians, wise Ganthet and his female counterpart Sayd warn that this war is the first sign of an ancient apocalyptic prophecy from the Forbidden Chapter of the sacred Book of Oa: The Blackest Night. The Guardians banish Ganthet and Sayd from the council for their heresy and rewrite the Book of Oa with ten new laws, the first of which enables the Lanterns to use lethal force.

Sinestro transports his Yellow Central Power Battery to the mechanized planet Warworld, built by Cyborg-Superman in exchange for the promise that the Anti-Monitor will grant him the death he has long sought. **The Sinestro Corps then pilots Warworld to their true target: the center of the Multiverse—Earth!**

GREEN LANTERN CORPS 16
Patrick Gleason
Tom Nguyen
Moose Baumann

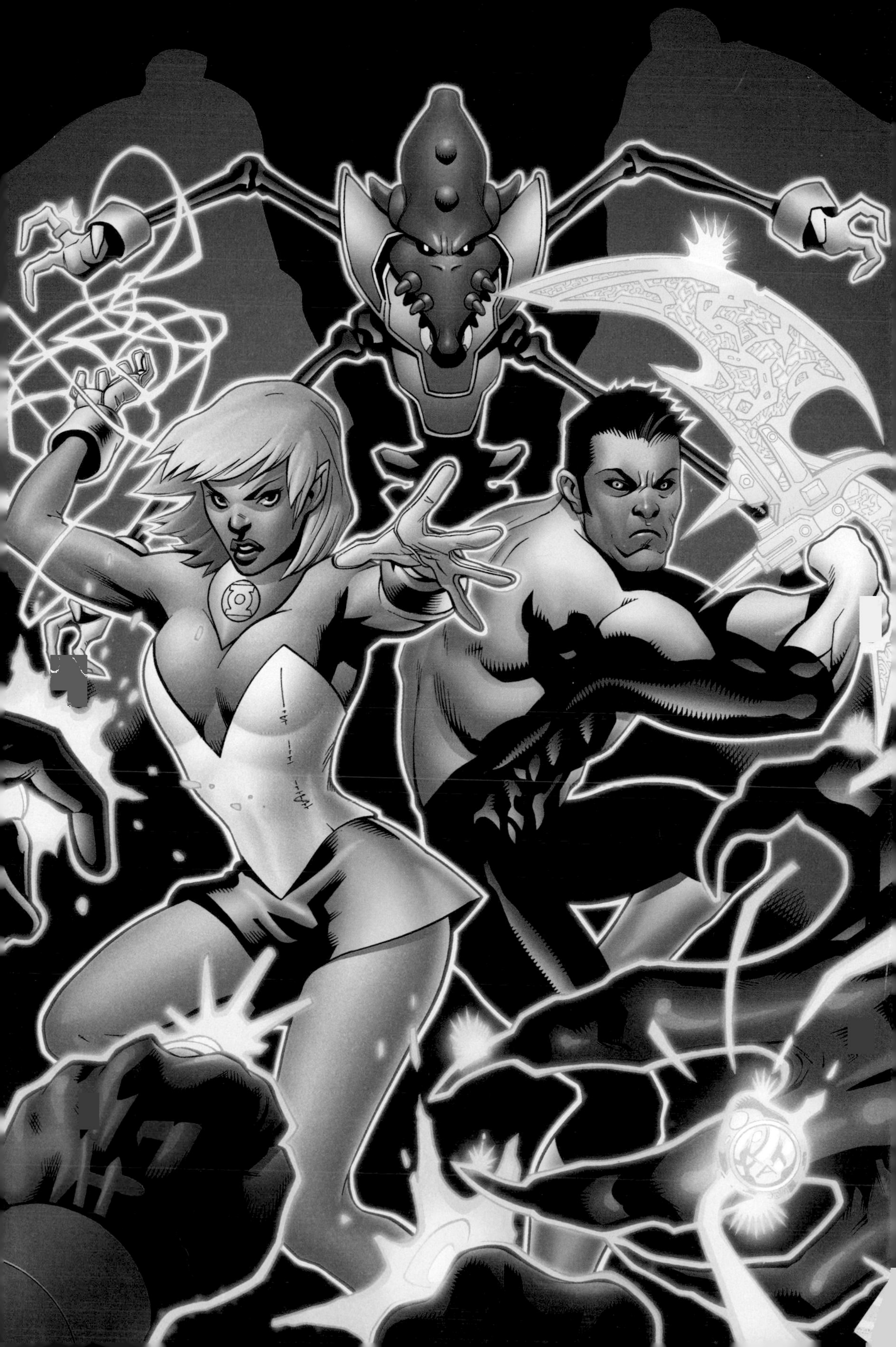

THE SINESTRO CORPS WAR
Chapter Six
THE BATTLE OF RANX
Writer: **Dave Gibbons**
Pencillers: **Patrick Gleason** and **Angel Unzueta**
Inkers: **Prentis Rollins, Drew Geraci** and **Vicente Cifuentes**
Colorist: **Guy Major**

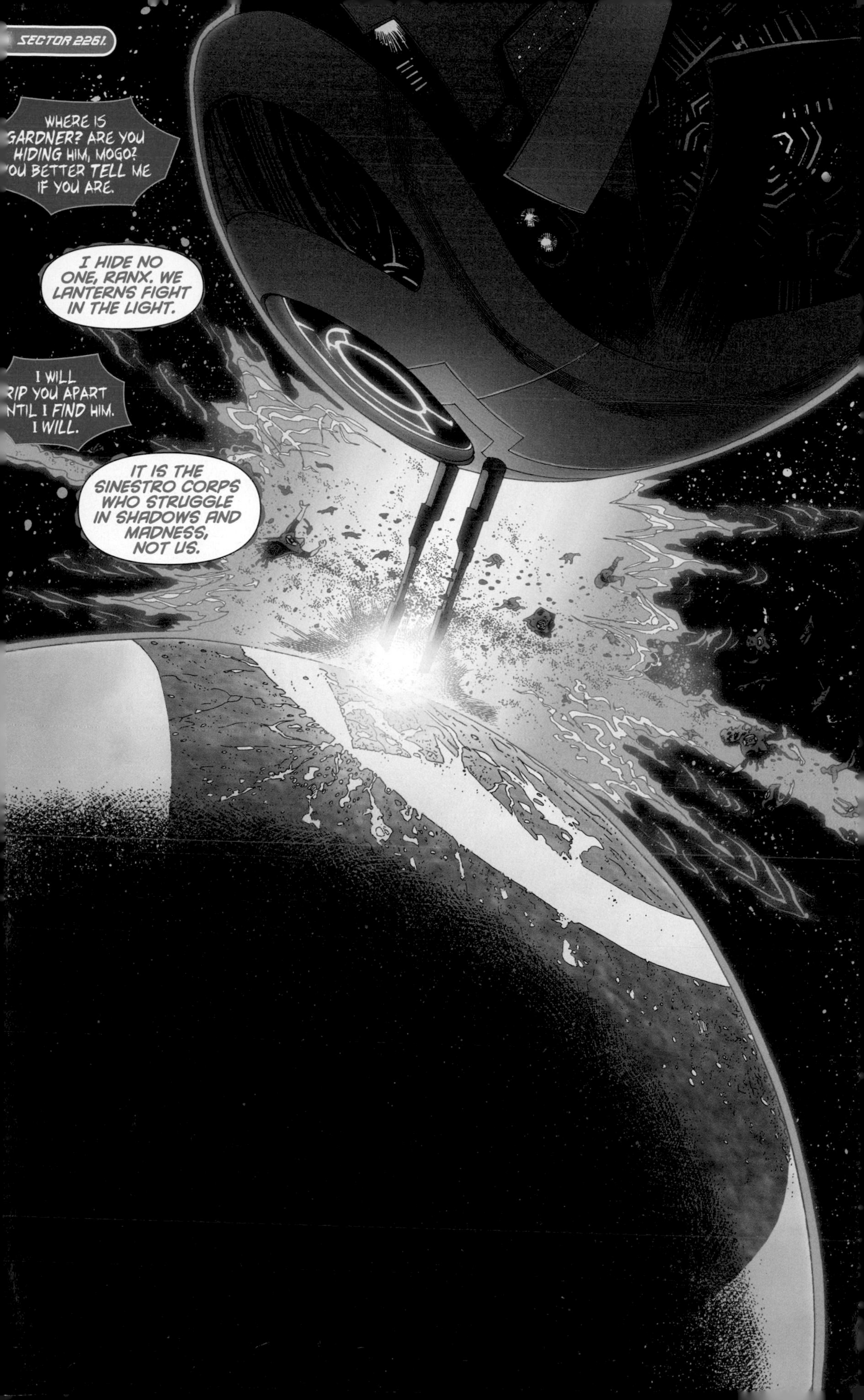
SECTOR 2261.
WHERE IS GARDNER? ARE YOU HIDING HIM, MOGO? YOU BETTER TELL ME IF YOU ARE.
I HIDE NO ONE, RANX. WE LANTERNS FIGHT IN THE LIGHT.
I WILL RIP YOU APART UNTIL I FIND HIM. I WILL.
IT IS THE SINESTRO CORPS WHO STRUGGLE IN SHADOWS AND MADNESS, NOT US.

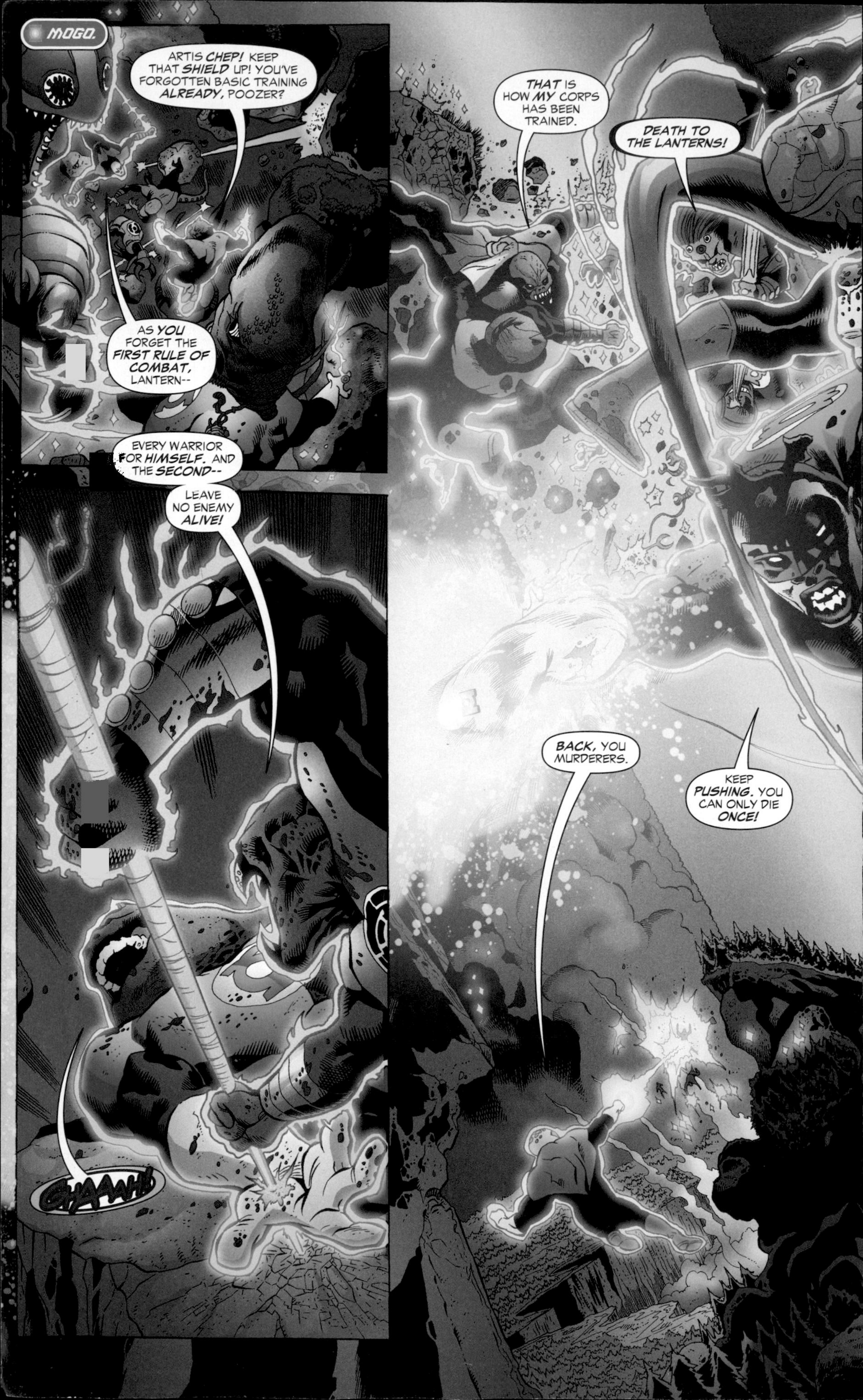
MOGO.
ARTIS CHEP! KEEP THAT SHIELD UP! YOU'VE FORGOTTEN BASIC TRAINING ALREADY, POOZER?
AS YOU FORGET THE FIRST RULE OF COMBAT, LANTERN--
EVERY WARRIOR FOR HIMSELF. AND THE SECOND--
LEAVE NO ENEMY ALIVE!
GHAAAH!
THAT IS HOW MY CORPS HAS BEEN TRAINED.
DEATH TO THE LANTERNS!
BACK, YOU MURDERERS.
KEEP PUSHING. YOU CAN ONLY DIE ONCE!

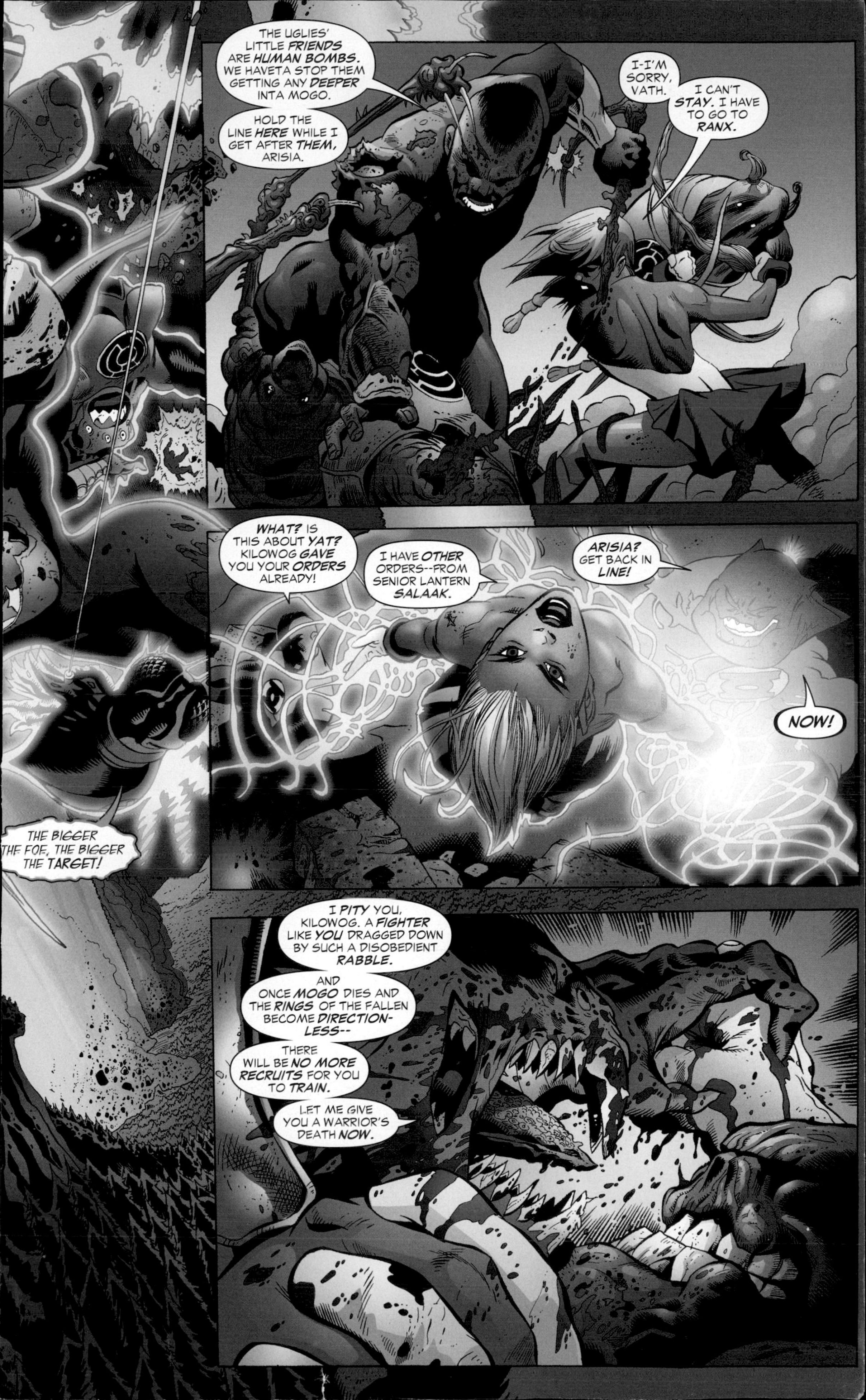

THE UGLIES' LITTLE FRIENDS ARE HUMAN BOMBS. WE HAVETA STOP THEM GETTING ANY DEEPER INTA MOGO.
HOLD THE LINE HERE WHILE I GET AFTER THEM, ARISIA.
I-I'M SORRY, VATH.
I CAN'T STAY. I HAVE TO GO TO RANX.
WHAT? IS THIS ABOUT YAT? KILOWOG GAVE YOU YOUR ORDERS ALREADY!
I HAVE OTHER ORDERS--FROM SENIOR LANTERN SALAAK.
ARISIA? GET BACK IN LINE!
NOW!
THE BIGGER THE FOE, THE BIGGER THE TARGET!
I PITY YOU, KILOWOG. A FIGHTER LIKE YOU DRAGGED DOWN BY SUCH A DISOBEDIENT RABBLE.
AND ONCE MOGO DIES AND THE RINGS OF THE FALLEN BECOME DIRECTION-LESS--
THERE WILL BE NO MORE RECRUITS FOR YOU TO TRAIN.
LET ME GIVE YOU A WARRIOR'S DEATH NOW.

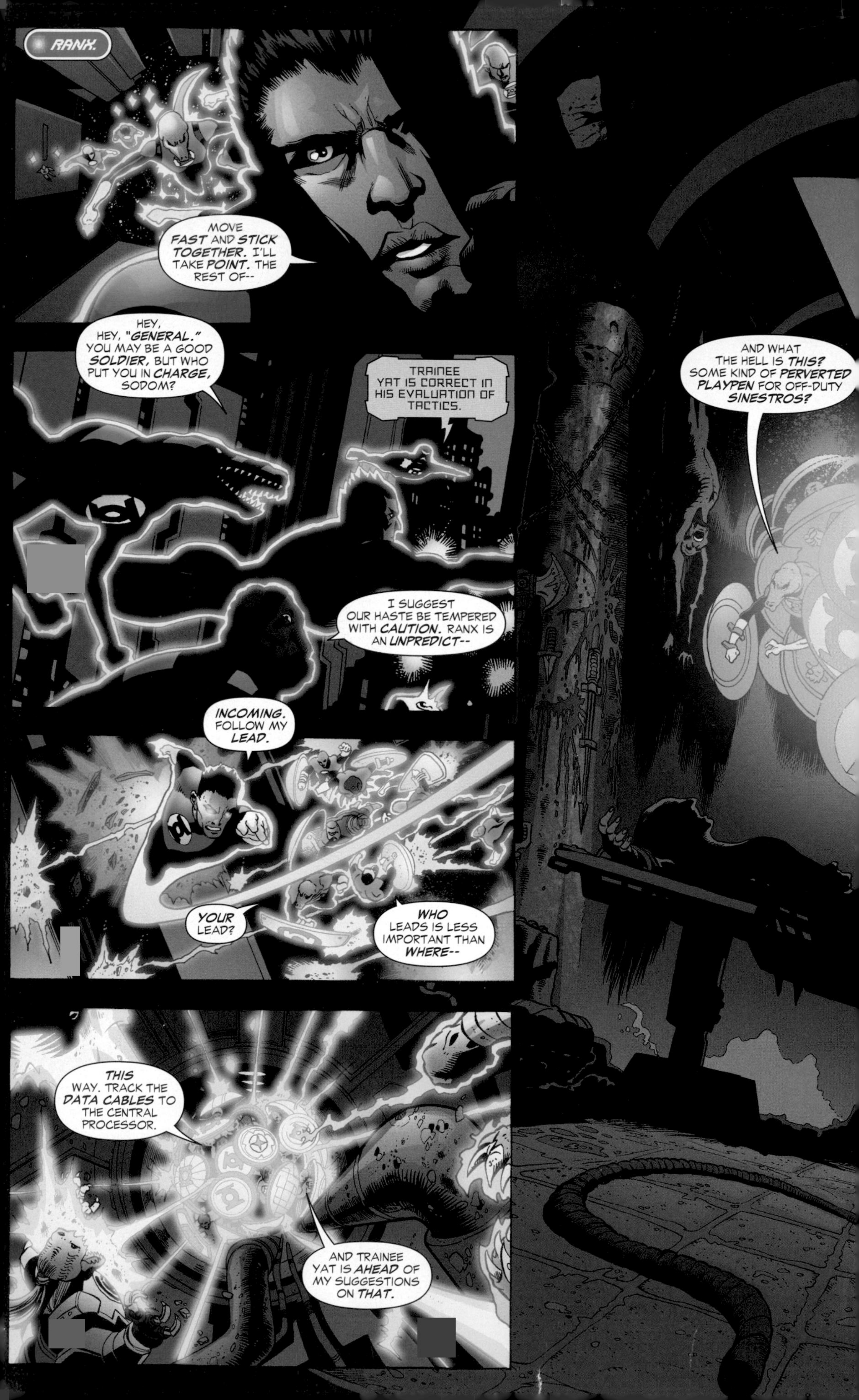
RANX.
MOVE FAST AND STICK TOGETHER. I'LL TAKE POINT. THE REST OF--
HEY, HEY, "GENERAL." YOU MAY BE A GOOD SOLDIER, BUT WHO PUT YOU IN CHARGE, SODOM?
TRAINEE YAT IS CORRECT IN HIS EVALUATION OF TACTICS.
I SUGGEST OUR HASTE BE TEMPERED WITH CAUTION. RANX IS AN UNPREDICT--
INCOMING. FOLLOW MY LEAD.
YOUR LEAD?
WHO LEADS IS LESS IMPORTANT THAN WHERE--
THIS WAY. TRACK THE DATA CABLES TO THE CENTRAL PROCESSOR.
AND TRAINEE YAT IS AHEAD OF MY SUGGESTIONS ON THAT.
AND WHAT THE HELL IS THIS? SOME KIND OF PERVERTED PLAYPEN FOR OFF-DUTY SINESTROS?

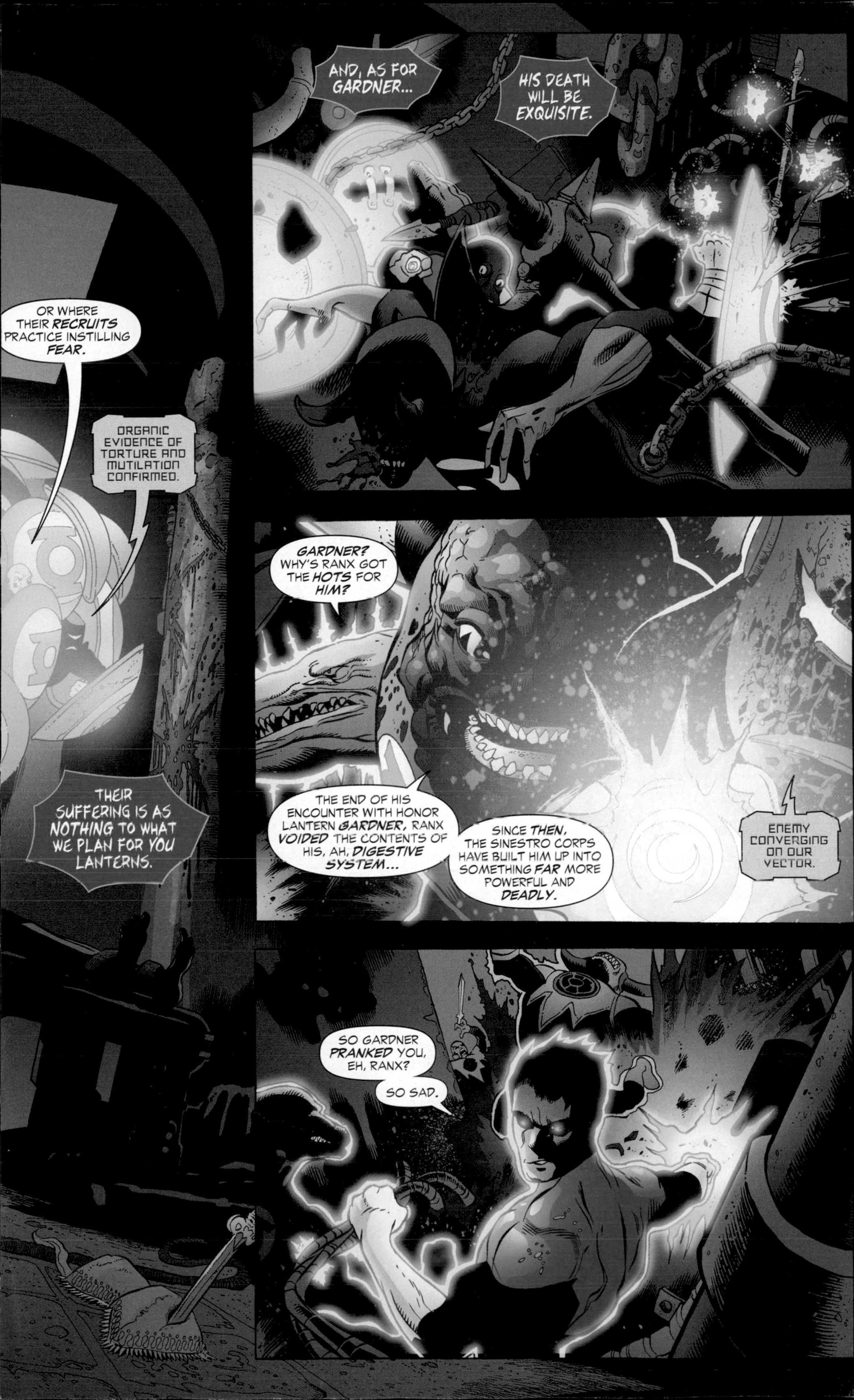
AND, AS FOR GARDNER...
HIS DEATH WILL BE EXQUISITE.
OR WHERE THEIR RECRUITS PRACTICE INSTILLING FEAR.
ORGANIC EVIDENCE OF TORTURE AND MUTILATION CONFIRMED.
GARDNER? WHY'S RANX GOT THE HOTS FOR HIM?
THE END OF HIS ENCOUNTER WITH HONOR LANTERN GARDNER, RANX VOIDED THE CONTENTS OF HIS, AH, DIGESTIVE SYSTEM...
SINCE THEN, THE SINESTRO CORPS HAVE BUILT HIM UP INTO SOMETHING FAR MORE POWERFUL AND DEADLY.
ENEMY CONVERGING ON OUR VECTOR.
THEIR SUFFERING IS AS NOTHING TO WHAT WE PLAN FOR YOU LANTERNS.
SO GARDNER PRANKED YOU, EH, RANX?
SO SAD.

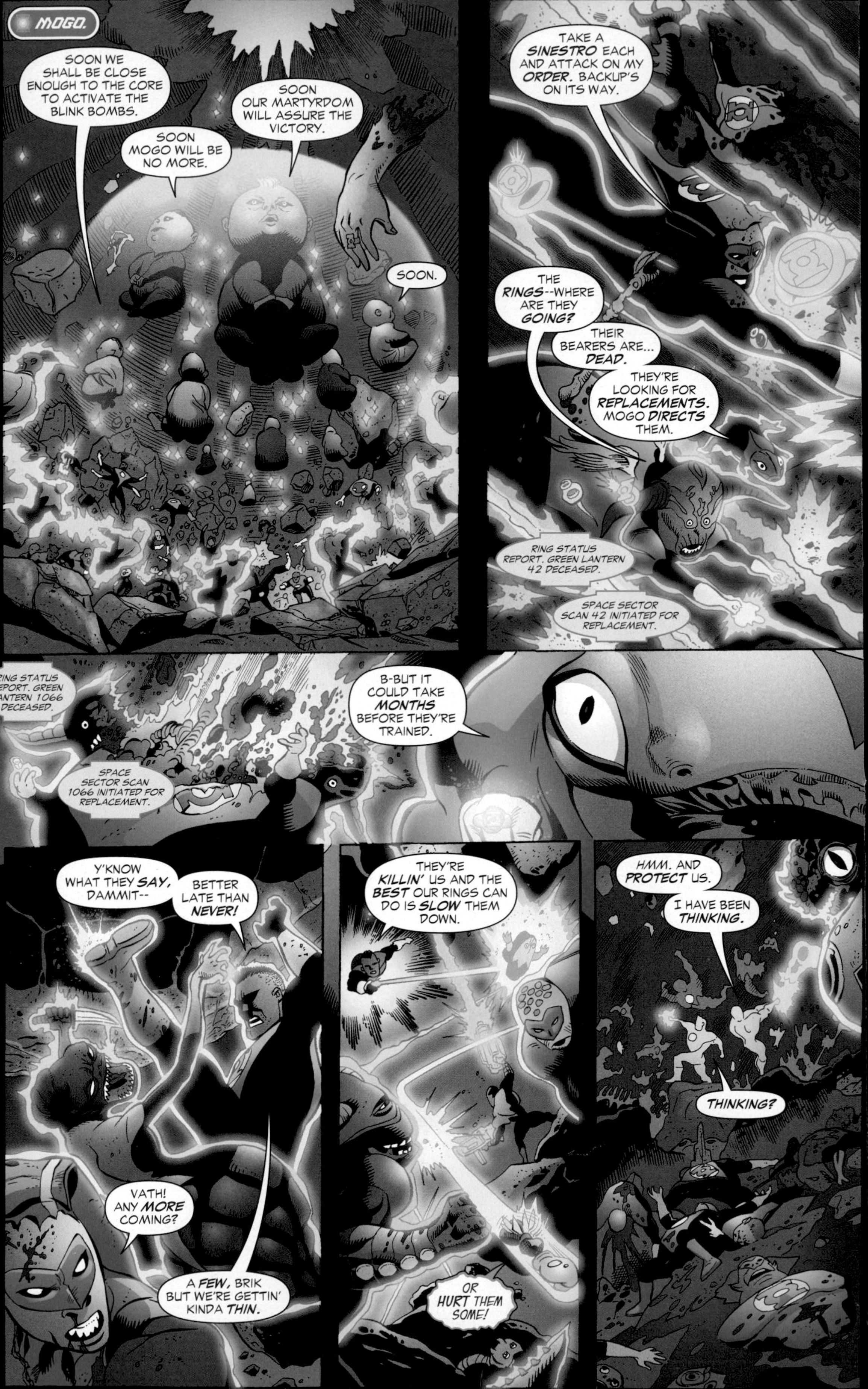
MOGO.
SOON WE SHALL BE CLOSE ENOUGH TO THE CORE TO ACTIVATE THE BLINK BOMBS.
SOON MOGO WILL BE NO MORE.
SOON OUR MARTYRDOM WILL ASSURE THE VICTORY.
SOON.
TAKE A SINESTRO EACH AND ATTACK ON MY ORDER. BACKUP'S ON ITS WAY.
THE RINGS--WHERE ARE THEY GOING?
THEIR BEARERS ARE... DEAD.
THEY'RE LOOKING FOR REPLACEMENTS. MOGO DIRECTS THEM.
RING STATUS REPORT. GREEN LANTERN 42 DECEASED.
SPACE SECTOR SCAN 42 INITIATED FOR REPLACEMENT.
RING STATUS REPORT. GREEN LANTERN 1066 DECEASED.
SPACE SECTOR SCAN 1066 INITIATED FOR REPLACEMENT.
B-BUT IT COULD TAKE MONTHS BEFORE THEY'RE TRAINED.
Y'KNOW WHAT THEY SAY, DAMMIT--
BETTER LATE THAN NEVER!
VATH! ANY MORE COMING?
A FEW, BRIK BUT WE'RE GETTIN' KINDA THIN.
THEY'RE KILLIN' US AND THE BEST OUR RINGS CAN DO IS SLOW THEM DOWN.
OR HURT THEM SOME!
HMM. AND PROTECT US.
I HAVE BEEN THINKING.
THINKING?

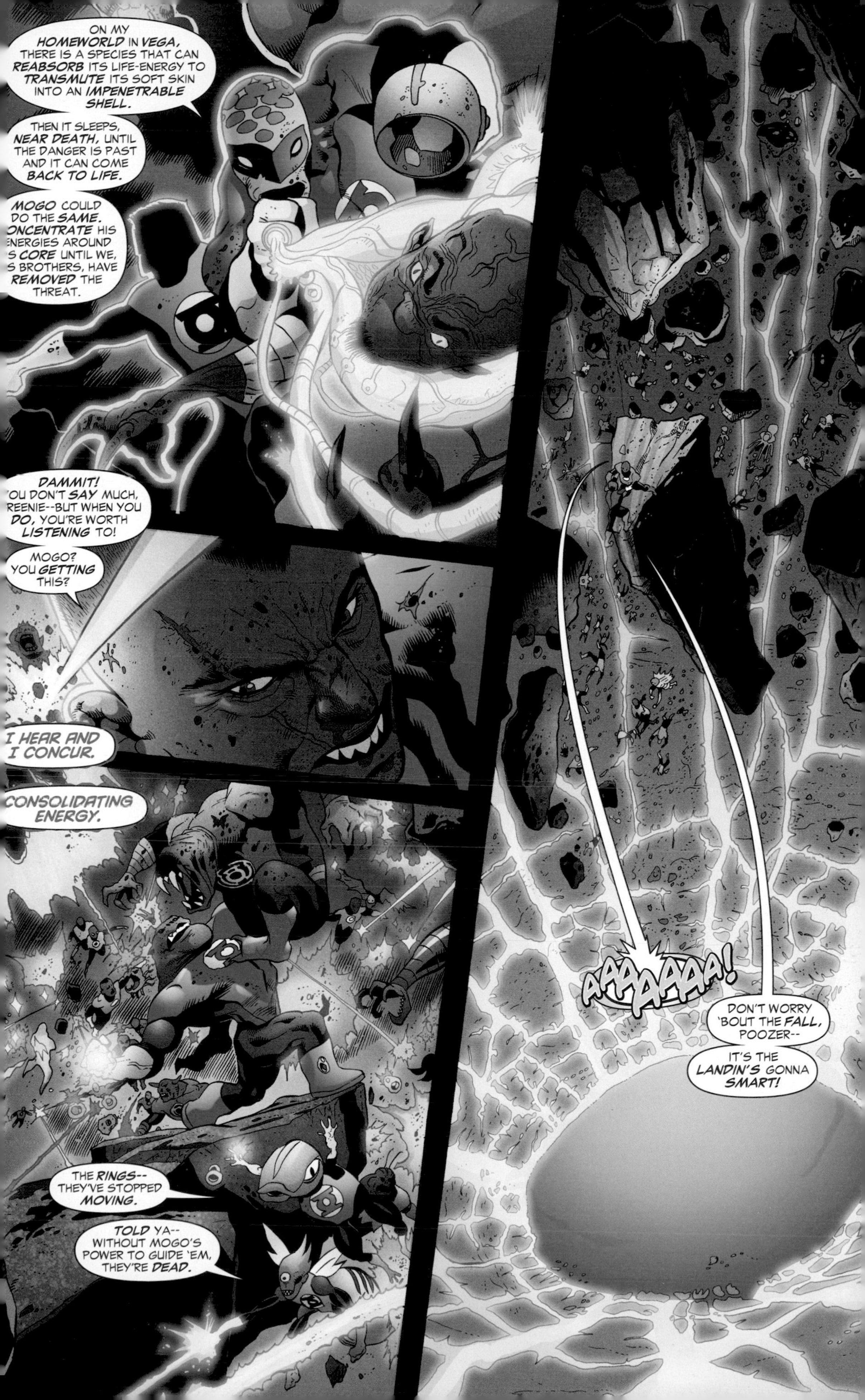
ON MY HOMEWORLD IN VEGA, THERE IS A SPECIES THAT CAN REABSORB ITS LIFE-ENERGY TO TRANSMUTE ITS SOFT SKIN INTO AN IMPENETRABLE SHELL.
THEN IT SLEEPS, NEAR DEATH, UNTIL THE DANGER IS PAST AND IT CAN COME BACK TO LIFE.
MOGO COULD DO THE SAME. ONCENTRATE HIS ENERGIES AROUND S CORE UNTIL WE, S BROTHERS, HAVE REMOVED THE THREAT.
DAMMIT! OU DON'T SAY MUCH, REENIE--BUT WHEN YOU DO, YOU'RE WORTH LISTENING TO!
MOGO? YOU GETTING THIS?
I HEAR AND I CONCUR.
CONSOLIDATING ENERGY.
THE RINGS-- THEY'VE STOPPED MOVING.
TOLD YA-- WITHOUT MOGO'S POWER TO GUIDE 'EM, THEY'RE DEAD.
AAAAAAA!
DON'T WORRY 'BOUT THE FALL, POOZER--
IT'S THE LANDIN'S GONNA SMART!

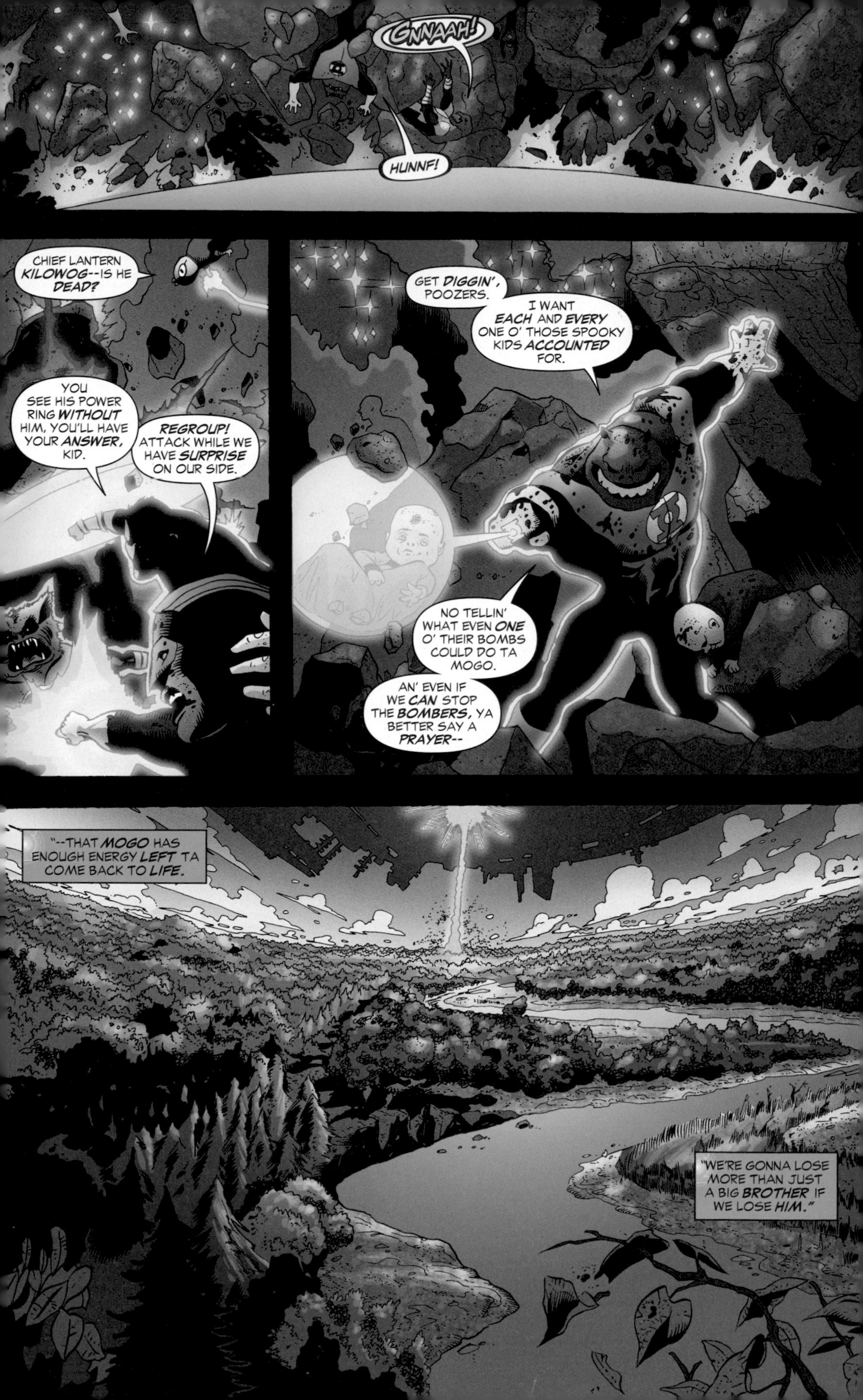
GNNAAH!
HUNNF!
CHIEF LANTERN KILOWOG--IS HE DEAD?
YOU SEE HIS POWER RING WITHOUT HIM, YOU'LL HAVE YOUR ANSWER, KID.
REGROUP! ATTACK WHILE WE HAVE SURPRISE ON OUR SIDE.
GET DIGGIN', POOZERS.
I WANT EACH AND EVERY ONE O' THOSE SPOOKY KIDS ACCOUNTED FOR.
NO TELLIN' WHAT EVEN ONE O' THEIR BOMBS COULD DO TA MOGO.
AN' EVEN IF WE CAN STOP THE BOMBERS, YA BETTER SAY A PRAYER--
"--THAT MOGO HAS ENOUGH ENERGY LEFT TA COME BACK TO LIFE.
"WE'RE GONNA LOSE MORE THAN JUST A BIG BROTHER IF WE LOSE HIM."

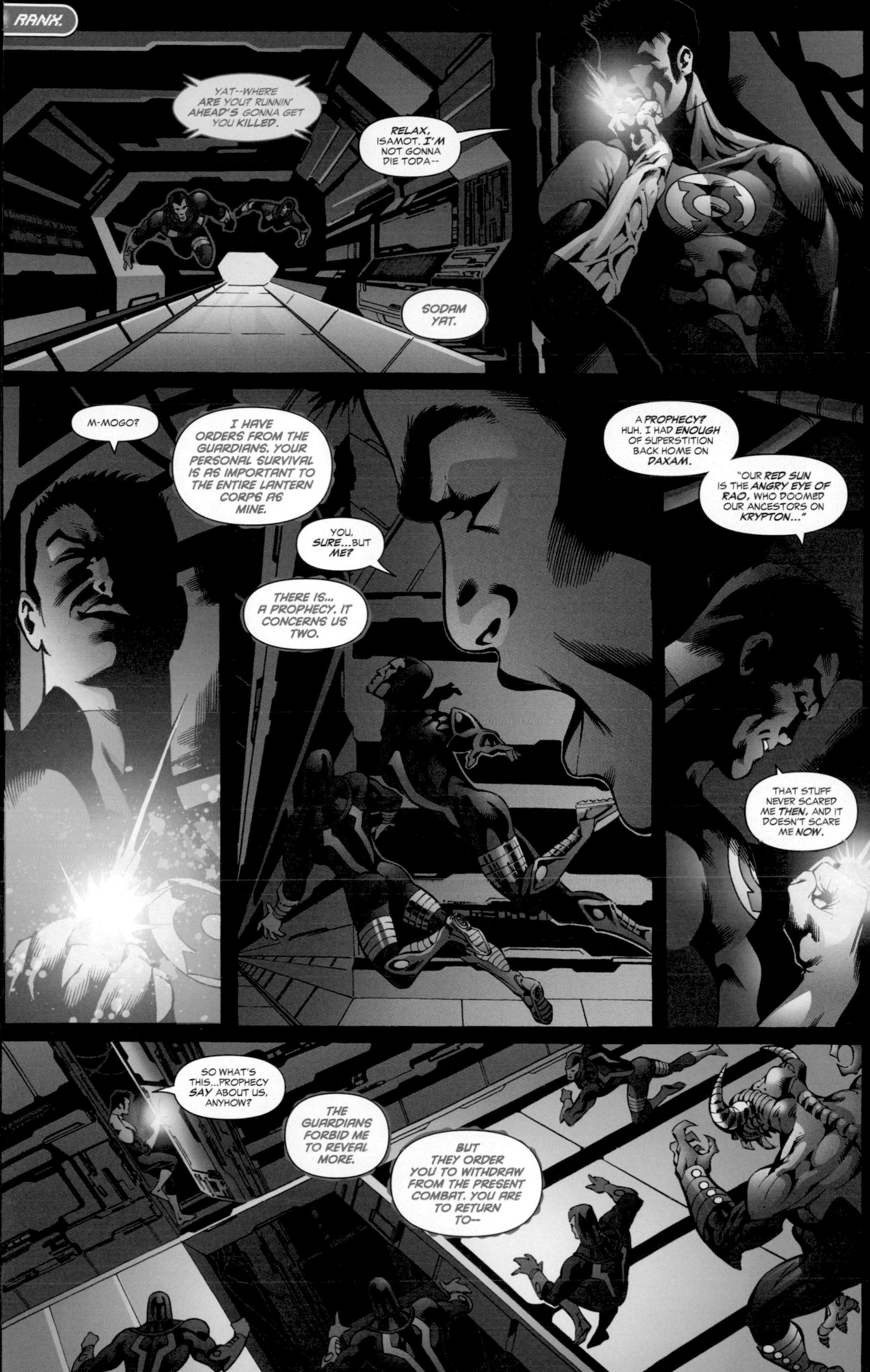
RANX.
YAT--WHERE ARE YOU? RUNNIN' AHEAD'S GONNA GET YOU KILLED.
RELAX, ISAMOT. I'M NOT GONNA DIE TODA--
SODAM YAT.
M-MOGO?
I HAVE ORDERS FROM THE GUARDIANS. YOUR PERSONAL SURVIVAL IS AS IMPORTANT TO THE ENTIRE LANTERN CORPS AS MINE.
YOU, SURE...BUT ME?
THERE IS... A PROPHECY. IT CONCERNS US TWO.
A PROPHECY? HUH. I HAD ENOUGH OF SUPERSTITION BACK HOME ON DAXAM.
"OUR RED SUN IS THE ANGRY EYE OF RAO, WHO DOOMED OUR ANCESTORS ON KRYPTON..."
THAT STUFF NEVER SCARED ME THEN, AND IT DOESN'T SCARE ME NOW.
SO WHAT'S THIS...PROPHECY SAY ABOUT US, ANYHOW?
THE GUARDIANS FORBID ME TO REVEAL MORE.
BUT THEY ORDER YOU TO WITHDRAW FROM THE PRESENT COMBAT. YOU ARE TO RETURN TO--

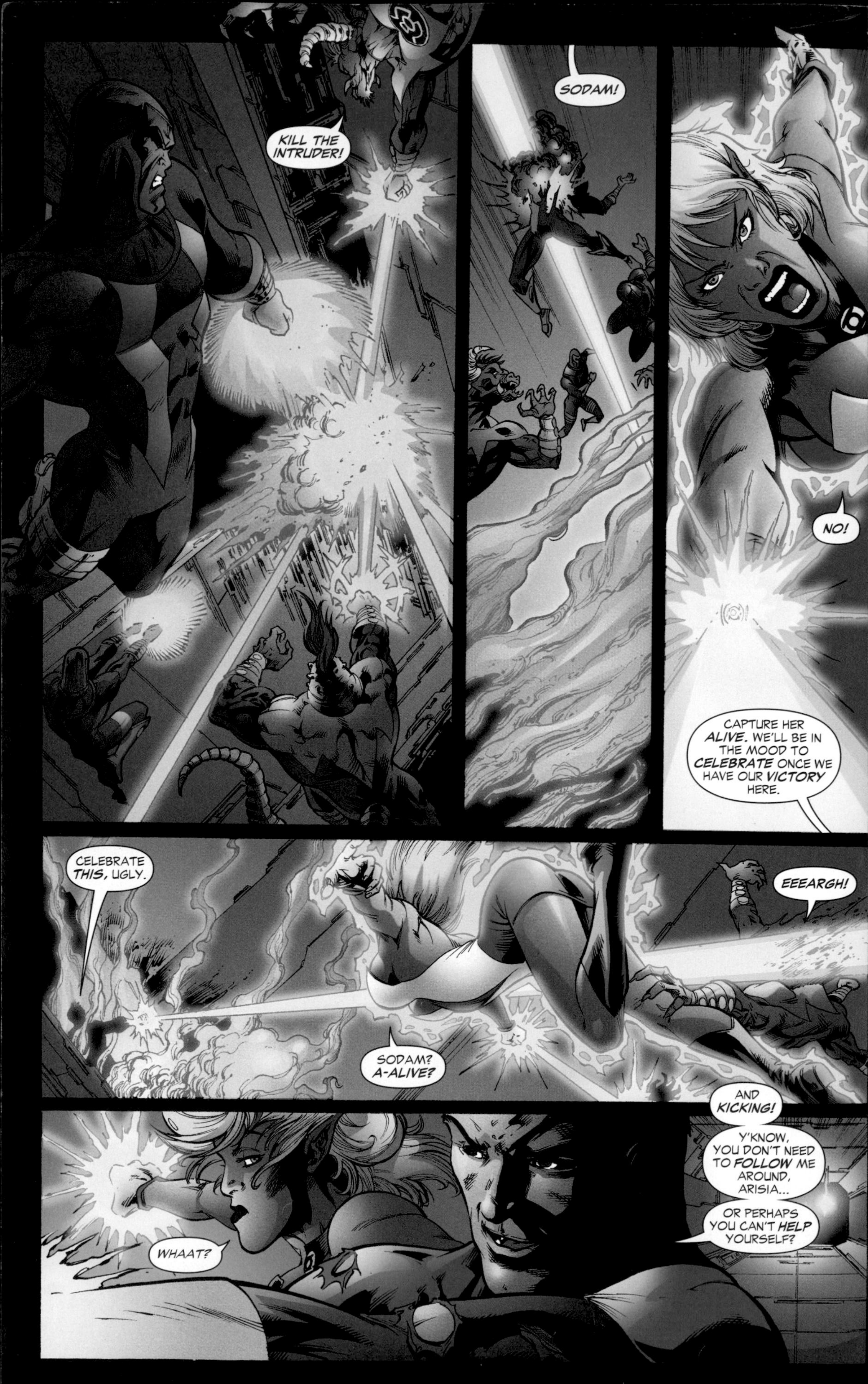
KILL THE INTRUDER!
SODAM!
NO!
CAPTURE HER ALIVE. WE'LL BE IN THE MOOD TO CELEBRATE ONCE WE HAVE OUR VICTORY HERE.
CELEBRATE THIS, UGLY.
EEEARGH!
SODAM? A-ALIVE?
AND KICKING!
Y'KNOW, YOU DON'T NEED TO FOLLOW ME AROUND, ARISIA...
OR PERHAPS YOU CAN'T HELP YOURSELF?
WHAAT?

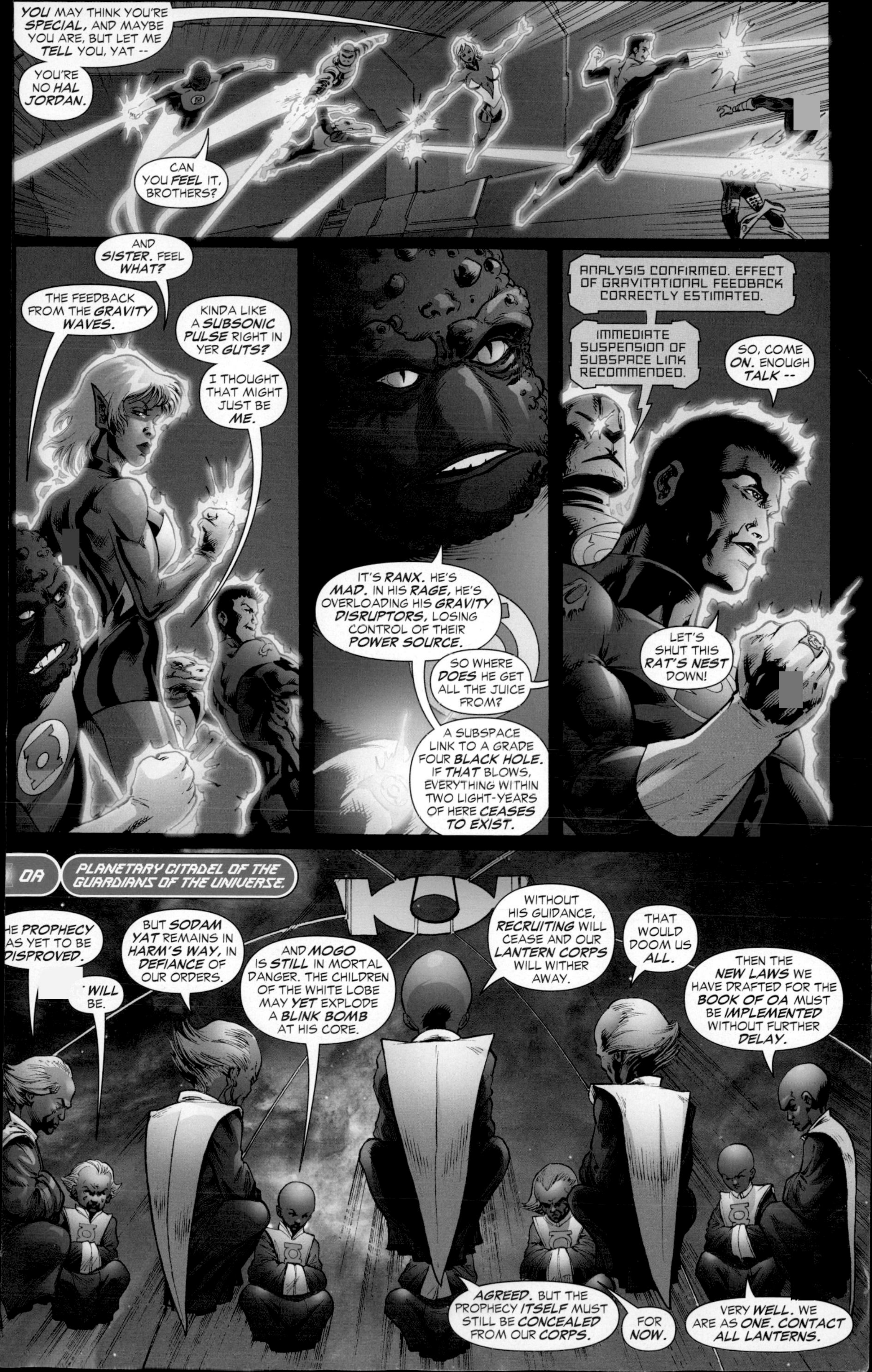
YOU MAY THINK YOU'RE SPECIAL, AND MAYBE YOU ARE, BUT LET ME TELL YOU, YAT --
YOU'RE NO HAL JORDAN.
CAN YOU FEEL IT, BROTHERS?
AND SISTER. FEEL WHAT?
THE FEEDBACK FROM THE GRAVITY WAVES.
KINDA LIKE A SUBSONIC PULSE RIGHT IN YER GUTS?
I THOUGHT THAT MIGHT JUST BE ME.
IT'S RANX. HE'S MAD. IN HIS RAGE, HE'S OVERLOADING HIS GRAVITY DISRUPTORS, LOSING CONTROL OF THEIR POWER SOURCE.
SO WHERE DOES HE GET ALL THE JUICE FROM?
A SUBSPACE LINK TO A GRADE FOUR BLACK HOLE. IF THAT BLOWS, EVERYTHING WITHIN TWO LIGHT-YEARS OF HERE CEASES TO EXIST.
ANALYSIS CONFIRMED. EFFECT OF GRAVITATIONAL FEEDBACK CORRECTLY ESTIMATED.
IMMEDIATE SUSPENSION OF SUBSPACE LINK RECOMMENDED.
SO, COME ON. ENOUGH TALK --
LET'S SHUT THIS RAT'S NEST DOWN!
OA
PLANETARY CITADEL OF THE GUARDIANS OF THE UNIVERSE.
HE PROPHECY AS YET TO BE DISPROVED.
WILL BE.
BUT SODAM YAT REMAINS IN HARM'S WAY, IN DEFIANCE OF OUR ORDERS.
AND MOGO IS STILL IN MORTAL DANGER. THE CHILDREN OF THE WHITE LOBE MAY YET EXPLODE A BLINK BOMB AT HIS CORE.
WITHOUT HIS GUIDANCE, RECRUITING WILL CEASE AND OUR LANTERN CORPS WILL WITHER AWAY.
THAT WOULD DOOM US ALL.
THEN THE NEW LAWS WE HAVE DRAFTED FOR THE BOOK OF OA MUST BE IMPLEMENTED WITHOUT FURTHER DELAY.
AGREED. BUT THE PROPHECY ITSELF MUST STILL BE CONCEALED FROM OUR CORPS.
FOR NOW.
VERY WELL. WE ARE AS ONE. CONTACT ALL LANTERNS.

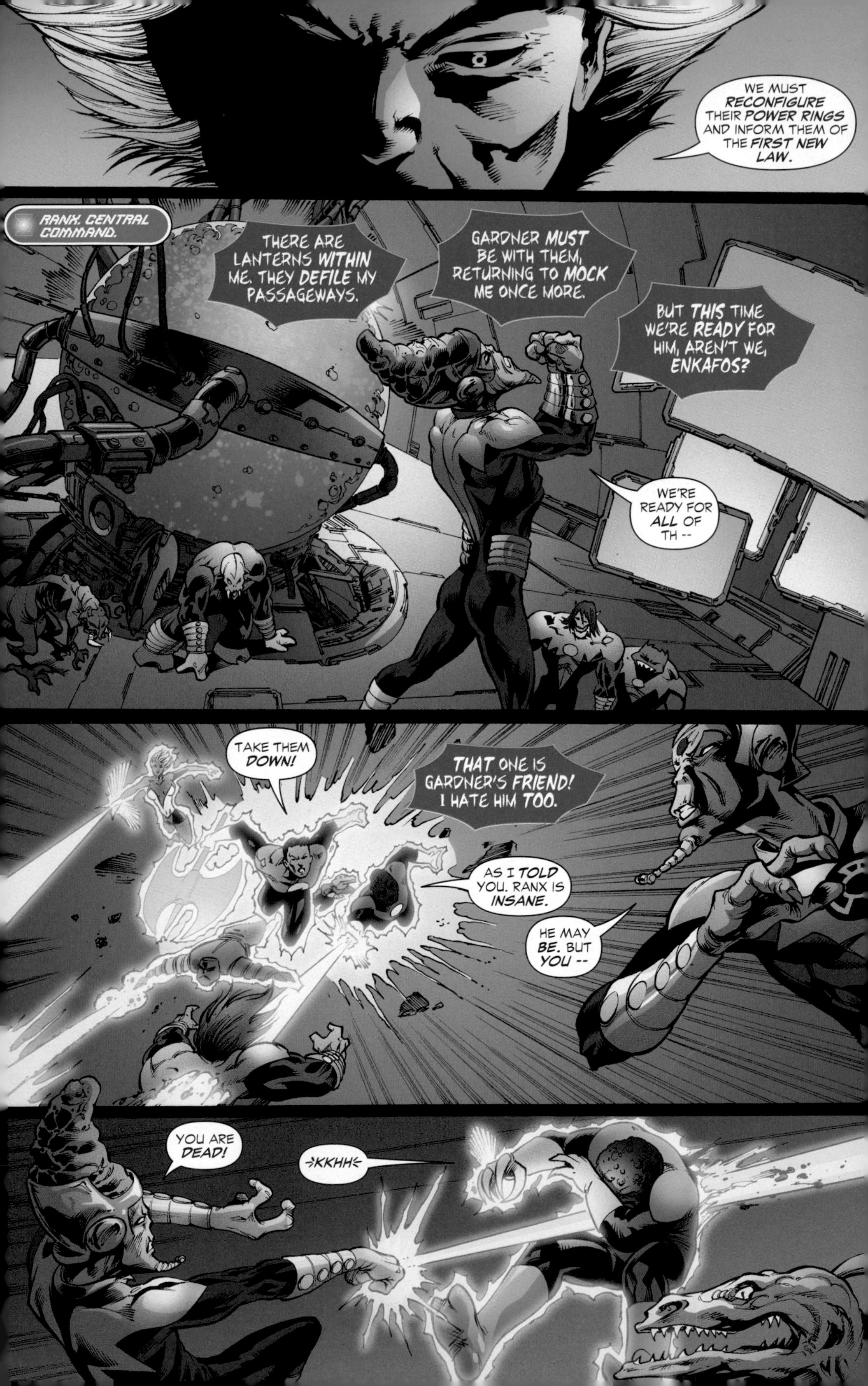
WE MUST RECONFIGURE THEIR POWER RINGS AND INFORM THEM OF THE FIRST NEW LAW.
RANX. CENTRAL COMMAND.
THERE ARE LANTERNS WITHIN ME. THEY DEFILE MY PASSAGEWAYS.
GARDNER MUST BE WITH THEM, RETURNING TO MOCK ME ONCE MORE.
BUT THIS TIME WE'RE READY FOR HIM, AREN'T WE, ENKAFOS?
WE'RE READY FOR ALL OF TH --
TAKE THEM DOWN!
THAT ONE IS GARDNER'S FRIEND! I HATE HIM TOO.
AS I TOLD YOU. RANX IS INSANE.
HE MAY BE. BUT YOU --
YOU ARE DEAD!
>KKHH<

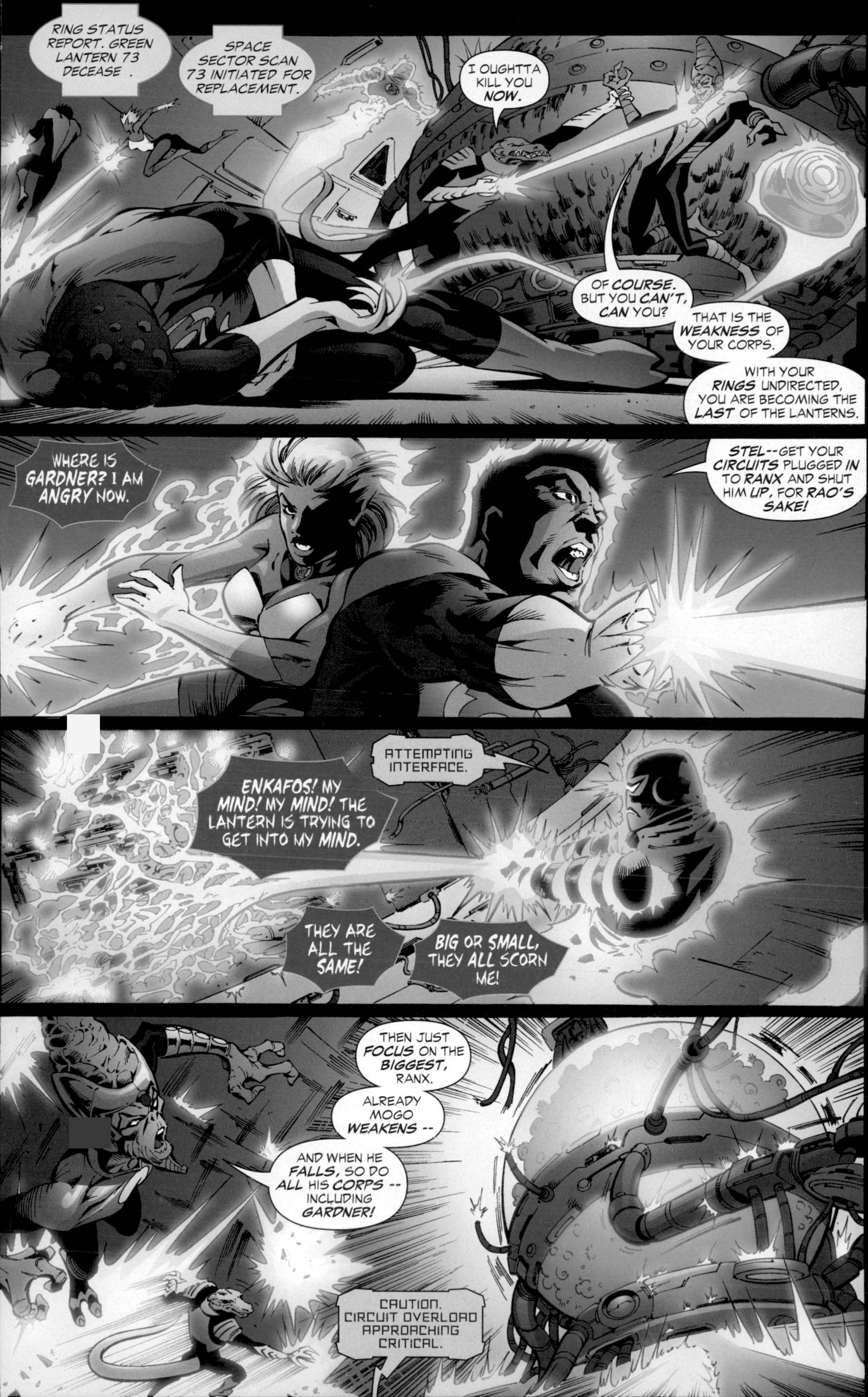
RING STATUS REPORT. GREEN LANTERN 73 DECEASE .
SPACE SECTOR SCAN 73 INITIATED FOR REPLACEMENT.
I OUGHTTA KILL YOU NOW.
OF COURSE. BUT YOU CAN'T, CAN YOU?
THAT IS THE WEAKNESS OF YOUR CORPS.
WITH YOUR RINGS UNDIRECTED, YOU ARE BECOMING THE LAST OF THE LANTERNS.
WHERE IS GARDNER? I AM ANGRY NOW.
STEL--GET YOUR CIRCUITS PLUGGED IN TO RANX AND SHUT HIM UP, FOR RAO'S SAKE!
ATTEMPTING INTERFACE.
ENKAFOS! MY MIND! MY MIND! THE LANTERN IS TRYING TO GET INTO MY MIND.
THEY ARE ALL THE SAME!
BIG OR SMALL, THEY ALL SCORN ME!
THEN JUST FOCUS ON THE BIGGEST, RANX.
ALREADY MOGO WEAKENS --
AND WHEN HE FALLS, SO DO ALL HIS CORPS -- INCLUDING GARDNER!
CAUTION. CIRCUIT OVERLOAD APPROACHING CRITICAL.

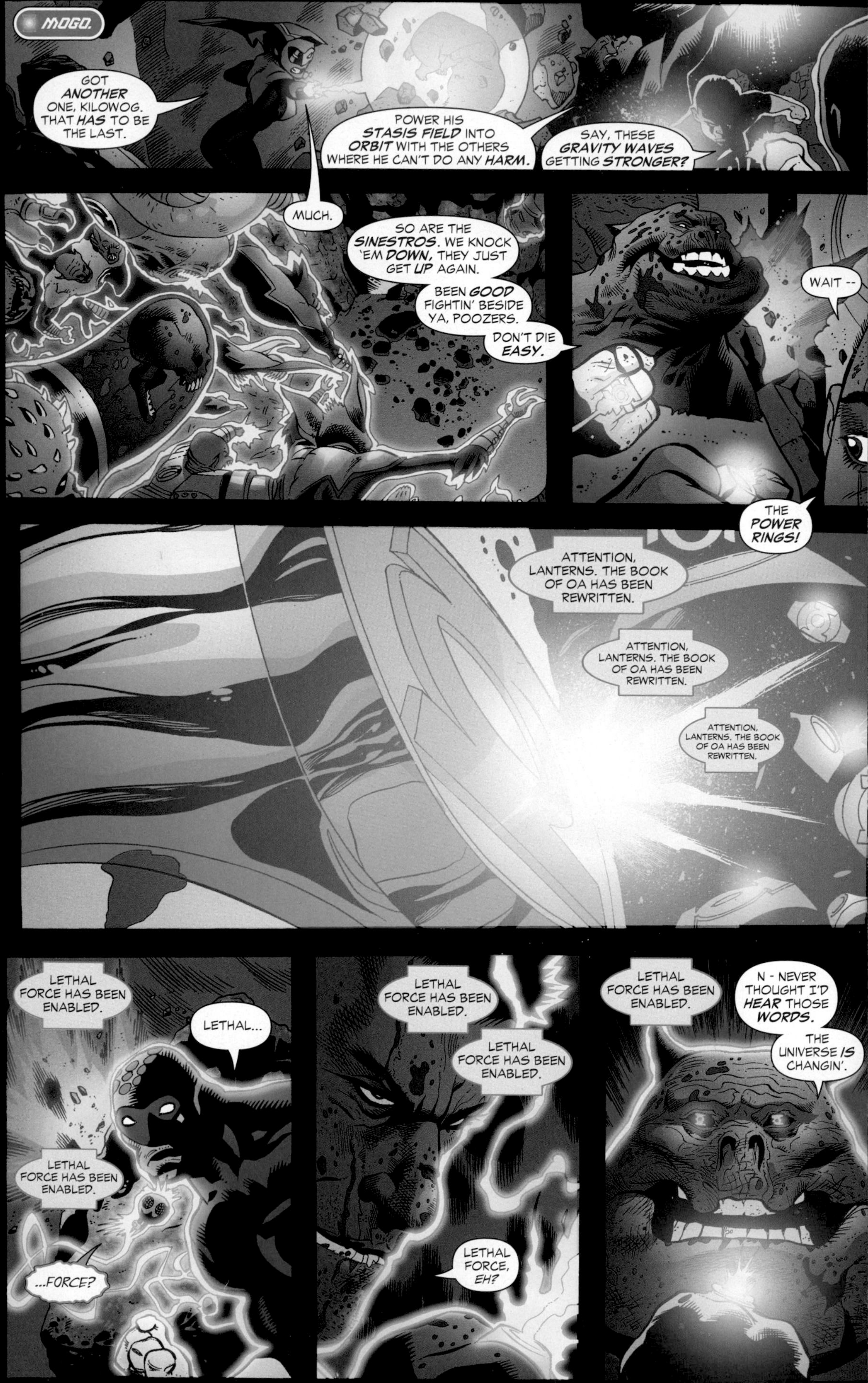
MOGO.
GOT ANOTHER ONE, KILOWOG. THAT HAS TO BE THE LAST.
POWER HIS STASIS FIELD INTO ORBIT WITH THE OTHERS WHERE HE CAN'T DO ANY HARM.
SAY, THESE GRAVITY WAVES GETTING STRONGER?
MUCH.
SO ARE THE SINESTROS. WE KNOCK 'EM DOWN, THEY JUST GET UP AGAIN.
BEEN GOOD FIGHTIN' BESIDE YA, POOZERS.
DON'T DIE EASY.
WAIT --
THE POWER RINGS!
ATTENTION, LANTERNS. THE BOOK OF OA HAS BEEN REWRITTEN.
ATTENTION, LANTERNS. THE BOOK OF OA HAS BEEN REWRITTEN.
ATTENTION, LANTERNS. THE BOOK OF OA HAS BEEN REWRITTEN.
LETHAL FORCE HAS BEEN ENABLED.
LETHAL...
LETHAL FORCE HAS BEEN ENABLED.
...FORCE?
LETHAL FORCE HAS BEEN ENABLED.
LETHAL FORCE HAS BEEN ENABLED.
LETHAL FORCE, EH?
LETHAL FORCE HAS BEEN ENABLED.
N - NEVER THOUGHT I'D HEAR THOSE WORDS.
THE UNIVERSE IS CHANGIN'.

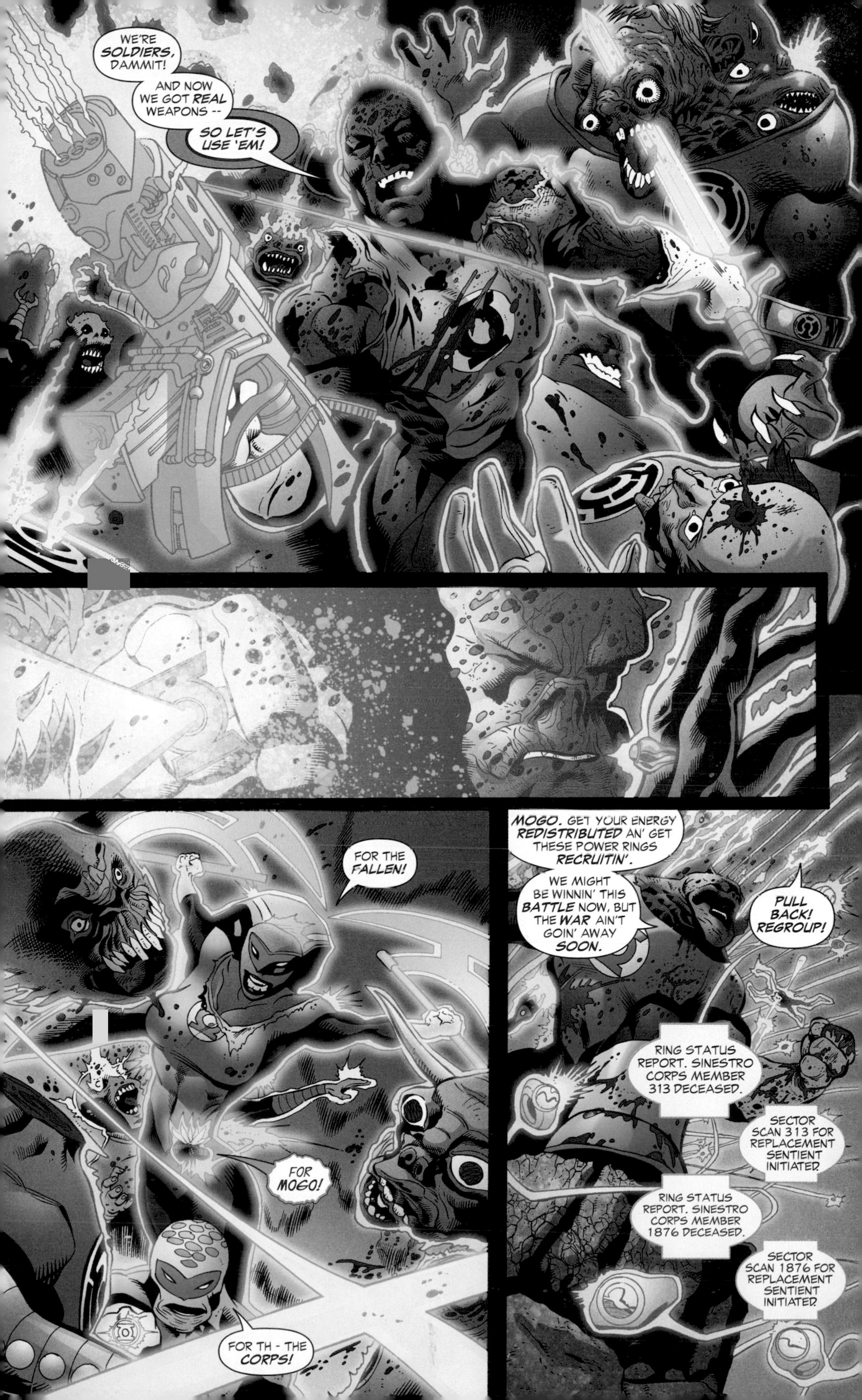
WE'RE SOLDIERS, DAMMIT!
AND NOW WE GOT REAL WEAPONS --
SO LET'S USE 'EM!
FOR THE FALLEN!
FOR MOGO!
FOR TH - THE CORPS!
MOGO. GET YOUR ENERGY REDISTRIBUTED AN' GET THESE POWER RINGS RECRUITIN'.
WE MIGHT BE WINNIN' THIS BATTLE NOW, BUT THE WAR AIN'T GOIN' AWAY SOON.
PULL BACK! REGROUP!
RING STATUS REPORT. SINESTRO CORPS MEMBER 313 DECEASED.
SECTOR SCAN 313 FOR REPLACEMENT SENTIENT INITIATED.
RING STATUS REPORT. SINESTRO CORPS MEMBER 1876 DECEASED.
SECTOR SCAN 1876 FOR REPLACEMENT SENTIENT INITIATED.

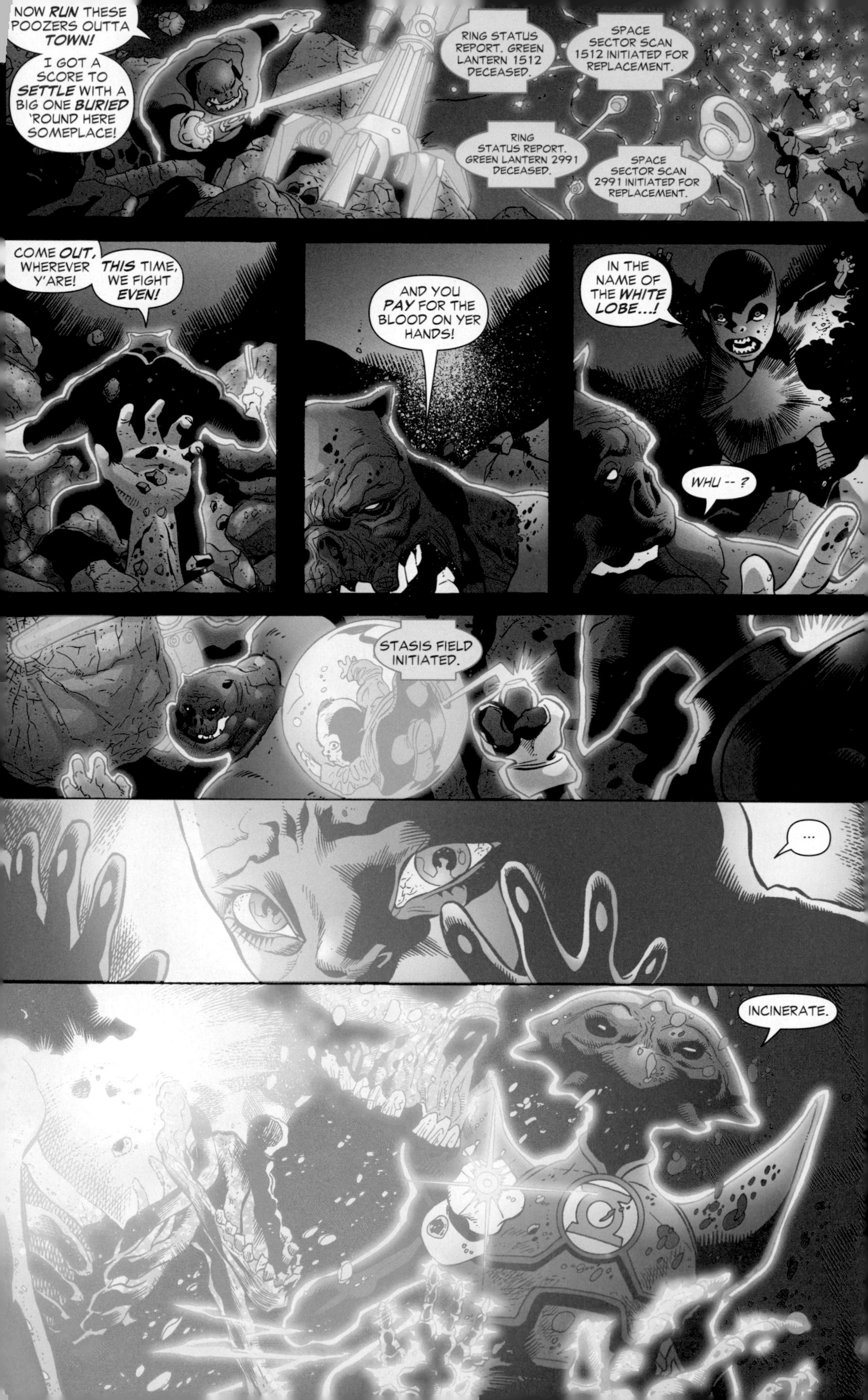

NOW RUN THESE POOZERS OUTTA TOWN!
I GOT A SCORE TO SETTLE WITH A BIG ONE BURIED 'ROUND HERE SOMEPLACE!
RING STATUS REPORT. GREEN LANTERN 1512 DECEASED.
SPACE SECTOR SCAN 1512 INITIATED FOR REPLACEMENT.
RING STATUS REPORT. GREEN LANTERN 2991 DECEASED.
SPACE SECTOR SCAN 2991 INITIATED FOR REPLACEMENT.
COME OUT, WHEREVER Y'ARE!
THIS TIME, WE FIGHT EVEN!
AND YOU PAY FOR THE BLOOD ON YER HANDS!
IN THE NAME OF THE WHITE LOBE...!
WHU -- ?
STASIS FIELD INITIATED.
...
INCINERATE.

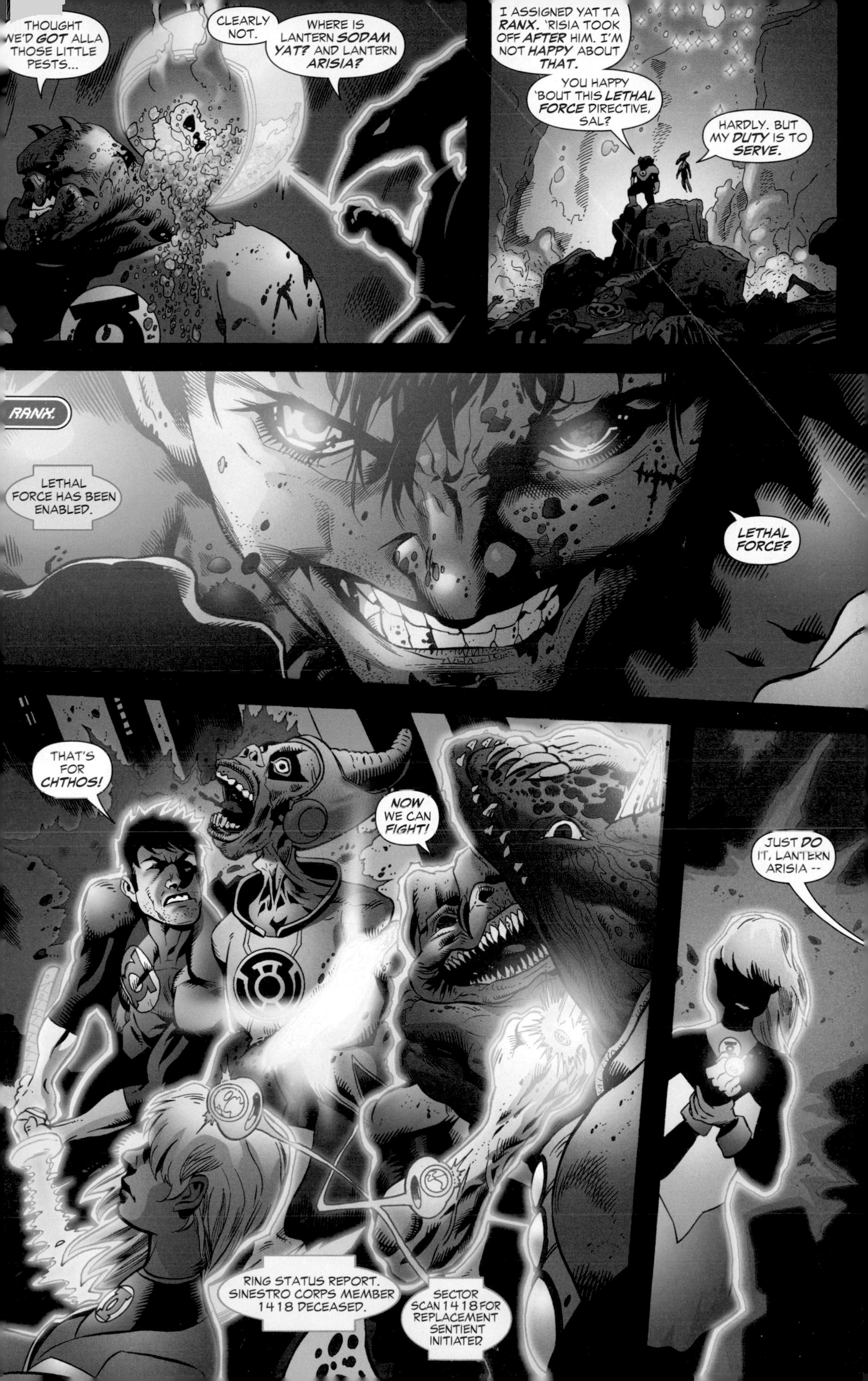
THOUGHT WE'D GOT ALLA THOSE LITTLE PESTS...
CLEARLY NOT.
WHERE IS LANTERN SODAM YAT? AND LANTERN ARISIA?
I ASSIGNED YAT TA RANX. 'RISIA TOOK OFF AFTER HIM. I'M NOT HAPPY ABOUT THAT.
YOU HAPPY 'BOUT THIS LETHAL FORCE DIRECTIVE, SAL?
HARDLY. BUT MY DUTY IS TO SERVE.
RANX.
LETHAL FORCE HAS BEEN ENABLED.
LETHAL FORCE?
THAT'S FOR CHTHOS!
NOW WE CAN FIGHT!
JUST DO IT, LANTERN ARISIA --
RING STATUS REPORT. SINESTRO CORPS MEMBER 1418 DECEASED.
SECTOR SCAN 1418 FOR REPLACEMENT SENTIENT INITIATED.

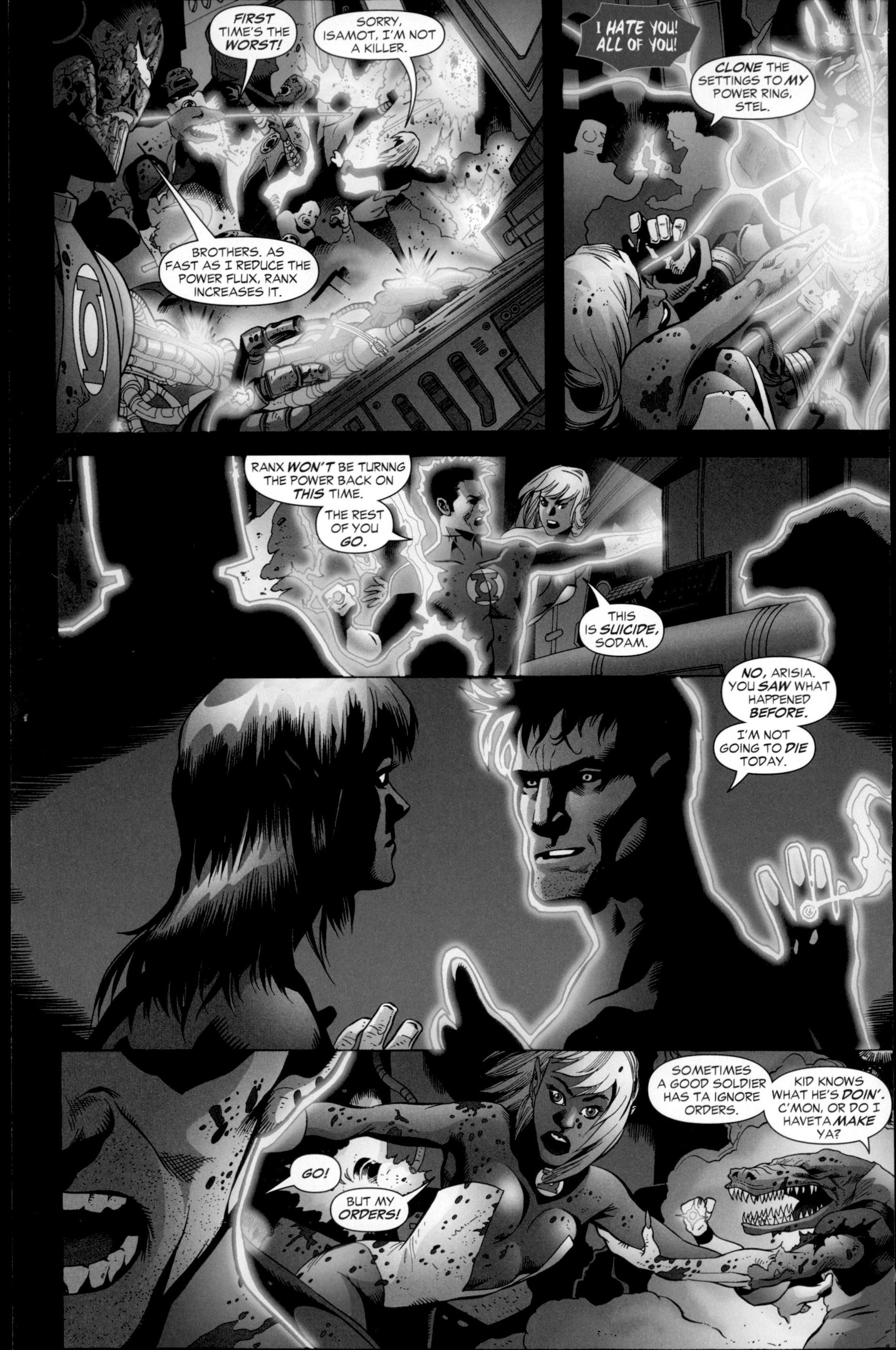
FIRST TIME'S THE WORST!
SORRY, ISAMOT, I'M NOT A KILLER.
BROTHERS. AS FAST AS I REDUCE THE POWER FLUX, RANX INCREASES IT.
I HATE YOU! ALL OF YOU!
CLONE THE SETTINGS TO MY POWER RING, STEL.
RANX WON'T BE TURNNG THE POWER BACK ON THIS TIME.
THE REST OF YOU GO.
THIS IS SUICIDE, SODAM.
NO, ARISIA. YOU SAW WHAT HAPPENED BEFORE.
I'M NOT GOING TO DIE TODAY.
SOMETIMES A GOOD SOLDIER HAS TA IGNORE ORDERS.
KID KNOWS WHAT HE'S DOIN'. C'MON, OR DO I HAVETA MAKE YA?
GO!
BUT MY ORDERS!

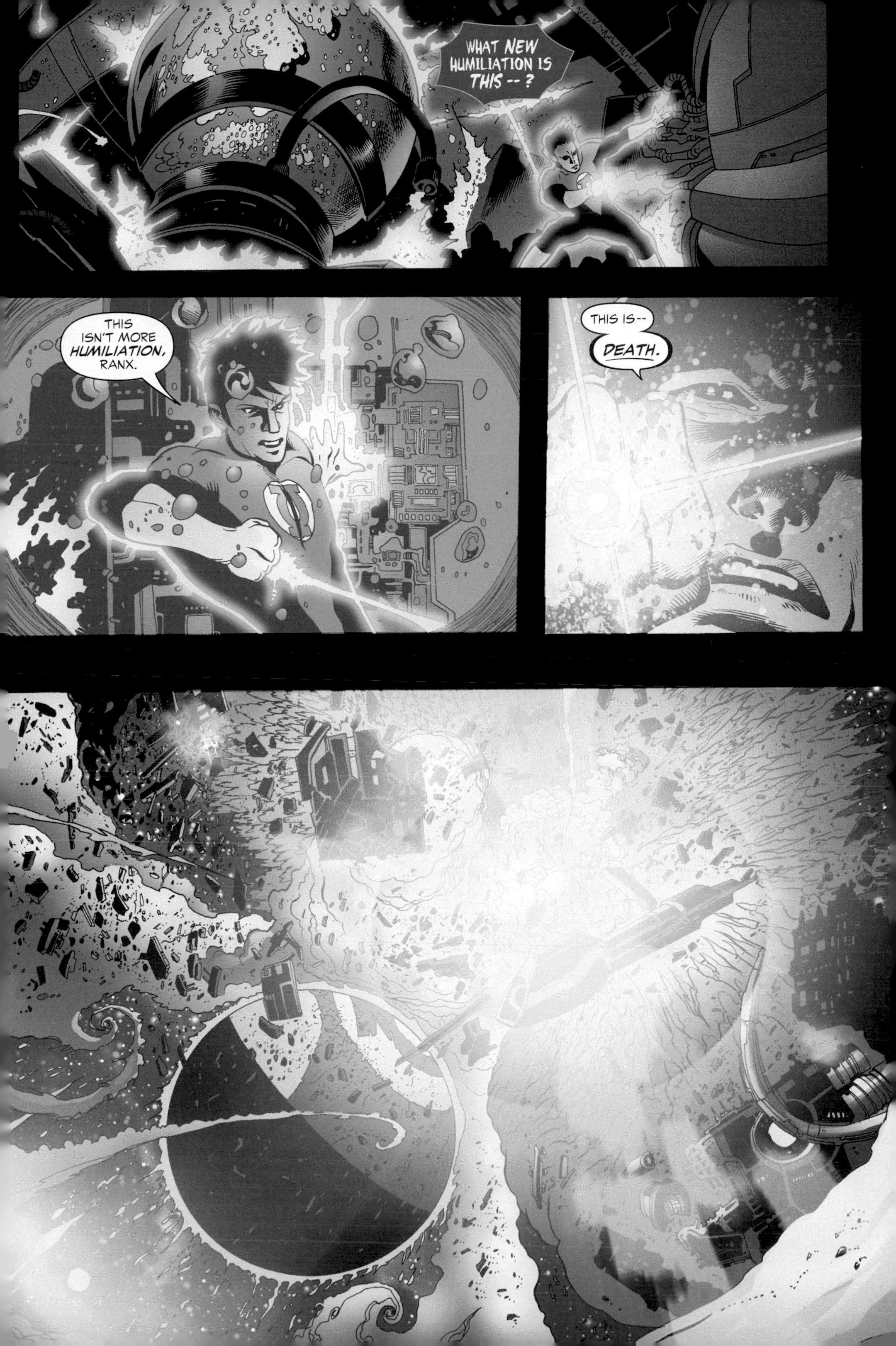
WHAT NEW HUMILIATION IS THIS -- ?
THIS ISN'T MORE HUMILIATION, RANX.
THIS IS--
DEATH.

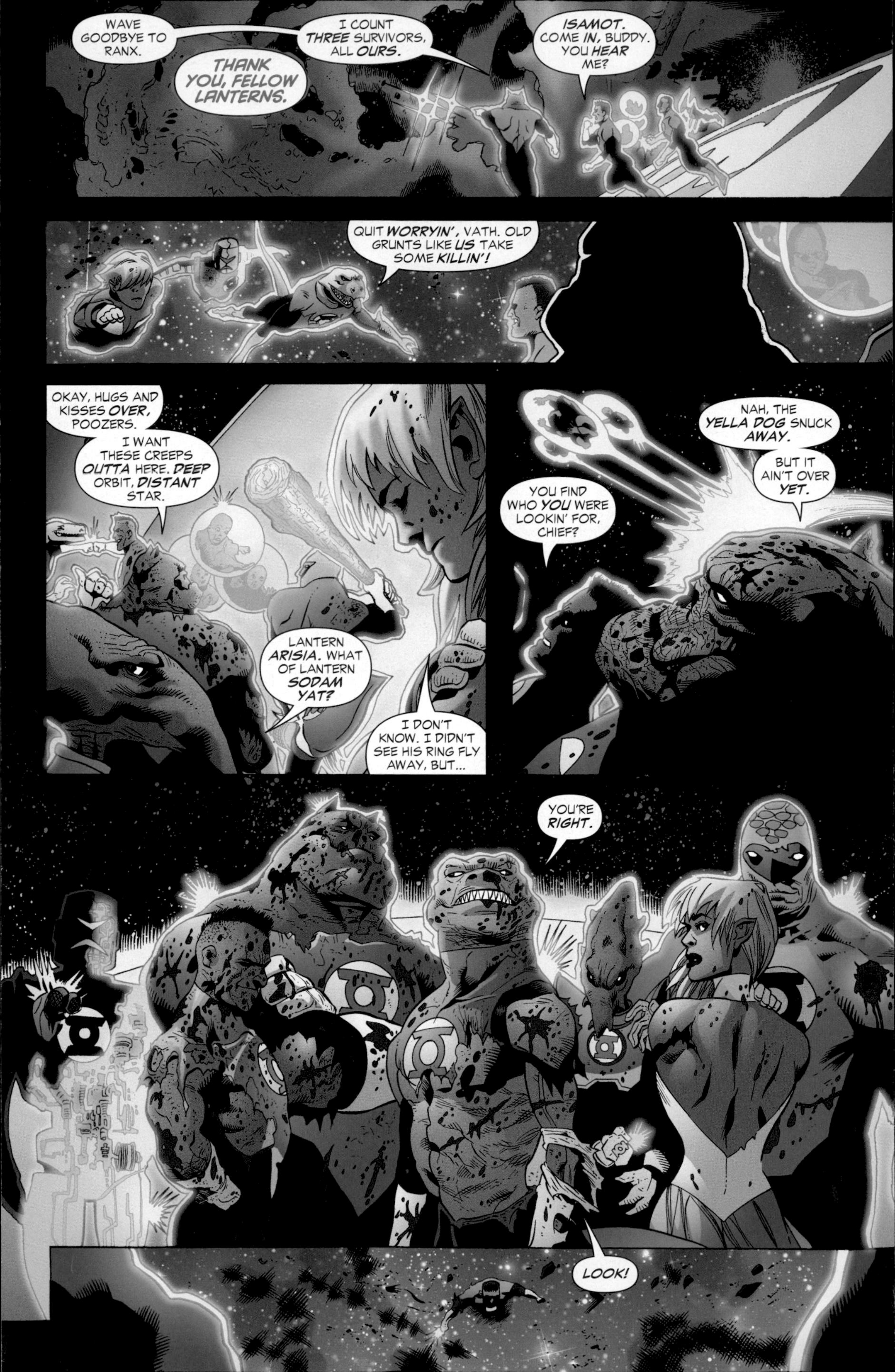
WAVE GOODBYE TO RANX.
I COUNT THREE SURVIVORS, ALL OURS.
THANK YOU, FELLOW LANTERNS.
ISAMOT. COME IN, BUDDY. YOU HEAR ME?
QUIT WORRYIN', VATH. OLD GRUNTS LIKE US TAKE SOME KILLIN'!
OKAY, HUGS AND KISSES OVER, POOZERS.
I WANT THESE CREEPS OUTTA HERE. DEEP ORBIT, DISTANT STAR.
LANTERN ARISIA. WHAT OF LANTERN SODAM YAT?
I DON'T KNOW. I DIDN'T SEE HIS RING FLY AWAY, BUT...
YOU FIND WHO YOU WERE LOOKIN' FOR, CHIEF?
NAH, THE YELLA DOG SNUCK AWAY.
BUT IT AIN'T OVER YET.
YOU'RE RIGHT.
LOOK!

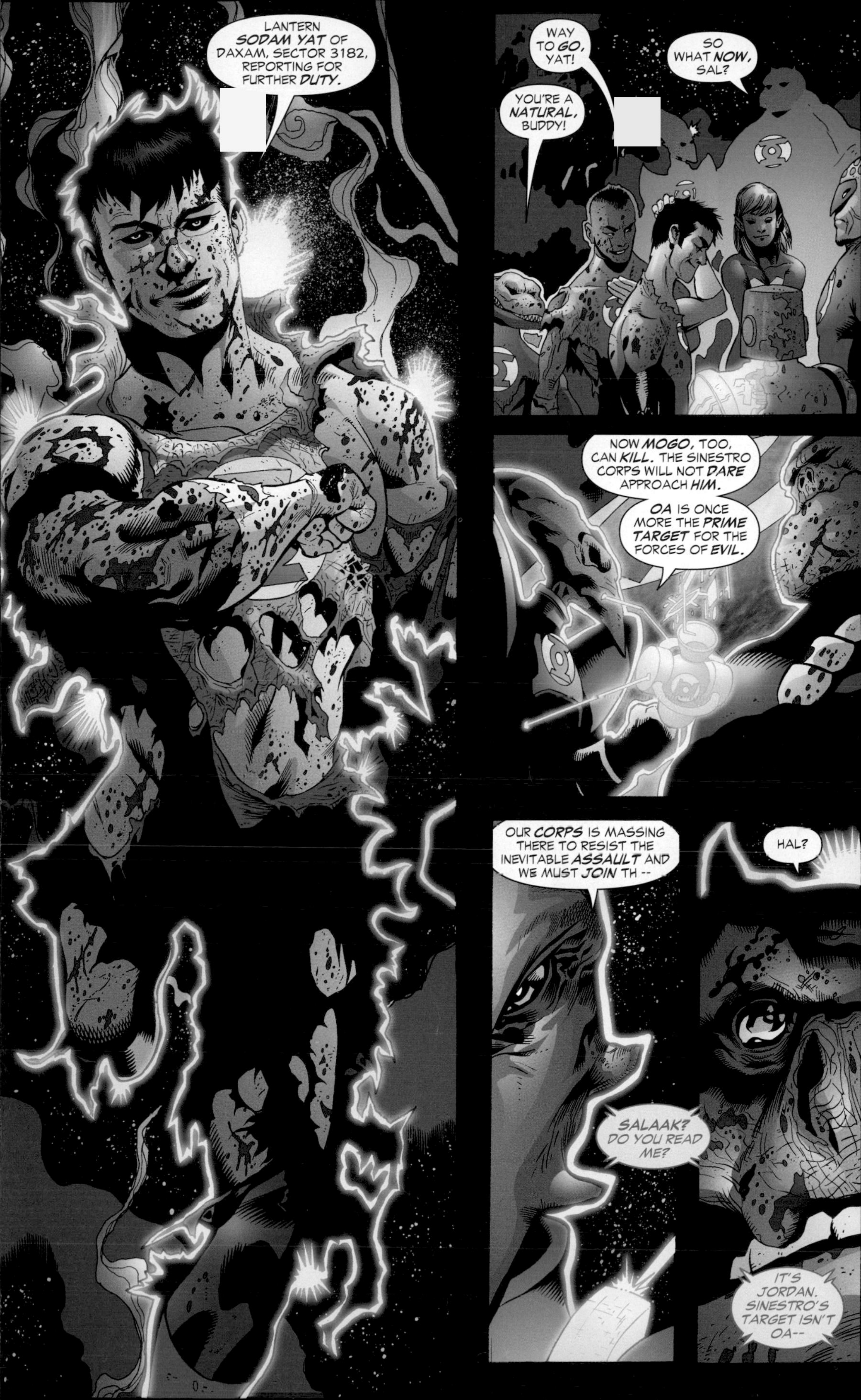
LANTERN SODAM YAT OF DAXAM, SECTOR 3182, REPORTING FOR FURTHER DUTY.
WAY TO GO, YAT!
YOU'RE A NATURAL, BUDDY!
SO WHAT NOW, SAL?
NOW MOGO, TOO, CAN KILL. THE SINESTRO CORPS WILL NOT DARE APPROACH HIM.
OA IS ONCE MORE THE PRIME TARGET FOR THE FORCES OF EVIL.
OUR CORPS IS MASSING THERE TO RESIST THE INEVITABLE ASSAULT AND WE MUST JOIN TH --
SALAAK? DO YOU READ ME?
HAL?
IT'S JORDAN. SINESTRO'S TARGET ISN'T OA--

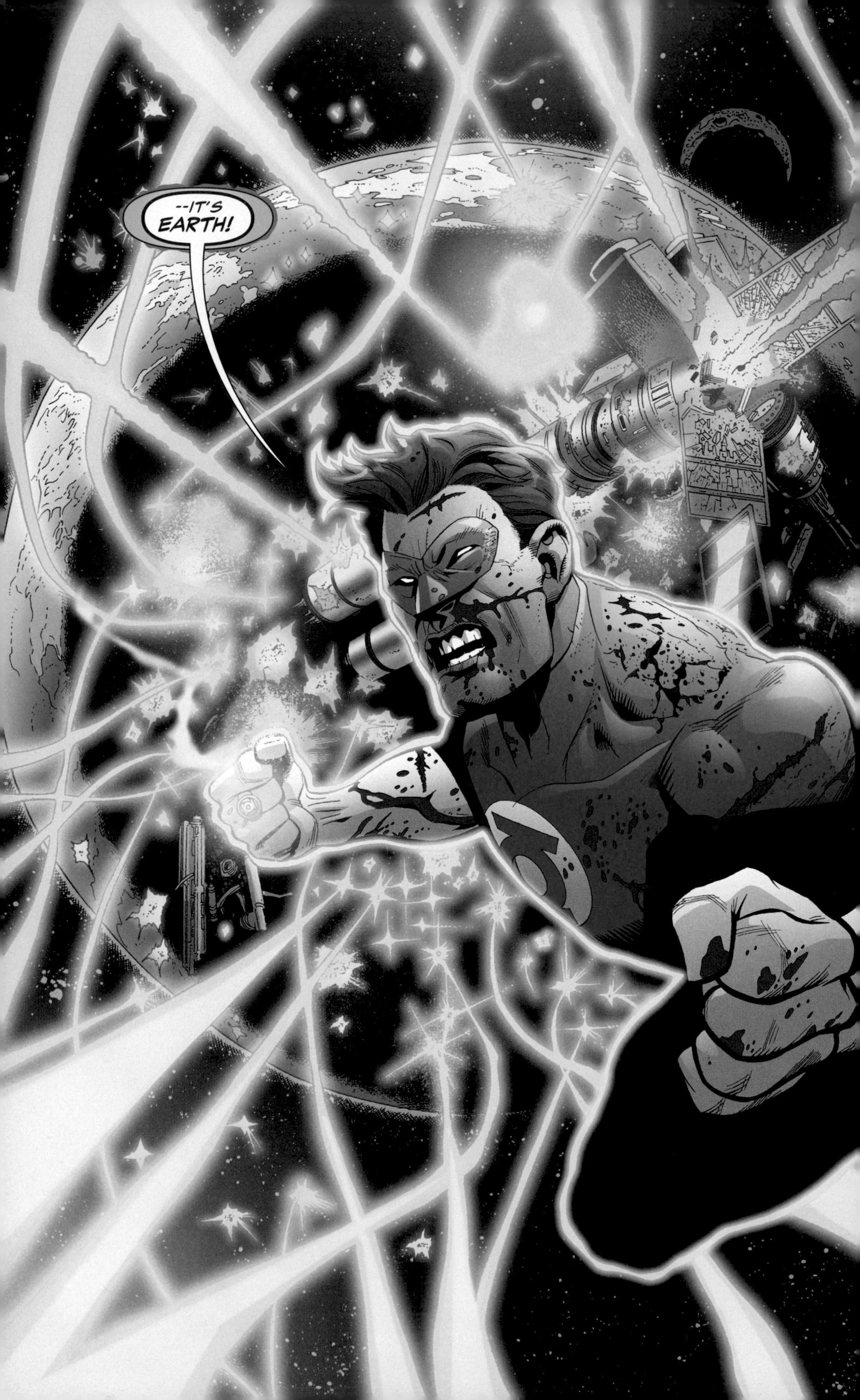
--IT'S EARTH!

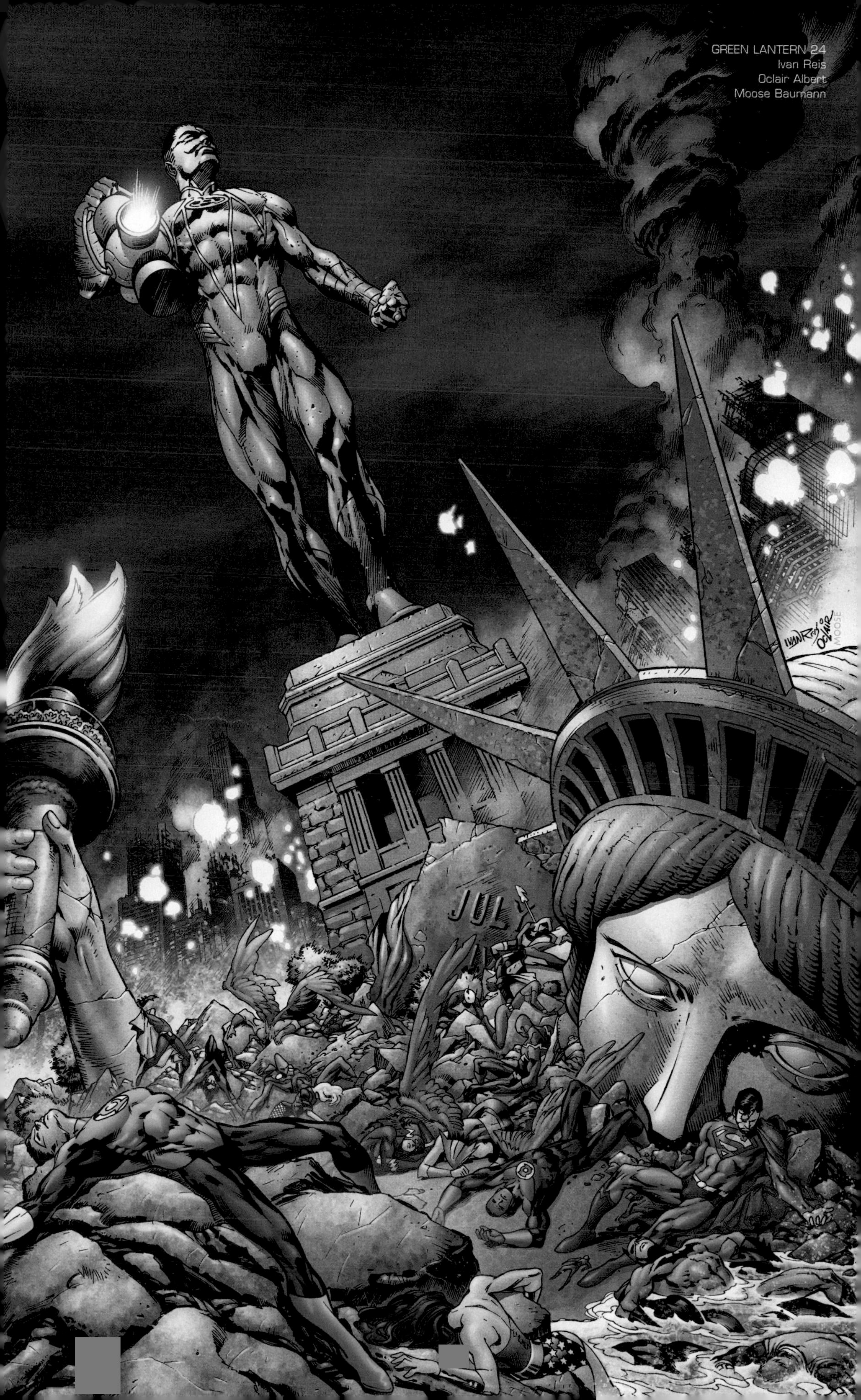
JUL
GREEN LANTERN 24
Ivan Reis
Oclair Albert
Moose Baumann

THE SINESTRO CORPS WAR
Chapter Seven
HOME INVASION
Writer: **Geoff Johns**
Penciller: **Ivan Reis**
Inkers: **Oclair Albert** and **Julio Ferreira**
Colorist: **Moose Baumann**

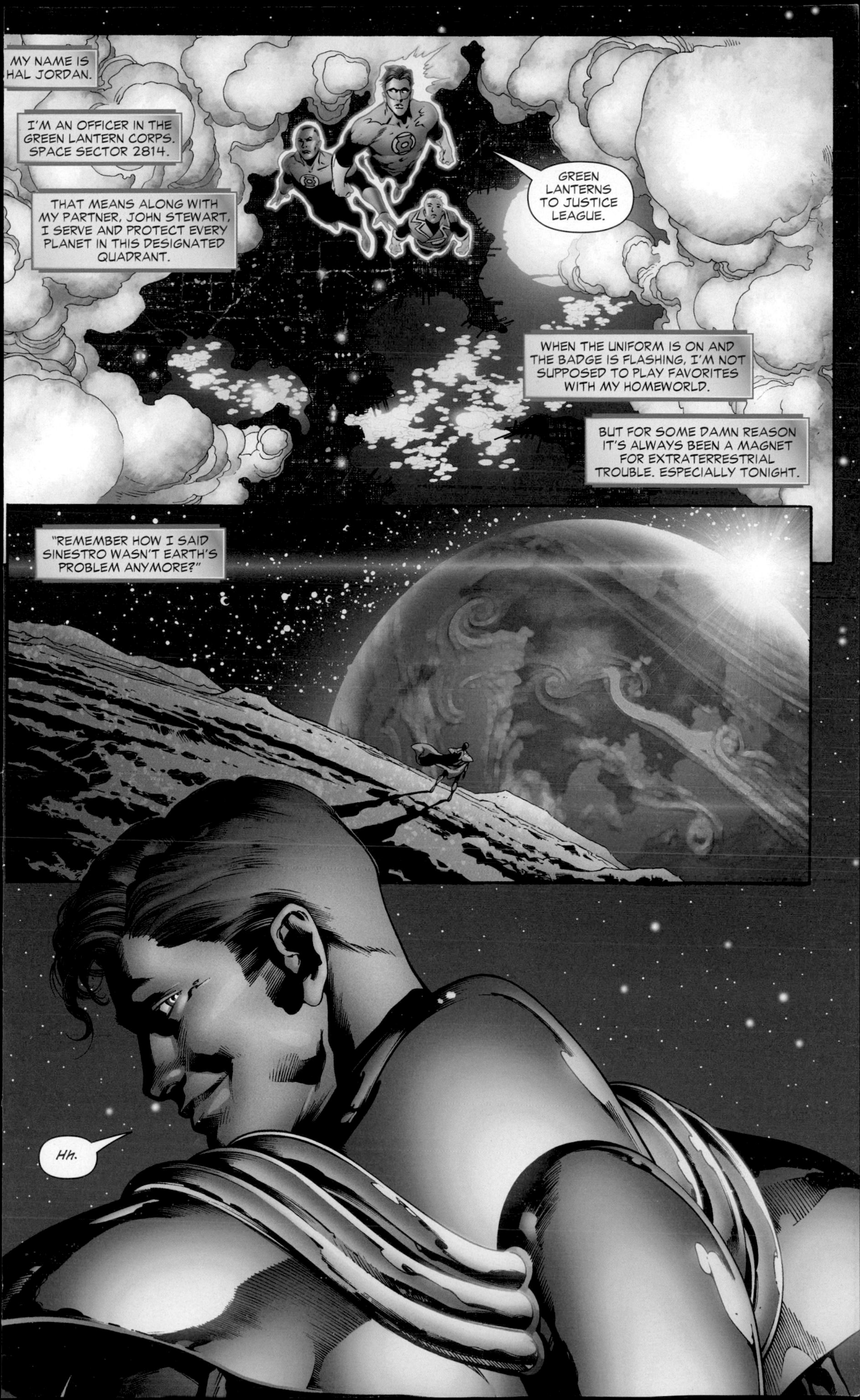

MY NAME IS HAL JORDAN.
I'M AN OFFICER IN THE GREEN LANTERN CORPS. SPACE SECTOR 2814.
GREEN LANTERNS TO JUSTICE LEAGUE.
THAT MEANS ALONG WITH MY PARTNER, JOHN STEWART, I SERVE AND PROTECT EVERY PLANET IN THIS DESIGNATED QUADRANT.
WHEN THE UNIFORM IS ON AND THE BADGE IS FLASHING, I'M NOT SUPPOSED TO PLAY FAVORITES WITH MY HOMEWORLD.
BUT FOR SOME DAMN REASON IT'S ALWAYS BEEN A MAGNET FOR EXTRATERRESTRIAL TROUBLE. ESPECIALLY TONIGHT.
"REMEMBER HOW I SAID SINESTRO WASN'T EARTH'S PROBLEM ANYMORE?"
Hh.

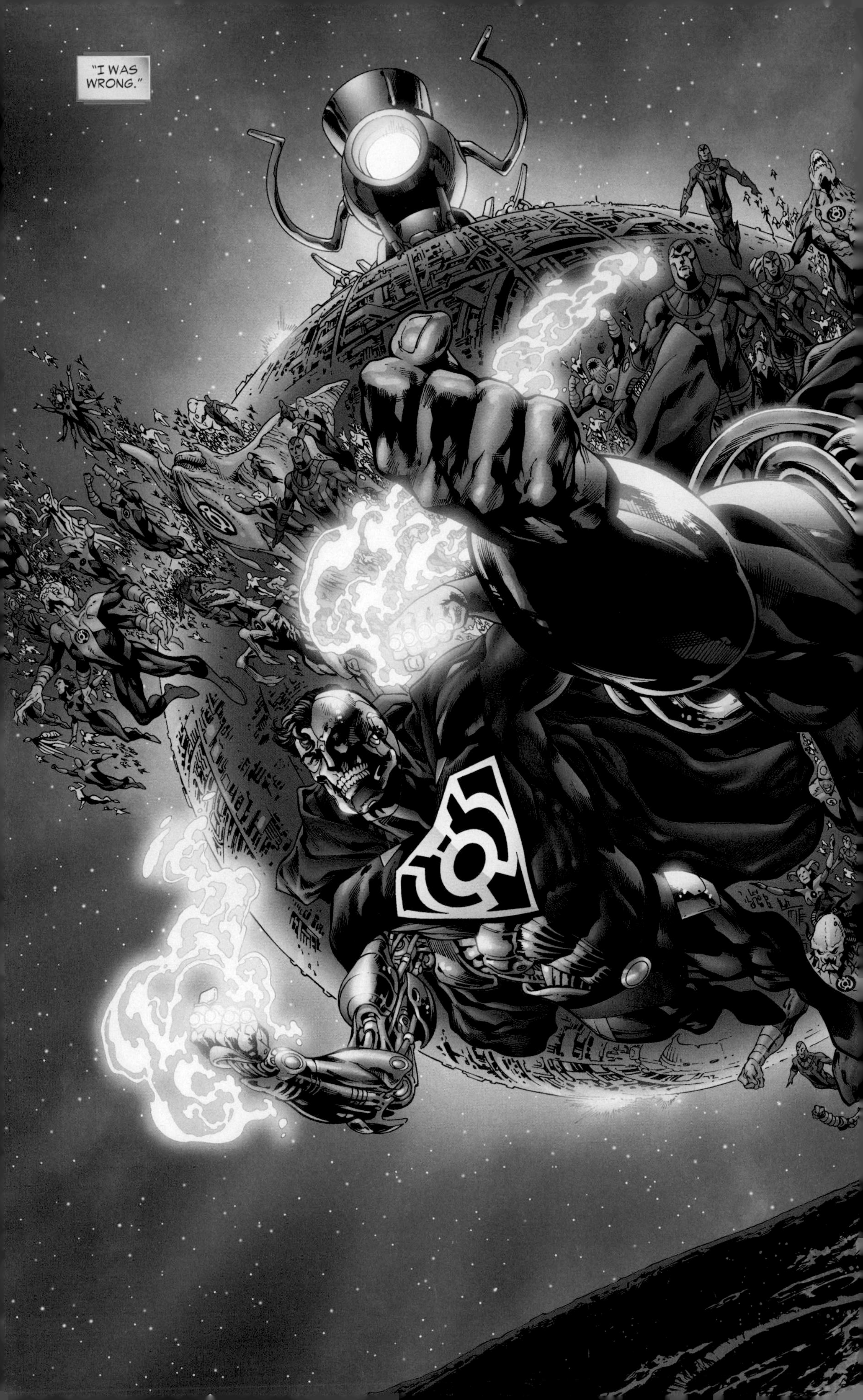
"I WAS WRONG."

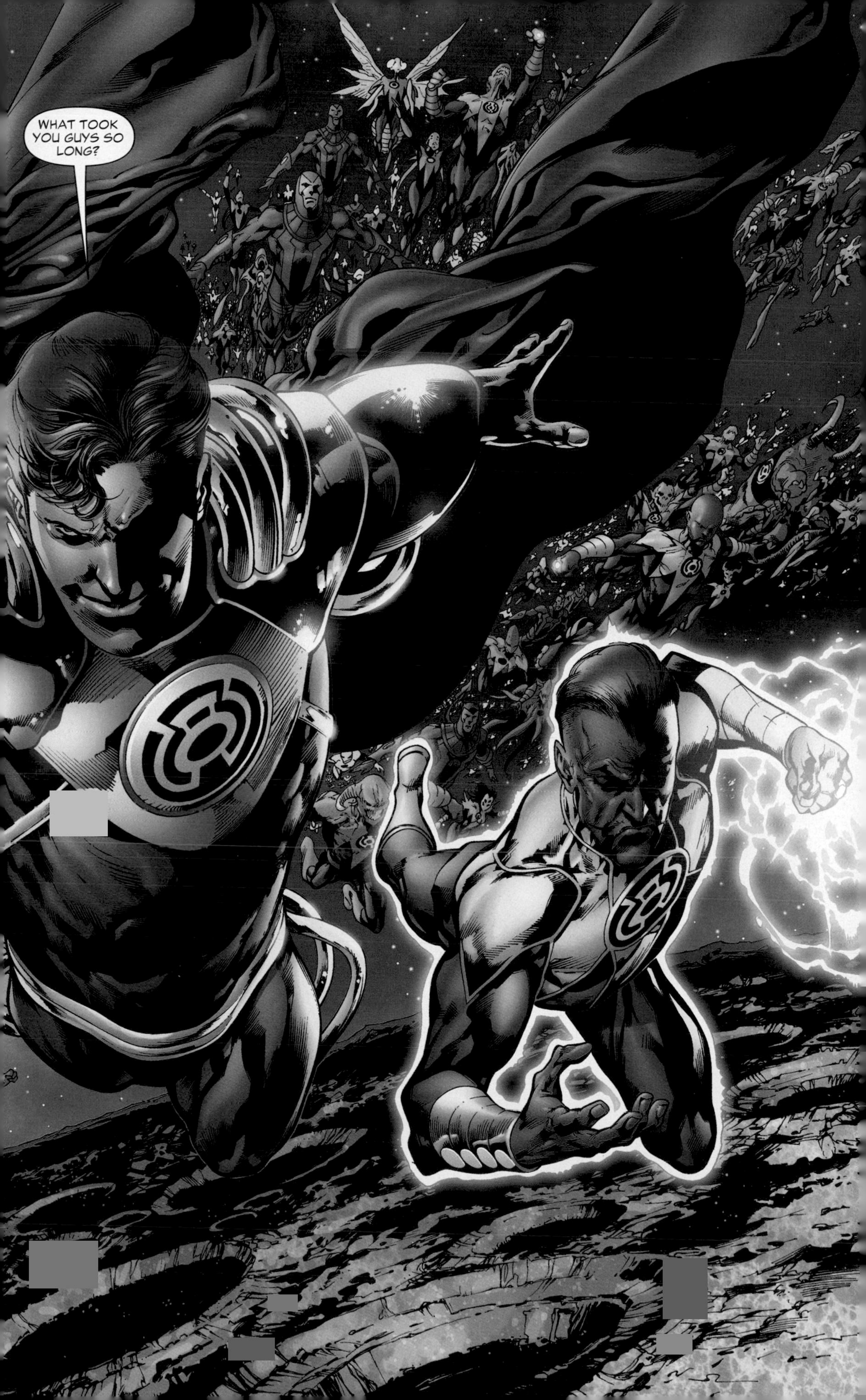
WHAT TOOK YOU GUYS SO LONG?

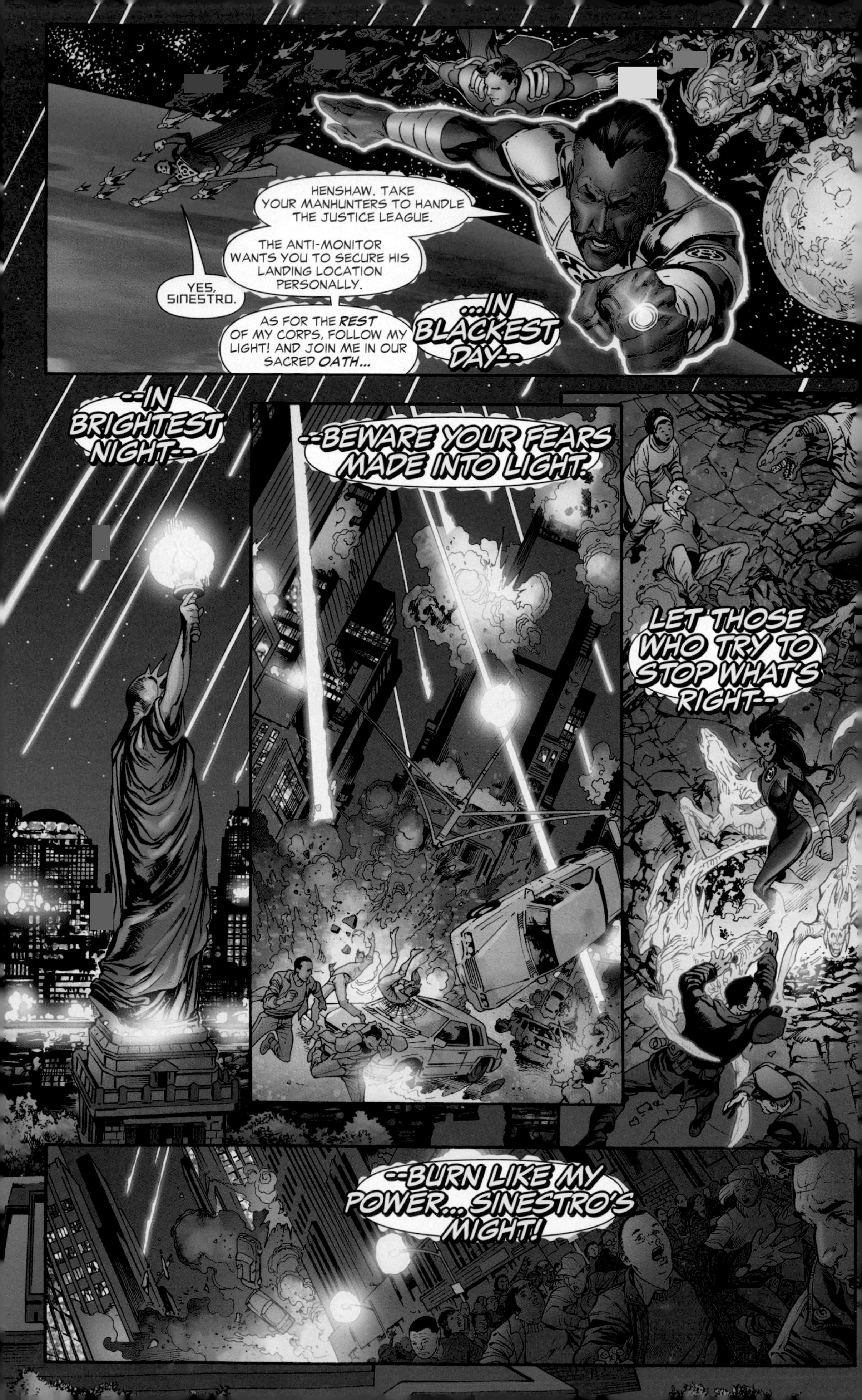
HENSHAW. TAKE YOUR MANHUNTERS TO HANDLE THE JUSTICE LEAGUE.
THE ANTI-MONITOR WANTS YOU TO SECURE HIS LANDING LOCATION PERSONALLY.
YES, SINESTRO.
AS FOR THE REST OF MY CORPS, FOLLOW MY LIGHT! AND JOIN ME IN OUR SACRED OATH...
...IN BLACKEST DAY--
--IN BRIGHTEST NIGHT--
--BEWARE YOUR FEARS MADE INTO LIGHT.
LET THOSE WHO TRY TO STOP WHAT'S RIGHT-
--BURN LIKE MY POWER... SINESTRO'S MIGHT!

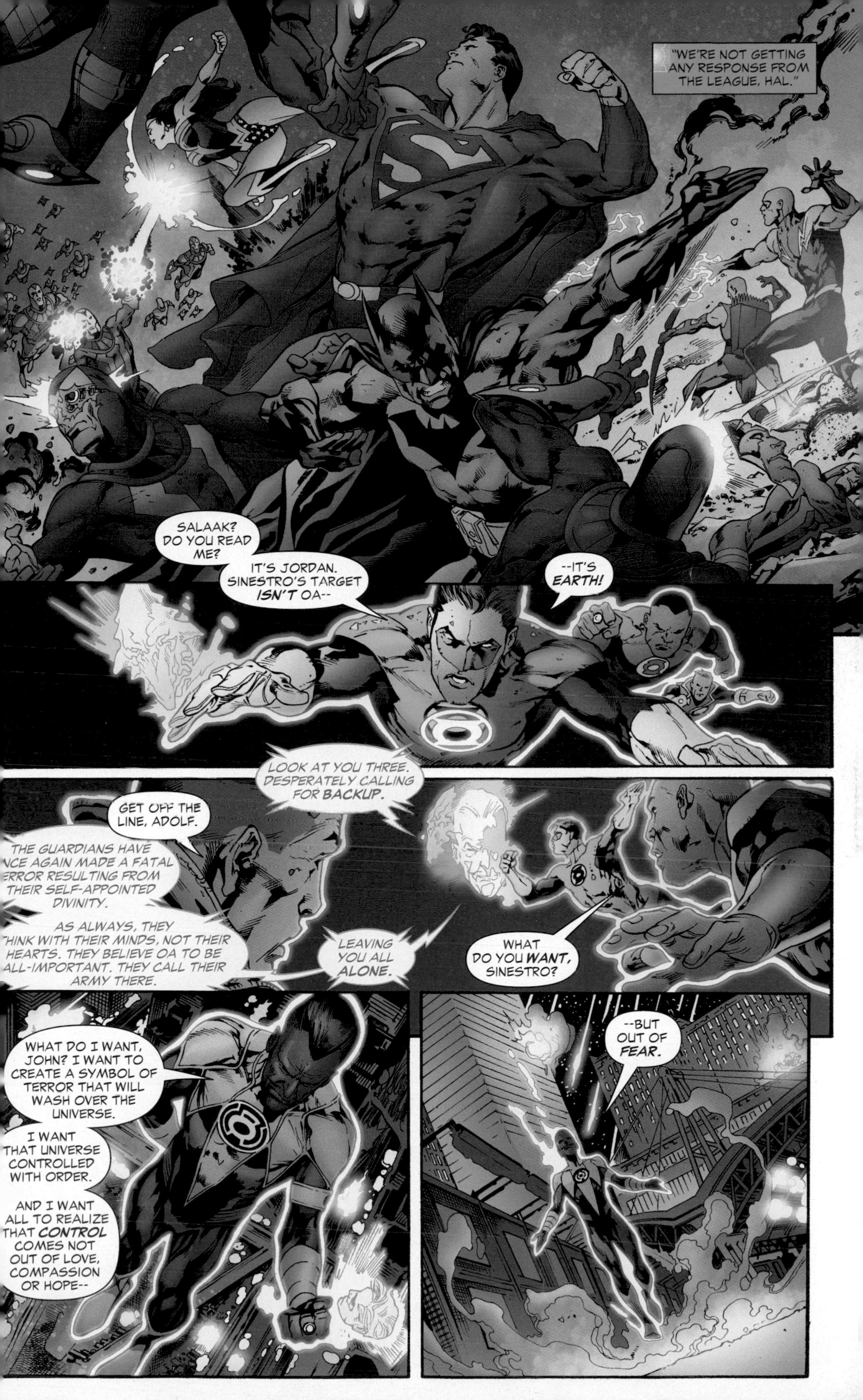
"WE'RE NOT GETTING ANY RESPONSE FROM THE LEAGUE, HAL."
SALAAK? DO YOU READ ME?
IT'S JORDAN. SINESTRO'S TARGET ISN'T OA--
--IT'S EARTH!
LOOK AT YOU THREE. DESPERATELY CALLING FOR BACKUP.
GET OFF THE LINE, ADOLF.
THE GUARDIANS HAVE NCE AGAIN MADE A FATAL RROR RESULTING FROM THEIR SELF-APPOINTED DIVINITY.
AS ALWAYS, THEY THINK WITH THEIR MINDS, NOT THEIR HEARTS. THEY BELIEVE OA TO BE ALL-IMPORTANT. THEY CALL THEIR ARMY THERE.
LEAVING YOU ALL ALONE.
WHAT DO YOU WANT, SINESTRO?
WHAT DO I WANT, JOHN? I WANT TO CREATE A SYMBOL OF TERROR THAT WILL WASH OVER THE UNIVERSE.
I WANT THAT UNIVERSE CONTROLLED WITH ORDER.
AND I WANT ALL TO REALIZE THAT CONTROL COMES NOT OUT OF LOVE, COMPASSION OR HOPE--
--BUT OUT OF FEAR.

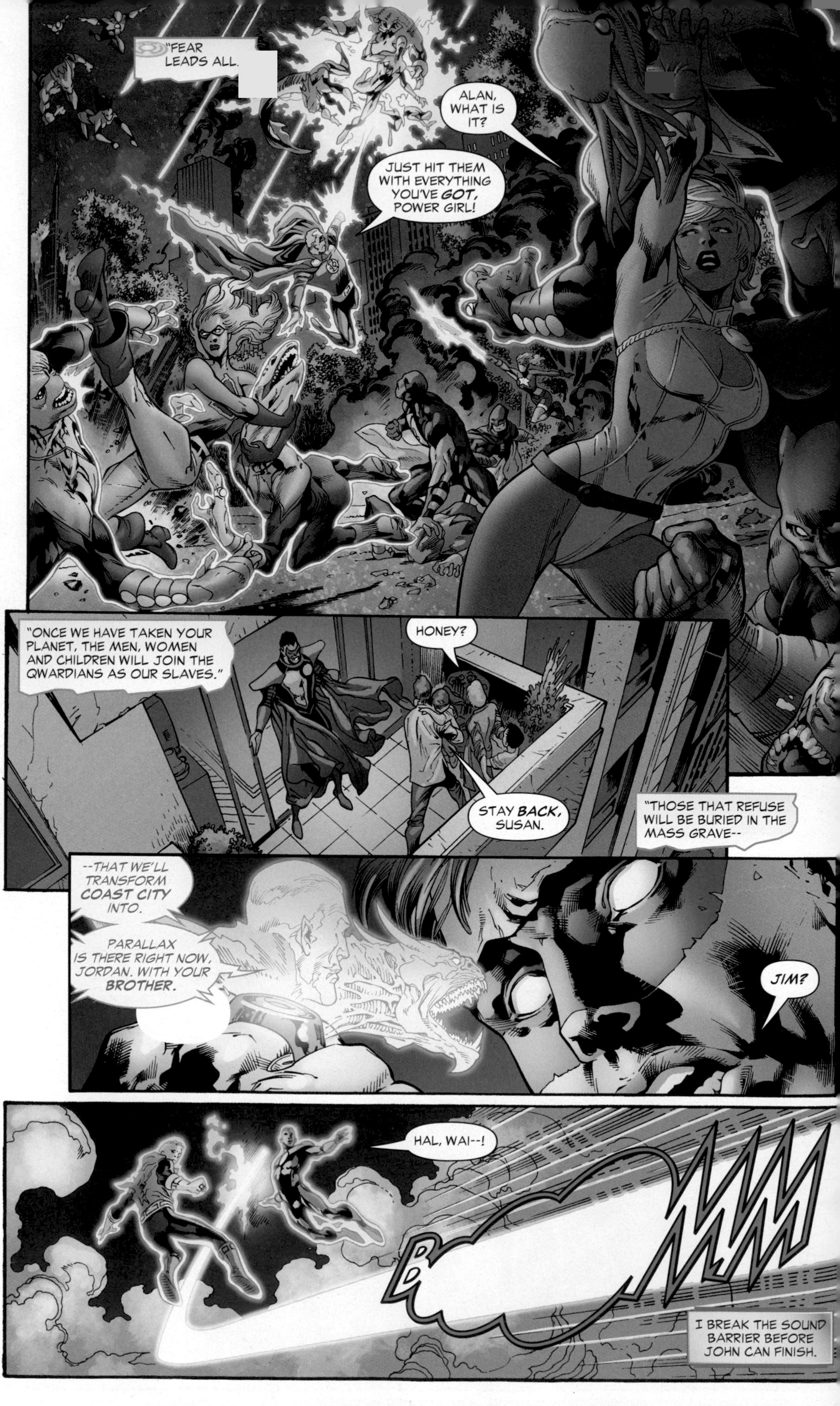
"FEAR LEADS ALL.
ALAN, WHAT IS IT?
JUST HIT THEM WITH EVERYTHING YOU'VE **GOT**, POWER GIRL!
"ONCE WE HAVE TAKEN YOUR PLANET, THE MEN, WOMEN AND CHILDREN WILL JOIN THE QWARDIANS AS OUR SLAVES."
HONEY?
STAY **BACK**, SUSAN.
"THOSE THAT REFUSE WILL BE BURIED IN THE MASS GRAVE--
--THAT WE'LL TRANSFORM **COAST CITY** INTO.
PARALLAX IS THERE RIGHT NOW, JORDAN. WITH YOUR **BROTHER**.
JIM?
HAL, WAI--!
I BREAK THE SOUND BARRIER BEFORE JOHN CAN FINISH.

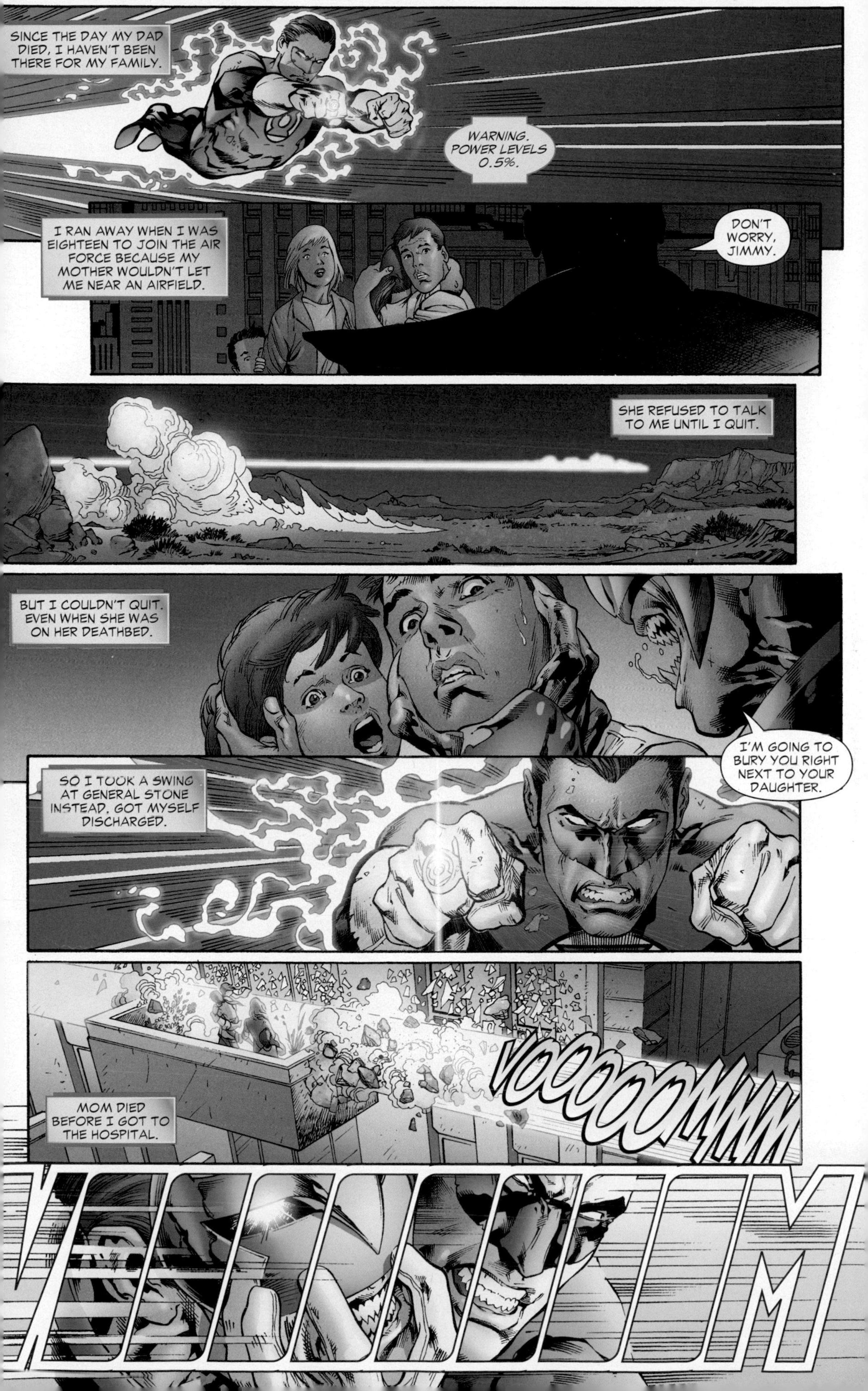

SINCE THE DAY MY DAD DIED, I HAVEN'T BEEN THERE FOR MY FAMILY.
WARNING. POWER LEVELS 0.5%.
I RAN AWAY WHEN I WAS EIGHTEEN TO JOIN THE AIR FORCE BECAUSE MY MOTHER WOULDN'T LET ME NEAR AN AIRFIELD.
DON'T WORRY, JIMMY.
SHE REFUSED TO TALK TO ME UNTIL I QUIT.
BUT I COULDN'T QUIT. EVEN WHEN SHE WAS ON HER DEATHBED.
I'M GOING TO BURY YOU RIGHT NEXT TO YOUR DAUGHTER.
SO I TOOK A SWING AT GENERAL STONE INSTEAD. GOT MYSELF DISCHARGED.
VOOOOOMMM
MOM DIED BEFORE I GOT TO THE HOSPITAL.

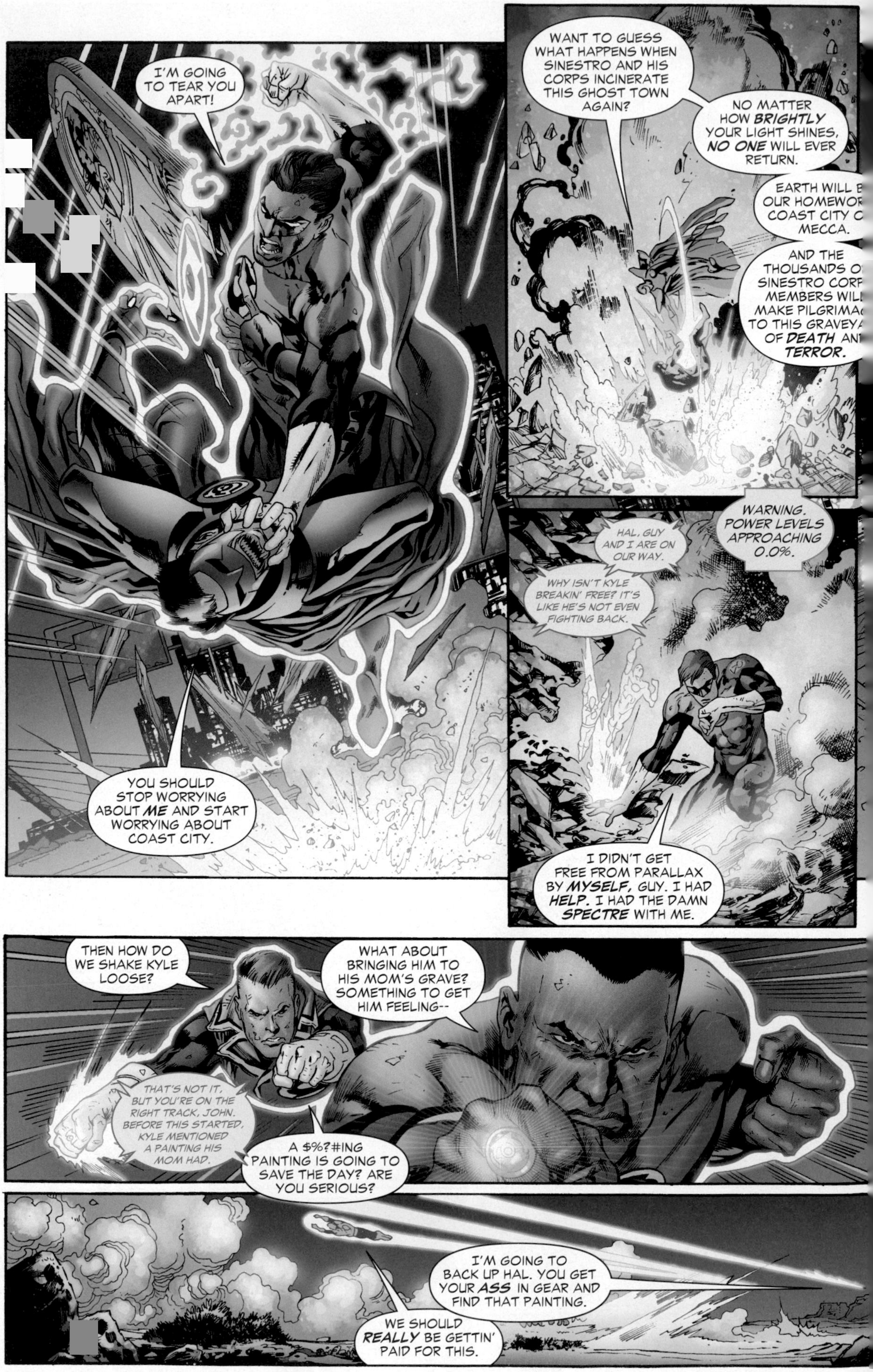
I'M GOING TO TEAR YOU APART!
YOU SHOULD STOP WORRYING ABOUT **ME** AND START WORRYING ABOUT COAST CITY.
WANT TO GUESS WHAT HAPPENS WHEN SINESTRO AND HIS CORPS INCINERATE THIS GHOST TOWN AGAIN?
NO MATTER HOW **BRIGHTLY** YOUR LIGHT SHINES, **NO ONE** WILL EVER RETURN.
EARTH WILL B OUR HOMEWOR COAST CITY O MECCA.
AND THE THOUSANDS O SINESTRO CORP MEMBERS WILL MAKE PILGRIMA TO THIS GRAVEYA OF **DEATH** AN **TERROR.**
WARNING. POWER LEVELS APPROACHING 0.0%.
HAL, GUY AND I ARE ON OUR WAY.
WHY ISN'T KYLE BREAKIN' FREE? IT'S LIKE HE'S NOT EVEN FIGHTING BACK.
I DIDN'T GET FREE FROM PARALLAX BY **MYSELF,** GUY. I HAD **HELP.** I HAD THE DAMN **SPECTRE** WITH ME.
THEN HOW DO WE SHAKE KYLE LOOSE?
WHAT ABOUT BRINGING HIM TO HIS MOM'S GRAVE? SOMETHING TO GET HIM FEELING--
THAT'S NOT IT, BUT YOU'RE ON THE RIGHT TRACK, JOHN. BEFORE THIS STARTED, KYLE MENTIONED A PAINTING HIS MOM HAD.
A $%?#ING PAINTING IS GOING TO SAVE THE DAY? ARE YOU SERIOUS?
I'M GOING TO BACK UP HAL. YOU GET YOUR **ASS** IN GEAR AND FIND THAT PAINTING.
WE SHOULD **REALLY** BE GETTIN' PAID FOR THIS.

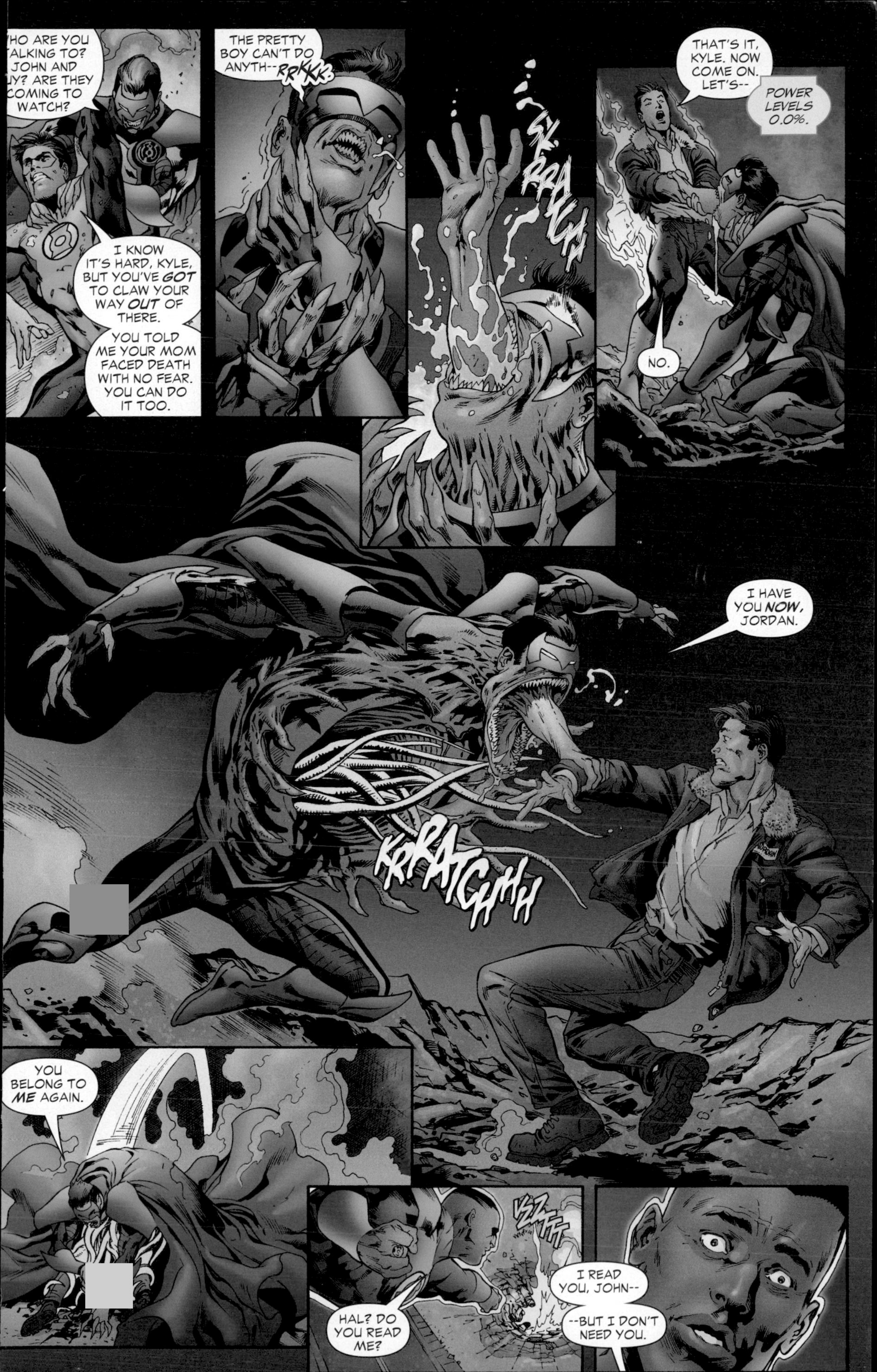

HO ARE YOU TALKING TO? JOHN AND UY? ARE THEY COMING TO WATCH?
I KNOW IT'S HARD, KYLE, BUT YOU'VE GOT TO CLAW YOUR WAY OUT OF THERE.
YOU TOLD ME YOUR MOM FACED DEATH WITH NO FEAR. YOU CAN DO IT TOO.
THE PRETTY BOY CAN'T DO ANYTH--RRKKK.
SKRRAUCH
THAT'S IT, KYLE. NOW COME ON. LET'S--
POWER LEVELS 0.0%.
NO.
I HAVE YOU NOW, JORDAN.
KRRRATCHHHH
YOU BELONG TO ME AGAIN.
VSZZZFFT
HAL? DO YOU READ ME?
I READ YOU, JOHN--
--BUT I DON'T NEED YOU.

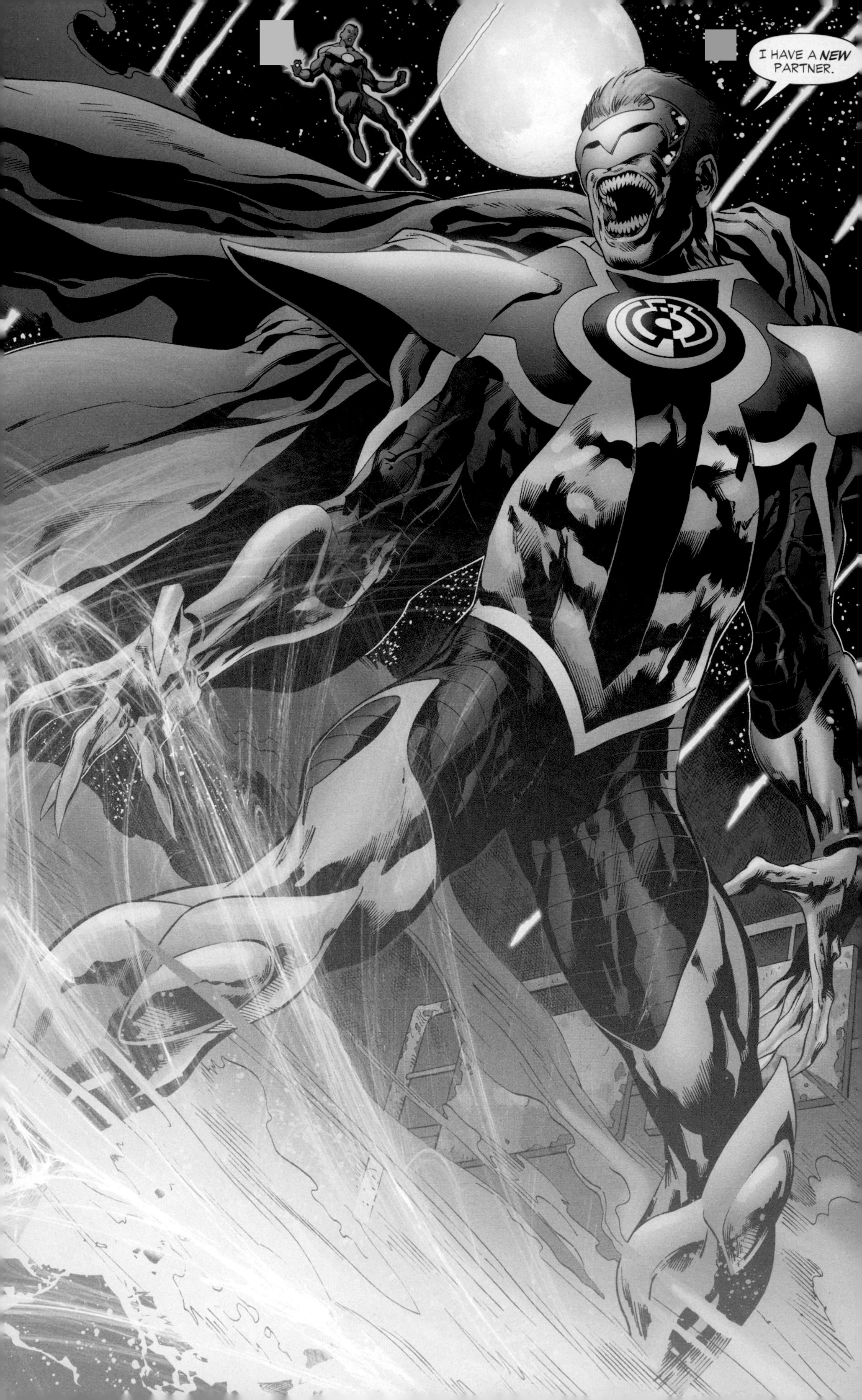
I HAVE A NEW PARTNER.

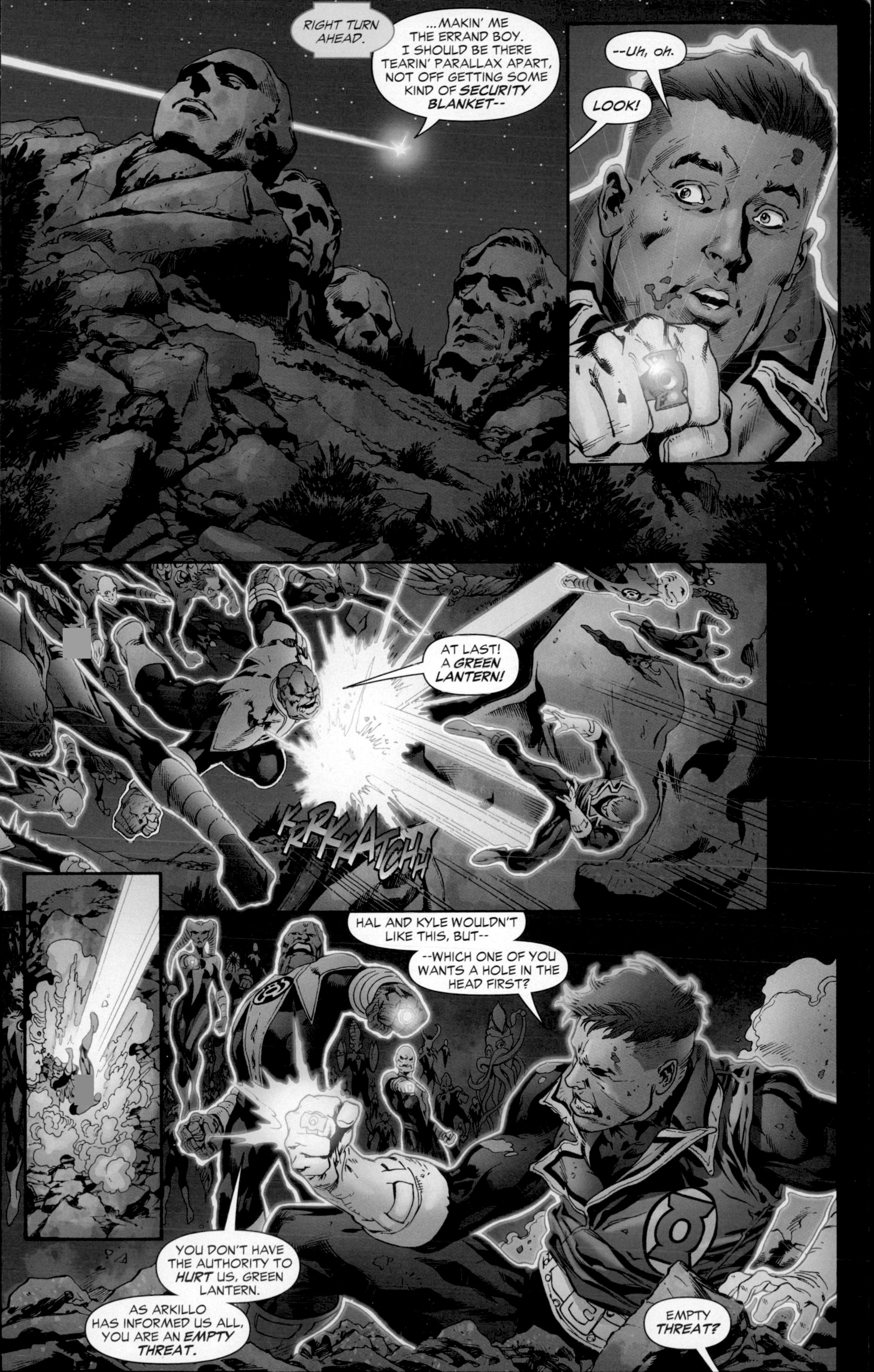

RIGHT TURN AHEAD.
...MAKIN' ME THE ERRAND BOY. I SHOULD BE THERE TEARIN' PARALLAX APART, NOT OFF GETTING SOME KIND OF SECURITY BLANKET--
--Uh, oh.
LOOK!
AT LAST! A GREEN LANTERN!
KRRKATCHH
HAL AND KYLE WOULDN'T LIKE THIS, BUT--
--WHICH ONE OF YOU WANTS A HOLE IN THE HEAD FIRST?
YOU DON'T HAVE THE AUTHORITY TO HURT US, GREEN LANTERN.
AS ARKILLO HAS INFORMED US ALL, YOU ARE AN EMPTY THREAT.
EMPTY THREAT?

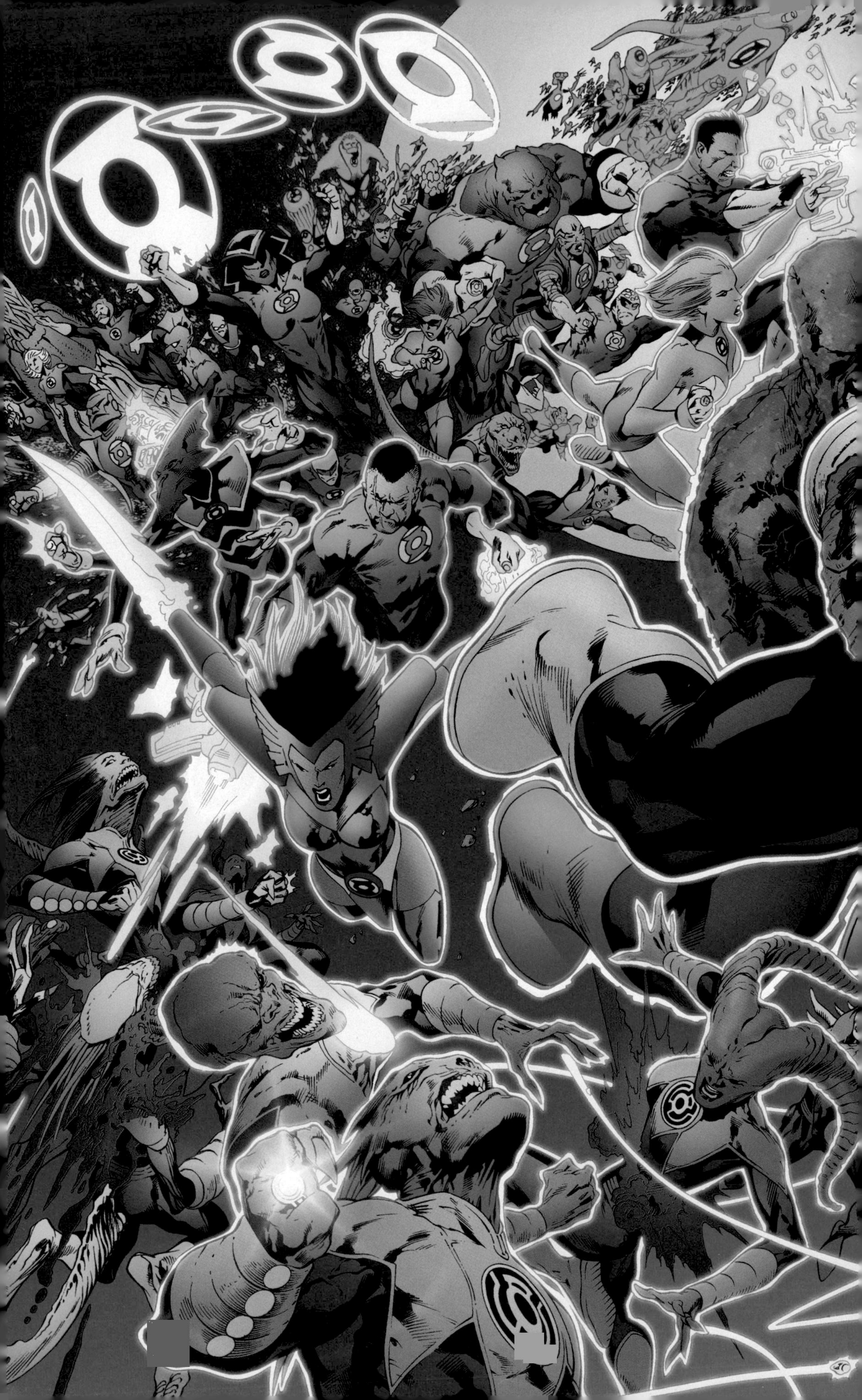

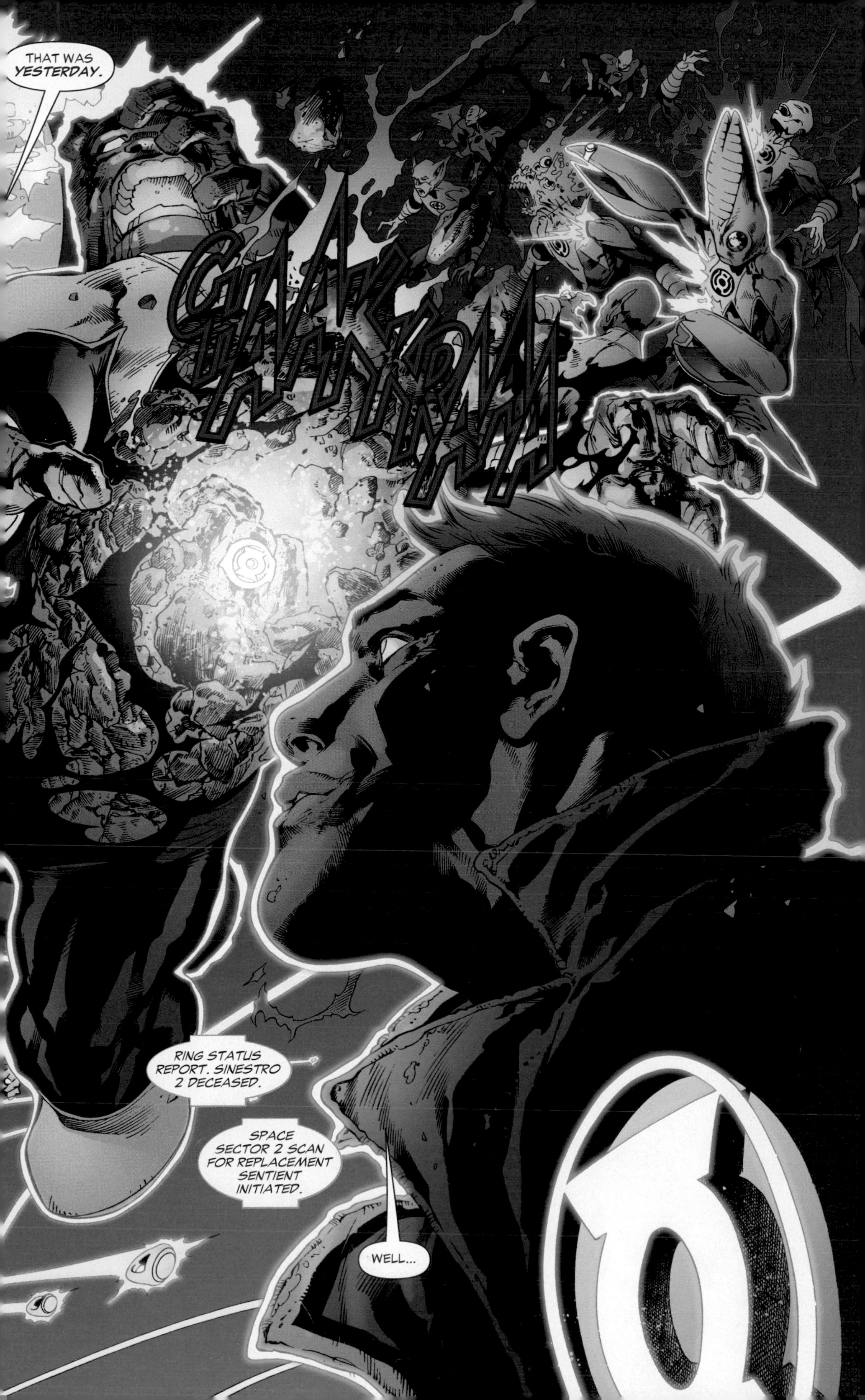
THAT WAS YESTERDAY.
RING STATUS REPORT. SINESTRO 2 DECEASED.
SPACE SECTOR 2 SCAN FOR REPLACEMENT SENTIENT INITIATED.
WELL...

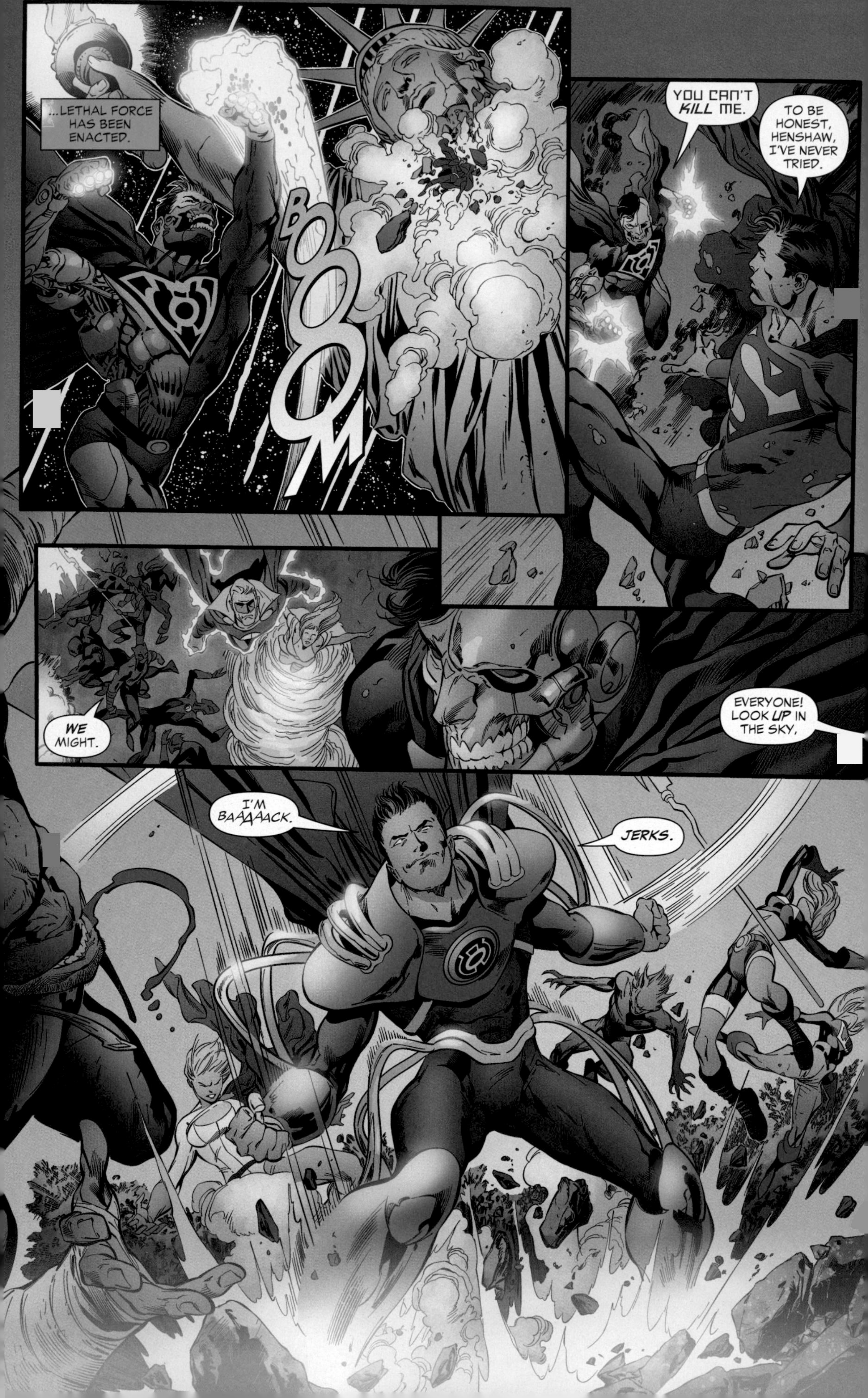
...LETHAL FORCE HAS BEEN ENACTED.
BOOOM
YOU CAN'T KILL ME.
TO BE HONEST, HENSHAW, I'VE NEVER TRIED.
WE MIGHT.
EVERYONE! LOOK UP IN THE SKY.
I'M BAAAAACK.
JERKS.

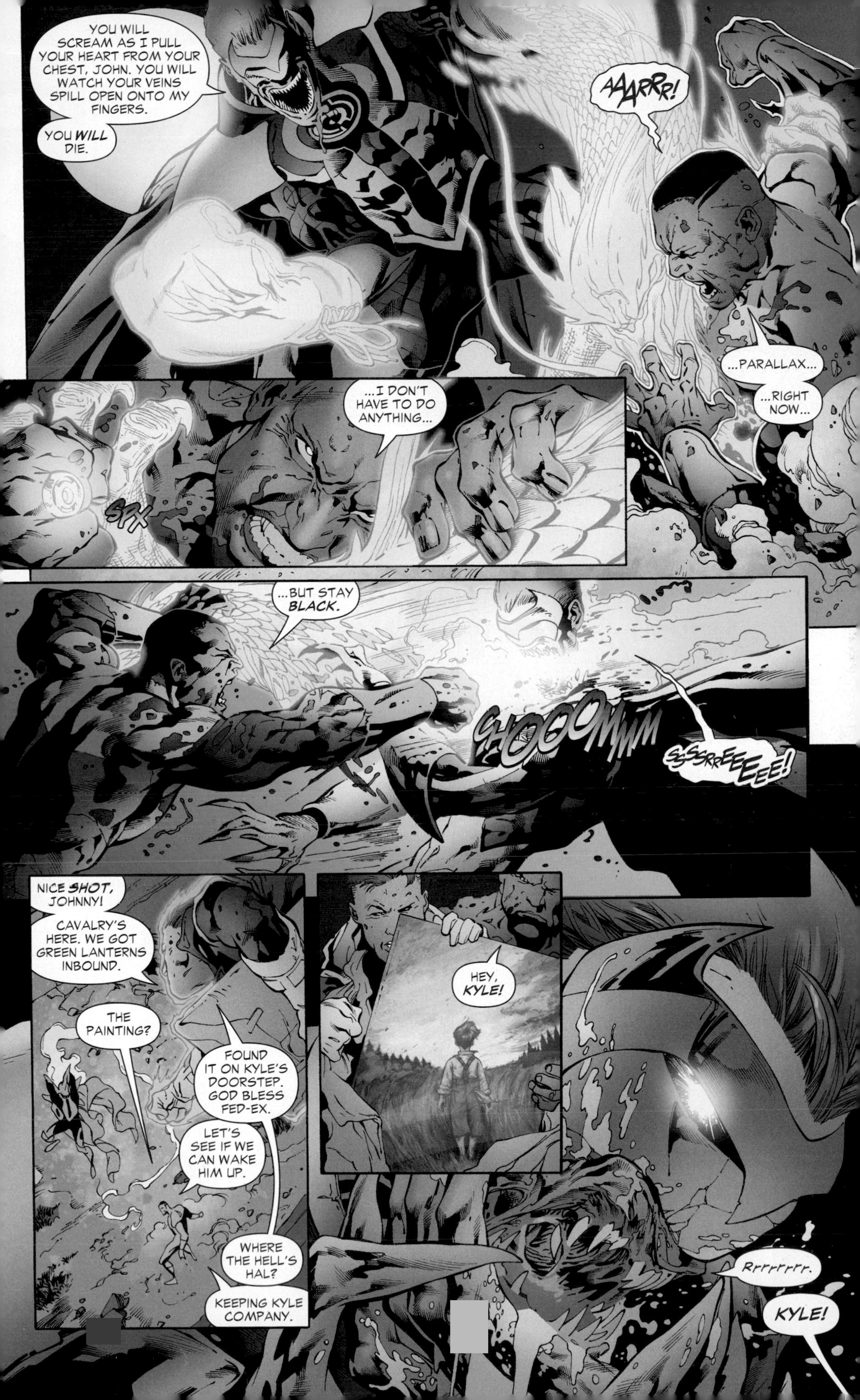
YOU WILL SCREAM AS I PULL YOUR HEART FROM YOUR CHEST, JOHN. YOU WILL WATCH YOUR VEINS SPILL OPEN ONTO MY FINGERS.
YOU *WILL* DIE.
AAARRR!
...PARALLAX...
...RIGHT NOW...
...I DON'T HAVE TO DO ANYTHING...
SPX
...BUT STAY *BLACK.*
CHOOOMMM
SSSRREEEEEE!
NICE *SHOT,* JOHNNY!
CAVALRY'S HERE. WE GOT GREEN LANTERNS INBOUND.
THE PAINTING?
FOUND IT ON KYLE'S DOORSTEP. GOD BLESS FED-EX.
LET'S SEE IF WE CAN WAKE HIM UP.
WHERE THE HELL'S HAL?
KEEPING KYLE COMPANY.
HEY, *KYLE!*
Rrrrrrrr.
KYLE!

KYLE!

HELLO?

IT'S ME.

IT'S HA

HAL...? I'VE BEEN TRYING TO FIND YOU... WHERE...?

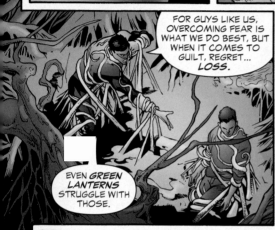

FOR GUYS LIKE US, OVERCOMING FEAR IS WHAT WE DO BEST, BUT WHEN IT COMES TO GUILT, REGRET... LOSS.

EVEN GREEN LANTERNS STRUGGLE WITH THOSE.

BUT WE DON'T HAVE TO DO IT ALONE.

YOU SEE THAT, JOHN?

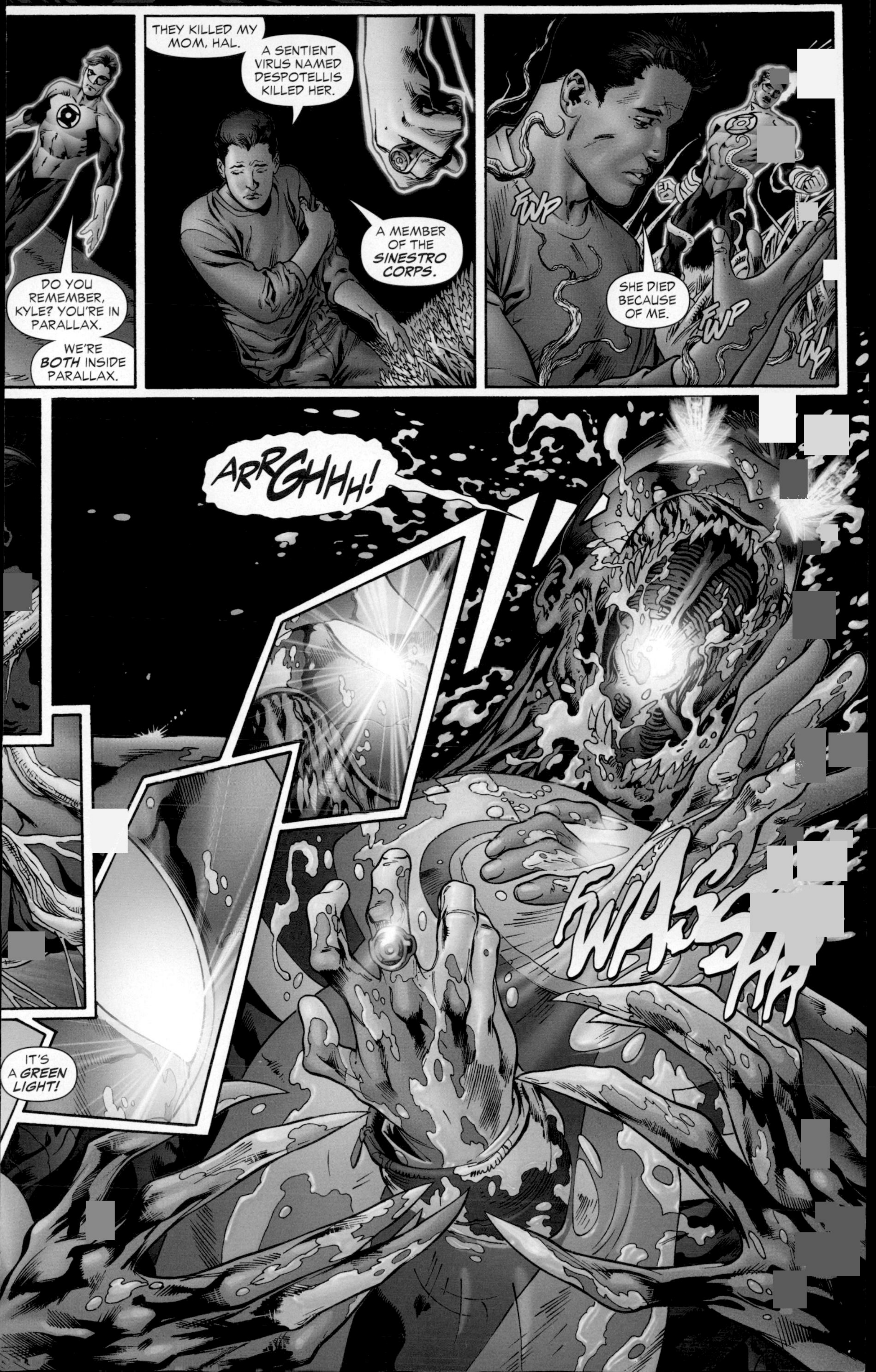
DO YOU REMEMBER, KYLE? YOU'RE IN PARALLAX.
WE'RE BOTH INSIDE PARALLAX.
THEY KILLED MY MOM, HAL.
A SENTIENT VIRUS NAMED DESPOTELLIS KILLED HER.
A MEMBER OF THE SINESTRO CORPS.
FWP
SHE DIED BECAUSE OF ME.
FWP
FWP
ARRGHHH!
FWASHH
IT'S A GREEN LIGHT!

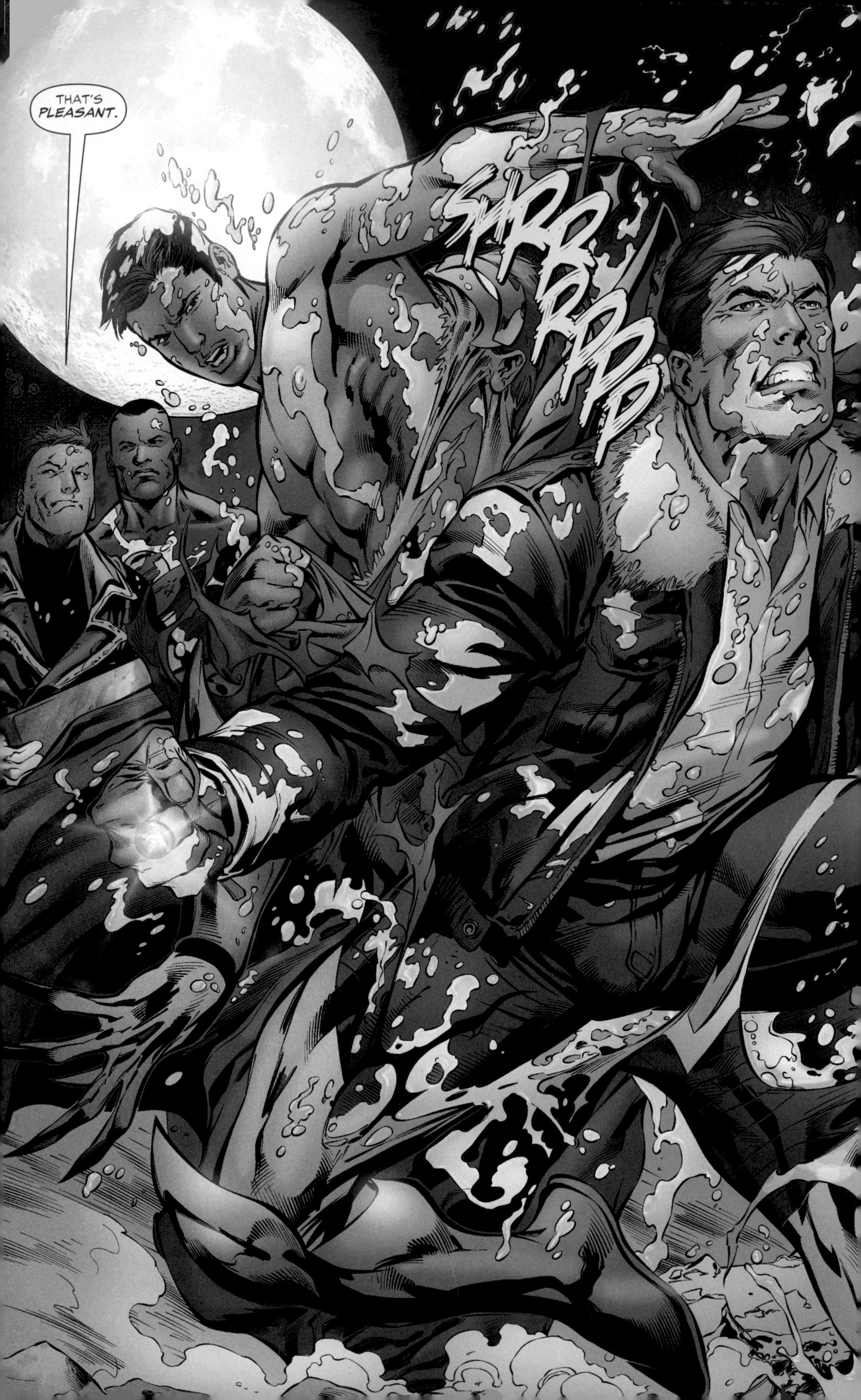
THAT'S PLEASANT.
SHRRRRRRP

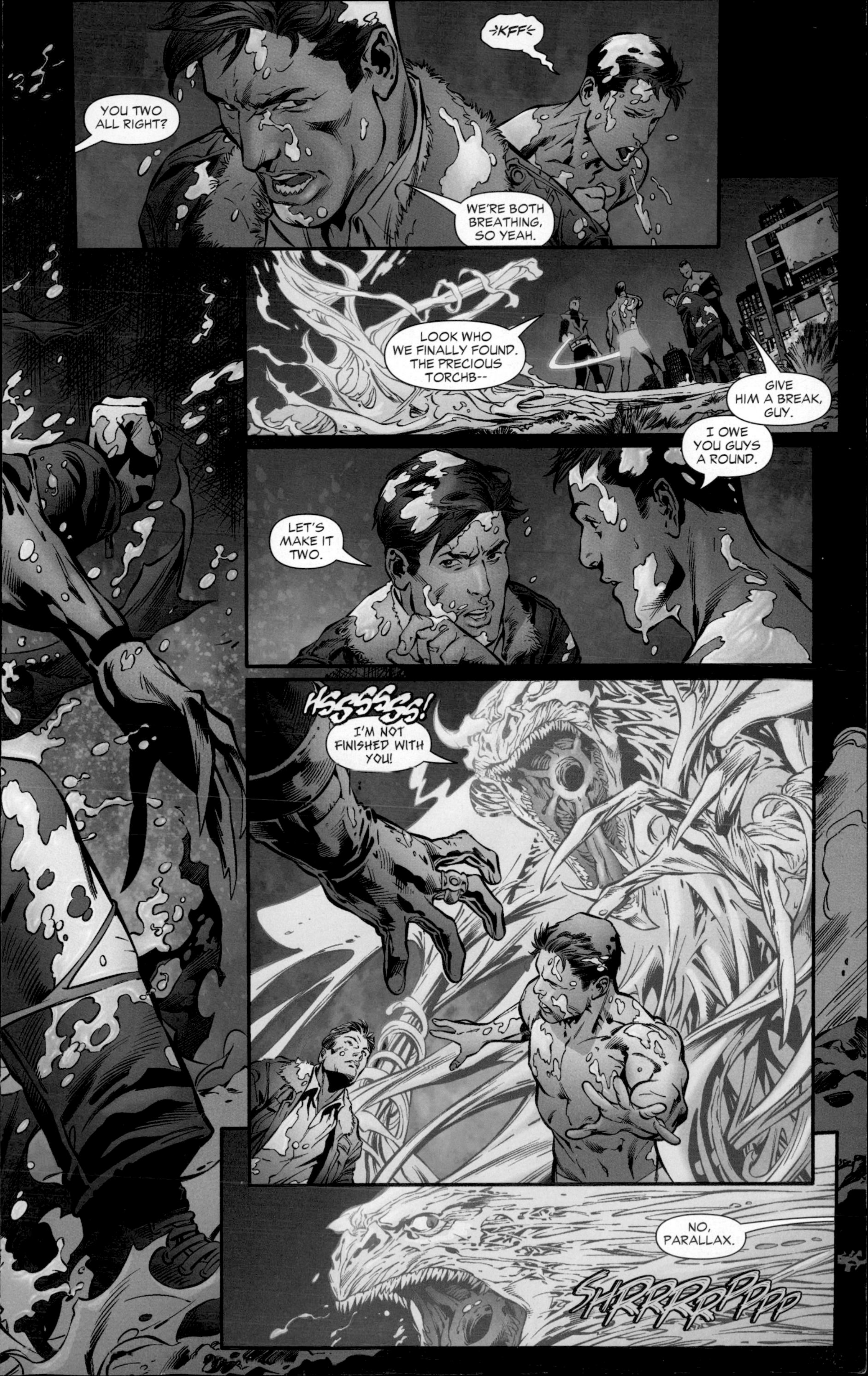

KFF
YOU TWO ALL RIGHT?
WE'RE BOTH BREATHING, SO YEAH.
LOOK WHO WE FINALLY FOUND. THE PRECIOUS TORCHB--
GIVE HIM A BREAK, GUY.
I OWE YOU GUYS A ROUND.
LET'S MAKE IT TWO.
HSSSSSS!
I'M NOT FINISHED WITH YOU!
NO, PARALLAX.
SHRRRRPPPP

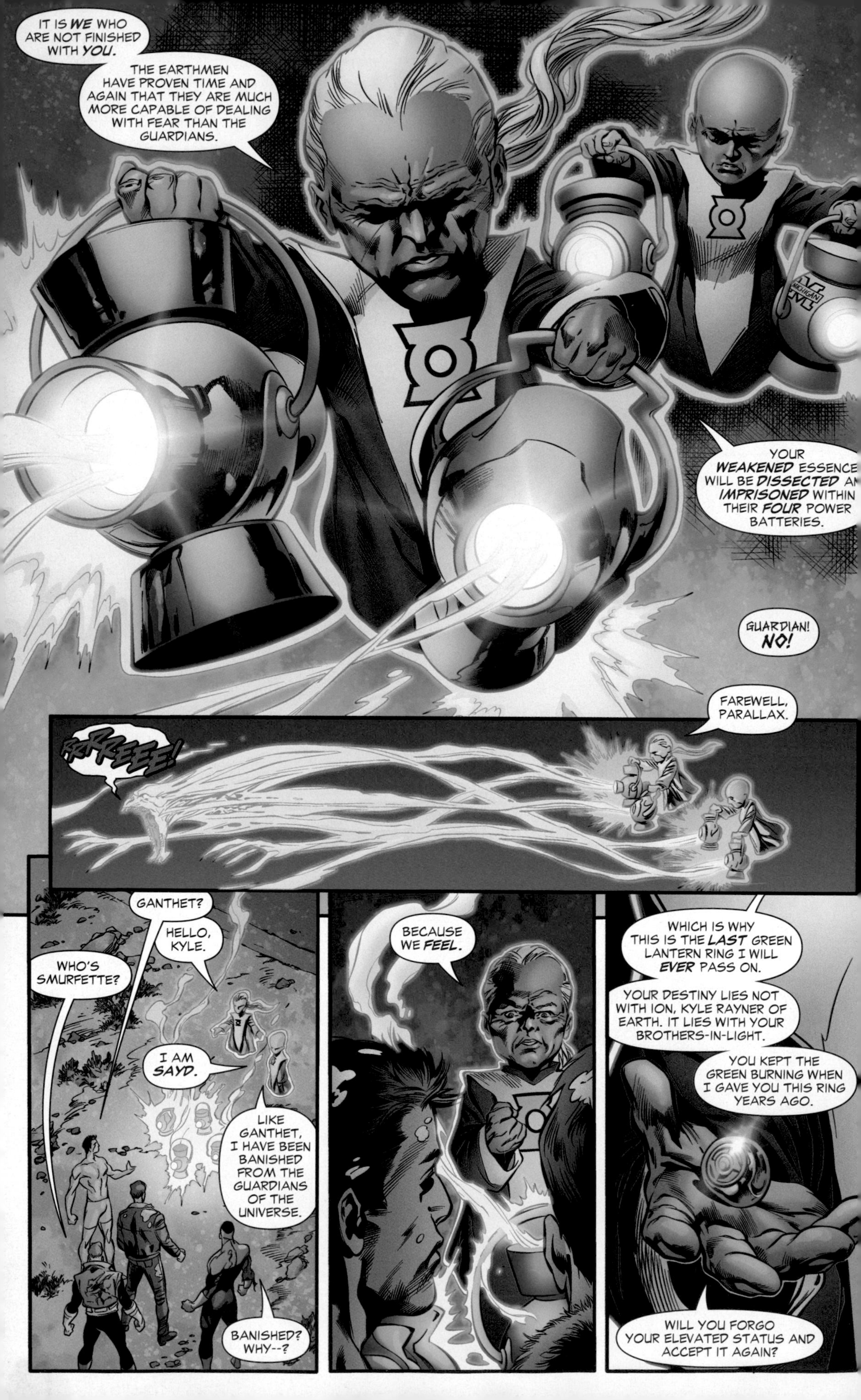
IT IS *WE* WHO ARE NOT FINISHED WITH *YOU*.
THE EARTHMEN HAVE PROVEN TIME AND AGAIN THAT THEY ARE MUCH MORE CAPABLE OF DEALING WITH FEAR THAN THE GUARDIANS.
YOUR *WEAKENED* ESSENCE WILL BE *DISSECTED* AN *IMPRISONED* WITHIN THEIR *FOUR* POWER BATTERIES.
GUARDIAN! **NO!**
FAREWELL, PARALLAX.
RRRREEEE!
GANTHET?
HELLO, KYLE.
WHO'S SMURFETTE?
I AM *SAYD*.
LIKE GANTHET, I HAVE BEEN BANISHED FROM THE GUARDIANS OF THE UNIVERSE.
BANISHED? WHY--?
BECAUSE WE *FEEL*.
WHICH IS WHY THIS IS THE *LAST* GREEN LANTERN RING I WILL *EVER* PASS ON.
YOUR DESTINY LIES NOT WITH ION, KYLE RAYNER OF EARTH. IT LIES WITH YOUR BROTHERS-IN-LIGHT.
YOU KEPT THE GREEN BURNING WHEN I GAVE YOU THIS RING YEARS AGO.
WILL YOU FORGO YOUR ELEVATED STATUS AND ACCEPT IT AGAIN?

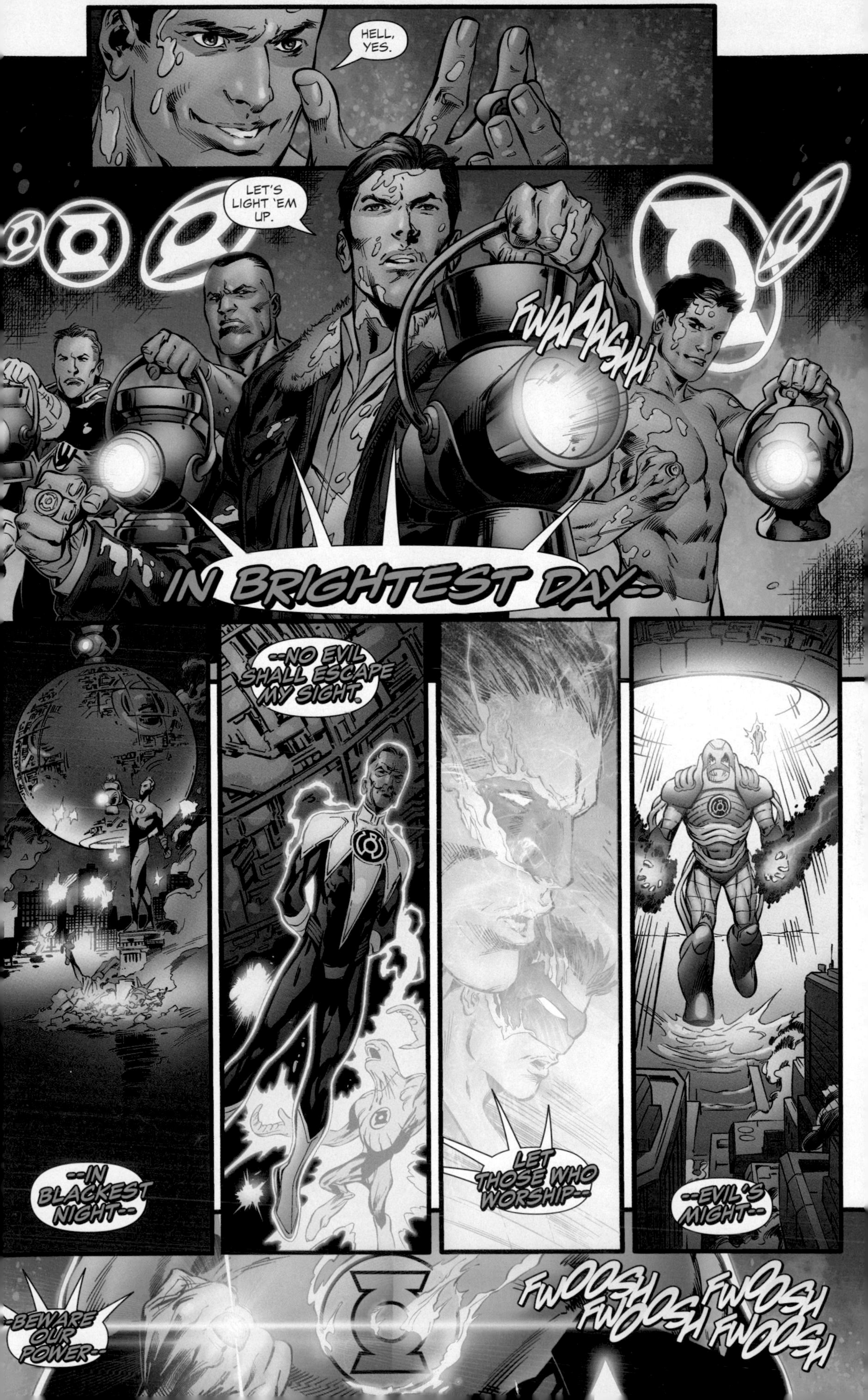
HELL, YES.
LET'S LIGHT 'EM UP.
FWAAAASHH
IN BRIGHTEST DAY--
--NO EVIL SHALL ESCAPE MY SIGHT.
--IN BLACKEST NIGHT--
LET THOSE WHO WORSHIP--
--EVIL'S MIGHT--
-BEWARE OUR POWER--
FWOOSH FWOOSH FWOOSH FWOOSH

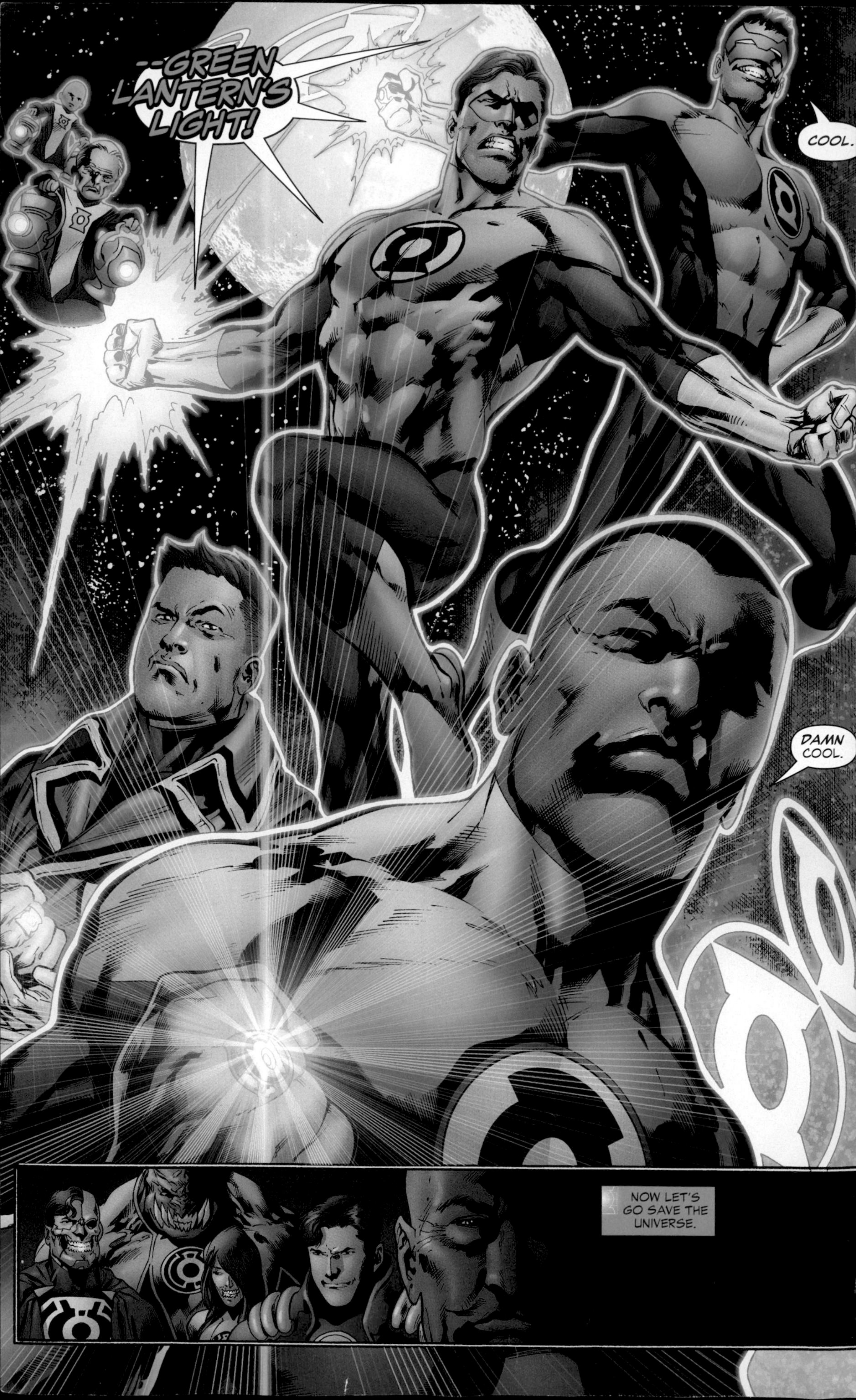
--GREEN LANTERN'S LIGHT!
COOL.
DAMN COOL.
NOW LET'S GO SAVE THE UNIVERSE.

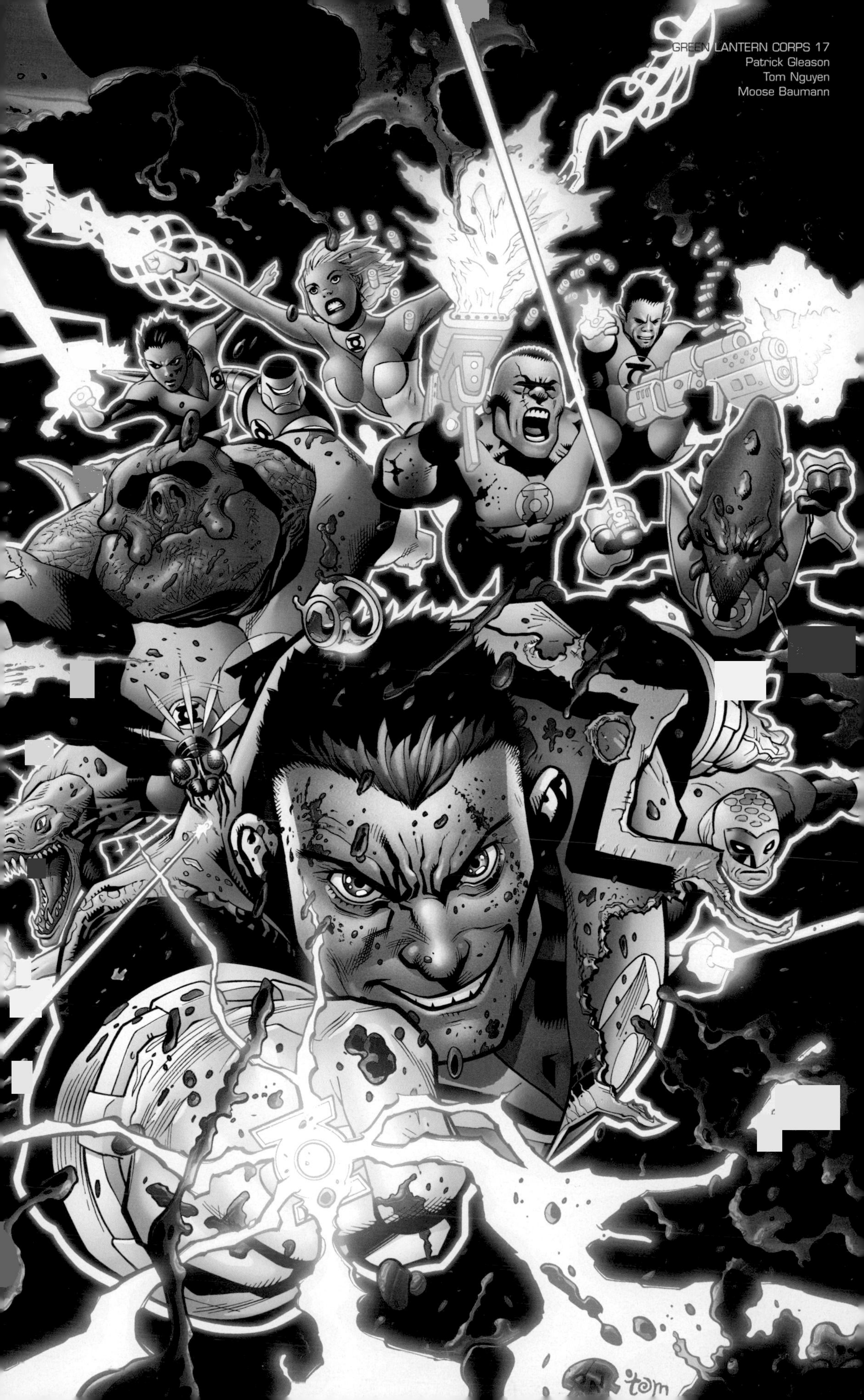
GREEN LANTERN CORPS 17
Patrick Gleason
Tom Nguyen
Moose Baumann

THE SINESTRO CORPS WAR
Chapter Eight
ENDGAME
Writer: **Dave Gibbons**
Pencillers: **Pascal Alixe, Angel Unzueta, Dustin Nguyen** and **Patrick Gleason**
Inkers: **Vicente Cifuentes, Rodney Ramos, Rob Hunter,**
Marlo Alquiza and **Prentis Rollins**
Colorist: **Guy Major**

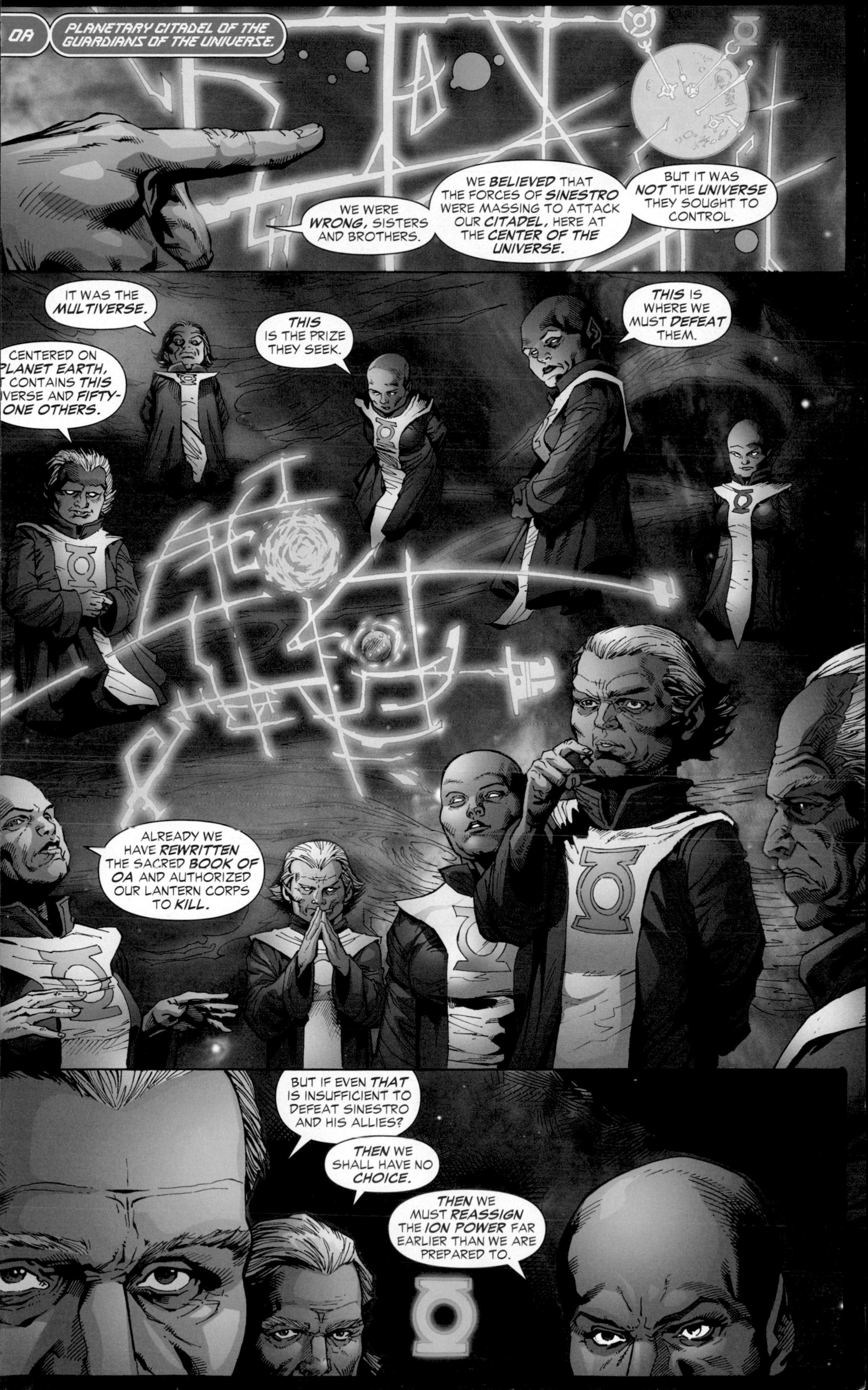
OA
PLANETARY CITADEL OF THE GUARDIANS OF THE UNIVERSE.
WE WERE WRONG, SISTERS AND BROTHERS.
WE BELIEVED THAT THE FORCES OF SINESTRO WERE MASSING TO ATTACK OUR CITADEL, HERE AT THE CENTER OF THE UNIVERSE.
BUT IT WAS NOT THE UNIVERSE THEY SOUGHT TO CONTROL.
IT WAS THE MULTIVERSE.
CENTERED ON PLANET EARTH, T CONTAINS THIS IVERSE AND FIFTY-ONE OTHERS.
THIS IS THE PRIZE THEY SEEK.
THIS IS WHERE WE MUST DEFEAT THEM.
ALREADY WE HAVE REWRITTEN THE SACRED BOOK OF OA AND AUTHORIZED OUR LANTERN CORPS TO KILL.
BUT IF EVEN THAT IS INSUFFICIENT TO DEFEAT SINESTRO AND HIS ALLIES?
THEN WE SHALL HAVE NO CHOICE.
THEN WE MUST REASSIGN THE ION POWER FAR EARLIER THAN WE ARE PREPARED TO.

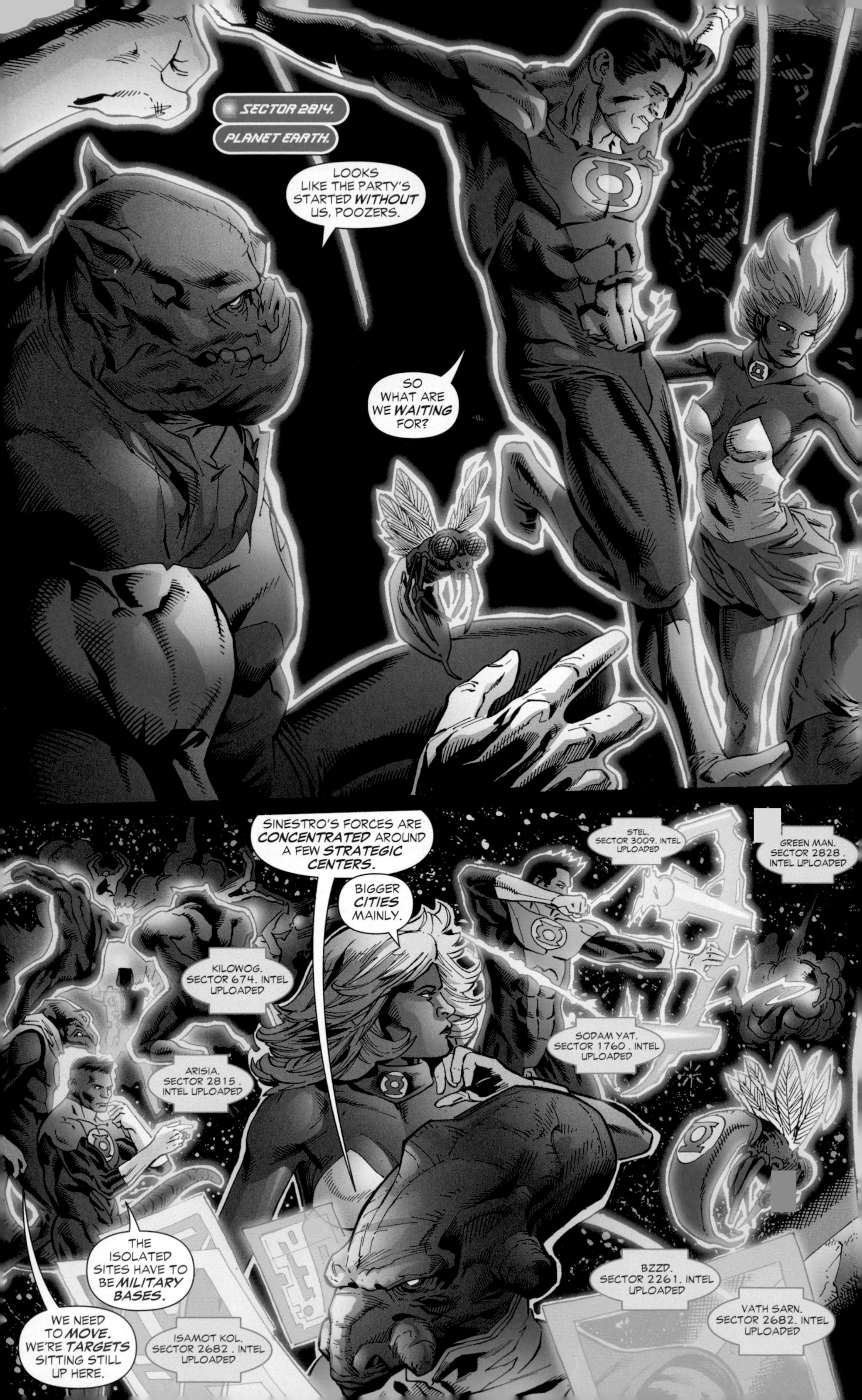
SECTOR 2814.
PLANET EARTH.
LOOKS LIKE THE PARTY'S STARTED WITHOUT US, POOZERS.
SO WHAT ARE WE WAITING FOR?
SINESTRO'S FORCES ARE CONCENTRATED AROUND A FEW STRATEGIC CENTERS.
BIGGER CITIES MAINLY.
STEL. SECTOR 3009. INTEL UPLOADED
GREEN MAN. SECTOR 2828 . INTEL UPLOADED
KILOWOG. SECTOR 674. INTEL UPLOADED
SODAM YAT. SECTOR 1760 . INTEL UPLOADED
ARISIA. SECTOR 2815 . INTEL UPLOADED
THE ISOLATED SITES HAVE TO BE MILITARY BASES.
WE NEED TO MOVE. WE'RE TARGETS SITTING STILL UP HERE.
ISAMOT KOL. SECTOR 2682 . INTEL UPLOADED
BZZD. SECTOR 2261. INTEL UPLOADED
VATH SARN. SECTOR 2682. INTEL UPLOADED

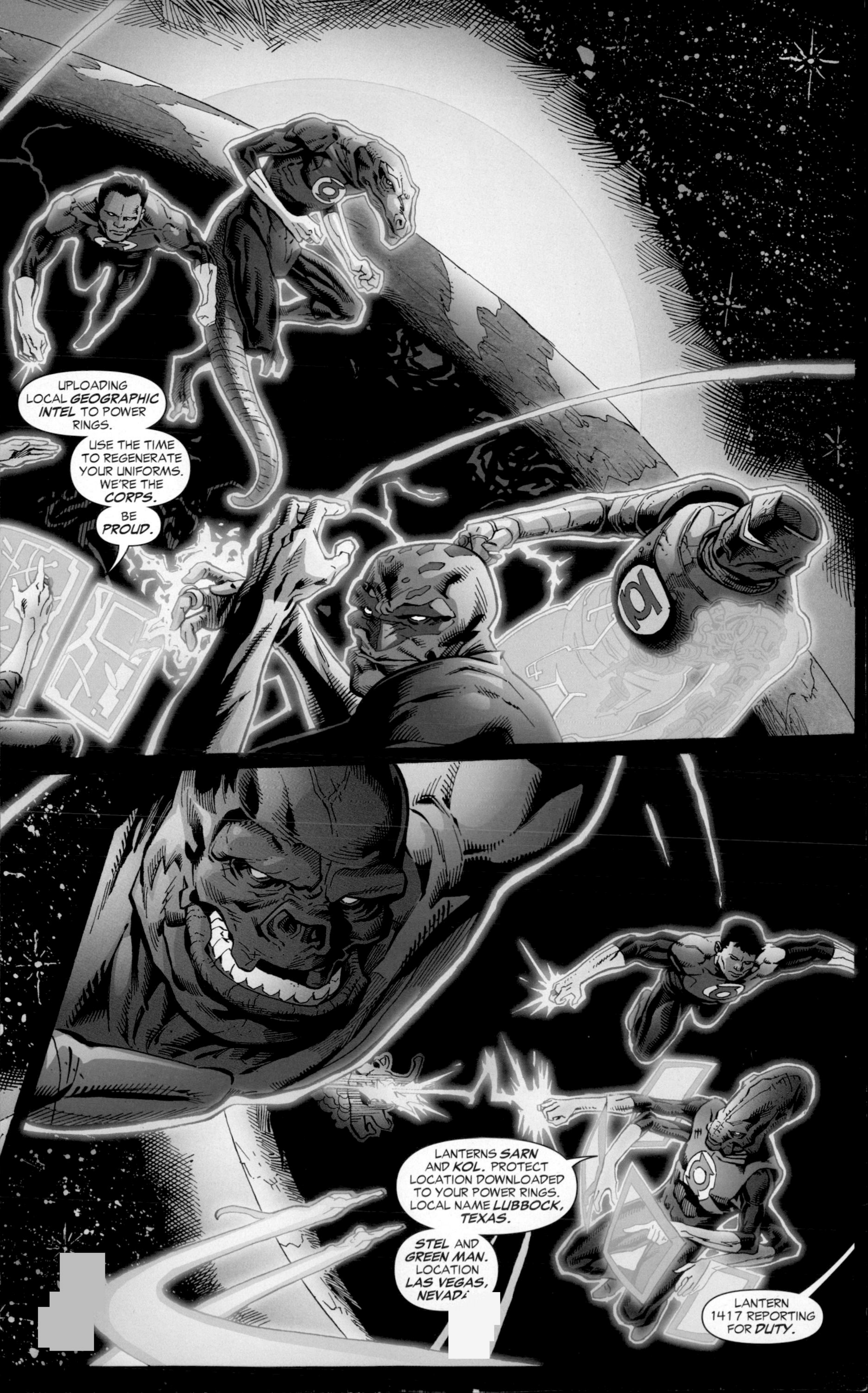
UPLOADING LOCAL GEOGRAPHIC INTEL TO POWER RINGS.
USE THE TIME TO REGENERATE YOUR UNIFORMS. WE'RE THE CORPS.
BE PROUD.
LANTERNS SARN AND KOL. PROTECT LOCATION DOWNLOADED TO YOUR POWER RINGS. LOCAL NAME LUBBOCK, TEXAS.
STEL AND GREEN MAN. LOCATION LAS VEGAS, NEVADA.
LANTERN 1417 REPORTING FOR DUTY.

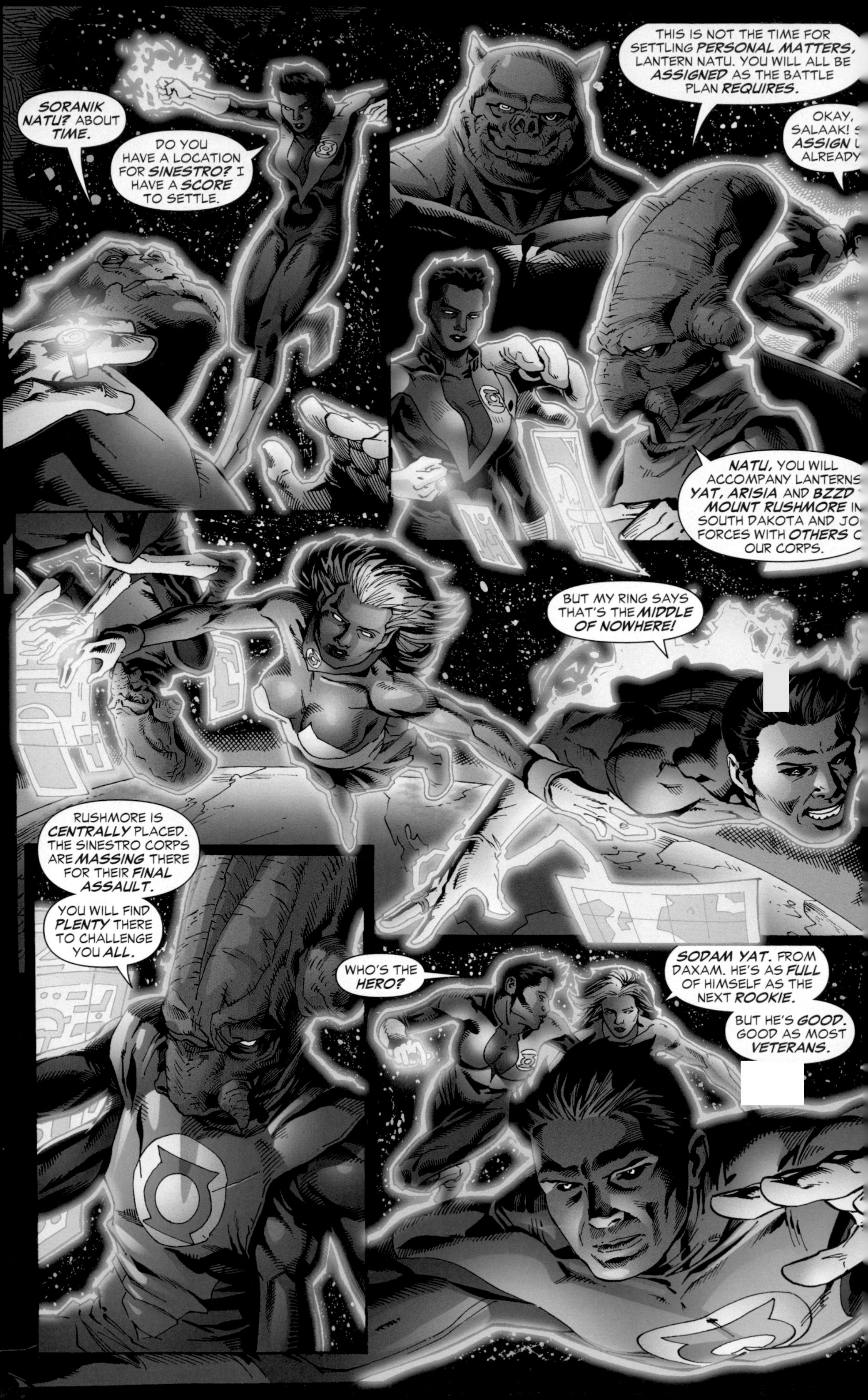
SORANIK NATU? ABOUT TIME.
DO YOU HAVE A LOCATION FOR SINESTRO? I HAVE A SCORE TO SETTLE.
THIS IS NOT THE TIME FOR SETTLING PERSONAL MATTERS, LANTERN NATU. YOU WILL ALL BE ASSIGNED AS THE BATTLE PLAN REQUIRES.
OKAY, SALAAK!
ALREADY
NATU, YOU WILL ACCOMPANY LANTERNS YAT, ARISIA AND BZZD
MOUNT RUSHMORE IN
SOUTH DAKOTA AND JO
FORCES WITH OTHERS
OUR CORPS.
BUT MY RING SAYS THAT'S THE MIDDLE OF NOWHERE!
RUSHMORE IS CENTRALLY PLACED. THE SINESTRO CORPS ARE MASSING THERE FOR THEIR FINAL ASSAULT.
YOU WILL FIND PLENTY THERE TO CHALLENGE YOU ALL.
WHO'S THE HERO?
SODAM YAT. FROM DAXAM. HE'S AS FULL OF HIMSELF AS THE NEXT ROOKIE.
BUT HE'S GOOD. GOOD AS MOST VETERANS.

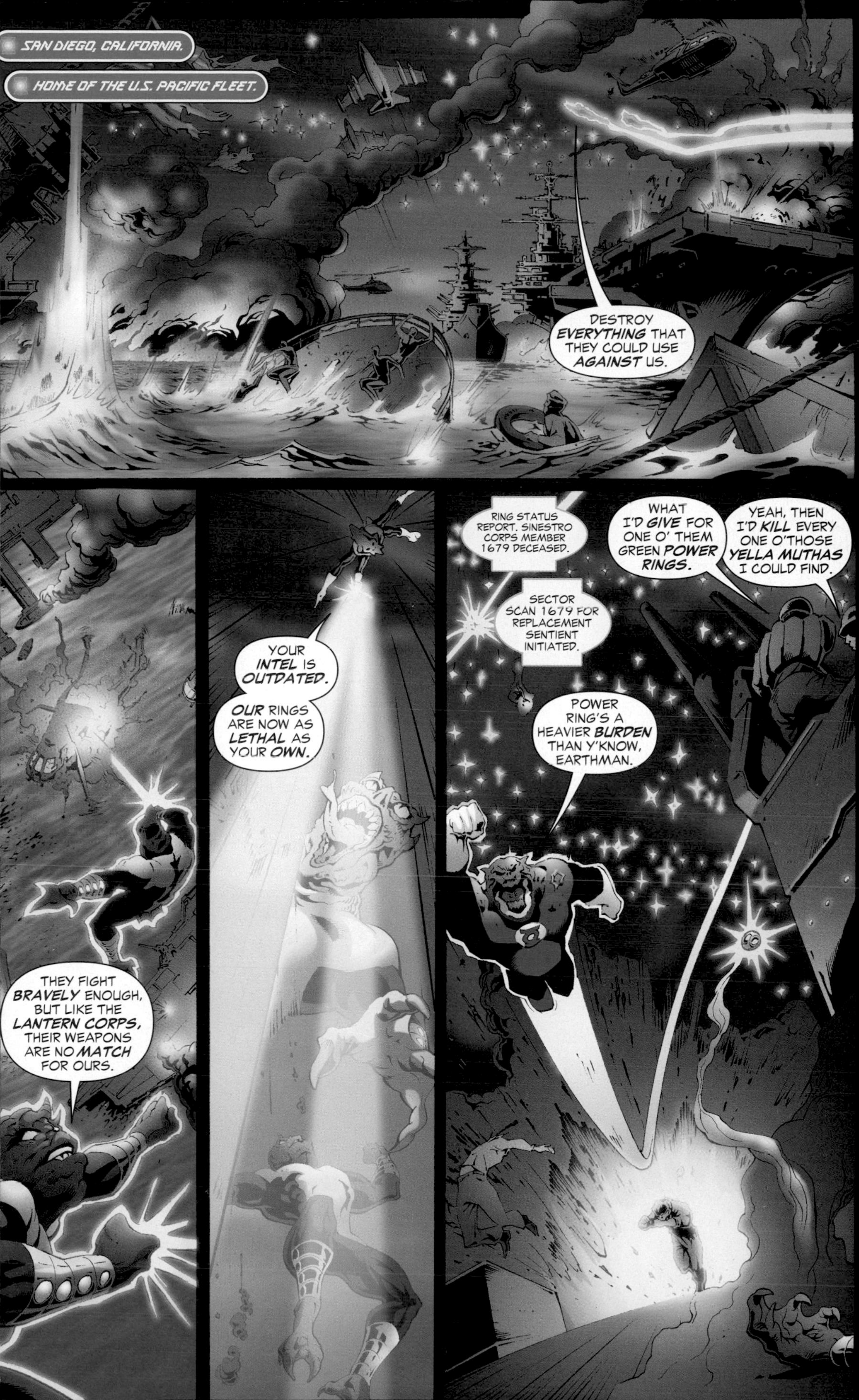
SAN DIEGO, CALIFORNIA.
HOME OF THE U.S. PACIFIC FLEET.
DESTROY EVERYTHING THAT THEY COULD USE AGAINST US.
THEY FIGHT BRAVELY ENOUGH, BUT LIKE THE LANTERN CORPS, THEIR WEAPONS ARE NO MATCH FOR OURS.
YOUR INTEL IS OUTDATED.
OUR RINGS ARE NOW AS LETHAL AS YOUR OWN.
RING STATUS REPORT. SINESTRO CORPS MEMBER 1679 DECEASED.
SECTOR SCAN 1679 FOR REPLACEMENT SENTIENT INITIATED.
WHAT I'D GIVE FOR ONE O' THEM GREEN POWER RINGS.
YEAH, THEN I'D KILL EVERY ONE O'THOSE YELLA MUTHAS I COULD FIND.
POWER RING'S A HEAVIER BURDEN THAN Y'KNOW, EARTHMAN.

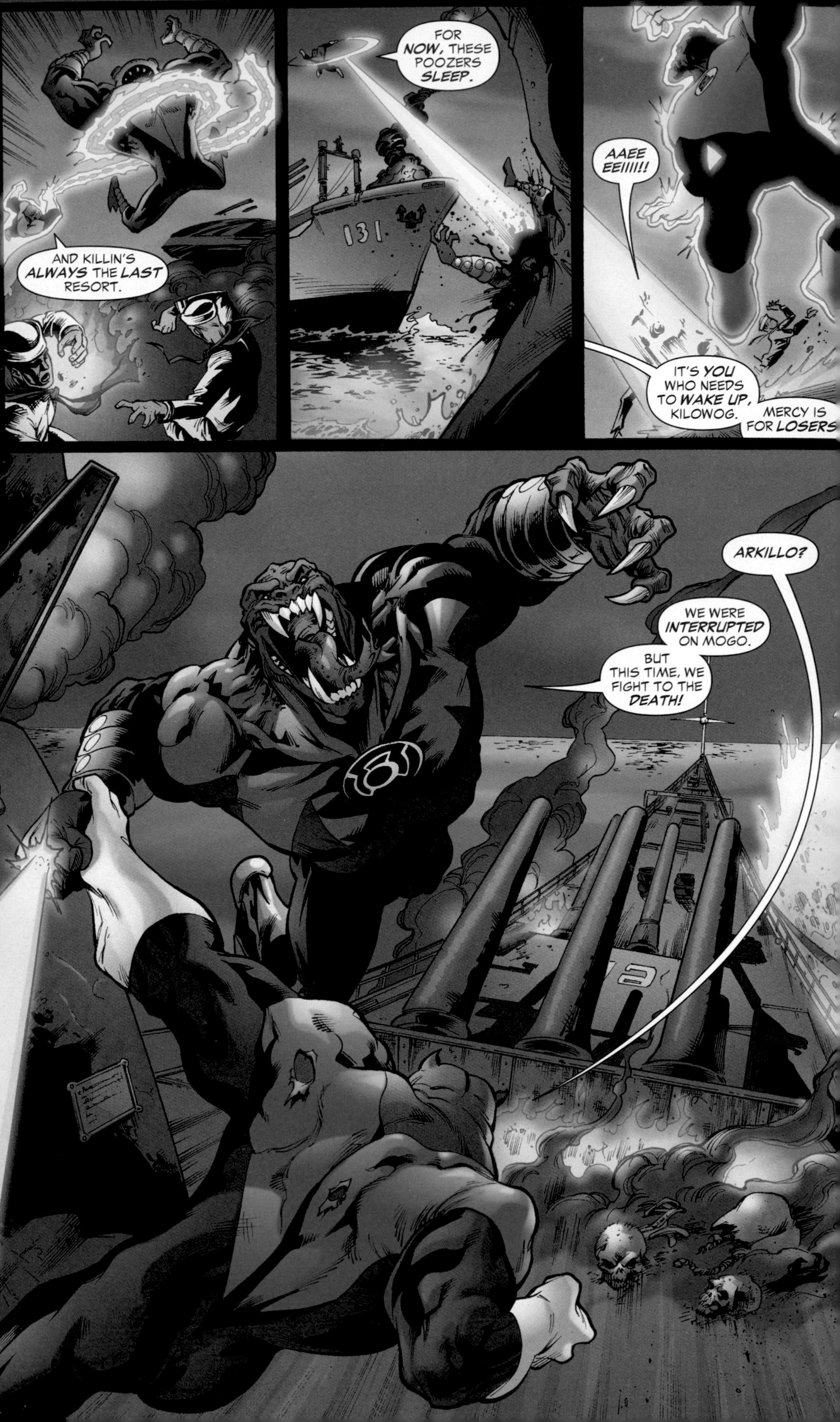
AND KILLIN'S ALWAYS THE LAST RESORT.
FOR NOW, THESE POOZERS SLEEP.
131
AAEE EE!!!!!!
IT'S YOU WHO NEEDS TO WAKE UP, KILOWOG.
MERCY IS FOR LOSERS
ARKILLO?
WE WERE INTERRUPTED ON MOGO.
BUT THIS TIME, WE FIGHT TO THE DEATH!

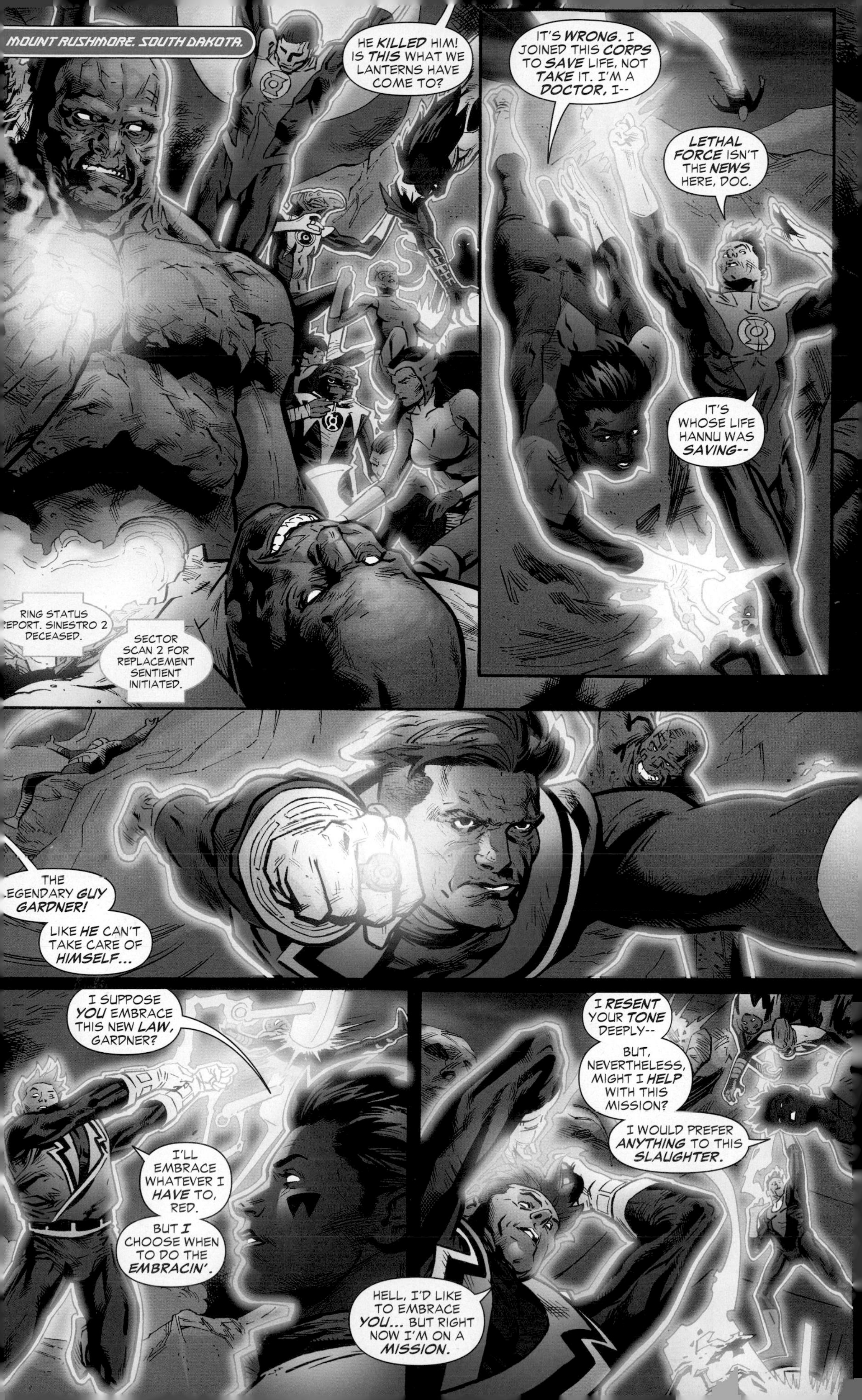
MOUNT RUSHMORE. SOUTH DAKOTA.
HE KILLED HIM! IS THIS WHAT WE LANTERNS HAVE COME TO?
IT'S WRONG. I JOINED THIS CORPS TO SAVE LIFE, NOT TAKE IT. I'M A DOCTOR, I--
LETHAL FORCE ISN'T THE NEWS HERE, DOC.
IT'S WHOSE LIFE HANNU WAS SAVING--
RING STATUS REPORT. SINESTRO 2 DECEASED.
SECTOR SCAN 2 FOR REPLACEMENT SENTIENT INITIATED.
THE LEGENDARY GUY GARDNER!
LIKE HE CAN'T TAKE CARE OF HIMSELF...
I SUPPOSE YOU EMBRACE THIS NEW LAW, GARDNER?
I'LL EMBRACE WHATEVER I HAVE TO, RED.
BUT I CHOOSE WHEN TO DO THE EMBRACIN'.
I RESENT YOUR TONE DEEPLY--
BUT, NEVERTHELESS, MIGHT I HELP WITH THIS MISSION?
I WOULD PREFER ANYTHING TO THIS SLAUGHTER.
HELL, I'D LIKE TO EMBRACE YOU... BUT RIGHT NOW I'M ON A MISSION.

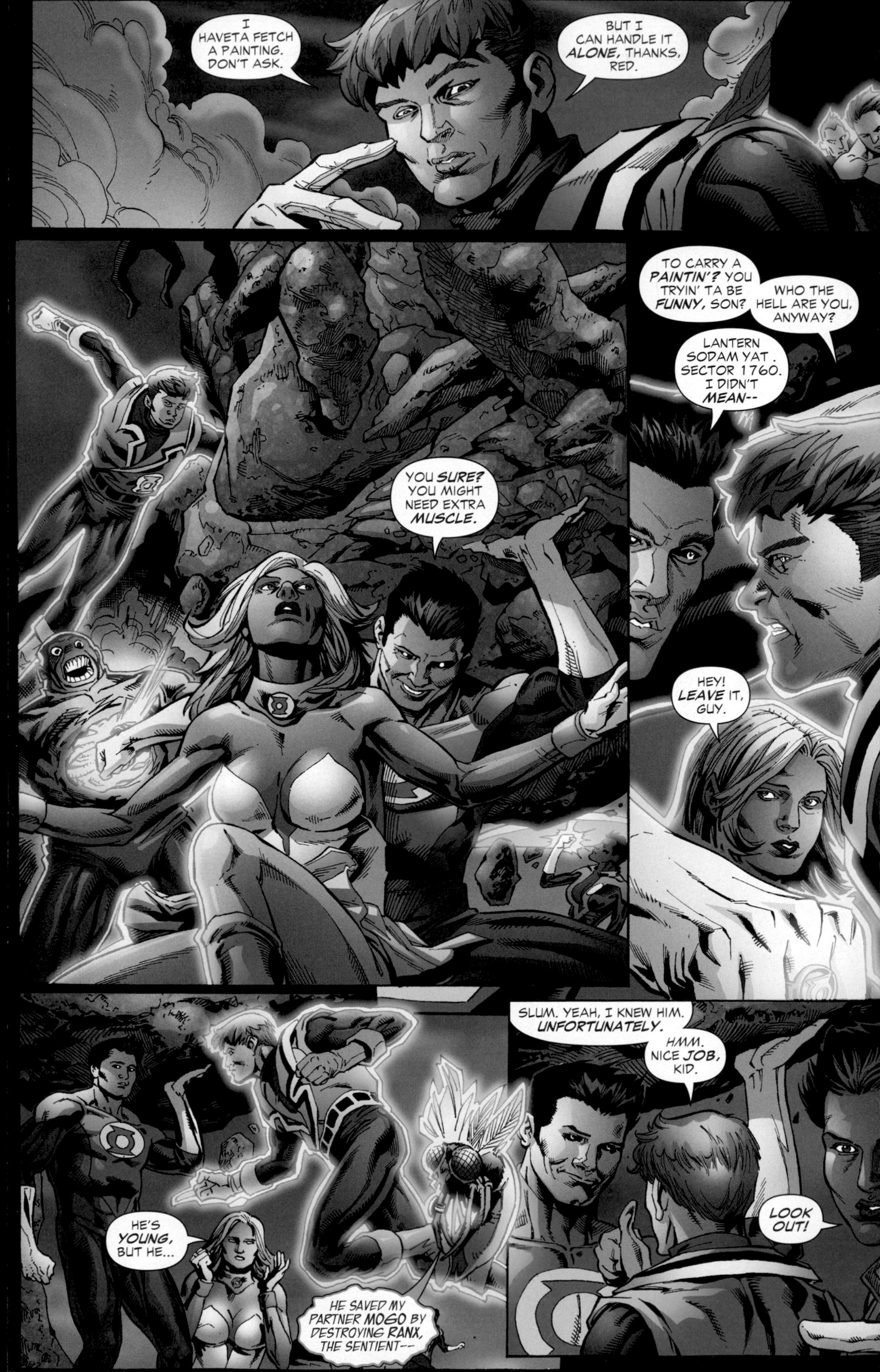
I HAVETA FETCH A PAINTING. DON'T ASK.
BUT I CAN HANDLE IT ALONE, THANKS, RED.
TO CARRY A PAINTIN'? YOU TRYIN' TA BE FUNNY, SON?
WHO THE HELL ARE YOU, ANYWAY?
LANTERN SODAM YAT. SECTOR 1760. I DIDN'T MEAN--
YOU SURE? YOU MIGHT NEED EXTRA MUSCLE.
HEY! LEAVE IT, GUY.
HE'S YOUNG, BUT HE...
HE SAVED MY PARTNER MOGO BY DESTROYING RANX, THE SENTIENT--
SLUM. YEAH, I KNEW HIM. UNFORTUNATELY.
HMM. NICE JOB, KID.
LOOK OUT!

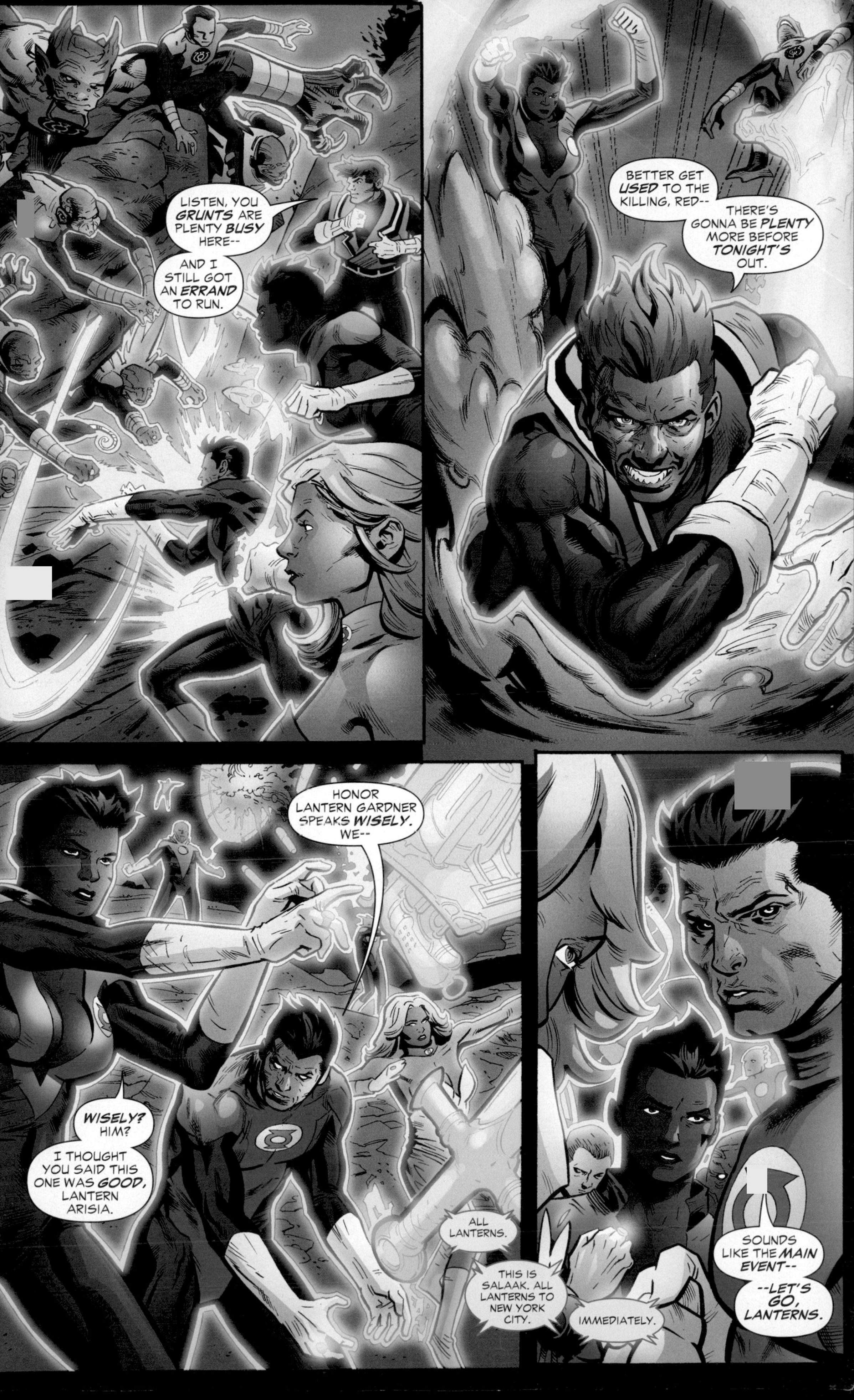
LISTEN, YOU GRUNTS ARE PLENTY BUSY HERE--
AND I STILL GOT AN ERRAND TO RUN.
BETTER GET USED TO THE KILLING, RED--
THERE'S GONNA BE PLENTY MORE BEFORE TONIGHT'S OUT.
HONOR LANTERN GARDNER SPEAKS WISELY. WE--
WISELY? HIM?
I THOUGHT YOU SAID THIS ONE WAS GOOD, LANTERN ARISIA.
ALL LANTERNS.
THIS IS SALAAK. ALL LANTERNS TO NEW YORK CITY.
IMMEDIATELY.
SOUNDS LIKE THE MAIN EVENT--
--LET'S GO, LANTERNS.

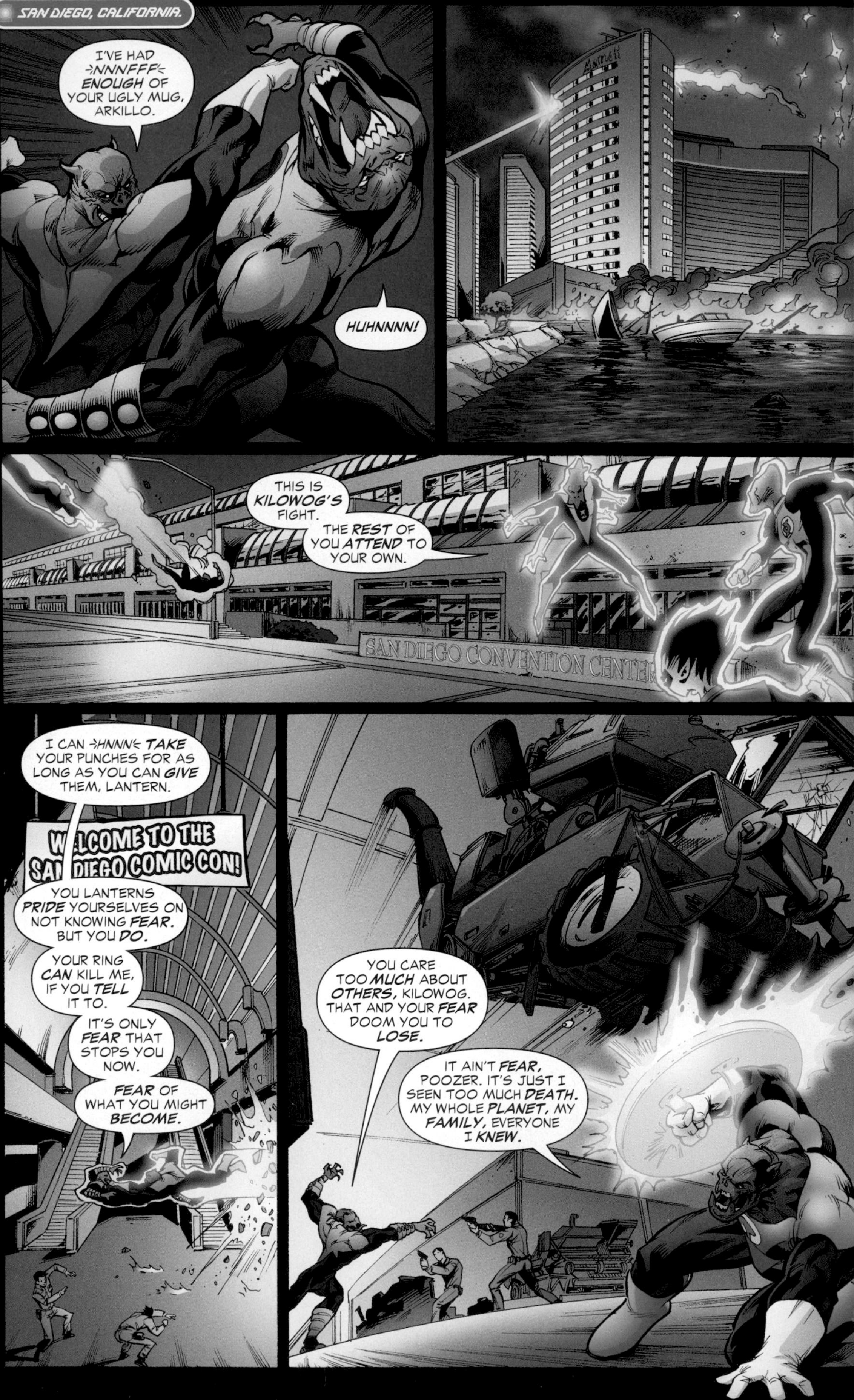
SAN DIEGO, CALIFORNIA.
I'VE HAD -NNNFFF- ENOUGH OF YOUR UGLY MUG, ARKILLO.
HUHNNNN!
THIS IS KILOWOG'S FIGHT.
THE REST OF YOU ATTEND TO YOUR OWN.
SAN DIEGO CONVENTION CENTER
I CAN -HNN- TAKE YOUR PUNCHES FOR AS LONG AS YOU CAN GIVE THEM, LANTERN.
WELCOME TO THE SAN DIEGO COMIC CON!
YOU LANTERNS PRIDE YOURSELVES ON NOT KNOWING FEAR. BUT YOU DO.
YOUR RING CAN KILL ME, IF YOU TELL IT TO.
IT'S ONLY FEAR THAT STOPS YOU NOW.
FEAR OF WHAT YOU MIGHT BECOME.
YOU CARE TOO MUCH ABOUT OTHERS, KILOWOG. THAT AND YOUR FEAR DOOM YOU TO LOSE.
IT AIN'T FEAR, POOZER. IT'S JUST I SEEN TOO MUCH DEATH. MY WHOLE PLANET, MY FAMILY, EVERYONE I KNEW.

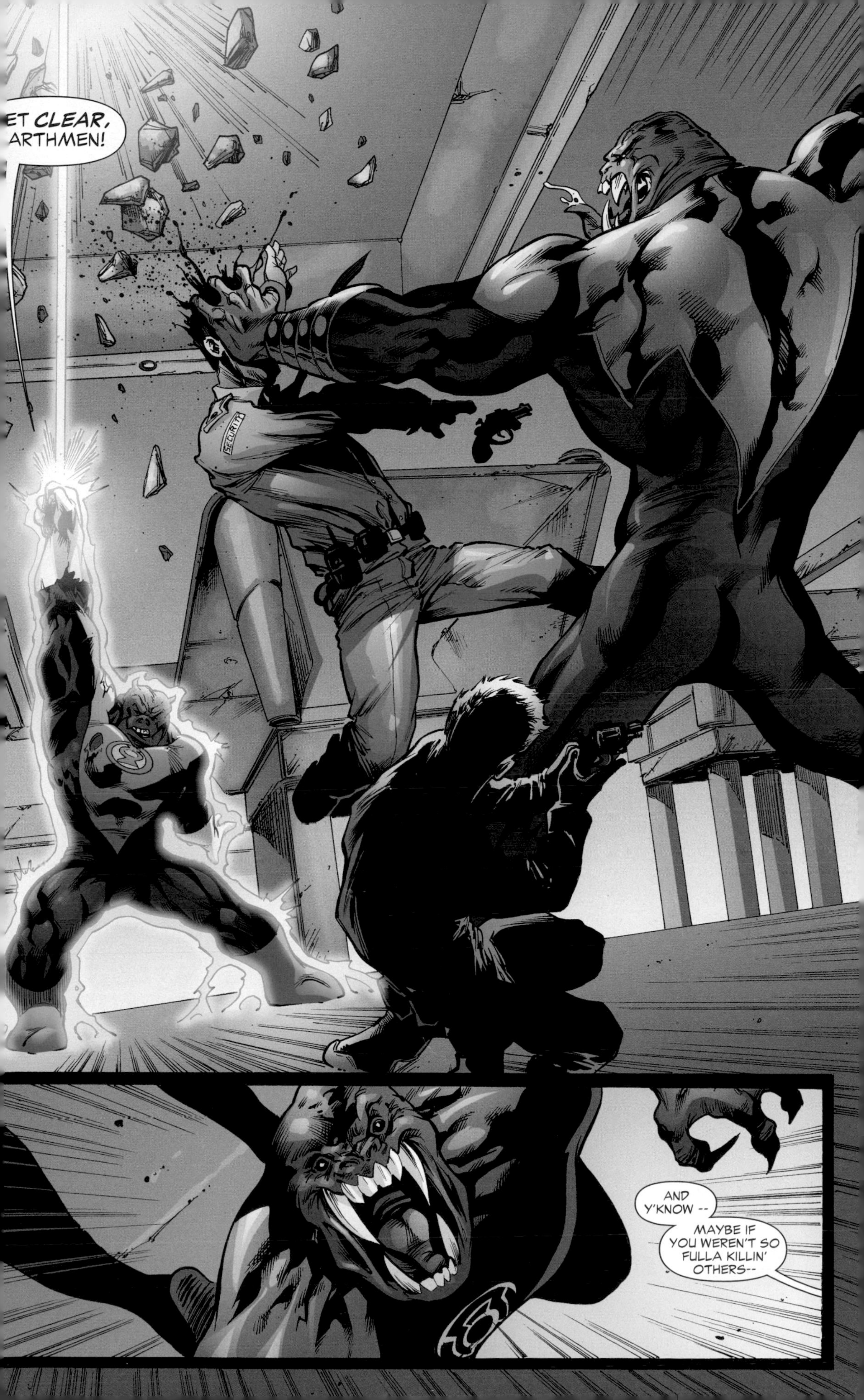

ET CLEAR,
ARTHMEN!
SECURITY
AND
Y'KNOW --
MAYBE IF
YOU WEREN'T SO
FULLA KILLIN'
OTHERS--

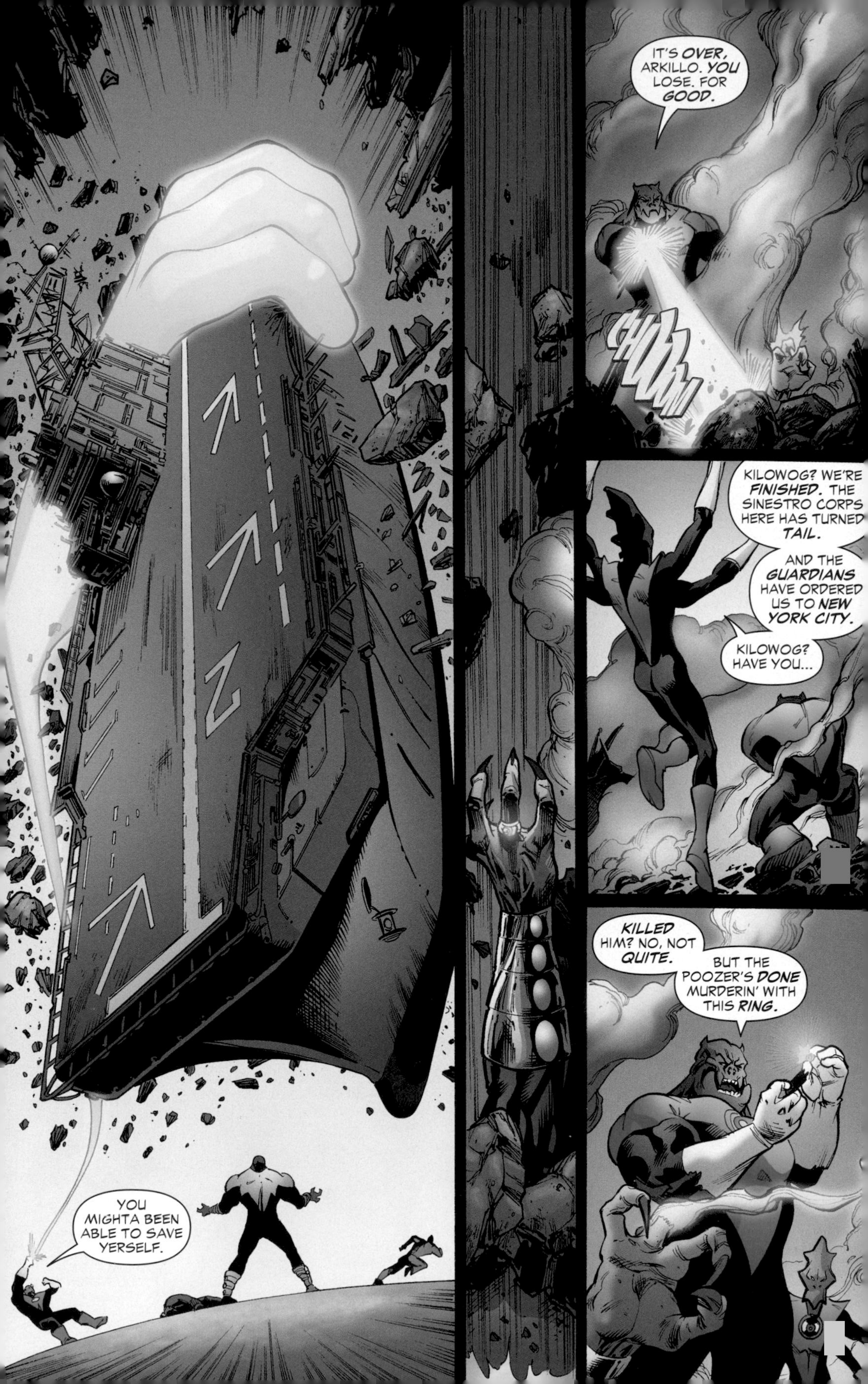
YOU MIGHTA BEEN ABLE TO SAVE YERSELF.
IT'S OVER, ARKILLO. YOU LOSE. FOR GOOD.
CHOOM
KILOWOG? WE'RE FINISHED. THE SINESTRO CORPS HERE HAS TURNED TAIL.
AND THE GUARDIANS HAVE ORDERED US TO NEW YORK CITY.
KILOWOG? HAVE YOU...
KILLED HIM? NO, NOT QUITE.
BUT THE POOZER'S DONE MURDERIN' WITH THIS RING.

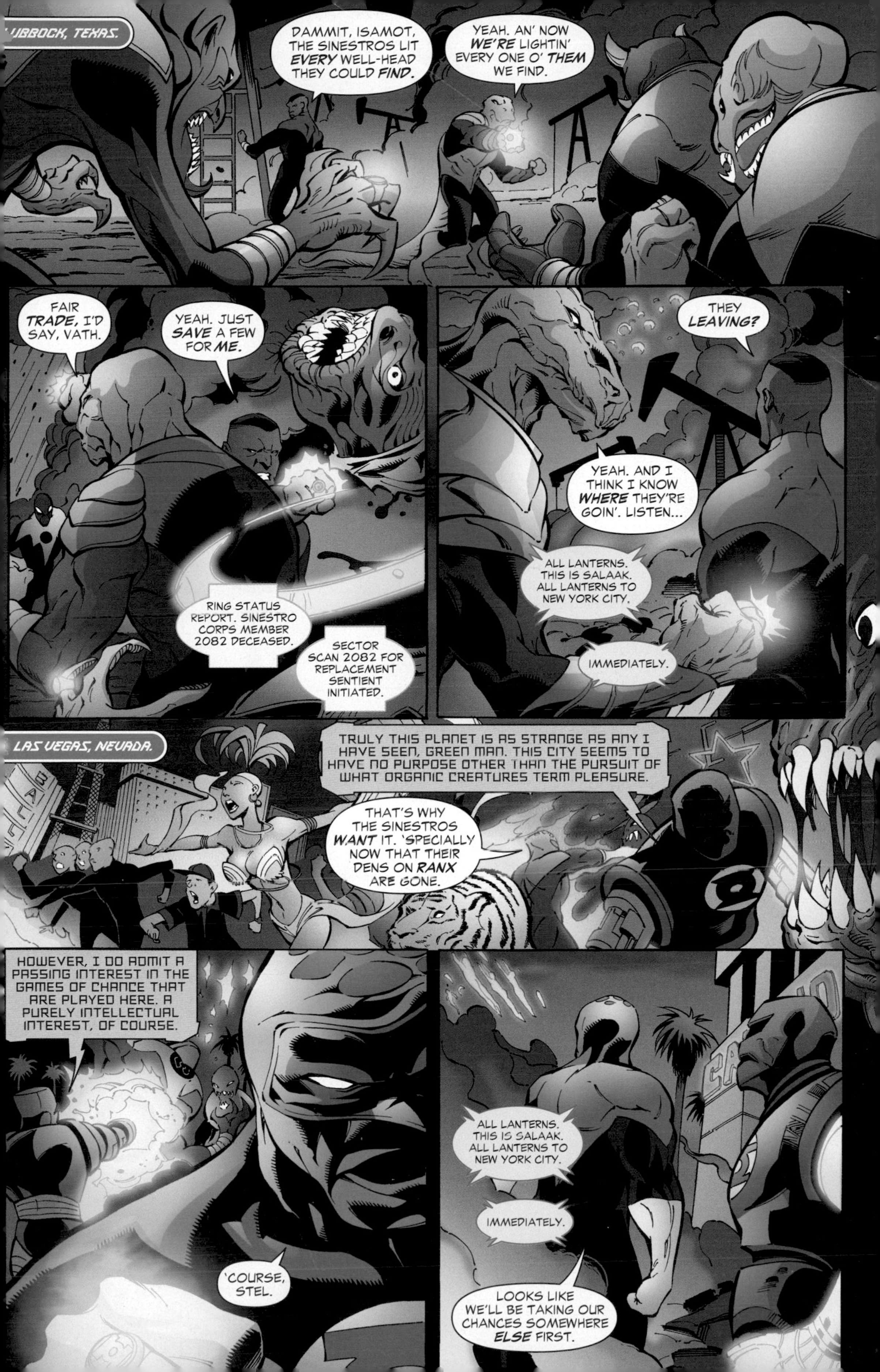
LUBBOCK, TEXAS.
DAMMIT, ISAMOT, THE SINESTROS LIT EVERY WELL-HEAD THEY COULD FIND.
YEAH. AN' NOW WE'RE LIGHTIN' EVERY ONE O' THEM WE FIND.
FAIR TRADE, I'D SAY, VATH.
YEAH. JUST SAVE A FEW FOR ME.
RING STATUS REPORT. SINESTRO CORPS MEMBER 2082 DECEASED.
SECTOR SCAN 2082 FOR REPLACEMENT SENTIENT INITIATED.
THEY LEAVING?
YEAH. AND I THINK I KNOW WHERE THEY'RE GOIN'. LISTEN...
ALL LANTERNS. THIS IS SALAAK. ALL LANTERNS TO NEW YORK CITY.
IMMEDIATELY.
LAS VEGAS, NEVADA.
TRULY THIS PLANET IS AS STRANGE AS ANY I HAVE SEEN, GREEN MAN. THIS CITY SEEMS TO HAVE NO PURPOSE OTHER THAN THE PURSUIT OF WHAT ORGANIC CREATURES TERM PLEASURE.
THAT'S WHY THE SINESTROS WANT IT. 'SPECIALLY NOW THAT THEIR DENS ON RANX ARE GONE.
HOWEVER, I DO ADMIT A PASSING INTEREST IN THE GAMES OF CHANCE THAT ARE PLAYED HERE. A PURELY INTELLECTUAL INTEREST, OF COURSE.
'COURSE, STEL.
ALL LANTERNS. THIS IS SALAAK. ALL LANTERNS TO NEW YORK CITY.
IMMEDIATELY.
LOOKS LIKE WE'LL BE TAKING OUR CHANCES SOMEWHERE ELSE FIRST.

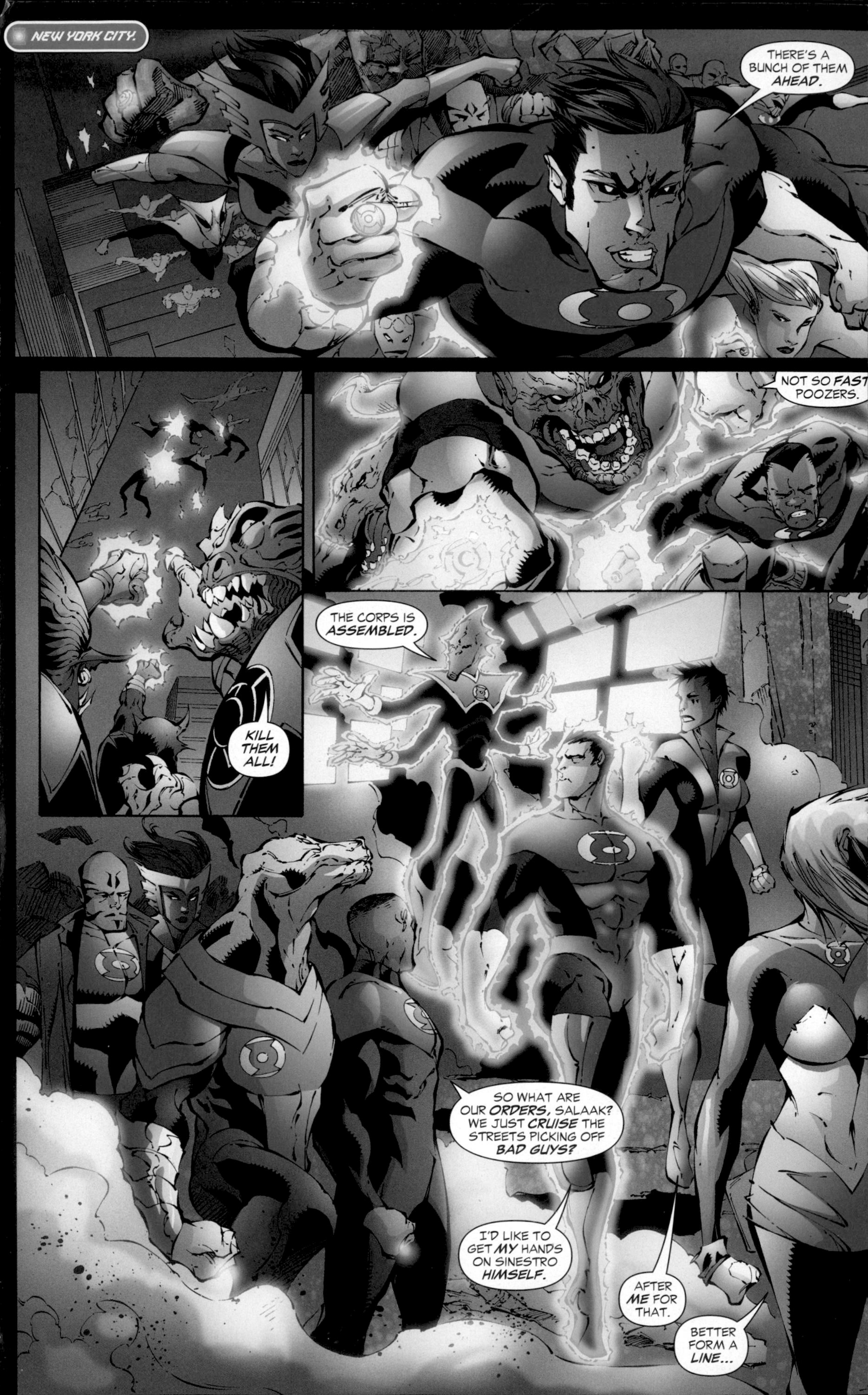
NEW YORK CITY.
THERE'S A BUNCH OF THEM AHEAD.
NOT SO FAST POOZERS.
KILL THEM ALL!
THE CORPS IS ASSEMBLED.
SO WHAT ARE OUR ORDERS, SALAAK? WE JUST CRUISE THE STREETS PICKING OFF BAD GUYS?
I'D LIKE TO GET MY HANDS ON SINESTRO HIMSELF.
AFTER ME FOR THAT.
BETTER FORM A LINE...

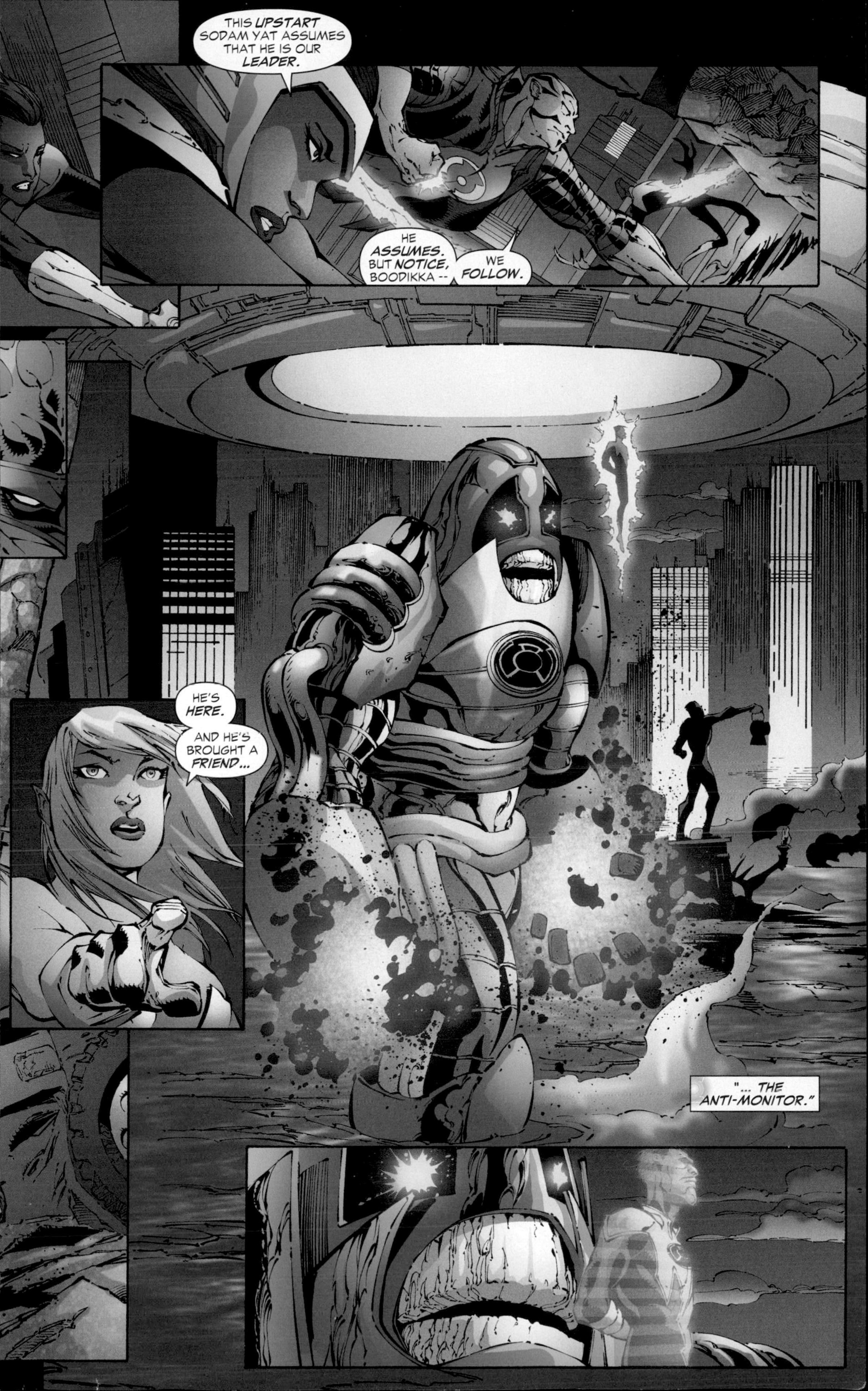
THIS UPSTART SODAM YAT ASSUMES THAT HE IS OUR LEADER.
HE ASSUMES. BUT NOTICE, BOODIKKA --
WE FOLLOW.
HE'S HERE.
AND HE'S BROUGHT A FRIEND...
"... THE ANTI-MONITOR."

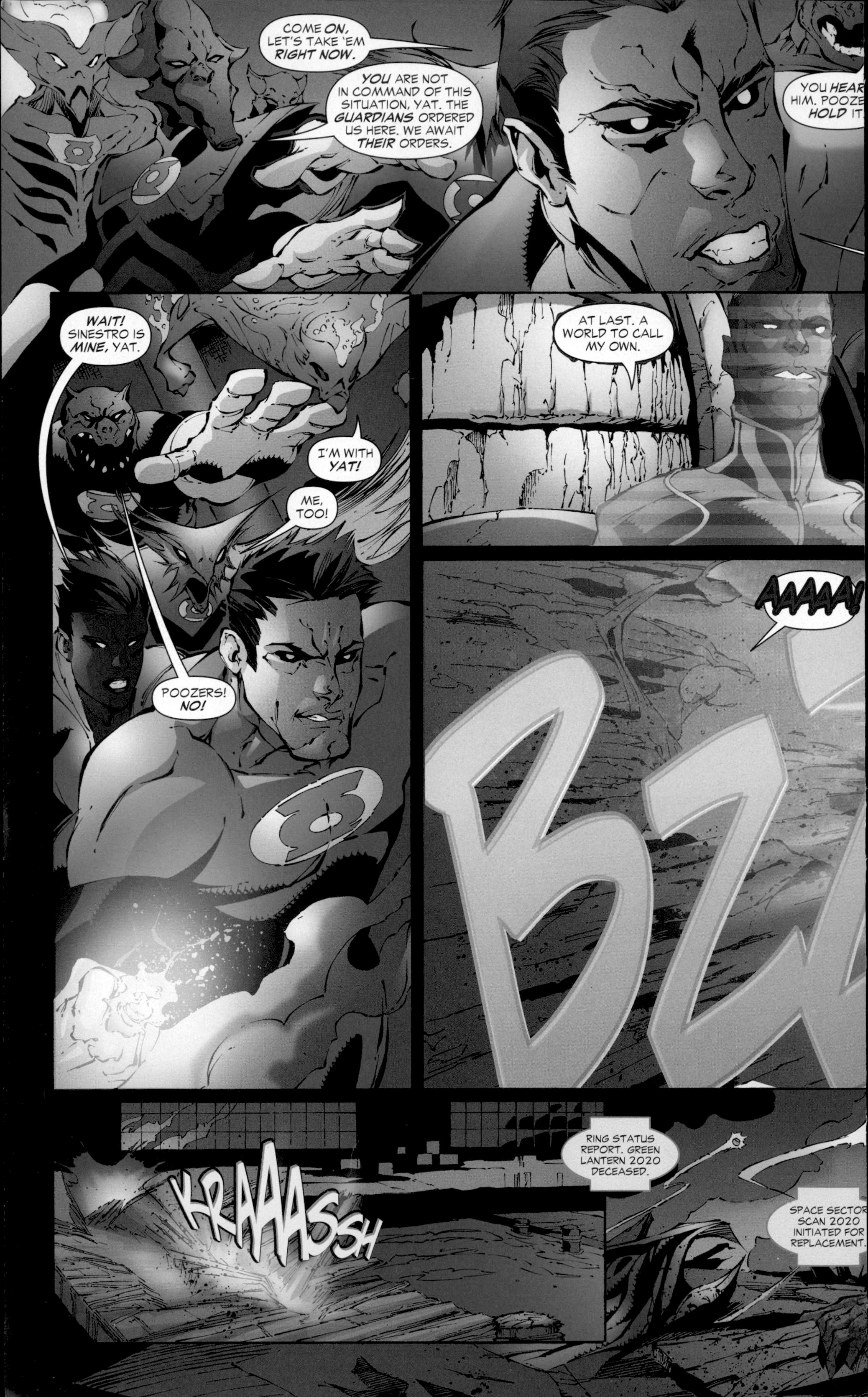
COME ON, LET'S TAKE 'EM RIGHT NOW.
YOU ARE NOT IN COMMAND OF THIS SITUATION, YAT. THE GUARDIANS ORDERED US HERE. WE AWAIT THEIR ORDERS.
YOU HEAR HIM. POOZE HOLD IT
WAIT! SINESTRO IS MINE, YAT.
I'M WITH YAT!
ME, TOO!
POOZERS! NO!
AT LAST. A WORLD TO CALL MY OWN.
AAAAA!
KRAAASSH
RING STATUS REPORT. GREEN LANTERN 2020 DECEASED.
SPACE SECTOR SCAN 2020 INITIATED FOR REPLACEMENT.

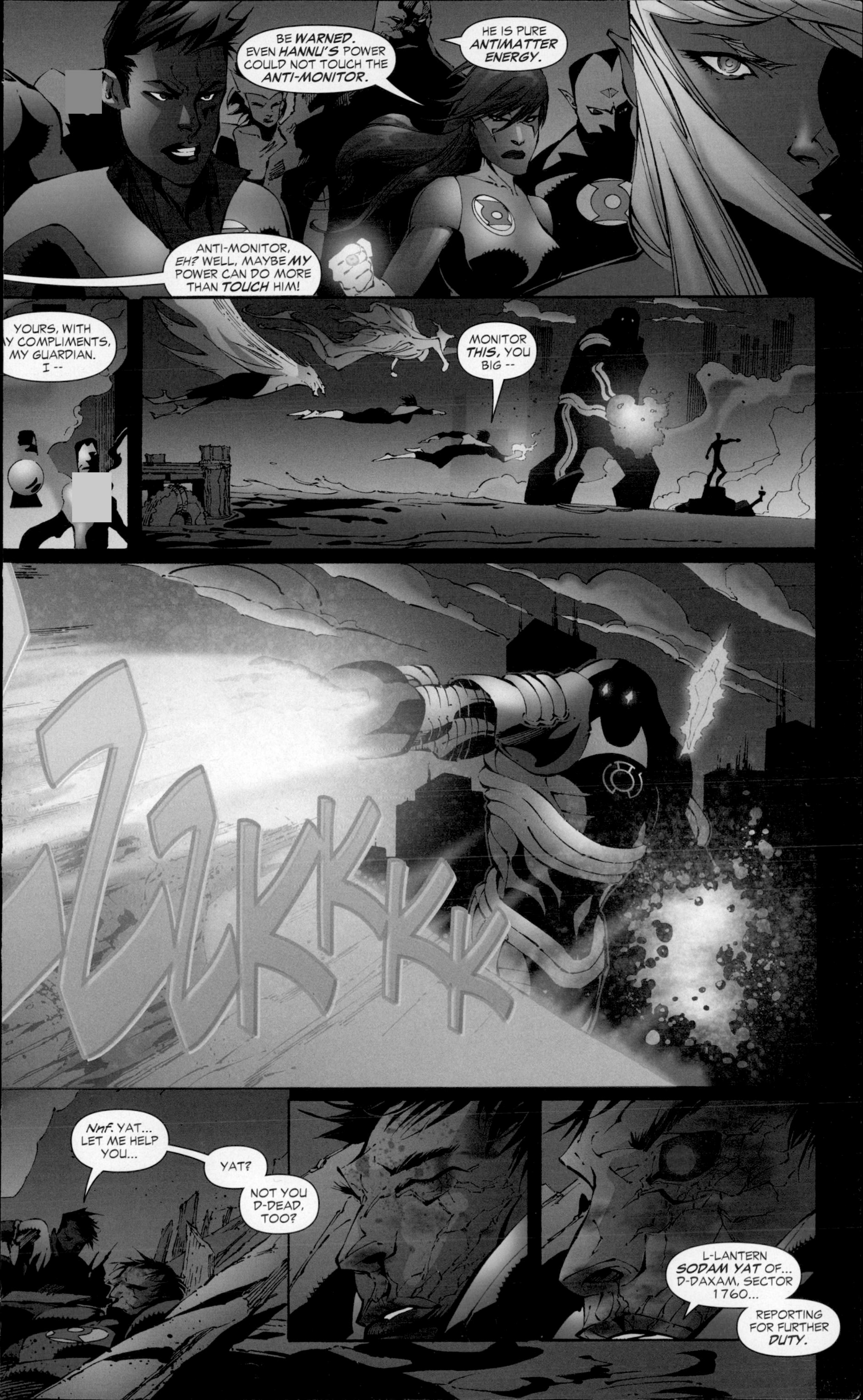
BE WARNED. EVEN HANNU'S POWER COULD NOT TOUCH THE ANTI-MONITOR.
HE IS PURE ANTIMATTER ENERGY.
ANTI-MONITOR, EH? WELL, MAYBE MY POWER CAN DO MORE THAN TOUCH HIM!
YOURS, WITH MY COMPLIMENTS, MY GUARDIAN. I --
MONITOR THIS, YOU BIG --
ZZKKKK
Nnf. YAT... LET ME HELP YOU...
YAT?
NOT YOU D-DEAD, TOO?
L-LANTERN SODAM YAT OF... D-DAXAM, SECTOR 1760...
REPORTING FOR FURTHER DUTY.

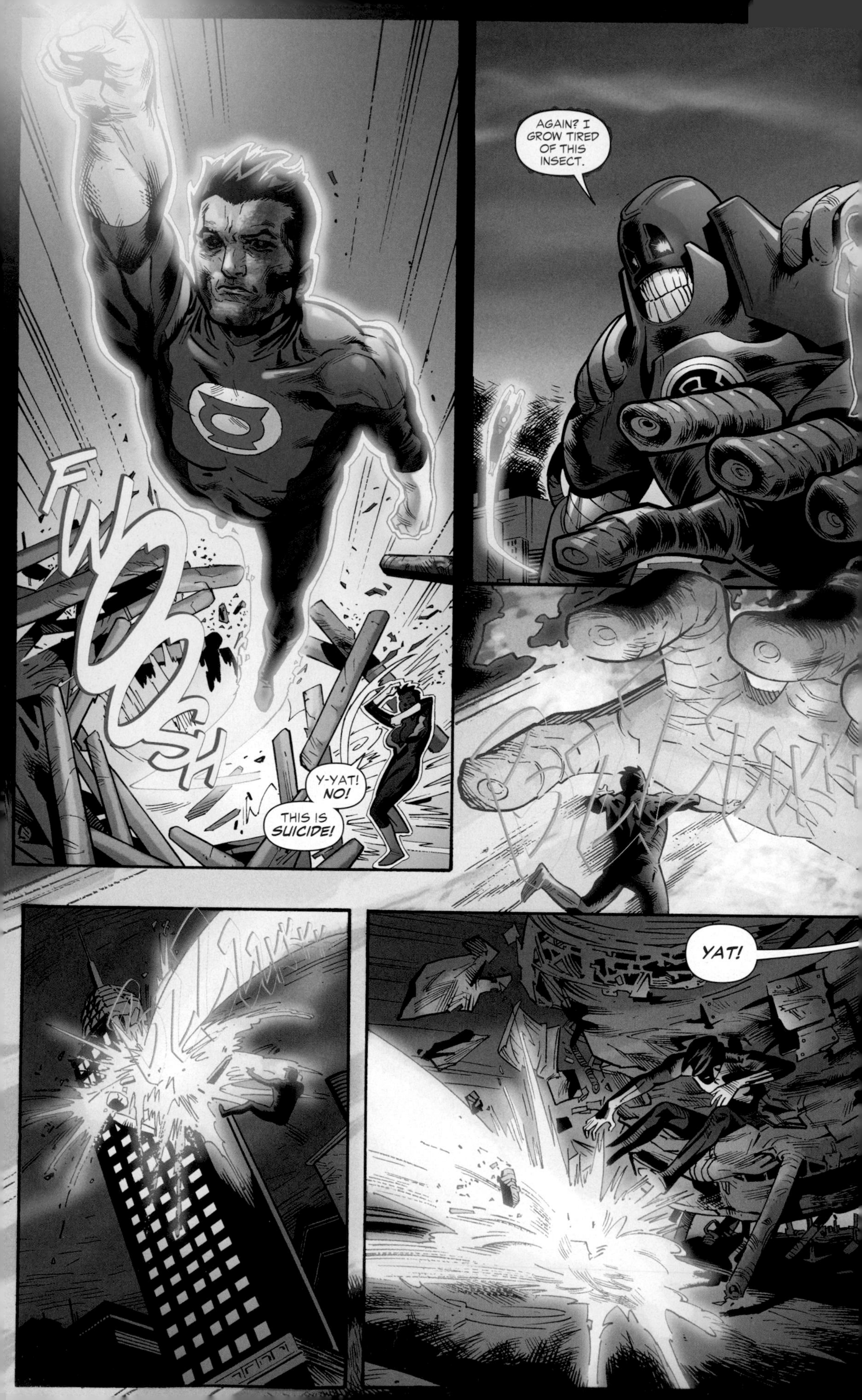
FWOOSH
Y-YAT! NO!
THIS IS SUICIDE!
AGAIN? I GROW TIRED OF THIS INSECT.
YAT!

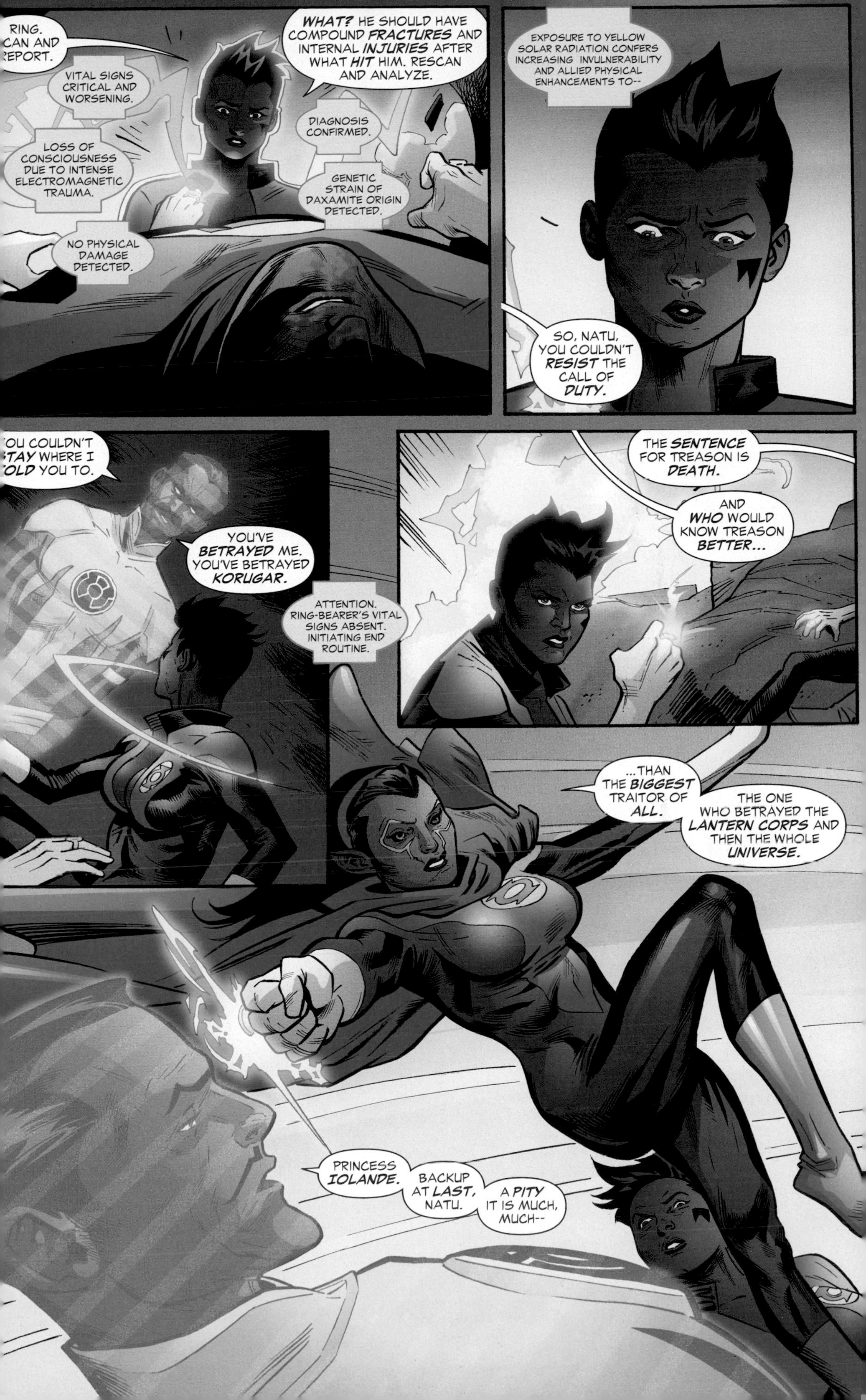
RING.
CAN AND
REPORT.
VITAL SIGNS CRITICAL AND WORSENING.
LOSS OF CONSCIOUSNESS DUE TO INTENSE ELECTROMAGNETIC TRAUMA.
NO PHYSICAL DAMAGE DETECTED.
WHAT? HE SHOULD HAVE COMPOUND FRACTURES AND INTERNAL INJURIES AFTER WHAT HIT HIM. RESCAN AND ANALYZE.
DIAGNOSIS CONFIRMED.
GENETIC STRAIN OF DAXAMITE ORIGIN DETECTED.
EXPOSURE TO YELLOW SOLAR RADIATION CONFERS INCREASING INVULNERABILITY AND ALLIED PHYSICAL ENHANCEMENTS TO--
SO, NATU, YOU COULDN'T RESIST THE CALL OF DUTY.
YOU COULDN'T STAY WHERE I TOLD YOU TO.
YOU'VE BETRAYED ME. YOU'VE BETRAYED KORUGAR.
ATTENTION. RING-BEARER'S VITAL SIGNS ABSENT. INITIATING END ROUTINE.
THE SENTENCE FOR TREASON IS DEATH.
AND WHO WOULD KNOW TREASON BETTER...
...THAN THE BIGGEST TRAITOR OF ALL.
THE ONE WHO BETRAYED THE LANTERN CORPS AND THEN THE WHOLE UNIVERSE.
PRINCESS IOLANDE.
BACKUP AT LAST, NATU.
A PITY IT IS MUCH, MUCH--

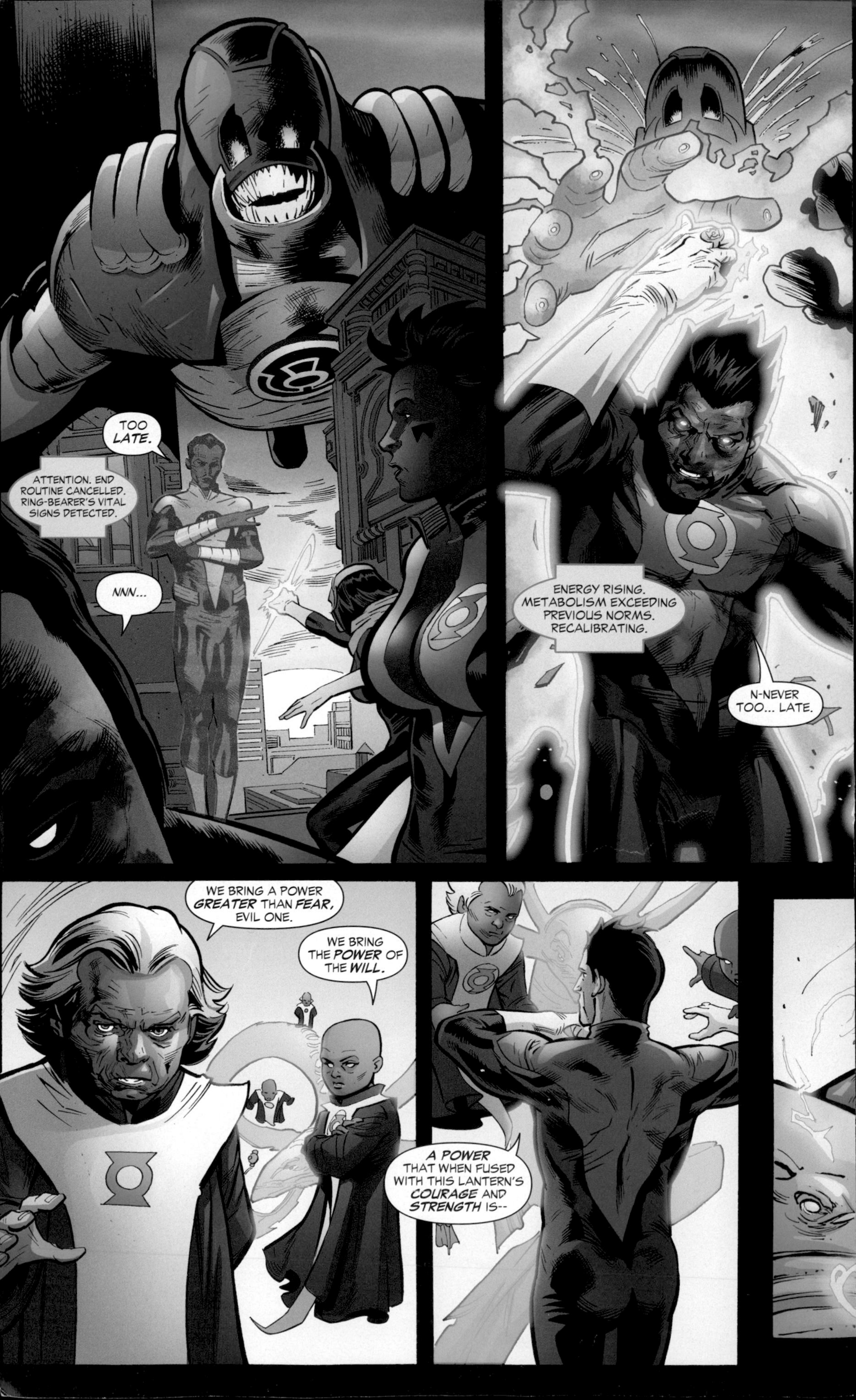
TOO LATE.
ATTENTION. END ROUTINE CANCELLED. RING-BEARER'S VITAL SIGNS DETECTED.
NNN...
ENERGY RISING. METABOLISM EXCEEDING PREVIOUS NORMS. RECALIBRATING.
N-NEVER TOO... LATE.
WE BRING A POWER GREATER THAN FEAR, EVIL ONE.
WE BRING THE POWER OF THE WILL.
A POWER THAT WHEN FUSED WITH THIS LANTERN'S COURAGE AND STRENGTH IS--

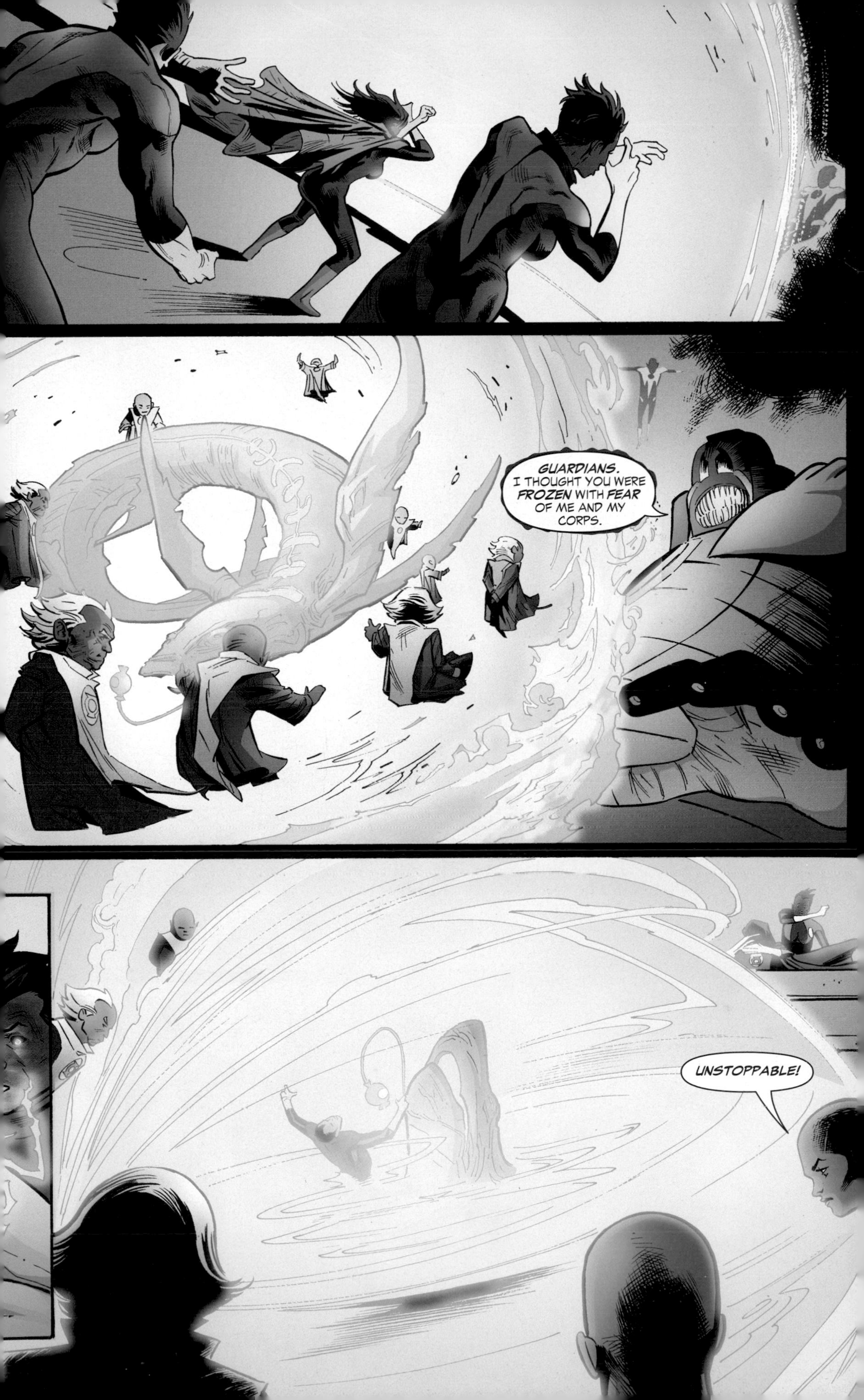
GUARDIANS. I THOUGHT YOU WERE FROZEN WITH FEAR OF ME AND MY CORPS.
UNSTOPPABLE!

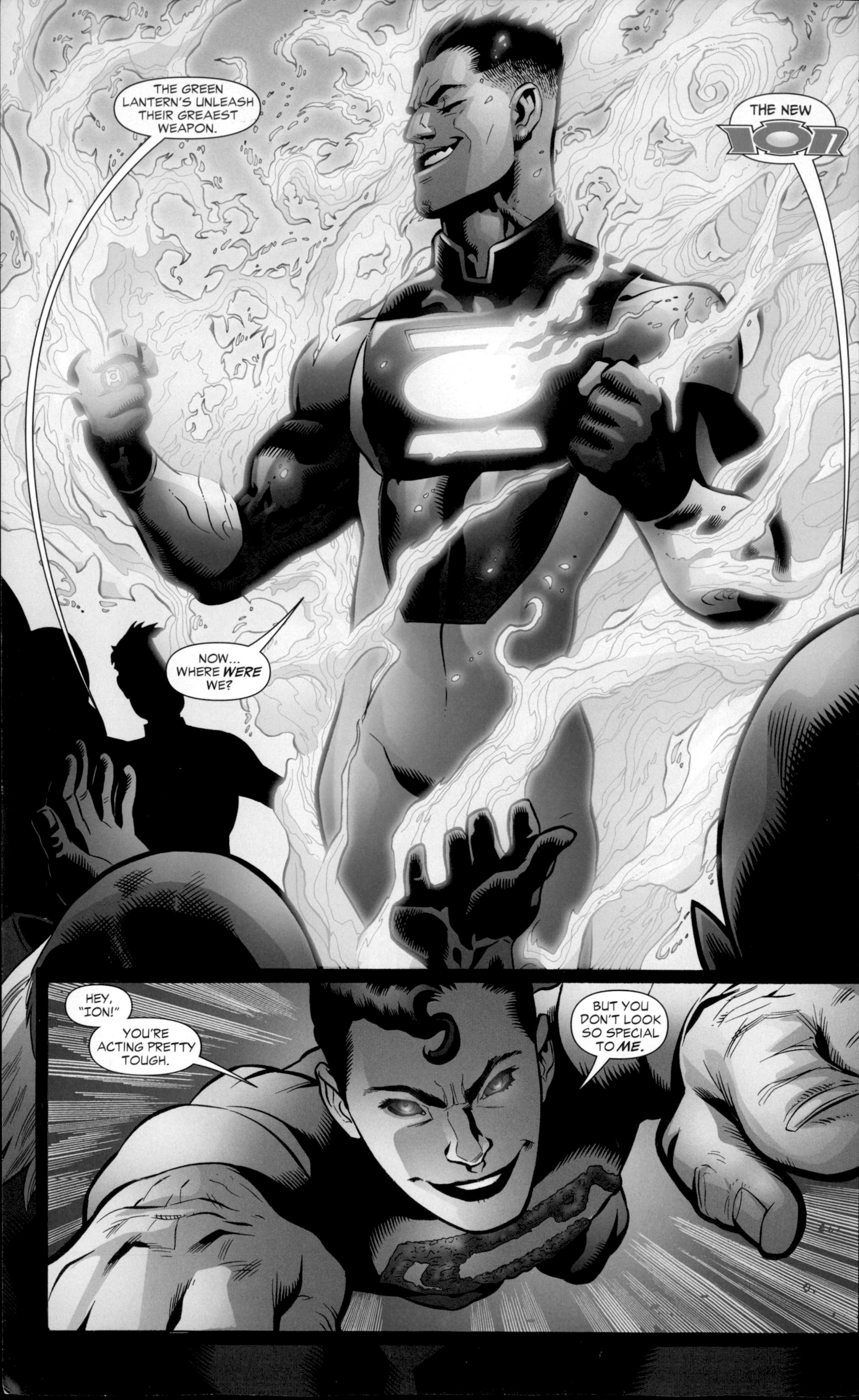
THE GREEN LANTERN'S UNLEASH THEIR GREAEST WEAPON.
THE NEW ION
NOW... WHERE *WERE* WE?
HEY, "ION!"
YOU'RE ACTING PRETTY TOUGH.
BUT YOU DON'T LOOK SO SPECIAL TO *ME*.

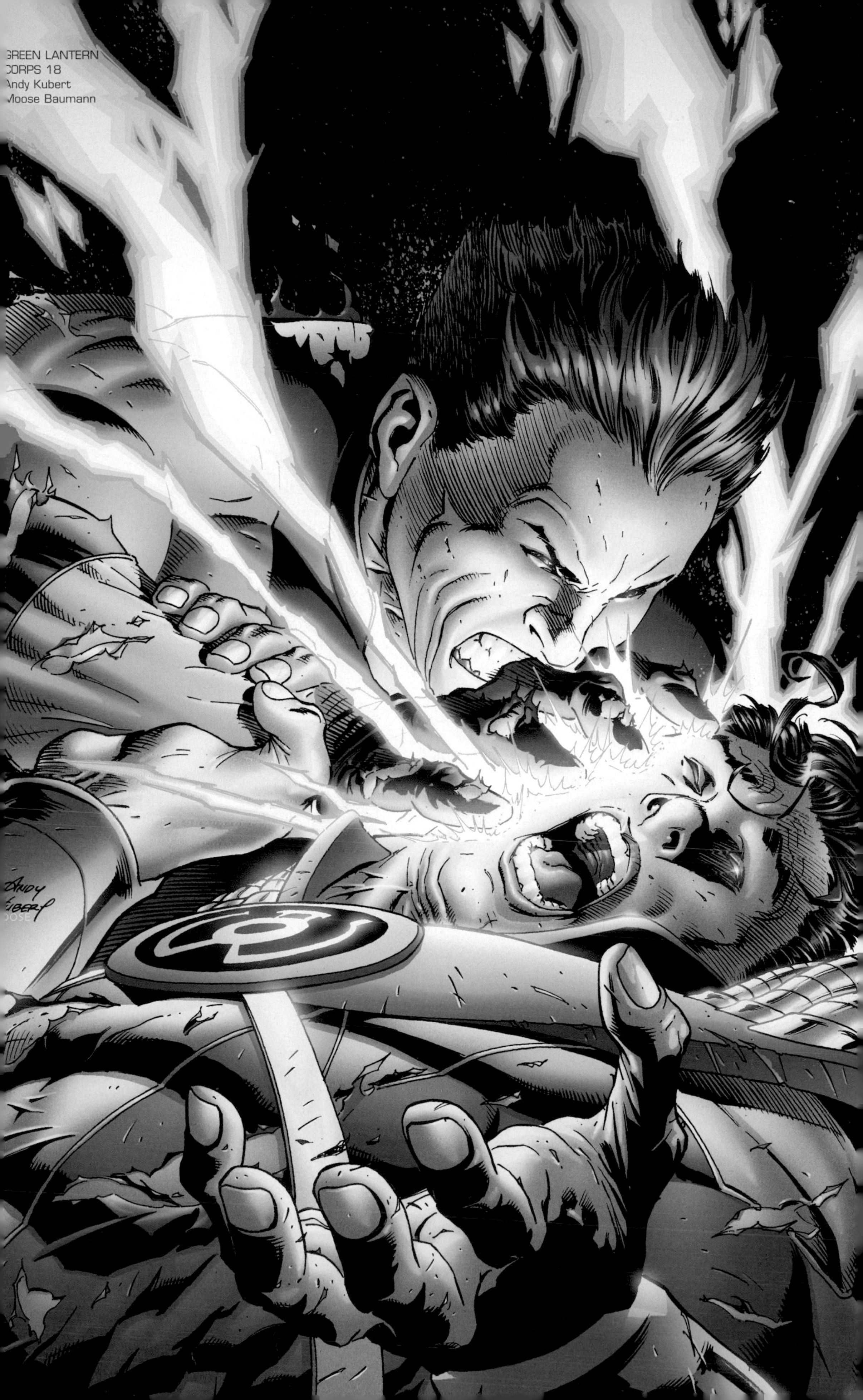

GREEN LANTERN
CORPS 18
Andy Kubert
Moose Baumann

THE SINESTRO CORPS WAR
Chapter Nine
HAMMER TO FALL
Writer: **Peter J. Tomasi**
Pencillers: **Patrick Gleason** and **Jamal Igle**
Inkers: **Prentis Rollins** and **Jerry Ordway**
Colorist: **Guy Major**

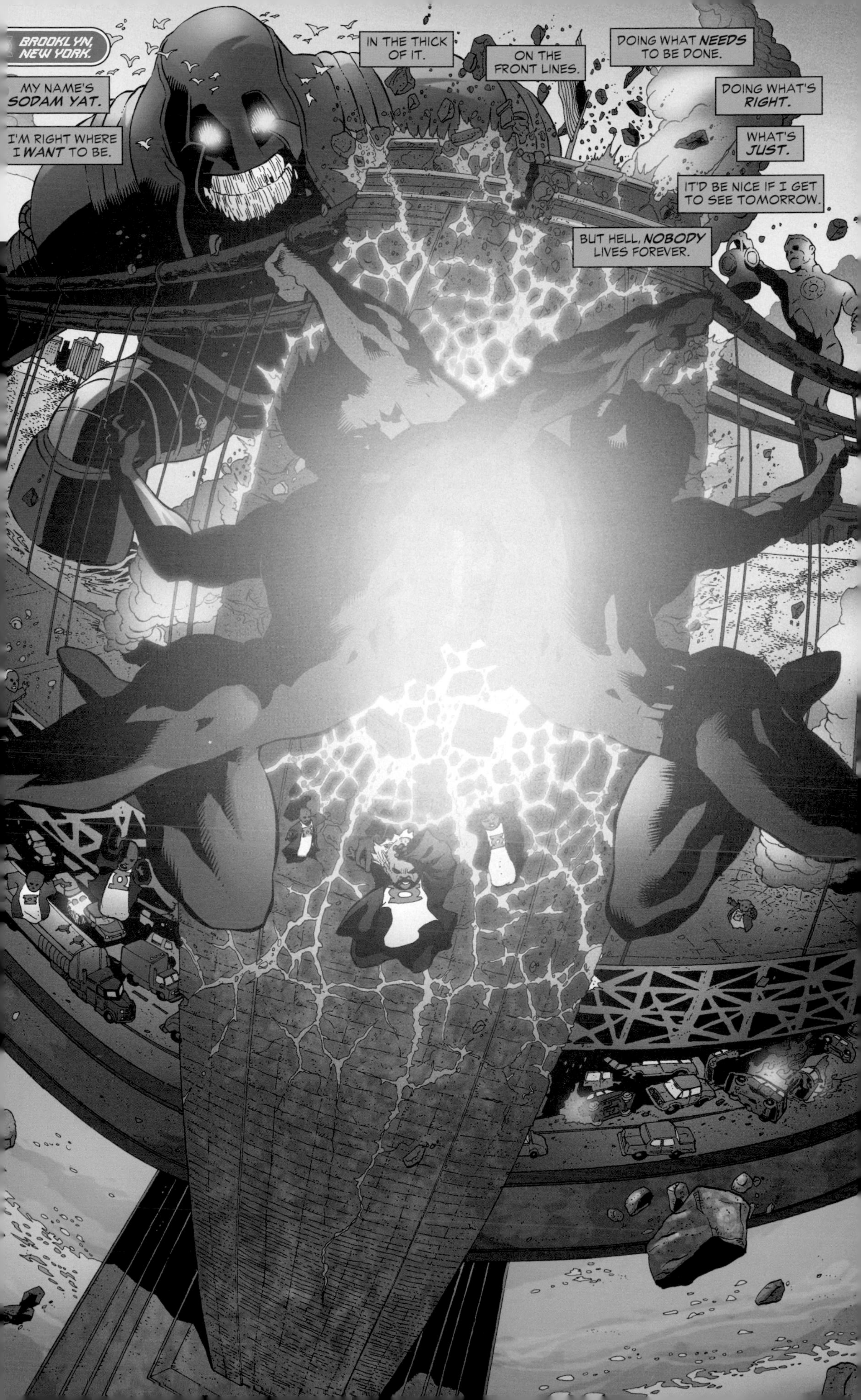
BROOKLYN, NEW YORK.
MY NAME'S SODAM YAT.
I'M RIGHT WHERE I WANT TO BE.
IN THE THICK OF IT.
ON THE FRONT LINES.
DOING WHAT NEEDS TO BE DONE.
DOING WHAT'S RIGHT.
WHAT'S JUST.
IT'D BE NICE IF I GET TO SEE TOMORROW.
BUT HELL, NOBODY LIVES FOREVER.

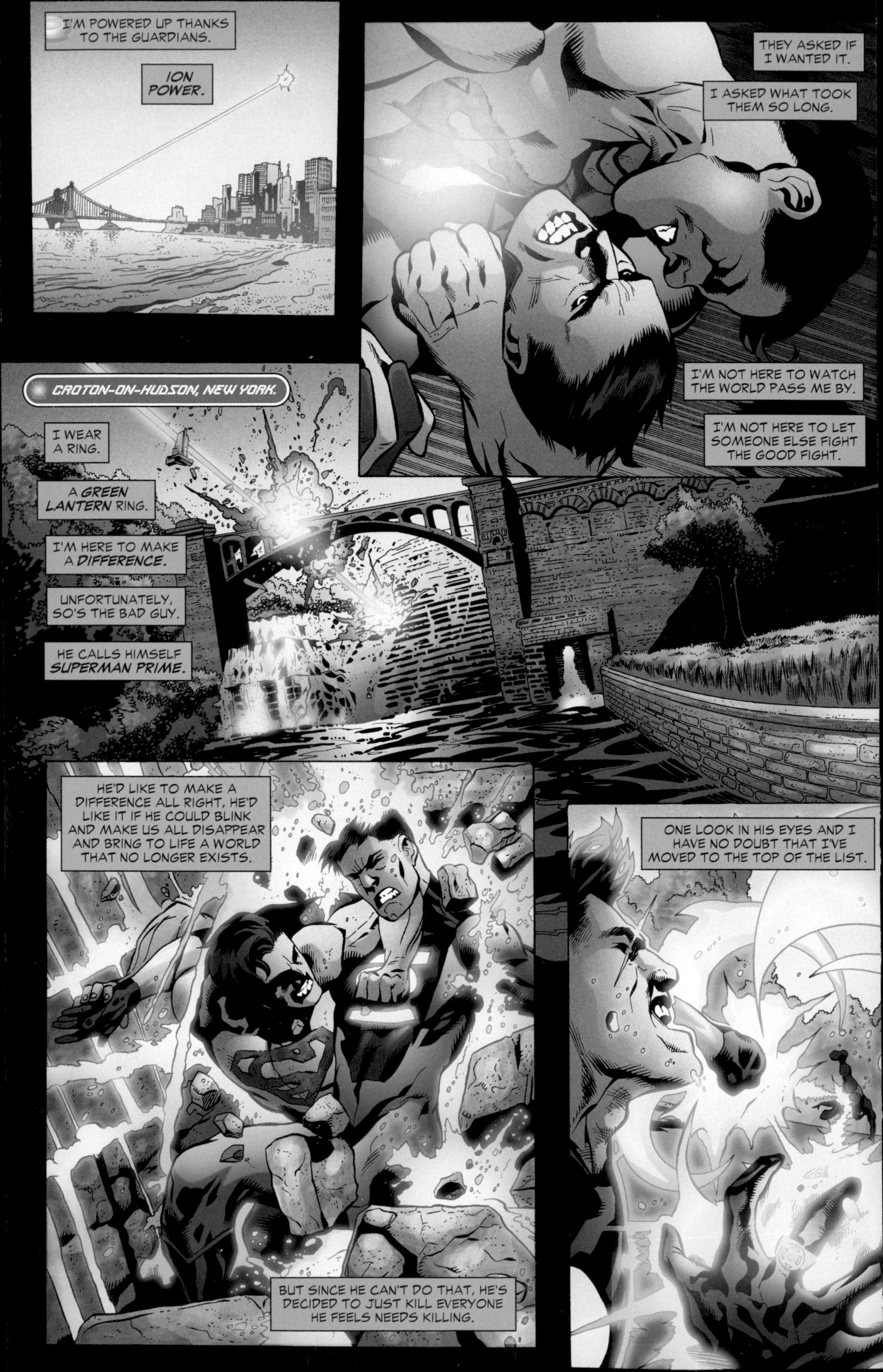
I'M POWERED UP THANKS TO THE GUARDIANS.
ION POWER.
THEY ASKED IF I WANTED IT.
I ASKED WHAT TOOK THEM SO LONG.
I'M NOT HERE TO WATCH THE WORLD PASS ME BY.
I'M NOT HERE TO LET SOMEONE ELSE FIGHT THE GOOD FIGHT.
CROTON-ON-HUDSON, NEW YORK.
I WEAR A RING.
A GREEN LANTERN RING.
I'M HERE TO MAKE A DIFFERENCE.
UNFORTUNATELY, SO'S THE BAD GUY.
HE CALLS HIMSELF SUPERMAN PRIME.
HE'D LIKE TO MAKE A DIFFERENCE ALL RIGHT, HE'D LIKE IT IF HE COULD BLINK AND MAKE US ALL DISAPPEAR AND BRING TO LIFE A WORLD THAT NO LONGER EXISTS.
BUT SINCE HE CAN'T DO THAT, HE'S DECIDED TO JUST KILL EVERYONE HE FEELS NEEDS KILLING.
ONE LOOK IN HIS EYES AND I HAVE NO DOUBT THAT I'VE MOVED TO THE TOP OF THE LIST.

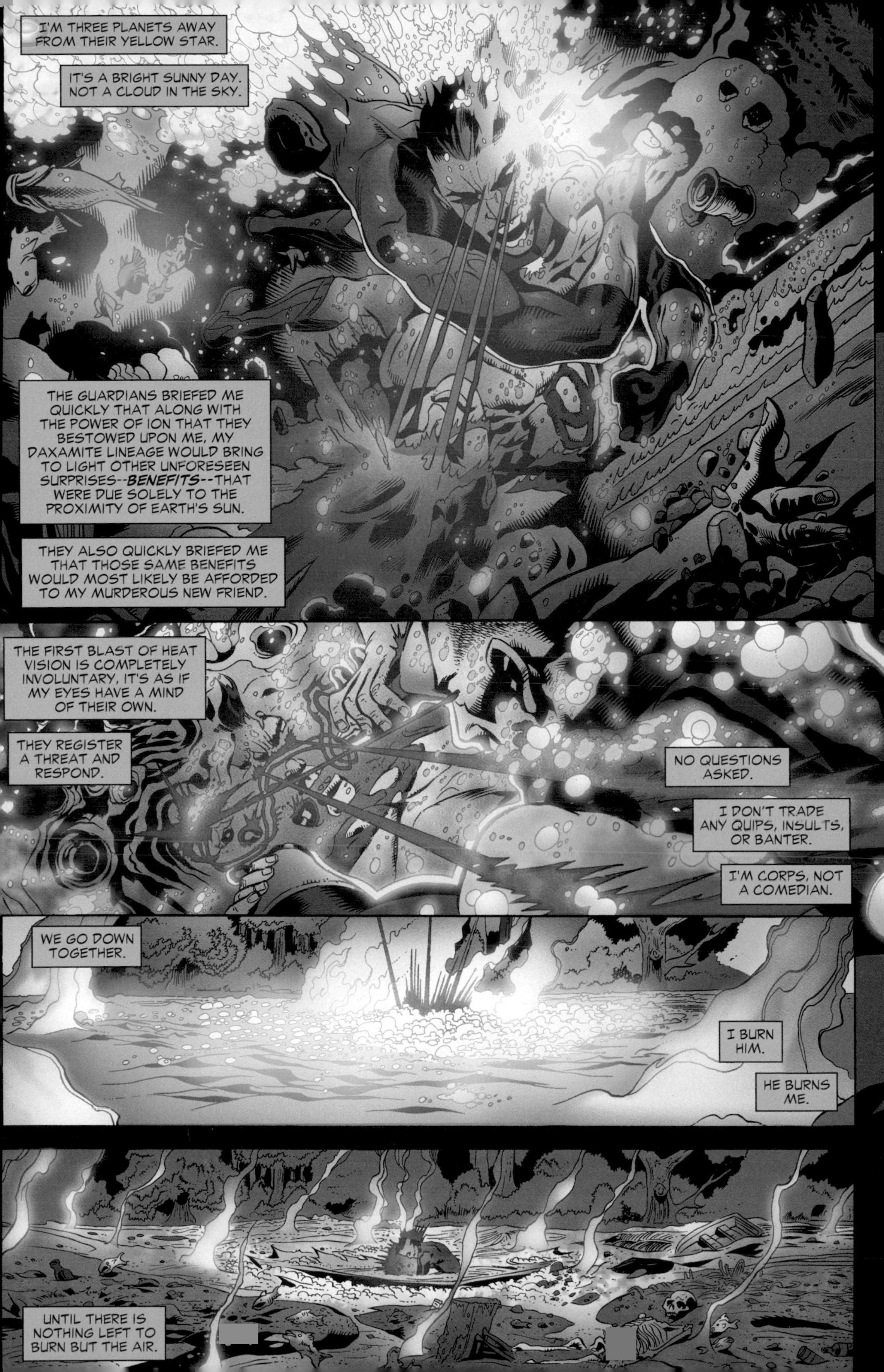
I'M THREE PLANETS AWAY FROM THEIR YELLOW STAR.
IT'S A BRIGHT SUNNY DAY. NOT A CLOUD IN THE SKY.
THE GUARDIANS BRIEFED ME QUICKLY THAT ALONG WITH THE POWER OF ION THAT THEY BESTOWED UPON ME, MY DAXAMITE LINEAGE WOULD BRING TO LIGHT OTHER UNFORESEEN SURPRISES--*BENEFITS*--THAT WERE DUE SOLELY TO THE PROXIMITY OF EARTH'S SUN.
THEY ALSO QUICKLY BRIEFED ME THAT THOSE SAME BENEFITS WOULD MOST LIKELY BE AFFORDED TO MY MURDEROUS NEW FRIEND.
THE FIRST BLAST OF HEAT VISION IS COMPLETELY INVOLUNTARY, IT'S AS IF MY EYES HAVE A MIND OF THEIR OWN.
THEY REGISTER A THREAT AND RESPOND.
NO QUESTIONS ASKED.
I DON'T TRADE ANY QUIPS, INSULTS, OR BANTER.
I'M CORPS, NOT A COMEDIAN.
WE GO DOWN TOGETHER.
I BURN HIM.
HE BURNS ME.
UNTIL THERE IS NOTHING LEFT TO BURN BUT THE AIR.

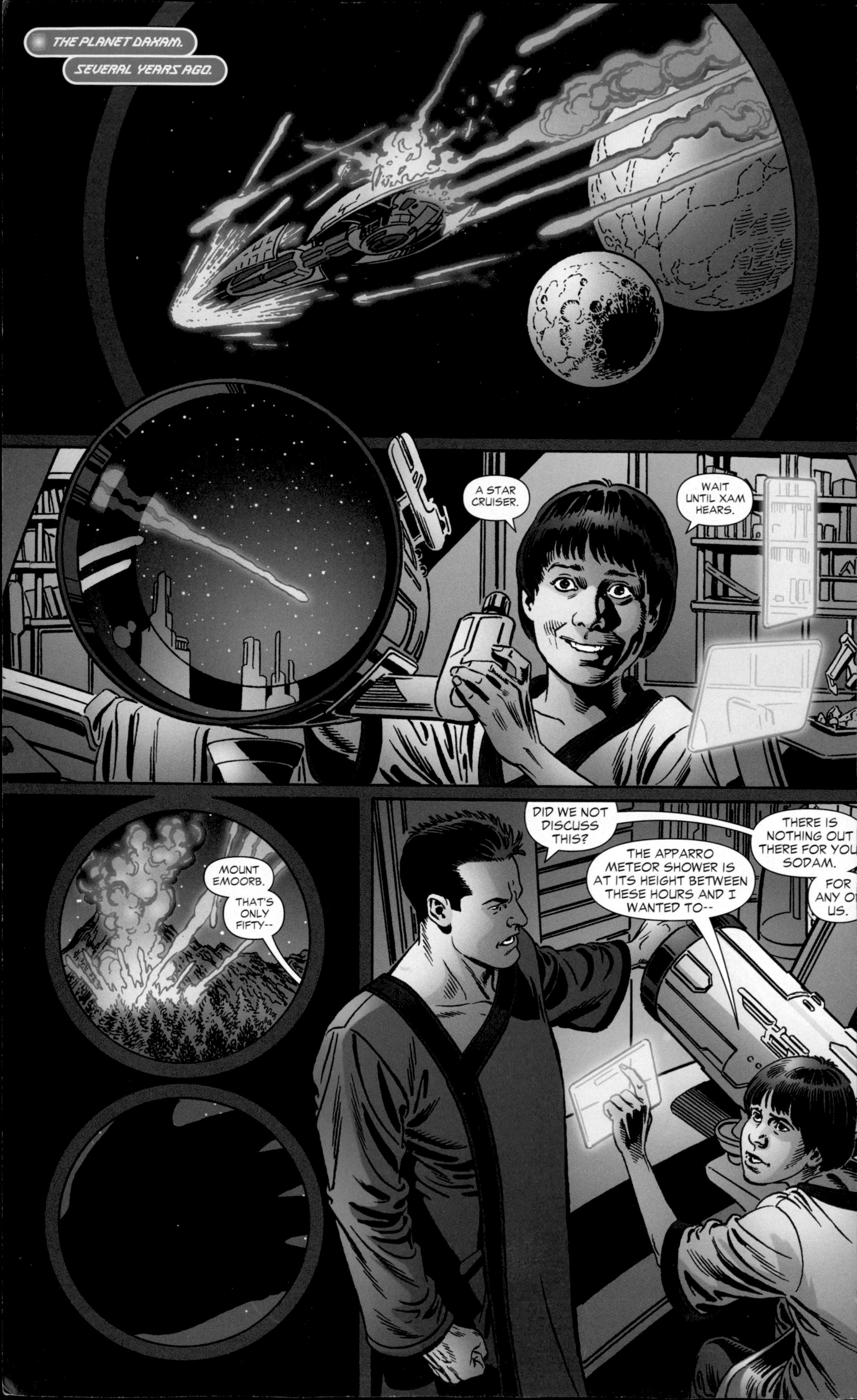
THE PLANET DAXAM.
SEVERAL YEARS AGO.
A STAR CRUISER.
WAIT UNTIL XAM HEARS.
MOUNT EMOORB.
THAT'S ONLY FIFTY--
DID WE NOT DISCUSS THIS?
THE APPARRO METEOR SHOWER IS AT ITS HEIGHT BETWEEN THESE HOURS AND I WANTED TO--
THERE IS NOTHING OUT THERE FOR YOU SODAM.
FOR ANY OF US.

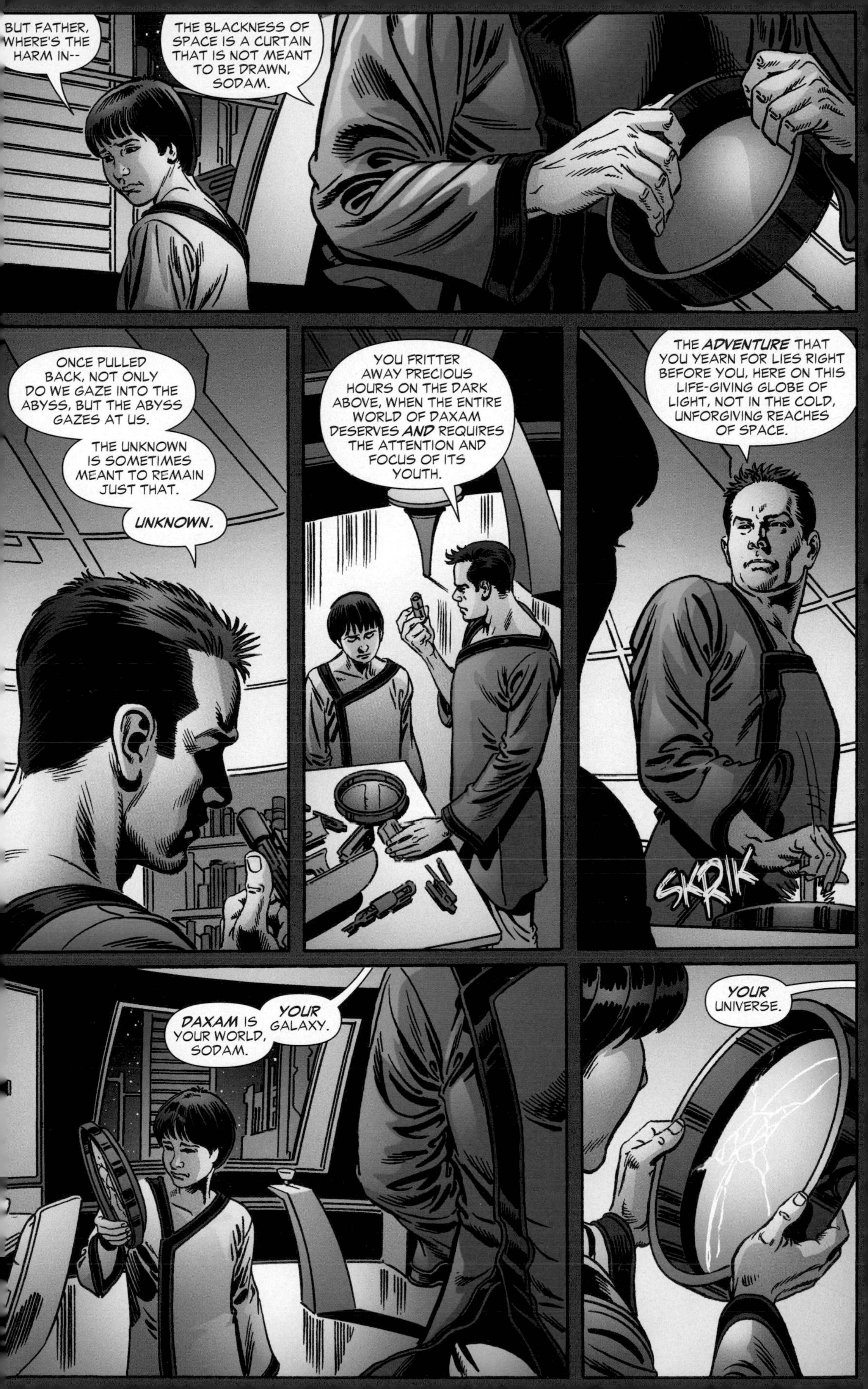
BUT FATHER, WHERE'S THE HARM IN--
THE BLACKNESS OF SPACE IS A CURTAIN THAT IS NOT MEANT TO BE DRAWN, SODAM.
ONCE PULLED BACK, NOT ONLY DO WE GAZE INTO THE ABYSS, BUT THE ABYSS GAZES AT US.
THE UNKNOWN IS SOMETIMES MEANT TO REMAIN JUST THAT.
UNKNOWN.
YOU FRITTER AWAY PRECIOUS HOURS ON THE DARK ABOVE, WHEN THE ENTIRE WORLD OF DAXAM DESERVES AND REQUIRES THE ATTENTION AND FOCUS OF ITS YOUTH.
THE ADVENTURE THAT YOU YEARN FOR LIES RIGHT BEFORE YOU, HERE ON THIS LIFE-GIVING GLOBE OF LIGHT, NOT IN THE COLD, UNFORGIVING REACHES OF SPACE.
SKRIK
DAXAM IS YOUR WORLD, SODAM.
YOUR GALAXY.
YOUR UNIVERSE.

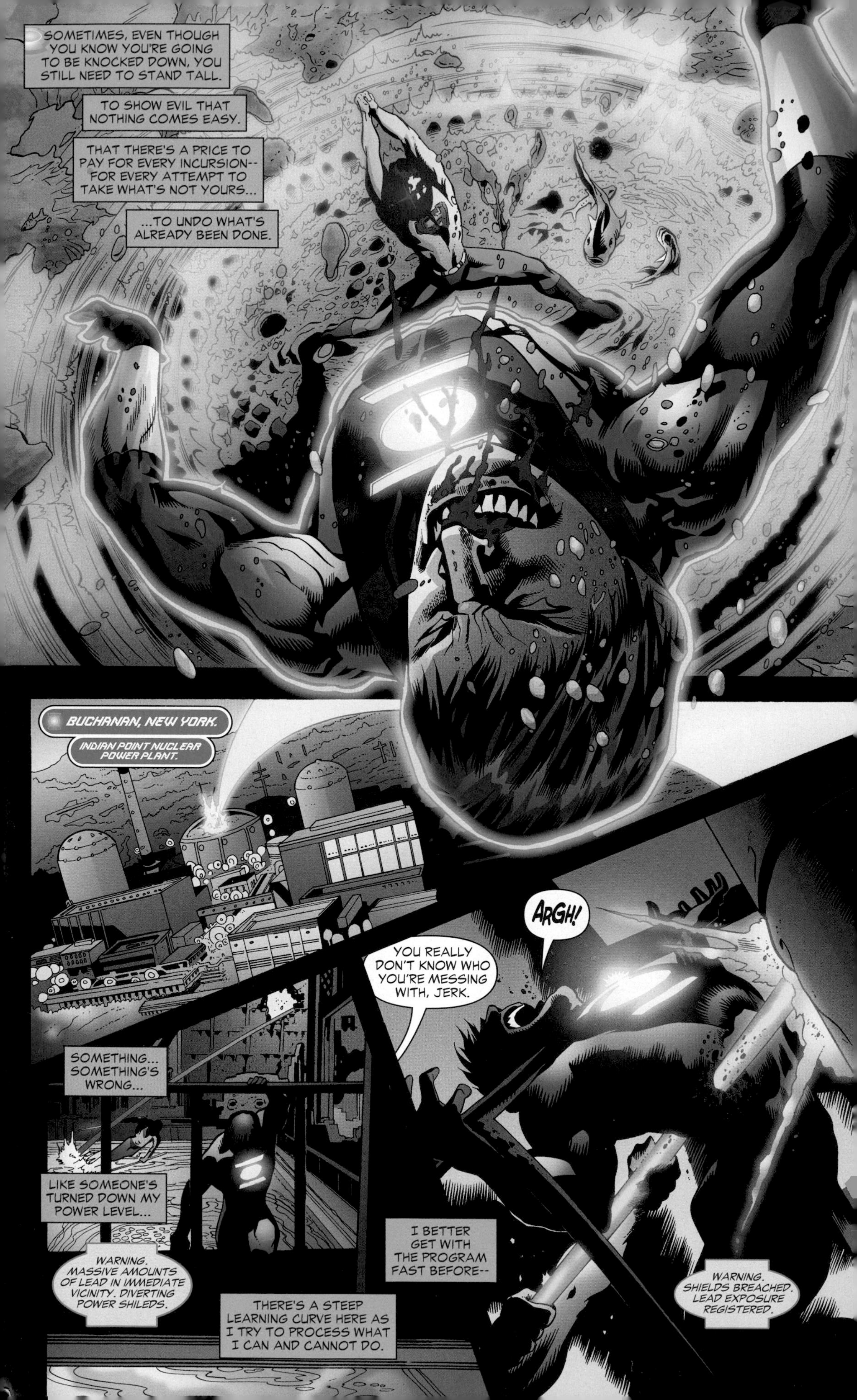
SOMETIMES, EVEN THOUGH YOU KNOW YOU'RE GOING TO BE KNOCKED DOWN, YOU STILL NEED TO STAND TALL.
TO SHOW EVIL THAT NOTHING COMES EASY.
THAT THERE'S A PRICE TO PAY FOR EVERY INCURSION-- FOR EVERY ATTEMPT TO TAKE WHAT'S NOT YOURS...
...TO UNDO WHAT'S ALREADY BEEN DONE.
BUCHANAN, NEW YORK.
INDIAN POINT NUCLEAR POWER PLANT.
SOMETHING... SOMETHING'S WRONG...
LIKE SOMEONE'S TURNED DOWN MY POWER LEVEL...
WARNING. MASSIVE AMOUNTS OF LEAD IN IMMEDIATE VICINITY. DIVERTING POWER SHILEDS.
THERE'S A STEEP LEARNING CURVE HERE AS I TRY TO PROCESS WHAT I CAN AND CANNOT DO.
I BETTER GET WITH THE PROGRAM FAST BEFORE--
ARGH!
YOU REALLY DON'T KNOW WHO YOU'RE MESSING WITH, JERK.
WARNING. SHIELDS BREACHED. LEAD EXPOSURE REGISTERED.

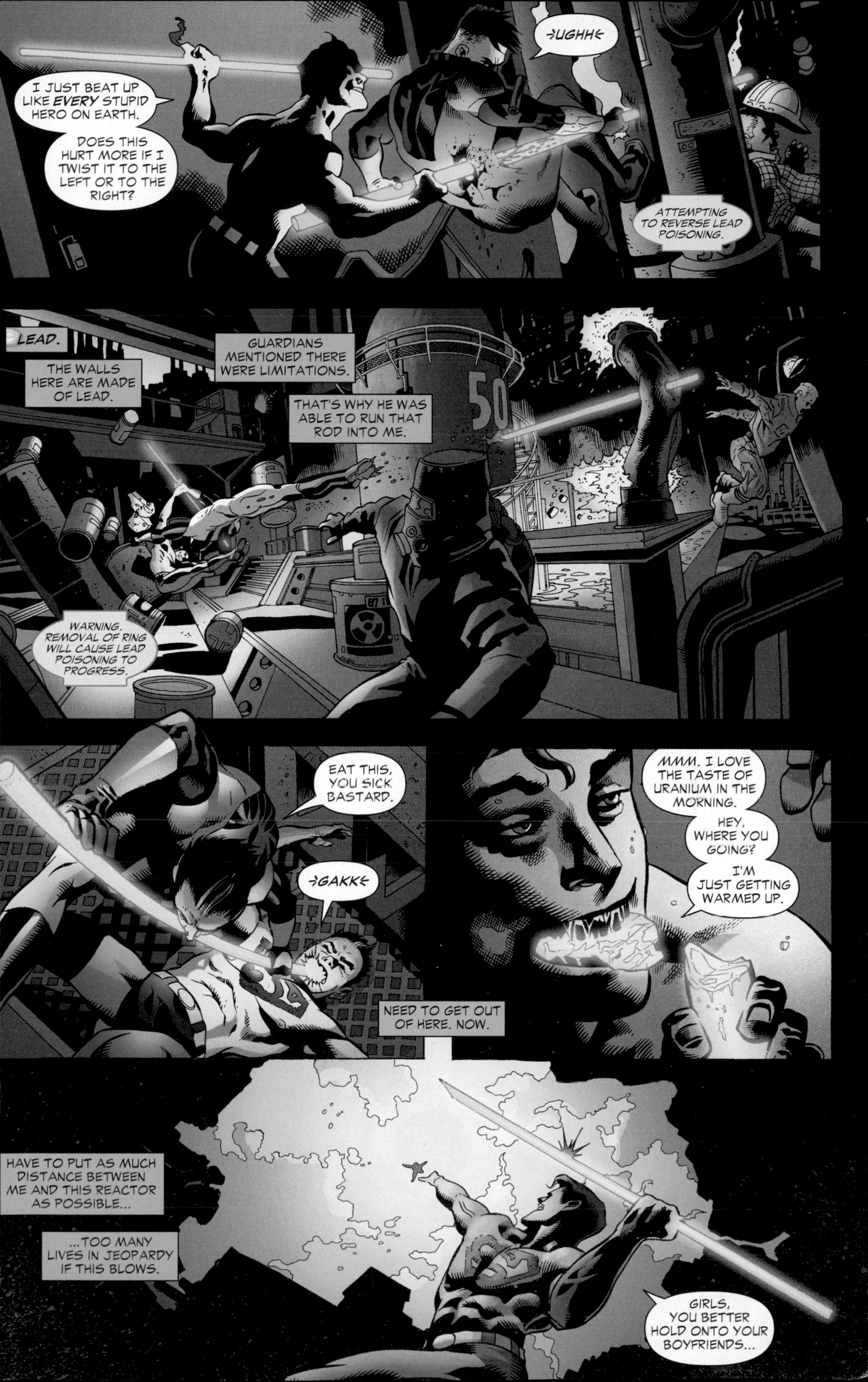
I JUST BEAT UP LIKE *EVERY* STUPID HERO ON EARTH.
DOES THIS HURT MORE IF I TWIST IT TO THE LEFT OR TO THE RIGHT?
UGHH
ATTEMPTING TO REVERSE LEAD POISONING.
LEAD.
THE WALLS HERE ARE MADE OF LEAD.
GUARDIANS MENTIONED THERE WERE LIMITATIONS.
THAT'S WHY HE WAS ABLE TO RUN THAT ROD INTO ME.
50
WARNING. REMOVAL OF RING WILL CAUSE LEAD POISONING TO PROGRESS.
EAT THIS, YOU SICK BASTARD.
GAKK
MMM. I LOVE THE TASTE OF URANIUM IN THE MORNING.
HEY, WHERE YOU GOING?
I'M JUST GETTING WARMED UP.
NEED TO GET OUT OF HERE. NOW.
HAVE TO PUT AS MUCH DISTANCE BETWEEN ME AND THIS REACTOR AS POSSIBLE...
...TOO MANY LIVES IN JEOPARDY IF THIS BLOWS.
GIRLS, YOU BETTER HOLD ONTO YOUR BOYFRIENDS...

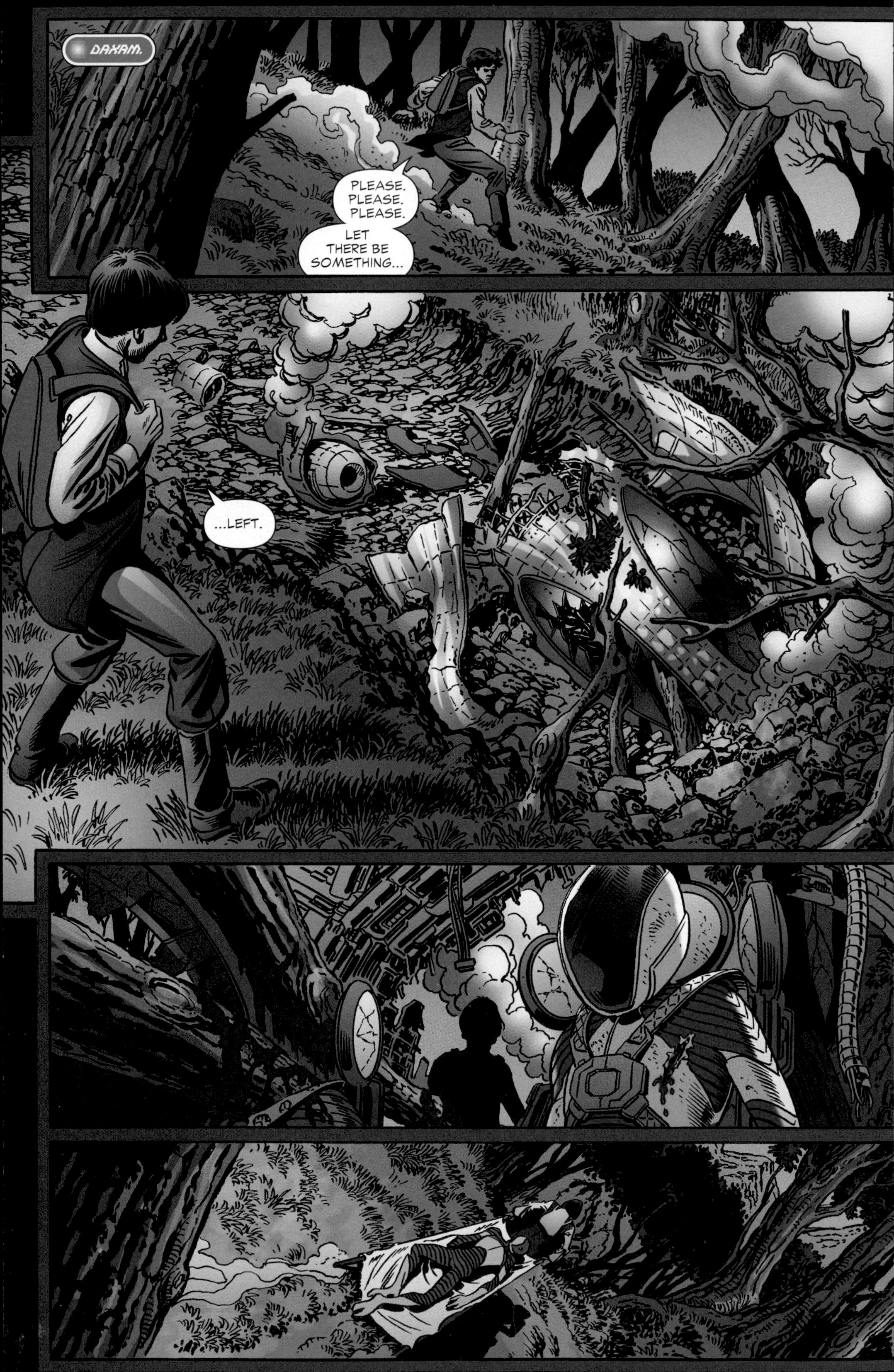
DAXAM.
PLEASE. PLEASE. PLEASE.
LET THERE BE SOMETHING...
...LEFT.

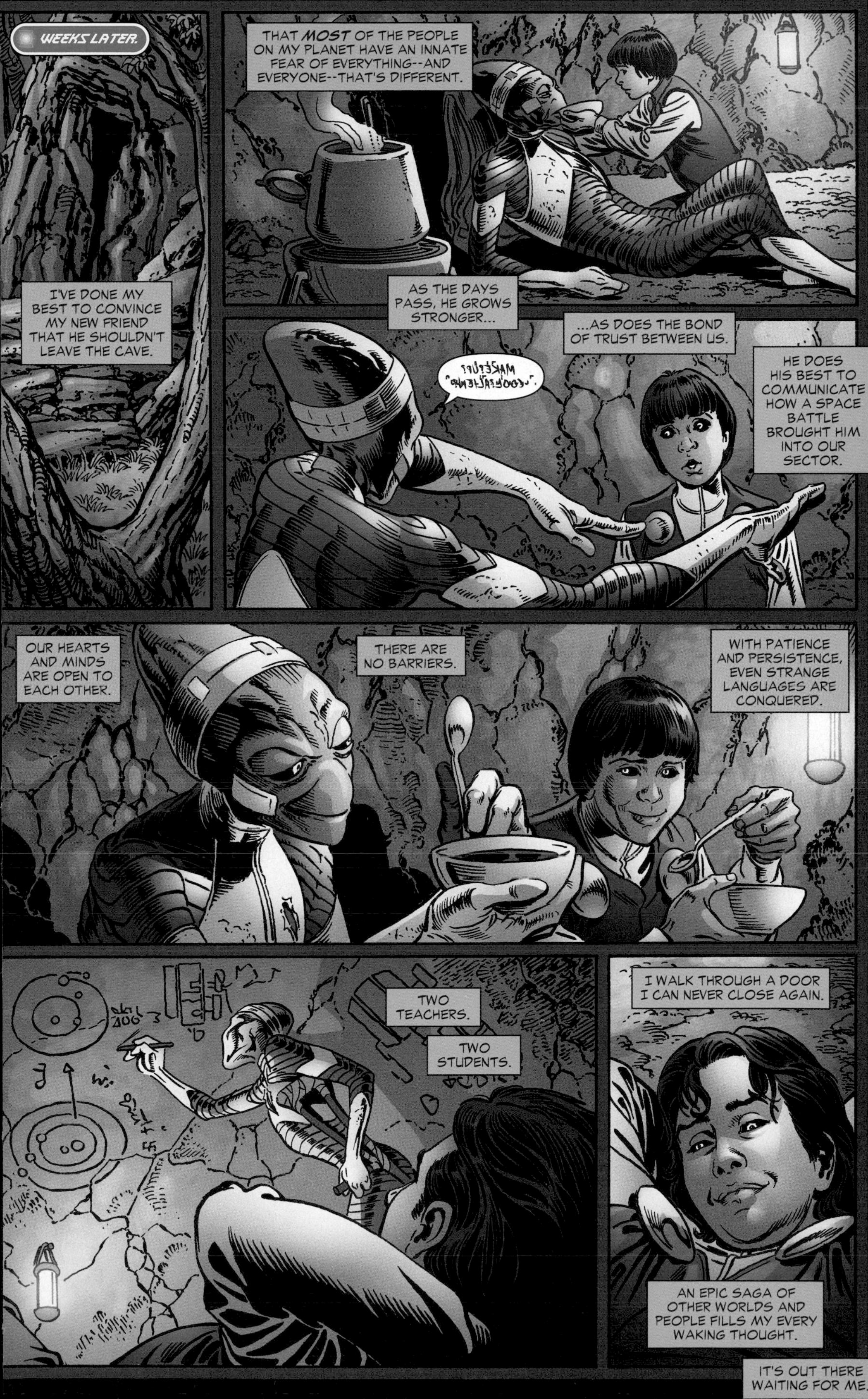
WEEKS LATER.
THAT MOST OF THE PEOPLE ON MY PLANET HAVE AN INNATE FEAR OF EVERYTHING--AND EVERYONE--THAT'S DIFFERENT.
I'VE DONE MY BEST TO CONVINCE MY NEW FRIEND THAT HE SHOULDN'T LEAVE THE CAVE.
AS THE DAYS PASS, HE GROWS STRONGER...
...AS DOES THE BOND OF TRUST BETWEEN US.
HE DOES HIS BEST TO COMMUNICATE HOW A SPACE BATTLE BROUGHT HIM INTO OUR SECTOR.
OUR HEARTS AND MINDS ARE OPEN TO EACH OTHER.
THERE ARE NO BARRIERS.
WITH PATIENCE AND PERSISTENCE, EVEN STRANGE LANGUAGES ARE CONQUERED.
TWO TEACHERS.
TWO STUDENTS.
I WALK THROUGH A DOOR I CAN NEVER CLOSE AGAIN.
AN EPIC SAGA OF OTHER WORLDS AND PEOPLE FILLS MY EVERY WAKING THOUGHT.
IT'S OUT THERE WAITING FOR ME

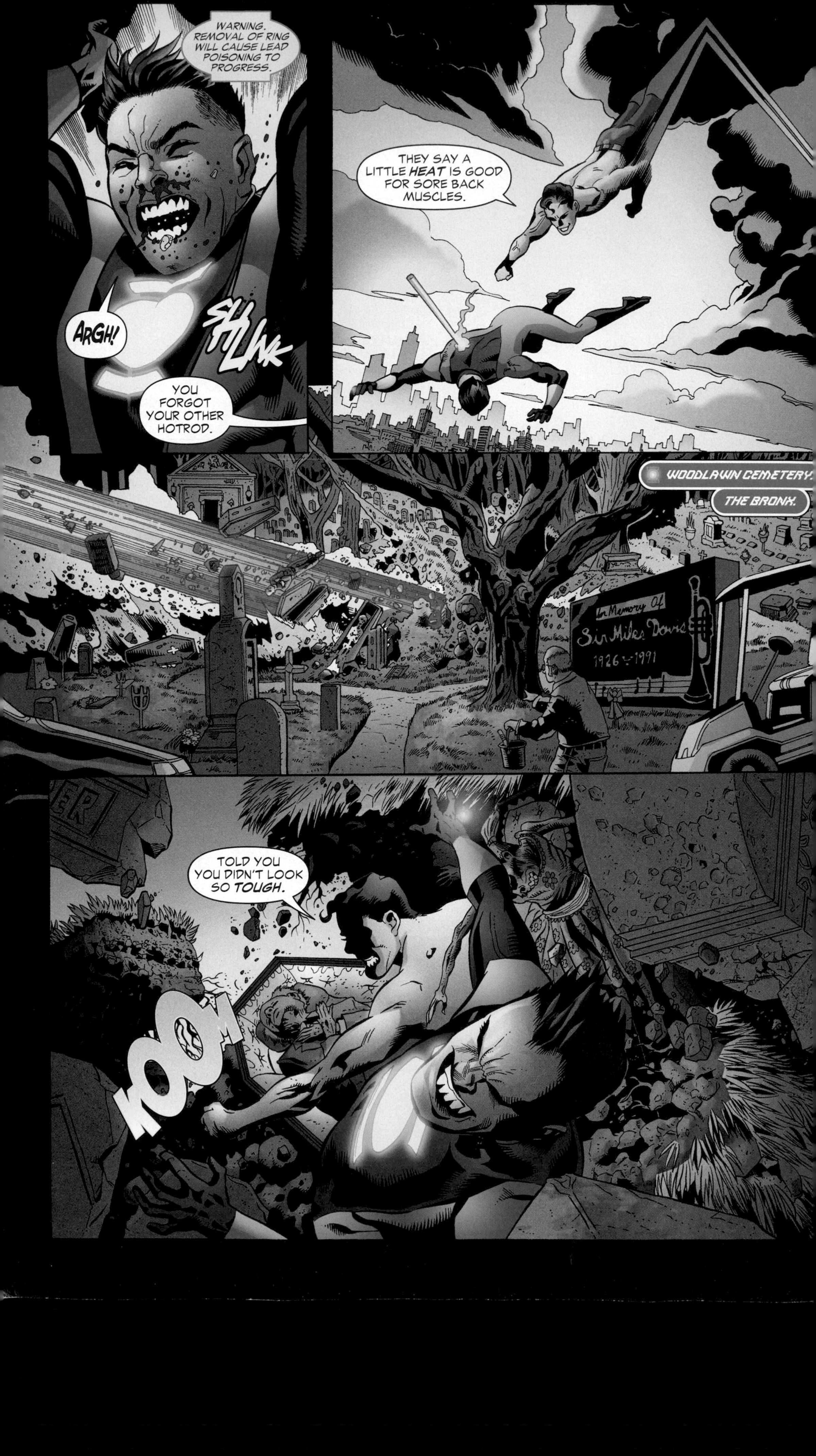
WARNING. REMOVAL OF RING WILL CAUSE LEAD POISONING TO PROGRESS.
ARGH!
SHLUNK
YOU FORGOT YOUR OTHER HOTROD.
THEY SAY A LITTLE HEAT IS GOOD FOR SORE BACK MUSCLES.
WOODLAWN CEMETERY.
THE BRONX.
In Memory Of
Sir Miles Davis
1926 - 1991
TOLD YOU YOU DIDN'T LOOK SO TOUGH.
KOOM

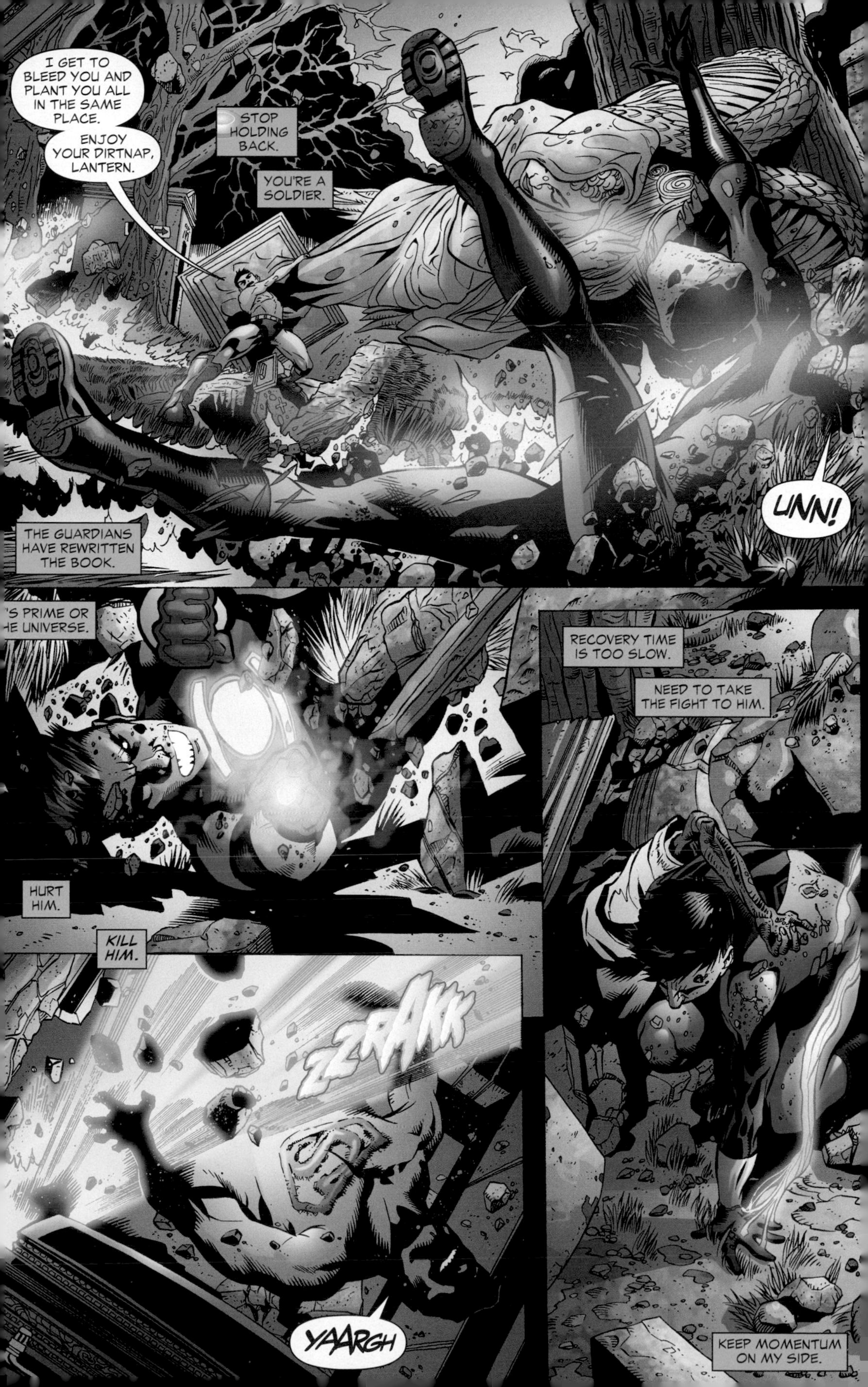
I GET TO BLEED YOU AND PLANT YOU ALL IN THE SAME PLACE.
ENJOY YOUR DIRTNAP, LANTERN.
STOP HOLDING BACK.
YOU'RE A SOLDIER.
THE GUARDIANS HAVE REWRITTEN THE BOOK.
UNN!
'S PRIME OR HE UNIVERSE.
HURT HIM.
KILL HIM.
ZZRAKK
YAARGH
RECOVERY TIME IS TOO SLOW.
NEED TO TAKE THE FIGHT TO HIM.
KEEP MOMENTUM ON MY SIDE.

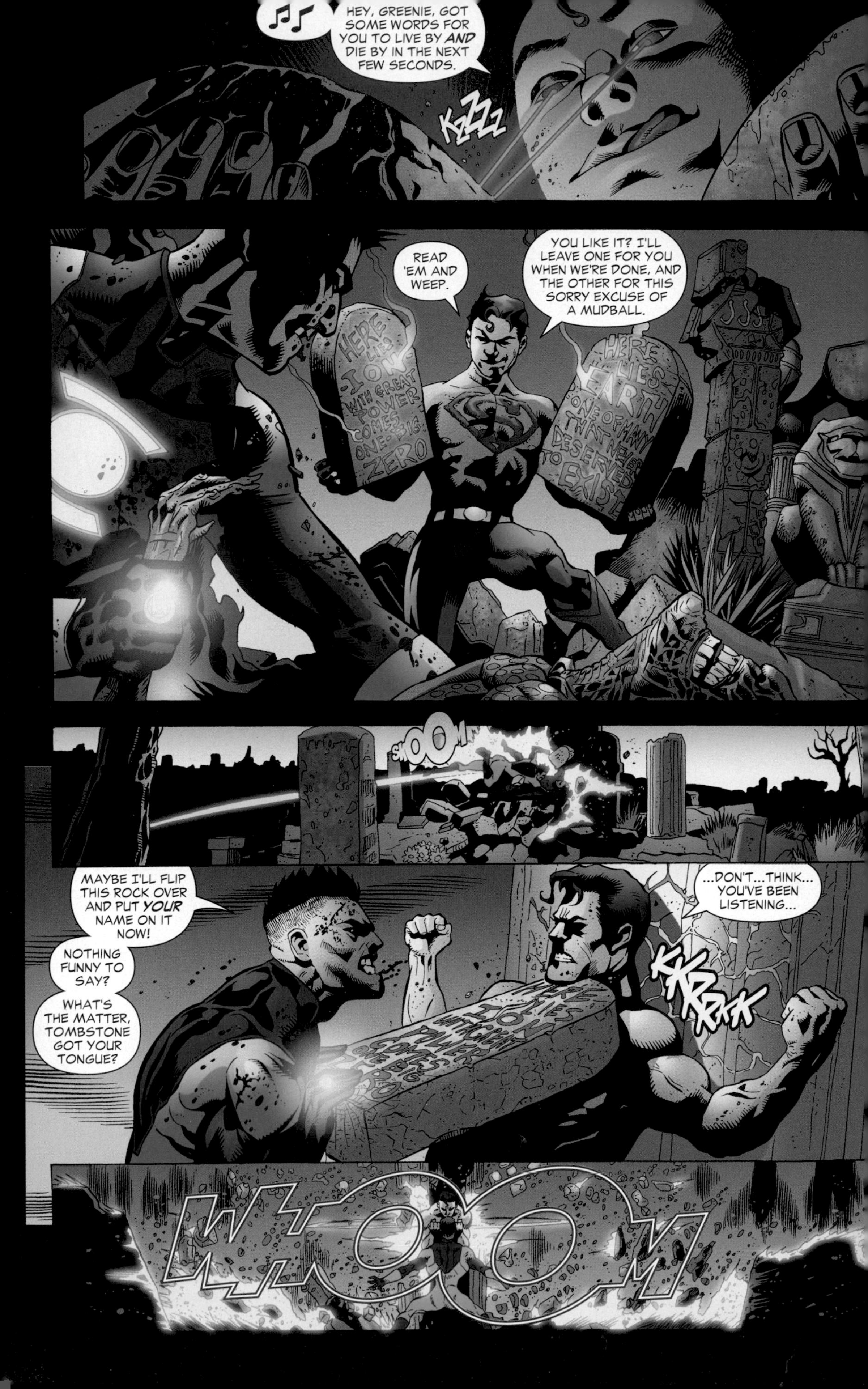

HEY, GREENIE, GOT SOME WORDS FOR YOU TO LIVE BY AND DIE BY IN THE NEXT FEW SECONDS.
KZZZZ
READ 'EM AND WEEP.
YOU LIKE IT? I'LL LEAVE ONE FOR YOU WHEN WE'RE DONE, AND THE OTHER FOR THIS SORRY EXCUSE OF A MUDBALL.
HERE LIES ION WITH GREAT POWER COMES ONE BIG ZERO
HERE LIES EARTH ONE OF MANY THAT NEVER DESERVED TO EXIST
SHOOOM
MAYBE I'LL FLIP THIS ROCK OVER AND PUT YOUR NAME ON IT NOW!
NOTHING FUNNY TO SAY?
WHAT'S THE MATTER, TOMBSTONE GOT YOUR TONGUE?
...DON'T...THINK... YOU'VE BEEN LISTENING...
KKRRKK
WHOOOM

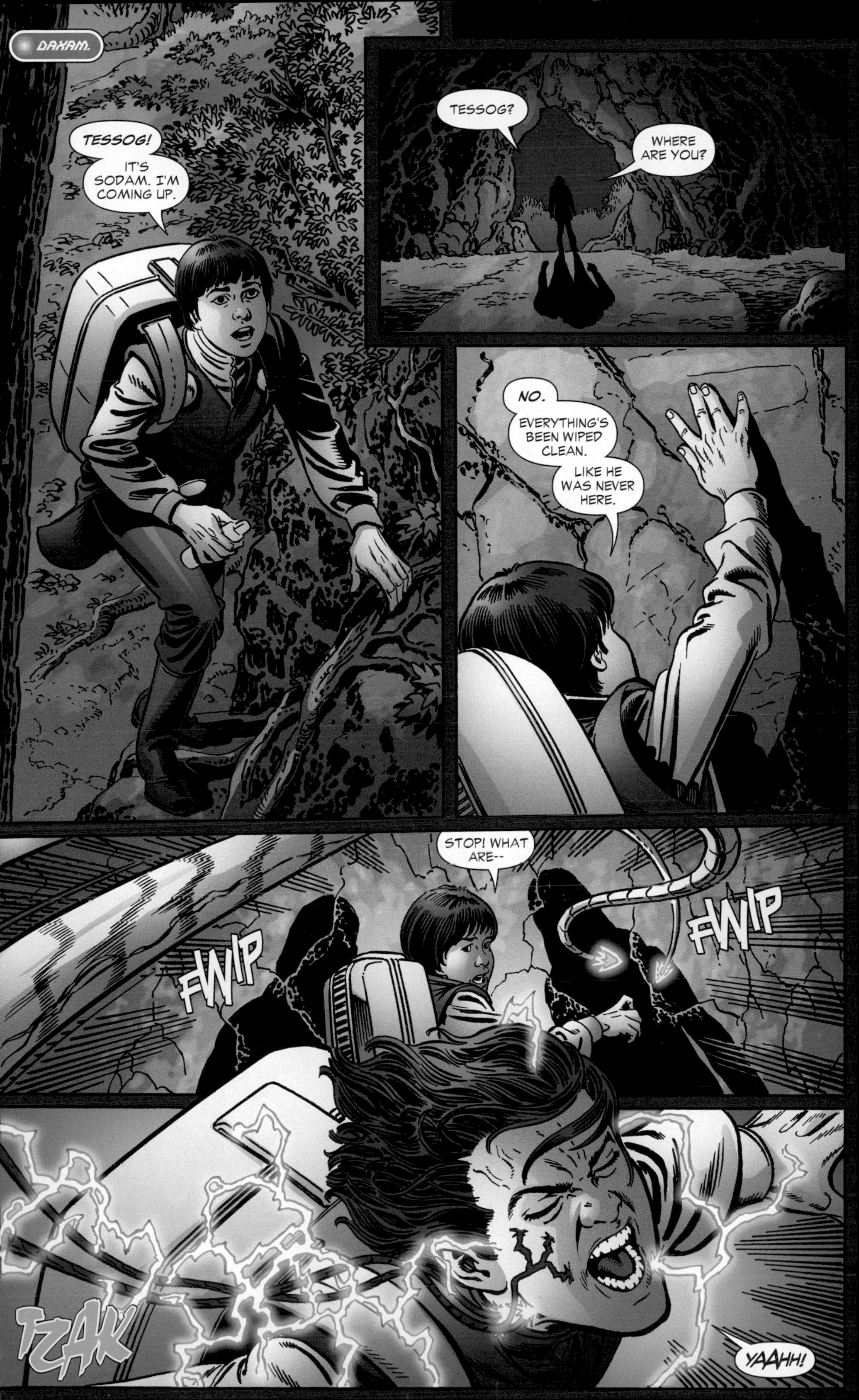
DAXAM.
TESSOG!
IT'S SODAM. I'M COMING UP.
TESSOG?
WHERE ARE YOU?
NO.
EVERYTHING'S BEEN WIPED CLEAN.
LIKE HE WAS NEVER HERE.
STOP! WHAT ARE--
FWIP
FWIP
TZAK
YAAHH!

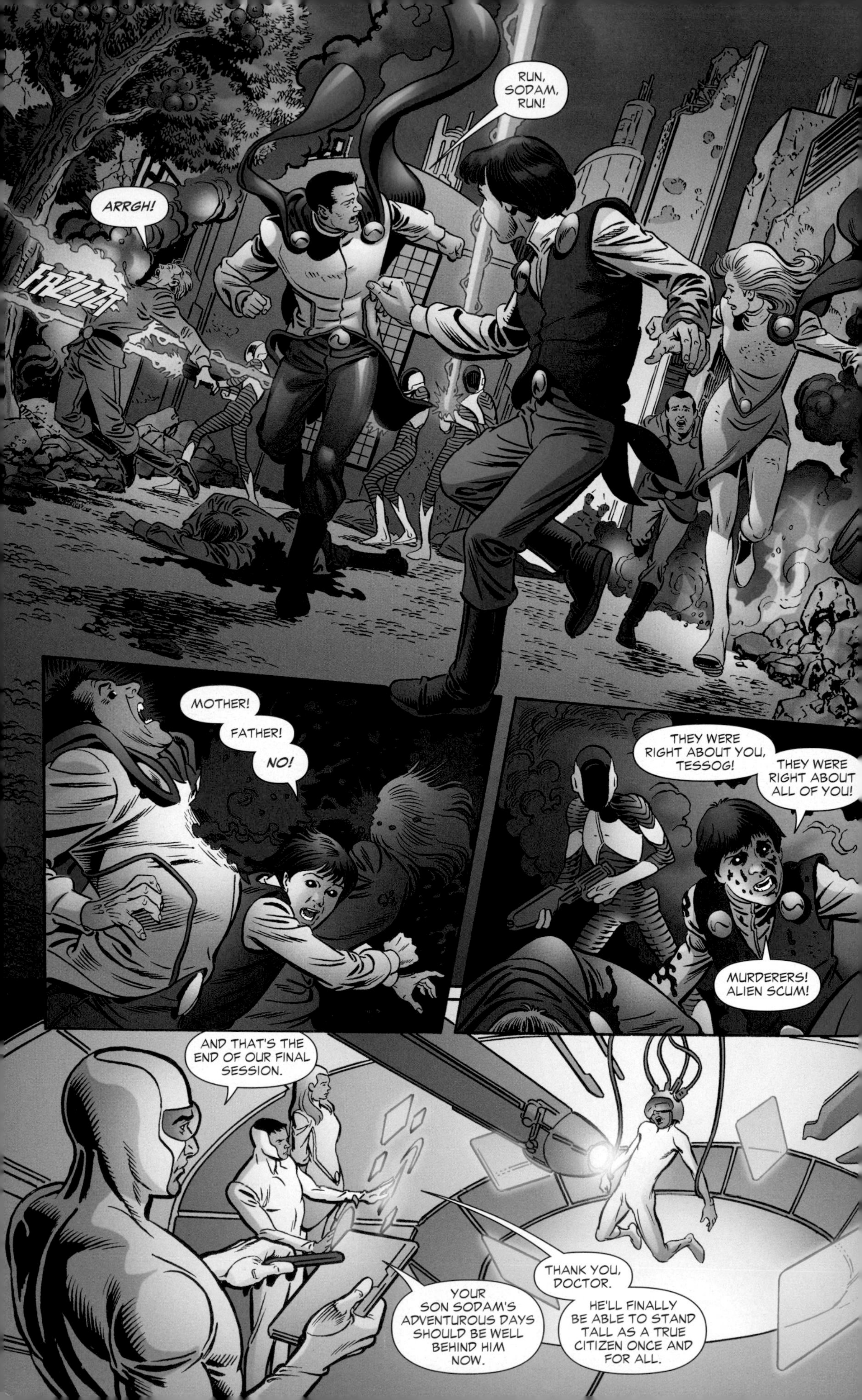
RUN, SODAM, RUN!
ARRGH!
FRZZZT
MOTHER!
FATHER!
NO!
THEY WERE RIGHT ABOUT YOU, TESSOG!
THEY WERE RIGHT ABOUT ALL OF YOU!
MURDERERS! ALIEN SCUM!
AND THAT'S THE END OF OUR FINAL SESSION.
YOUR SON SODAM'S ADVENTUROUS DAYS SHOULD BE WELL BEHIND HIM NOW.
THANK YOU, DOCTOR.
HE'LL FINALLY BE ABLE TO STAND TALL AS A TRUE CITIZEN ONCE AND FOR ALL.

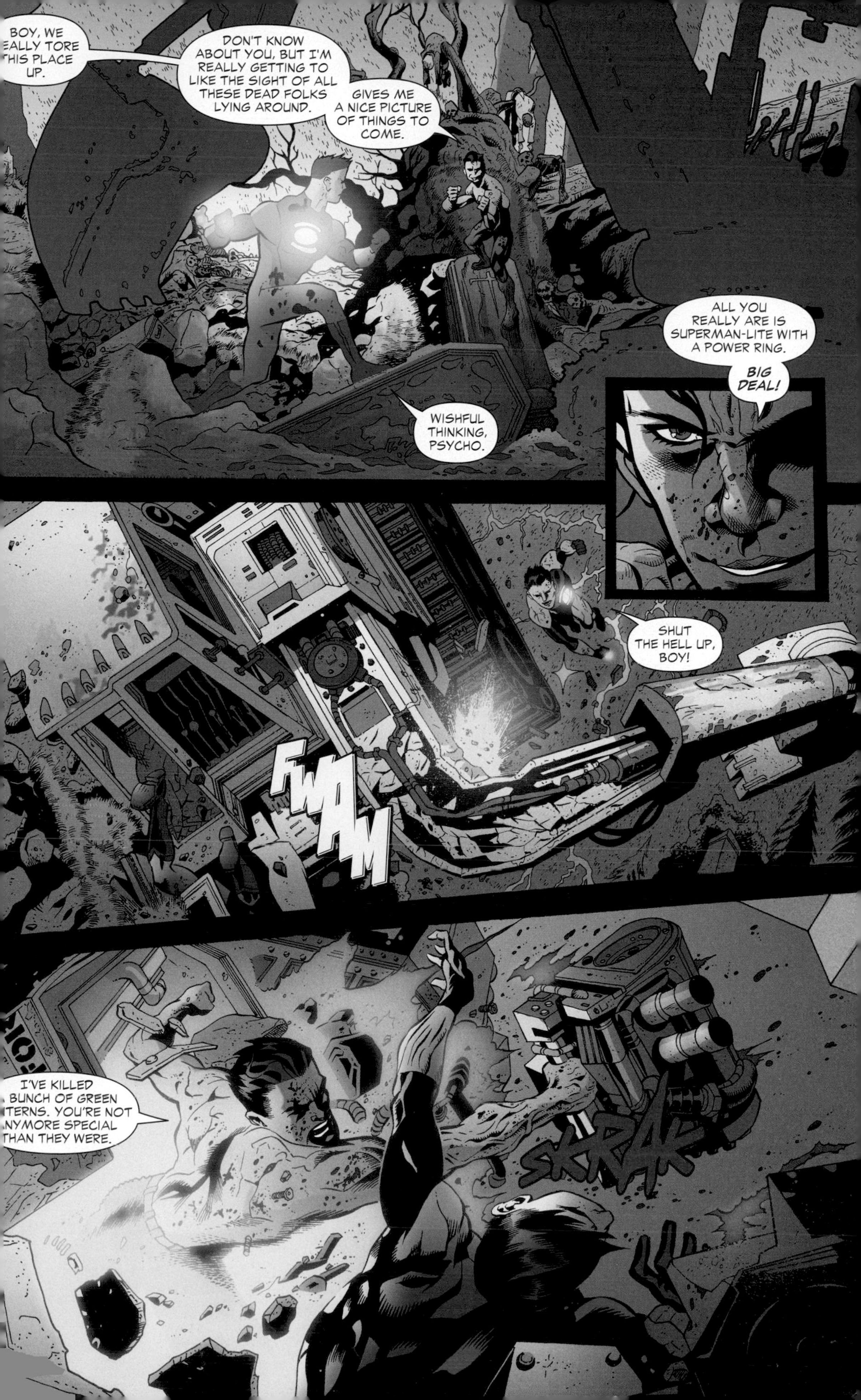

BOY, WE EALLY TORE THIS PLACE UP.
DON'T KNOW ABOUT YOU, BUT I'M REALLY GETTING TO LIKE THE SIGHT OF ALL THESE DEAD FOLKS LYING AROUND.
GIVES ME A NICE PICTURE OF THINGS TO COME.
WISHFUL THINKING, PSYCHO.
ALL YOU REALLY ARE IS SUPERMAN-LITE WITH A POWER RING.
BIG DEAL!
SHUT THE HELL UP, BOY!
FWAAM
I'VE KILLED BUNCH OF GREEN TERNS. YOU'RE NOT NYMORE SPECIAL THAN THEY WERE.
SKRAK

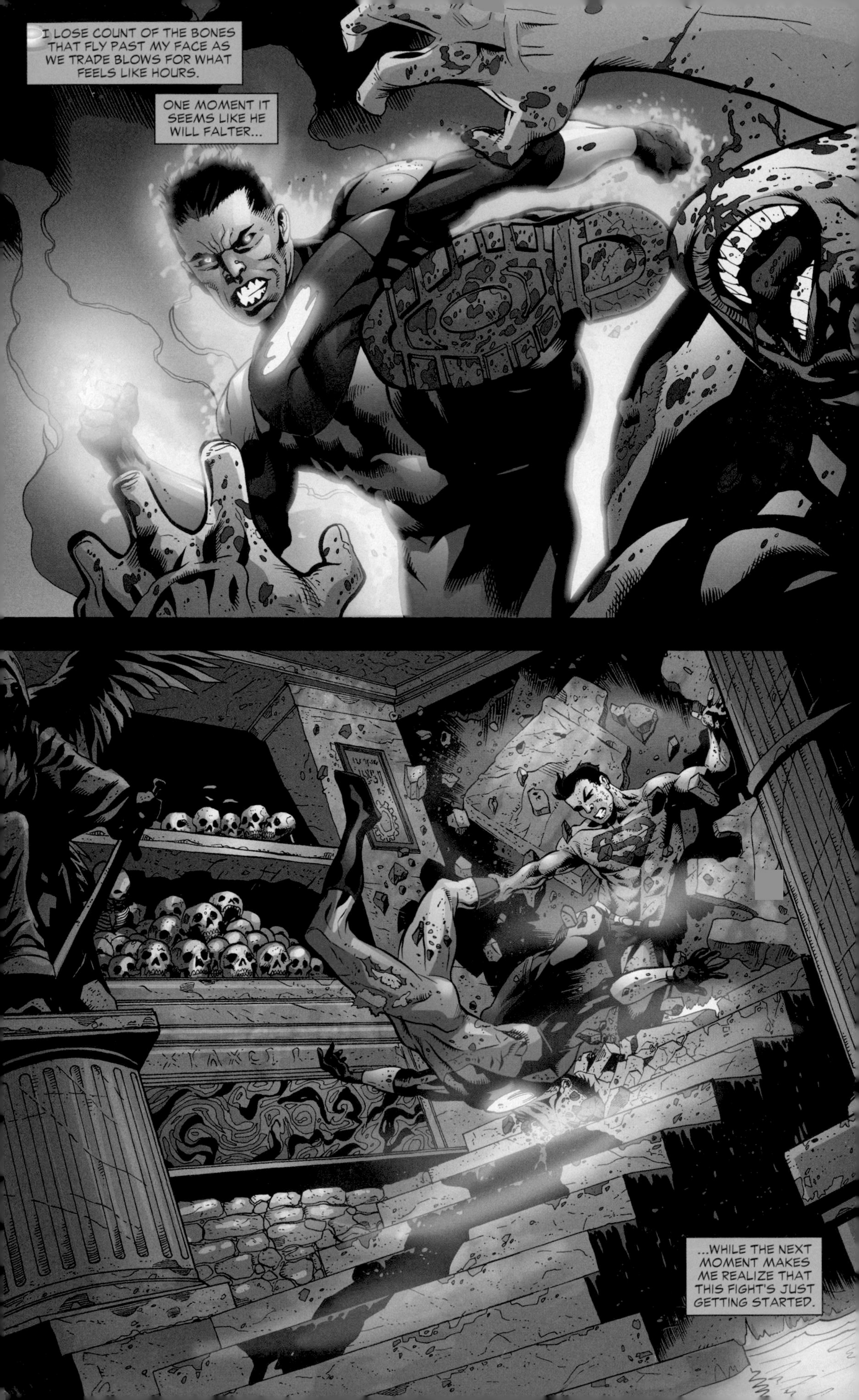
I LOSE COUNT OF THE BONES THAT FLY PAST MY FACE AS WE TRADE BLOWS FOR WHAT FEELS LIKE HOURS.
ONE MOMENT IT SEEMS LIKE HE WILL FALTER...
...WHILE THE NEXT MOMENT MAKES ME REALIZE THAT THIS FIGHT'S JUST GETTING STARTED.

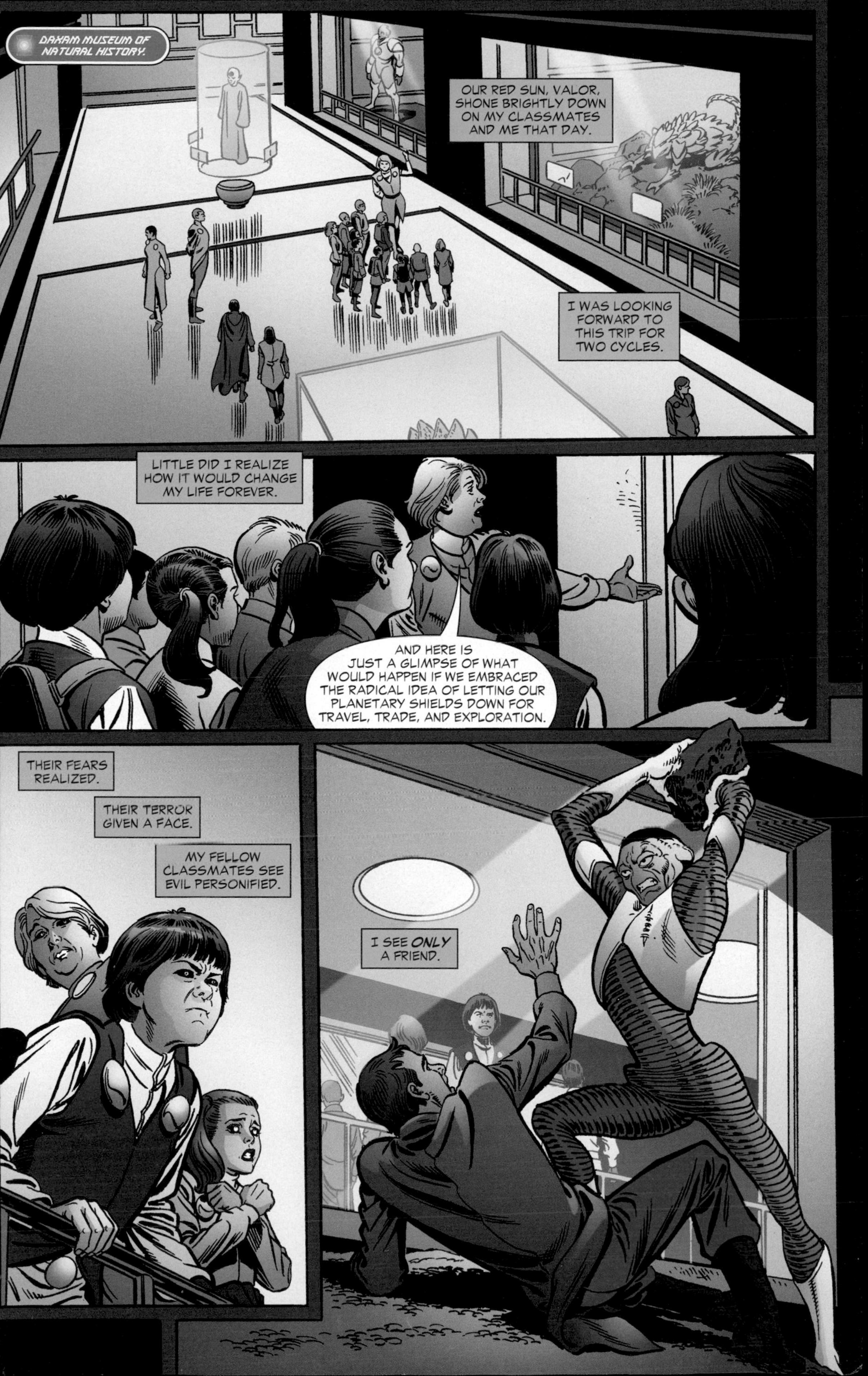
DAXAM MUSEUM OF NATURAL HISTORY.
OUR RED SUN, VALOR, SHONE BRIGHTLY DOWN ON MY CLASSMATES AND ME THAT DAY.
I WAS LOOKING FORWARD TO THIS TRIP FOR TWO CYCLES.
LITTLE DID I REALIZE HOW IT WOULD CHANGE MY LIFE FOREVER.
AND HERE IS JUST A GLIMPSE OF WHAT WOULD HAPPEN IF WE EMBRACED THE RADICAL IDEA OF LETTING OUR PLANETARY SHIELDS DOWN FOR TRAVEL, TRADE, AND EXPLORATION.
THEIR FEARS REALIZED.
THEIR TERROR GIVEN A FACE.
MY FELLOW CLASSMATES SEE EVIL PERSONIFIED.
I SEE *ONLY* A FRIEND.

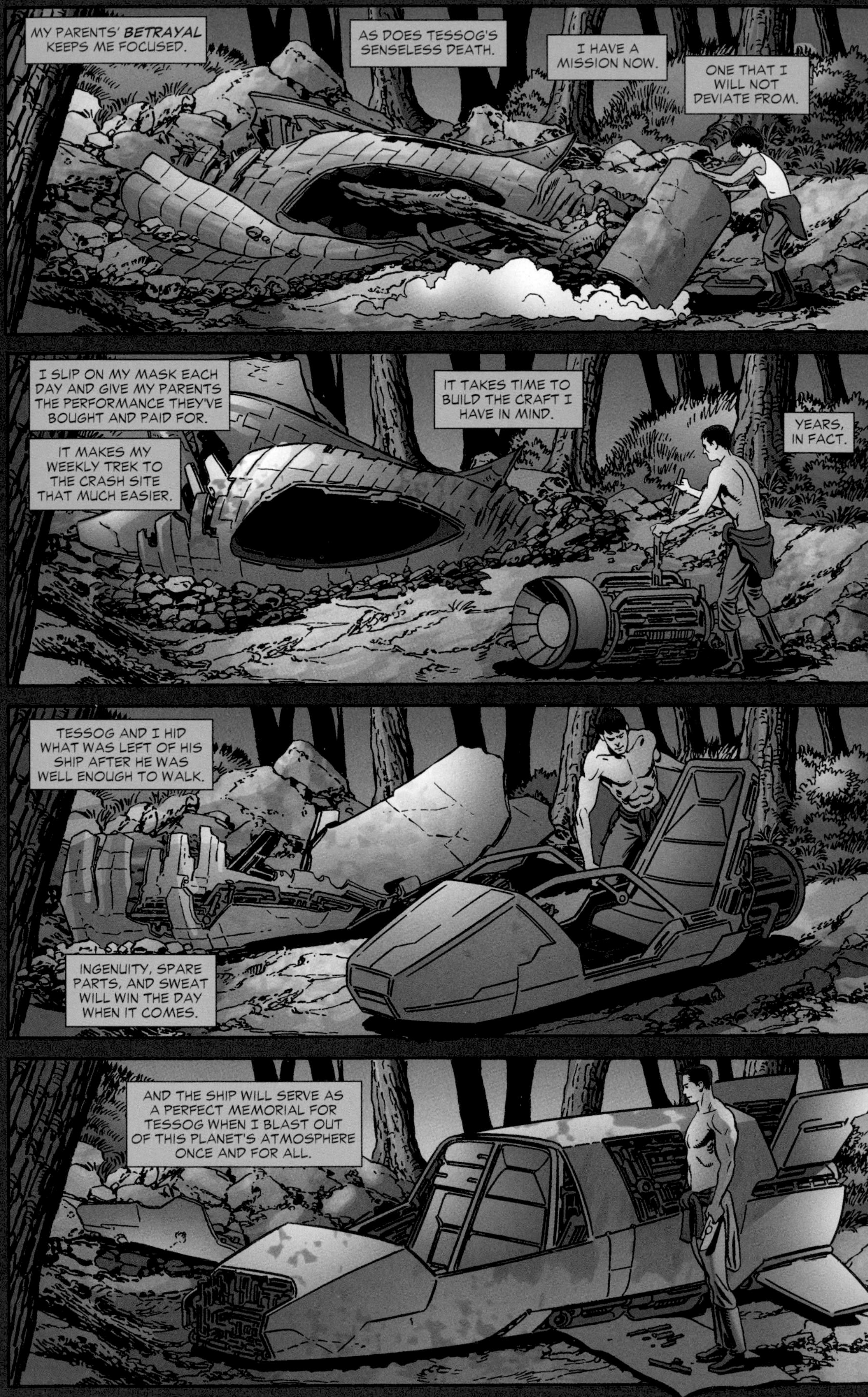
MY PARENTS' BETRAYAL KEEPS ME FOCUSED.
AS DOES TESSOG'S SENSELESS DEATH.
I HAVE A MISSION NOW.
ONE THAT I WILL NOT DEVIATE FROM.
I SLIP ON MY MASK EACH DAY AND GIVE MY PARENTS THE PERFORMANCE THEY'VE BOUGHT AND PAID FOR.
IT MAKES MY WEEKLY TREK TO THE CRASH SITE THAT MUCH EASIER.
IT TAKES TIME TO BUILD THE CRAFT I HAVE IN MIND.
YEARS, IN FACT.
TESSOG AND I HID WHAT WAS LEFT OF HIS SHIP AFTER HE WAS WELL ENOUGH TO WALK.
INGENUITY, SPARE PARTS, AND SWEAT WILL WIN THE DAY WHEN IT COMES.
AND THE SHIP WILL SERVE AS A PERFECT MEMORIAL FOR TESSOG WHEN I BLAST OUT OF THIS PLANET'S ATMOSPHERE ONCE AND FOR ALL.

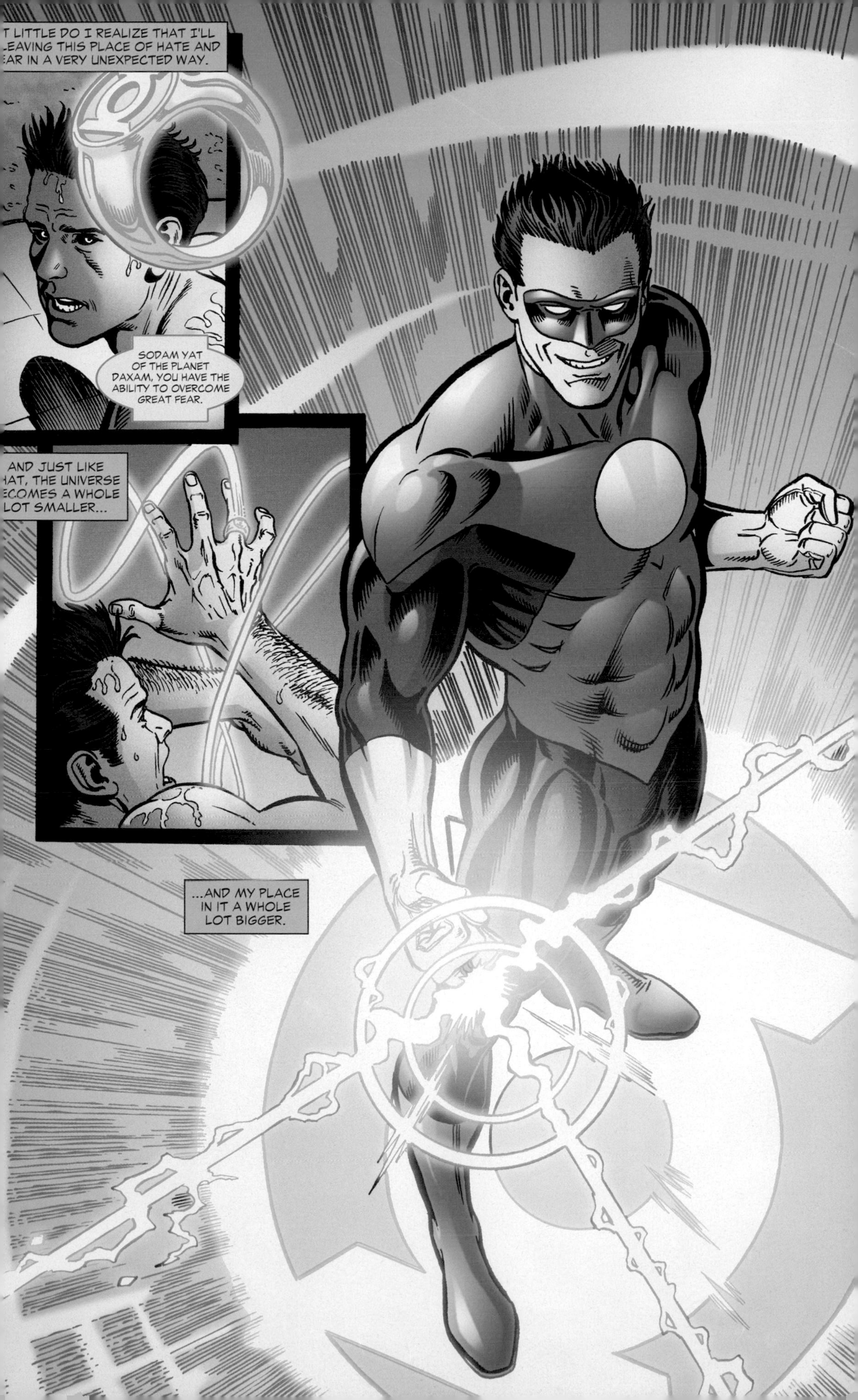
T LITTLE DO I REALIZE THAT I'LL
LEAVING THIS PLACE OF HATE AND
EAR IN A VERY UNEXPECTED WAY.
SODAM YAT OF THE PLANET DAXAM, YOU HAVE THE ABILITY TO OVERCOME GREAT FEAR.
AND JUST LIKE HAT, THE UNIVERSE ECOMES A WHOLE LOT SMALLER...
...AND MY PLACE IN IT A WHOLE LOT BIGGER.

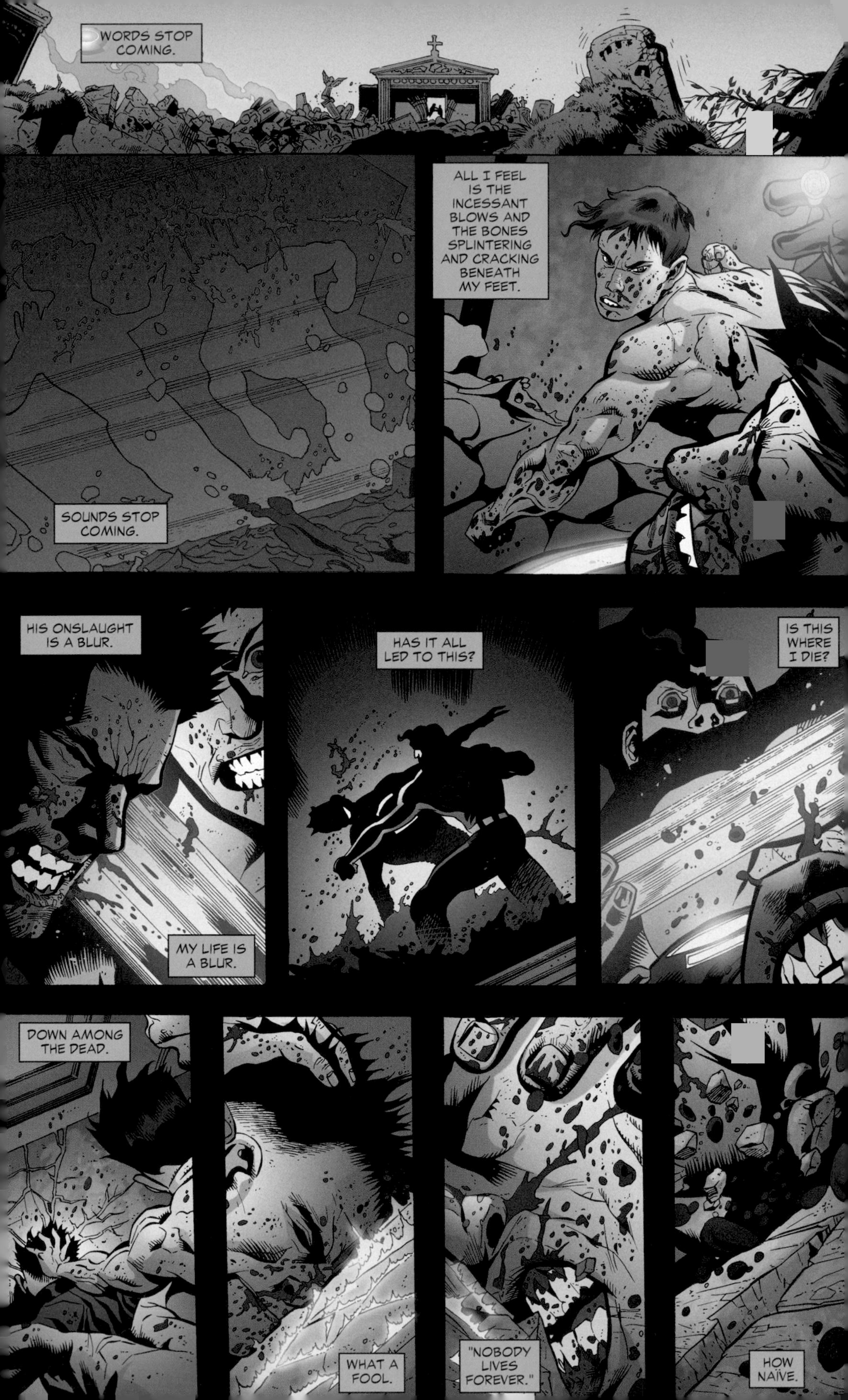
WORDS STOP COMING.
SOUNDS STOP COMING.
ALL I FEEL IS THE INCESSANT BLOWS AND THE BONES SPLINTERING AND CRACKING BENEATH MY FEET.
HIS ONSLAUGHT IS A BLUR.
MY LIFE IS A BLUR.
HAS IT ALL LED TO THIS?
IS THIS WHERE I DIE?
DOWN AMONG THE DEAD.
WHAT A FOOL.
"NOBODY LIVES FOREVER."
HOW NAÏVE.

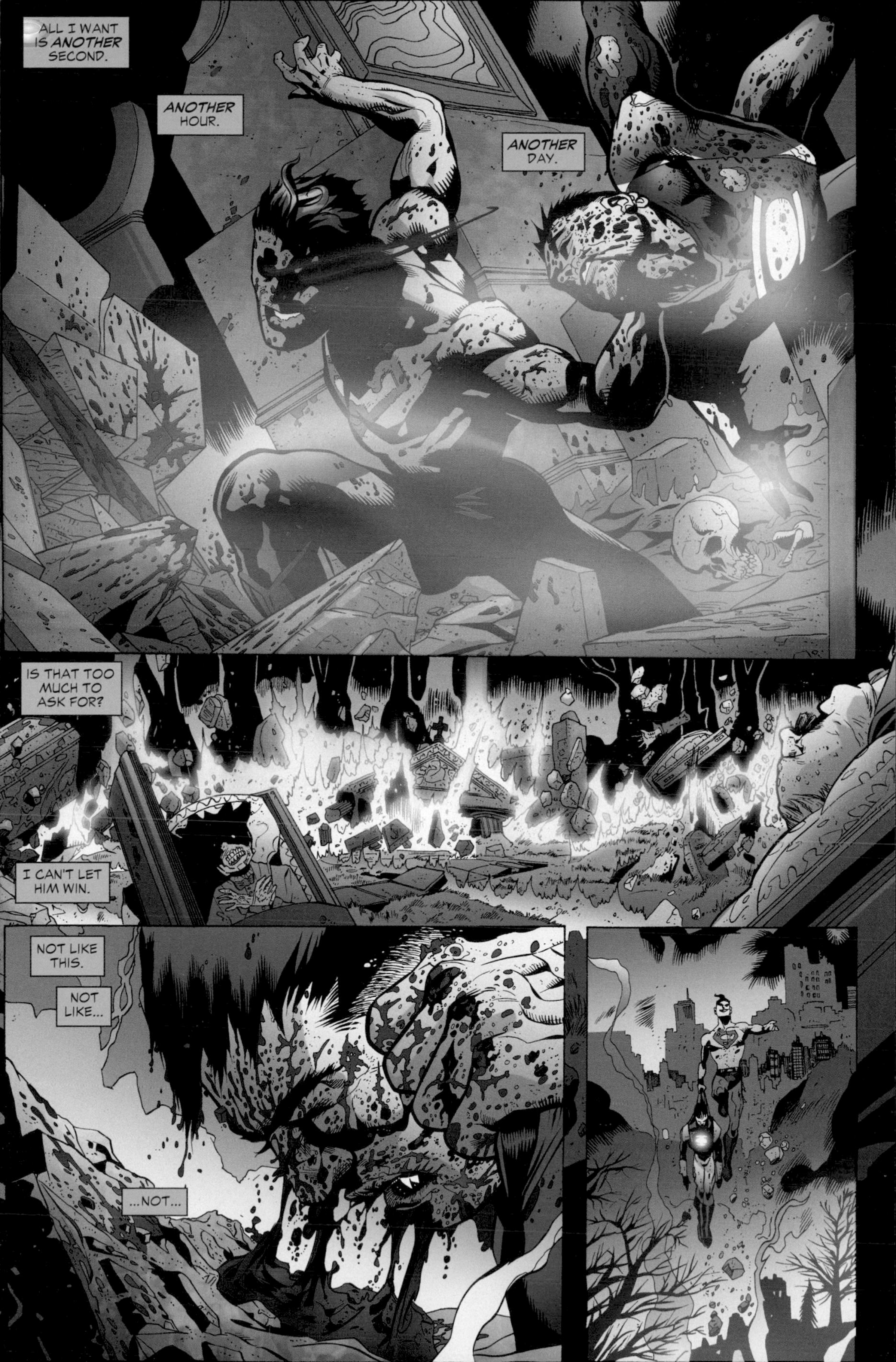
ALL I WANT IS ANOTHER SECOND.
ANOTHER HOUR.
ANOTHER DAY.
IS THAT TOO MUCH TO ASK FOR?
I CAN'T LET HIM WIN.
NOT LIKE THIS.
NOT LIKE...
...NOT...

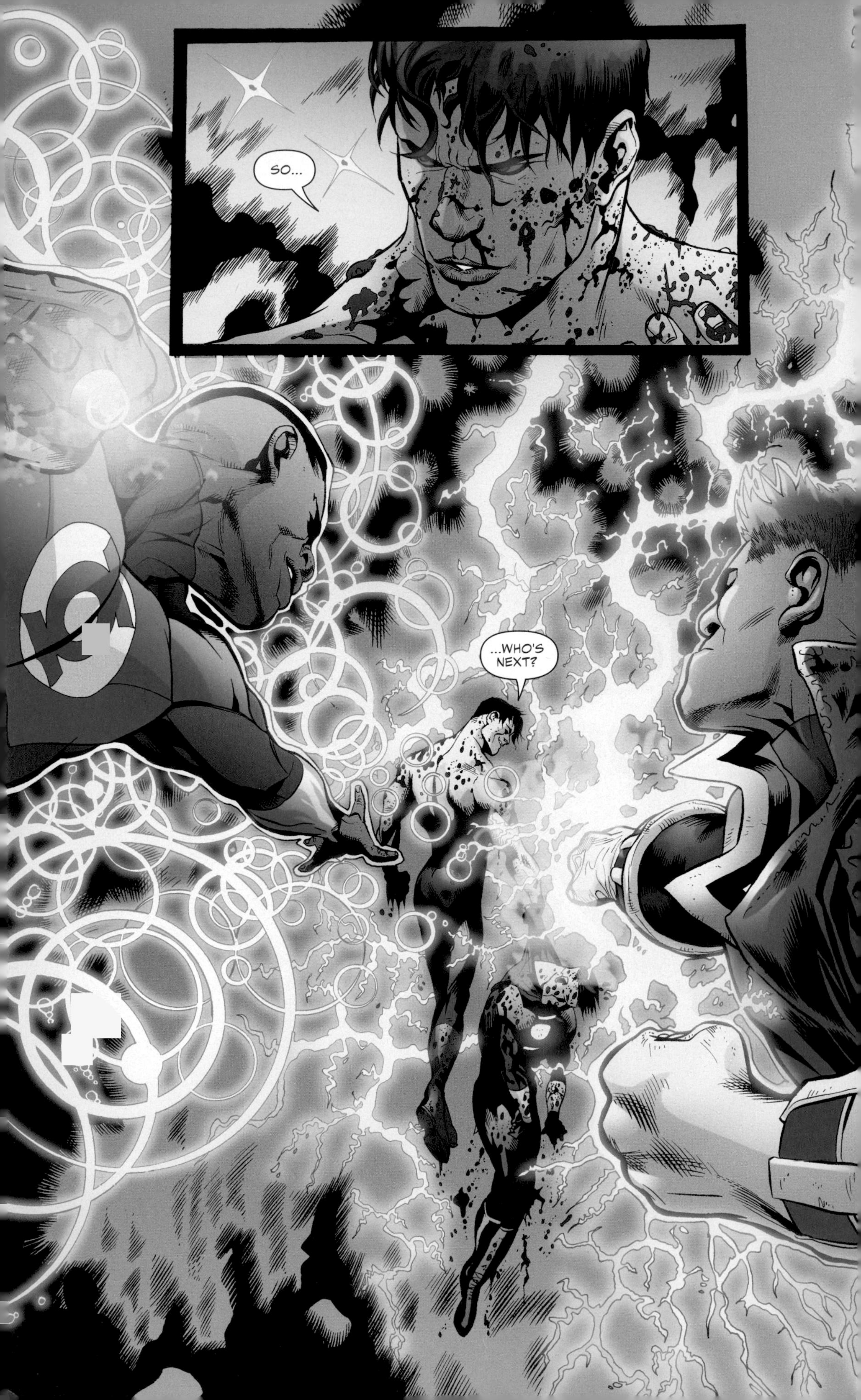
SO...
...WHO'S NEXT?

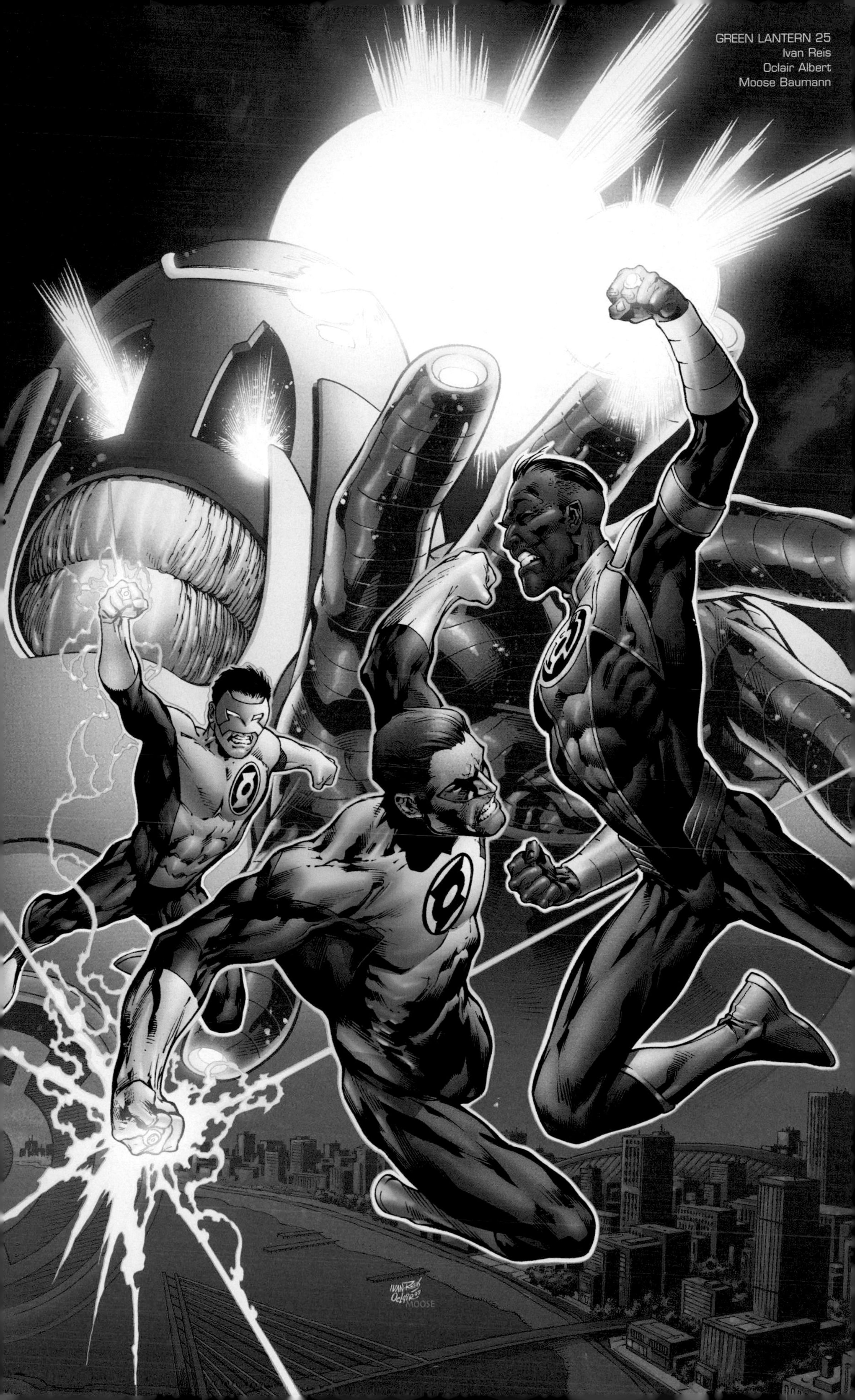

GREEN LANTERN 25
Ivan Reis
Oclair Albert
Moose Baumann

THE SINESTRO CORPS WAR
Chapter Ten
THE BIRTH OF THE BLACK LANTERN
Writer: **Geoff Johns**
Pencillers: **Ivan Reis** and **Ethan Van Sciver**
Inkers: **Oclair Albert, Julio Ferreira** and **Rod Reis**
Colorist: **Moose Baumann**

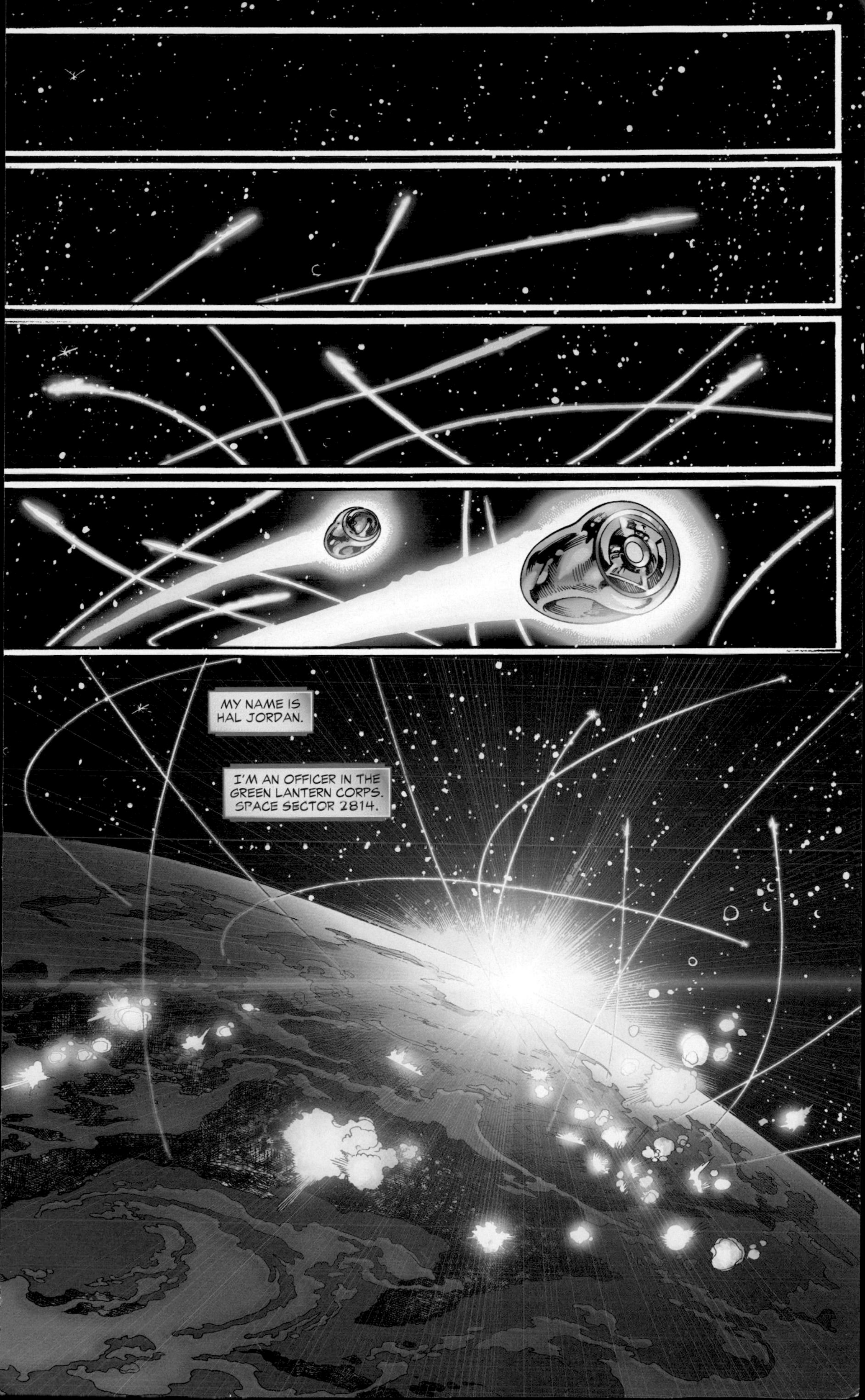
MY NAME IS HAL JORDAN.
I'M AN OFFICER IN THE GREEN LANTERN CORPS. SPACE SECTOR 2814.

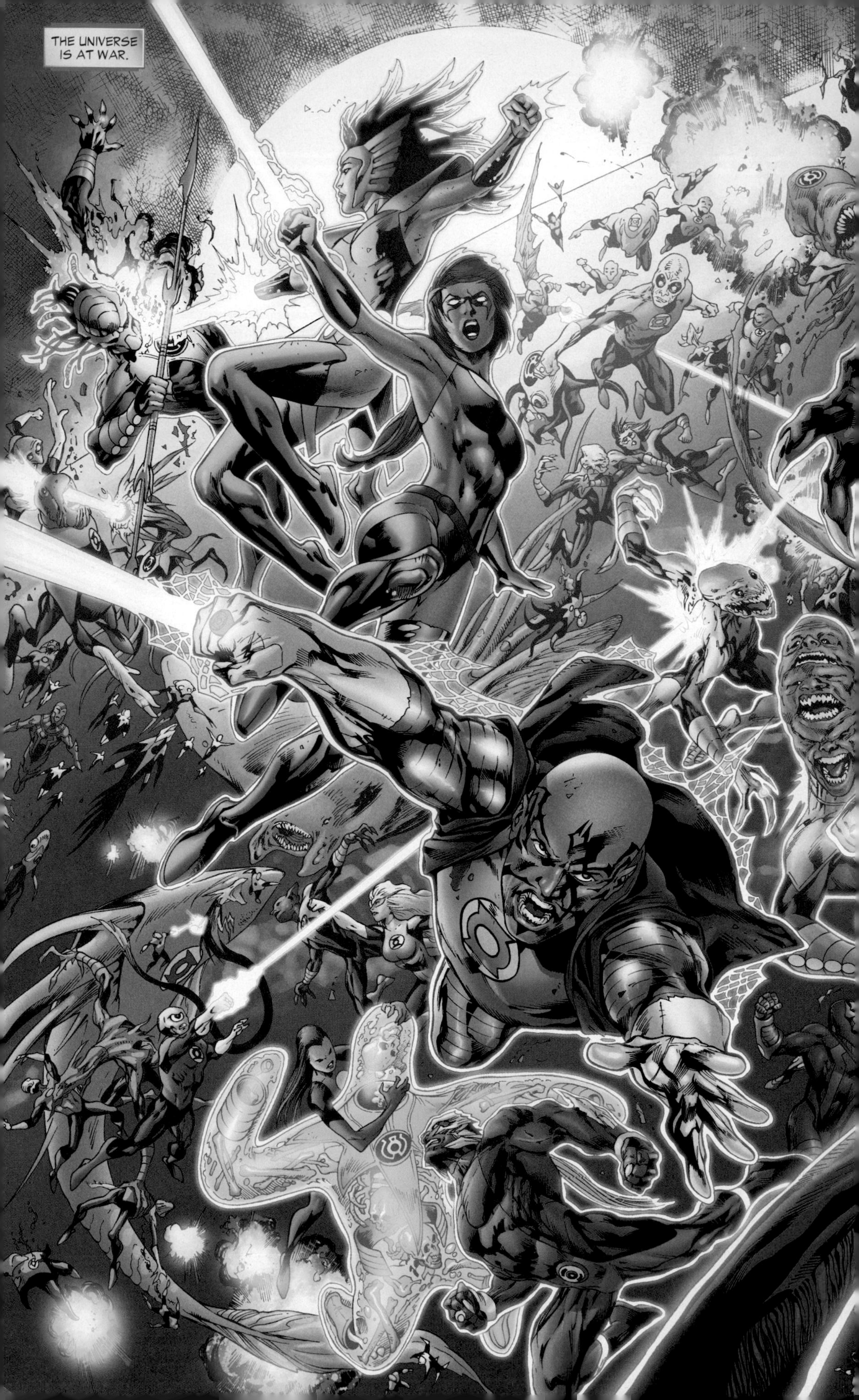
THE UNIVERSE IS AT WAR.

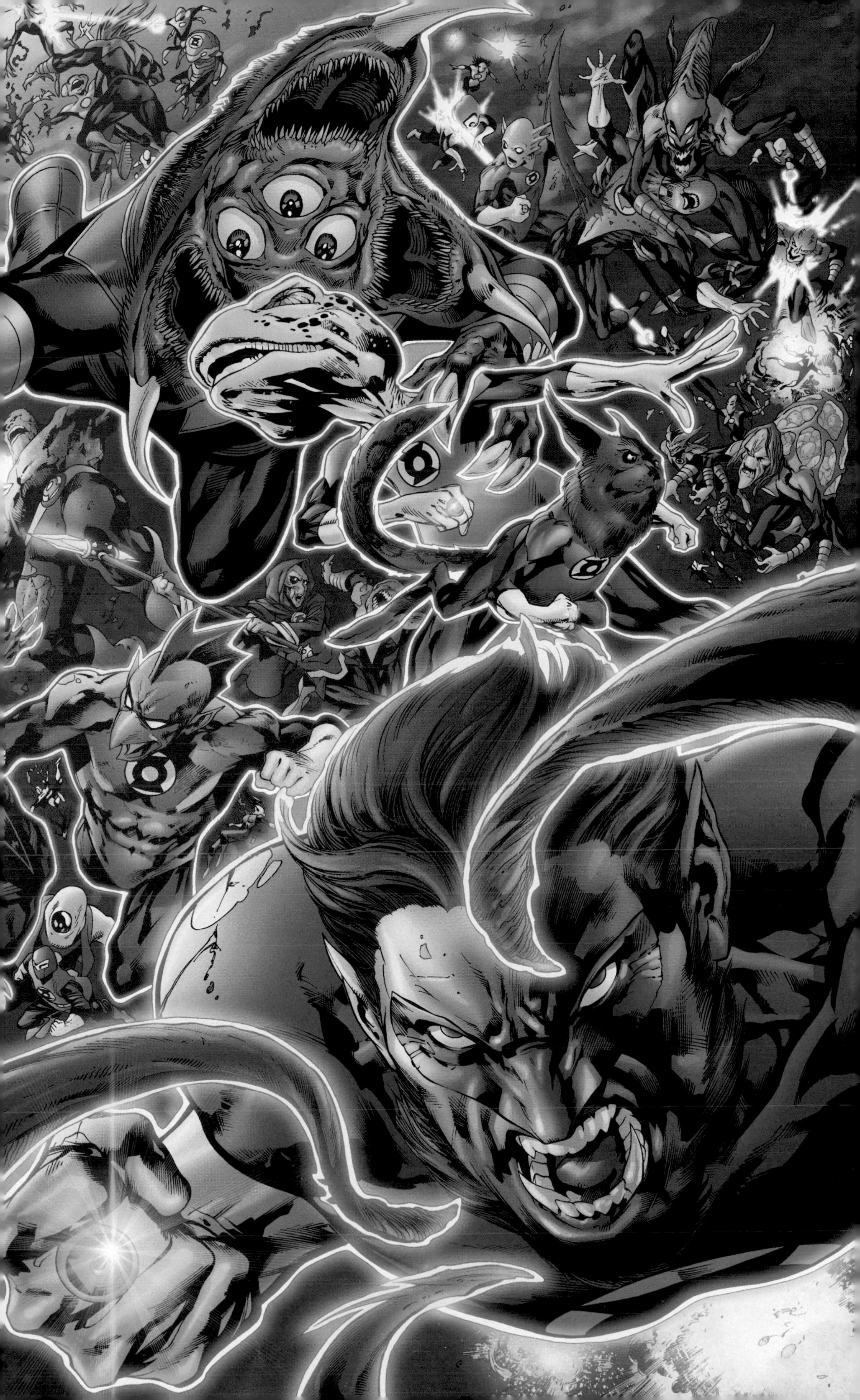

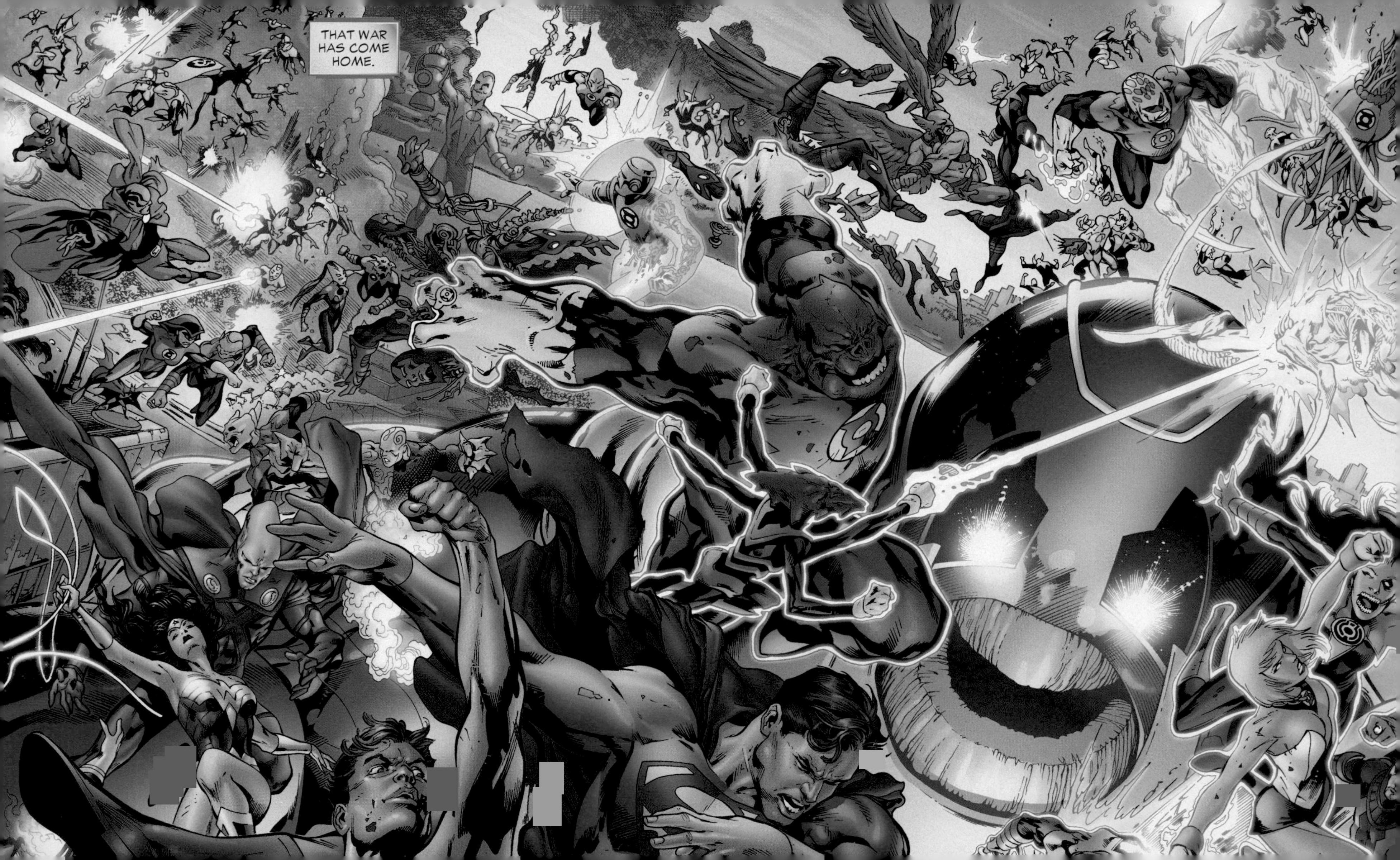
THAT WAR HAS COME HOME.

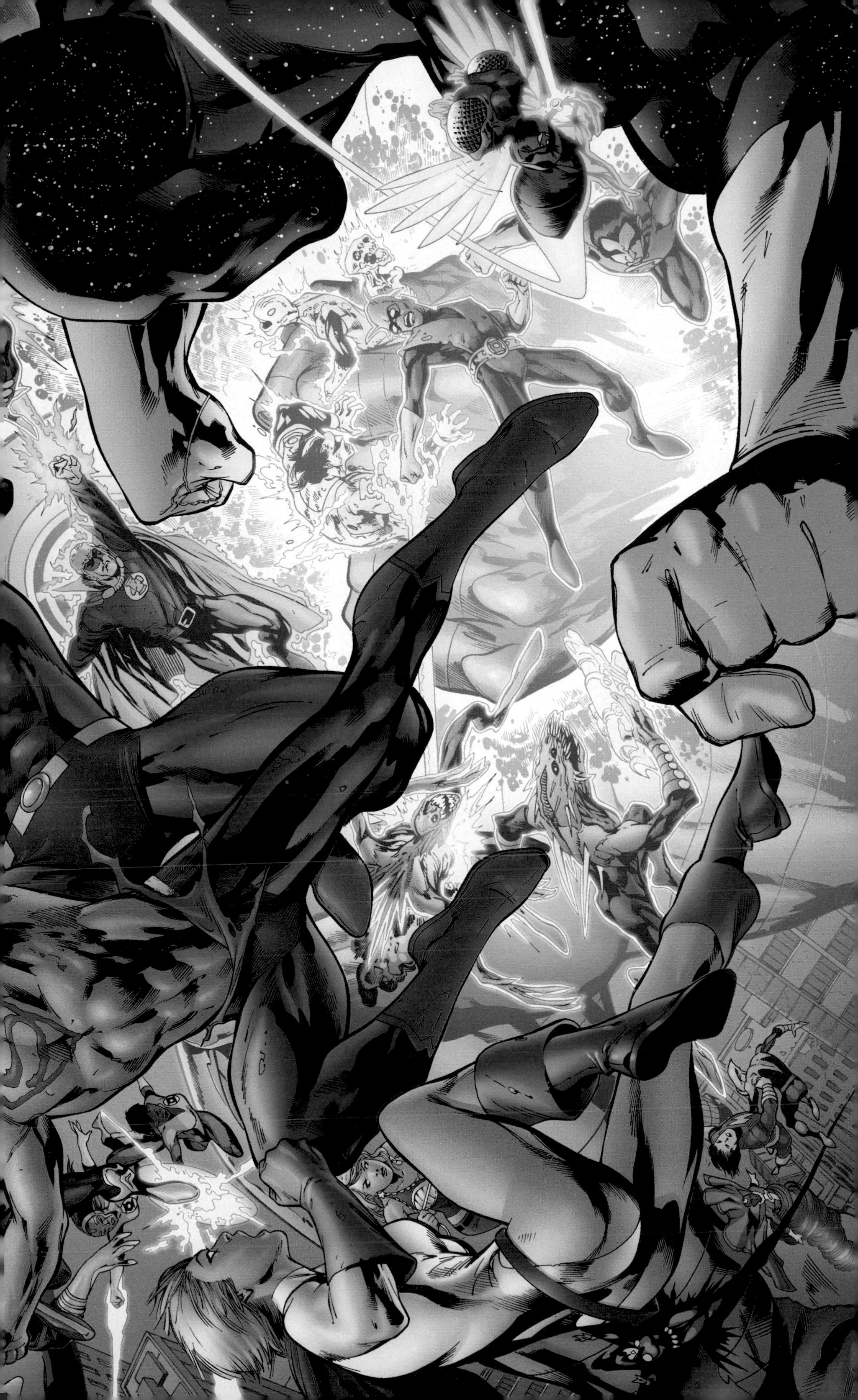

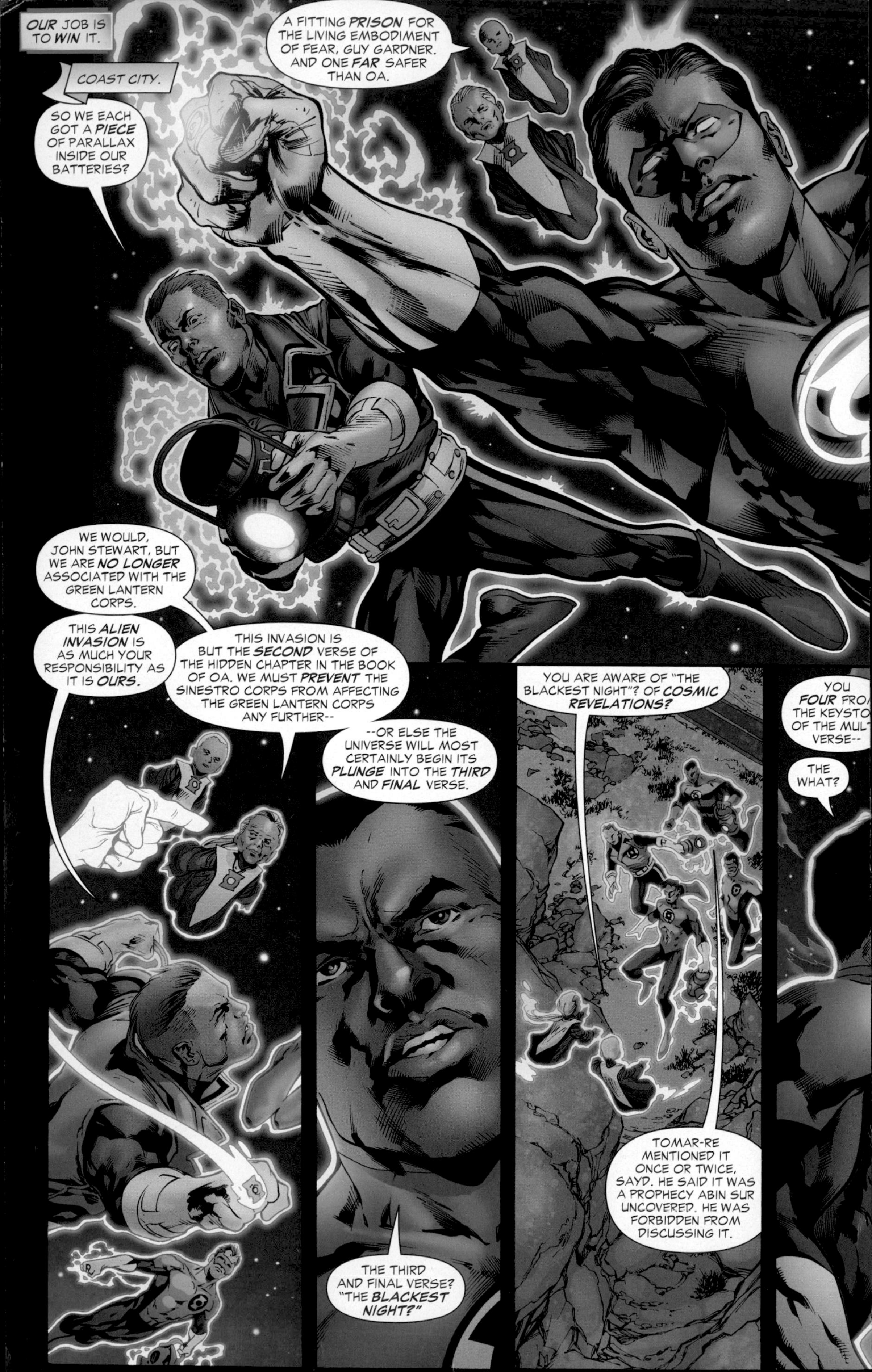
OUR JOB IS TO WIN IT.
COAST CITY.
A FITTING PRISON FOR THE LIVING EMBODIMENT OF FEAR, GUY GARDNER. AND ONE FAR SAFER THAN OA.
SO WE EACH GOT A PIECE OF PARALLAX INSIDE OUR BATTERIES?
WE WOULD, JOHN STEWART, BUT WE ARE NO LONGER ASSOCIATED WITH THE GREEN LANTERN CORPS.
THIS ALIEN INVASION IS AS MUCH YOUR RESPONSIBILITY AS IT IS OURS.
THIS INVASION IS BUT THE SECOND VERSE OF THE HIDDEN CHAPTER IN THE BOOK OF OA. WE MUST PREVENT THE SINESTRO CORPS FROM AFFECTING THE GREEN LANTERN CORPS ANY FURTHER--
--OR ELSE THE UNIVERSE WILL MOST CERTAINLY BEGIN ITS PLUNGE INTO THE THIRD AND FINAL VERSE.
THE THIRD AND FINAL VERSE? "THE BLACKEST NIGHT?"
YOU ARE AWARE OF "THE BLACKEST NIGHT"? OF COSMIC REVELATIONS?
TOMAR-RE MENTIONED IT ONCE OR TWICE, SAYD. HE SAID IT WAS A PROPHECY ABIN SUR UNCOVERED. HE WAS FORBIDDEN FROM DISCUSSING IT.
YOU FOUR FROM THE KEYSTO OF THE MULT VERSE--
THE WHAT?

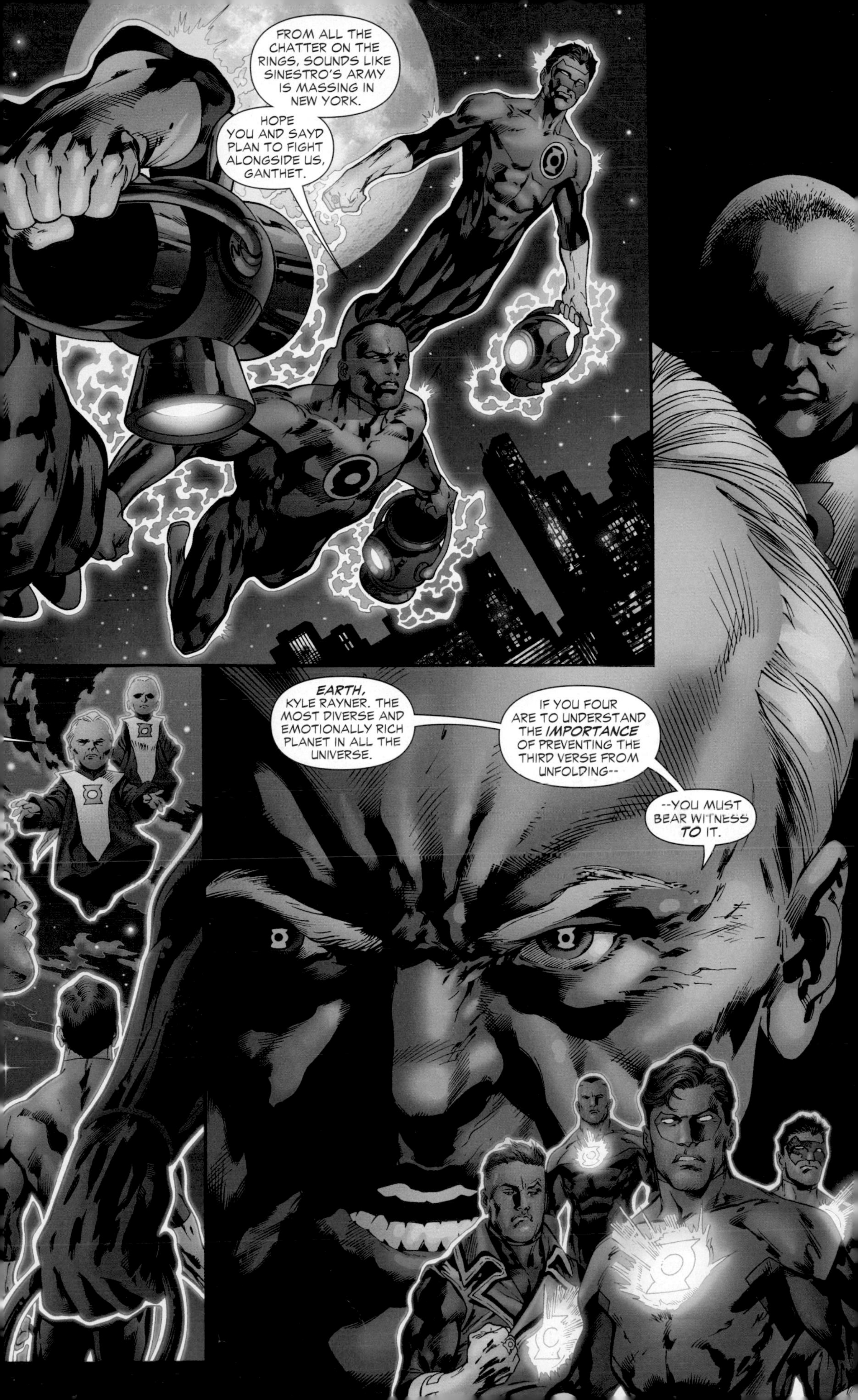
FROM ALL THE CHATTER ON THE RINGS, SOUNDS LIKE SINESTRO'S ARMY IS MASSING IN NEW YORK.
HOPE YOU AND SAYD PLAN TO FIGHT ALONGSIDE US, GANTHET.
EARTH, KYLE RAYNER. THE MOST DIVERSE AND EMOTIONALLY RICH PLANET IN ALL THE UNIVERSE.
IF YOU FOUR ARE TO UNDERSTAND THE IMPORTANCE OF PREVENTING THE THIRD VERSE FROM UNFOLDING--
--YOU MUST BEAR WITNESS TO IT.

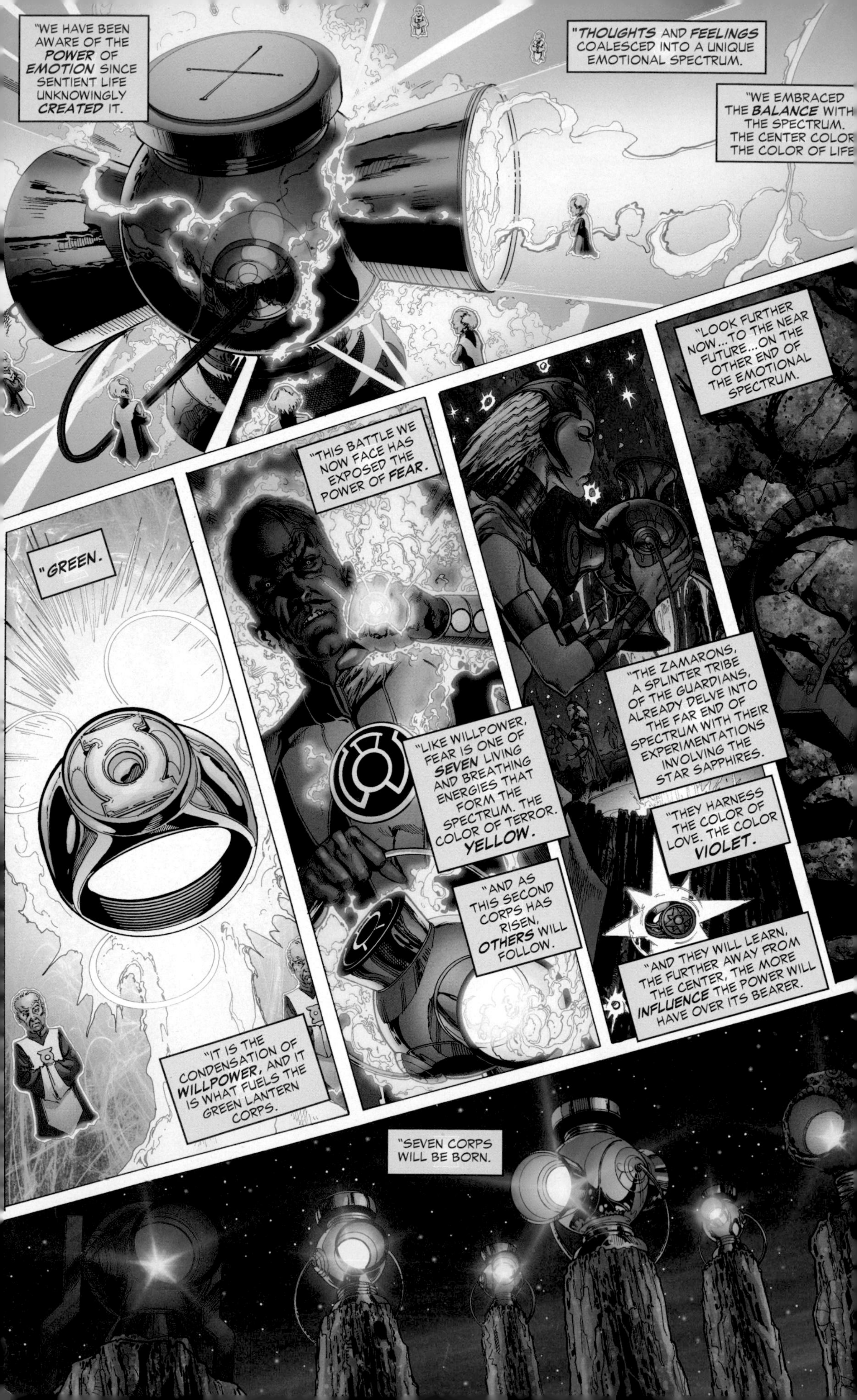
"WE HAVE BEEN AWARE OF THE POWER OF EMOTION SINCE SENTIENT LIFE UNKNOWINGLY CREATED IT.
"THOUGHTS AND FEELINGS COALESCED INTO A UNIQUE EMOTIONAL SPECTRUM.
"WE EMBRACED THE BALANCE WITH THE SPECTRUM. THE CENTER COLOR THE COLOR OF LIFE
"LOOK FURTHER NOW...TO THE NEAR FUTURE...ON THE OTHER END OF THE EMOTIONAL SPECTRUM.
"THIS BATTLE WE NOW FACE HAS EXPOSED THE POWER OF FEAR.
"GREEN.
"IT IS THE CONDENSATION OF WILLPOWER, AND IT IS WHAT FUELS THE GREEN LANTERN CORPS.
"LIKE WILLPOWER, FEAR IS ONE OF SEVEN LIVING AND BREATHING ENERGIES THAT FORM THE SPECTRUM. THE COLOR OF TERROR. YELLOW.
"AND AS THIS SECOND CORPS HAS RISEN, OTHERS WILL FOLLOW.
"THE ZAMARONS, A SPLINTER TRIBE OF THE GUARDIANS, ALREADY DELVE INTO THE FAR END OF SPECTRUM WITH THEIR EXPERIMENTATIONS INVOLVING THE STAR SAPPHIRES.
"THEY HARNESS THE COLOR OF LOVE. THE COLOR VIOLET.
"AND THEY WILL LEARN, THE FURTHER AWAY FROM THE CENTER, THE MORE INFLUENCE THE POWER WILL HAVE OVER ITS BEARER.
"SEVEN CORPS WILL BE BORN.

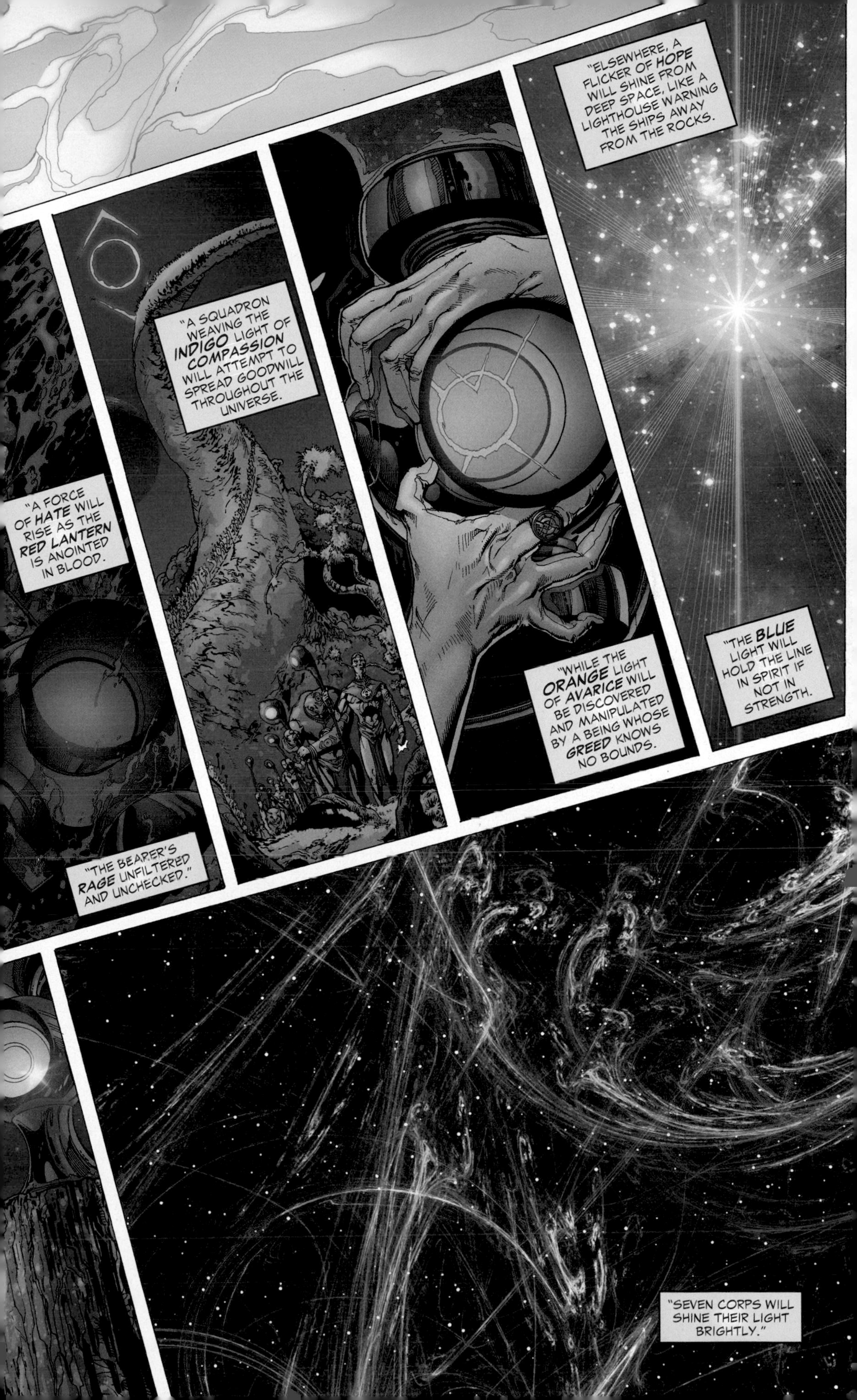
"A FORCE OF HATE WILL RISE AS THE RED LANTERN IS ANOINTED IN BLOOD.
"THE BEARER'S RAGE UNFILTERED AND UNCHECKED."
"A SQUADRON WEAVING THE INDIGO LIGHT OF COMPASSION WILL ATTEMPT TO SPREAD GOODWILL THROUGHOUT THE UNIVERSE.
"WHILE THE ORANGE LIGHT OF AVARICE WILL BE DISCOVERED AND MANIPULATED BY A BEING WHOSE GREED KNOWS NO BOUNDS.
"ELSEWHERE, A FLICKER OF HOPE WILL SHINE FROM DEEP SPACE, LIKE A LIGHTHOUSE WARNING THE SHIPS AWAY FROM THE ROCKS.
"THE BLUE LIGHT WILL HOLD THE LINE IN SPIRIT IF NOT IN STRENGTH.
"SEVEN CORPS WILL SHINE THEIR LIGHT BRIGHTLY."

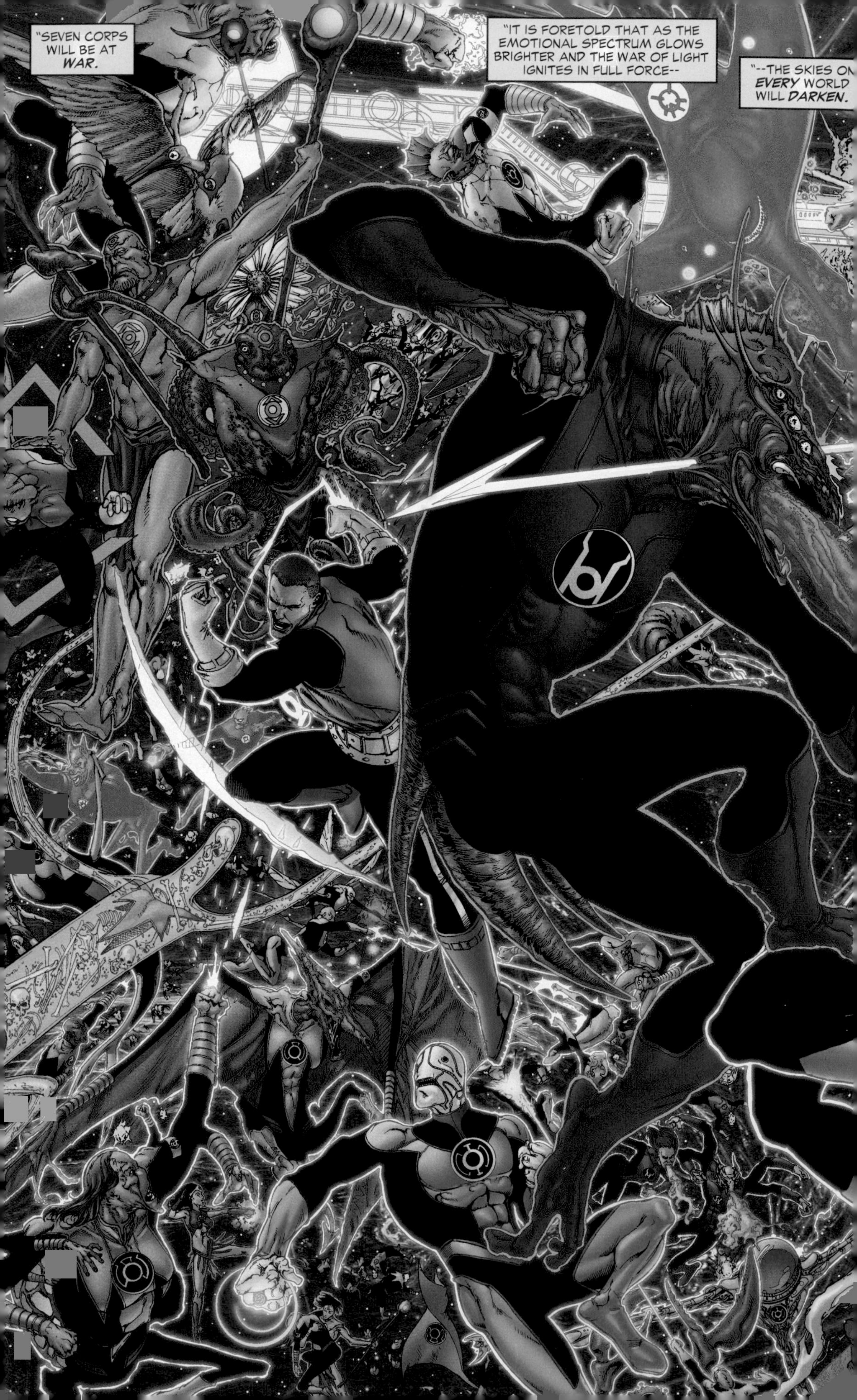
"SEVEN CORPS WILL BE AT **WAR**.
"IT IS FORETOLD THAT AS THE EMOTIONAL SPECTRUM GLOWS BRIGHTER AND THE WAR OF LIGHT IGNITES IN FULL FORCE--
"--THE SKIES ON **EVERY** WORLD WILL **DARKEN**.

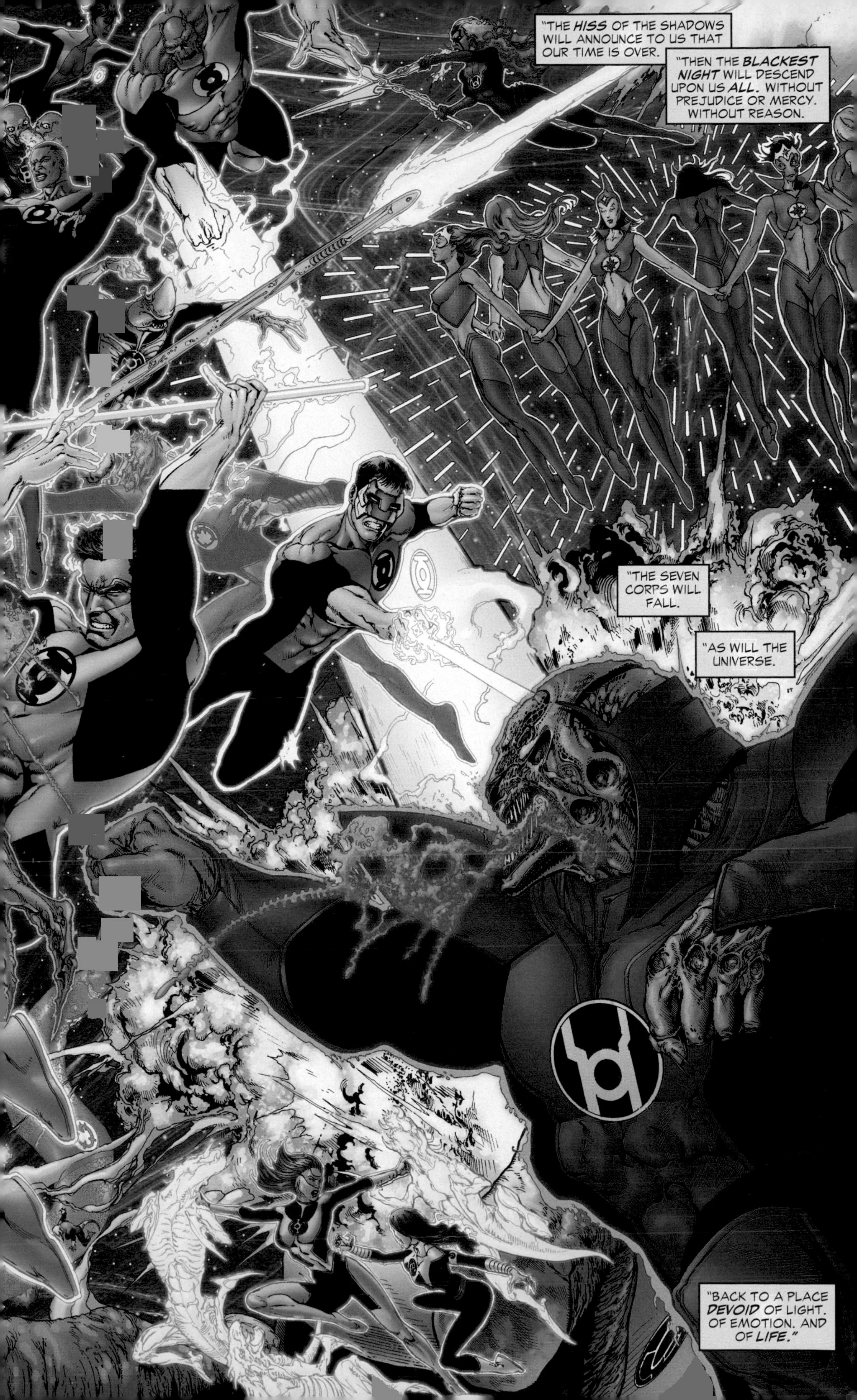
"THE HISS OF THE SHADOWS WILL ANNOUNCE TO US THAT OUR TIME IS OVER.
"THEN THE BLACKEST NIGHT WILL DESCEND UPON US ALL. WITHOUT PREJUDICE OR MERCY. WITHOUT REASON.
"THE SEVEN CORPS WILL FALL.
"AS WILL THE UNIVERSE.
"BACK TO A PLACE DEVOID OF LIGHT. OF EMOTION. AND OF LIFE."

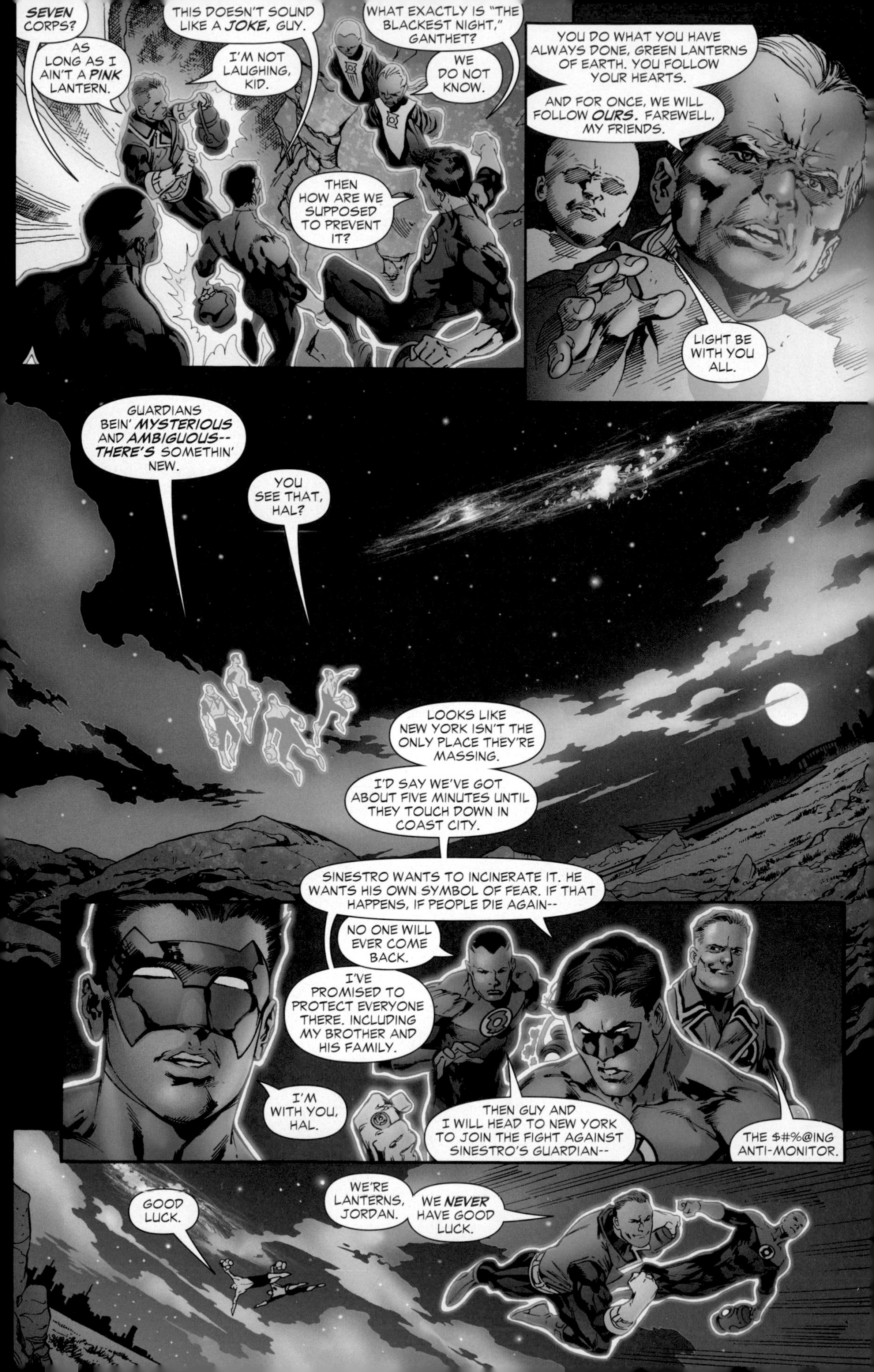
SEVEN CORPS?
AS LONG AS I AIN'T A PINK LANTERN.
THIS DOESN'T SOUND LIKE A JOKE, GUY.
I'M NOT LAUGHING, KID.
WHAT EXACTLY IS "THE BLACKEST NIGHT," GANTHET?
WE DO NOT KNOW.
THEN HOW ARE WE SUPPOSED TO PREVENT IT?
YOU DO WHAT YOU HAVE ALWAYS DONE, GREEN LANTERNS OF EARTH. YOU FOLLOW YOUR HEARTS.
AND FOR ONCE, WE WILL FOLLOW OURS. FAREWELL, MY FRIENDS.
LIGHT BE WITH YOU ALL.
GUARDIANS BEIN' MYSTERIOUS AND AMBIGUOUS-- THERE'S SOMETHIN' NEW.
YOU SEE THAT, HAL?
LOOKS LIKE NEW YORK ISN'T THE ONLY PLACE THEY'RE MASSING.
I'D SAY WE'VE GOT ABOUT FIVE MINUTES UNTIL THEY TOUCH DOWN IN COAST CITY.
SINESTRO WANTS TO INCINERATE IT. HE WANTS HIS OWN SYMBOL OF FEAR. IF THAT HAPPENS, IF PEOPLE DIE AGAIN--
NO ONE WILL EVER COME BACK.
I'VE PROMISED TO PROTECT EVERYONE THERE. INCLUDING MY BROTHER AND HIS FAMILY.
I'M WITH YOU, HAL.
THEN GUY AND I WILL HEAD TO NEW YORK TO JOIN THE FIGHT AGAINST SINESTRO'S GUARDIAN--
THE $#%@ING ANTI-MONITOR.
GOOD LUCK.
WE'RE LANTERNS, JORDAN.
WE NEVER HAVE GOOD LUCK.

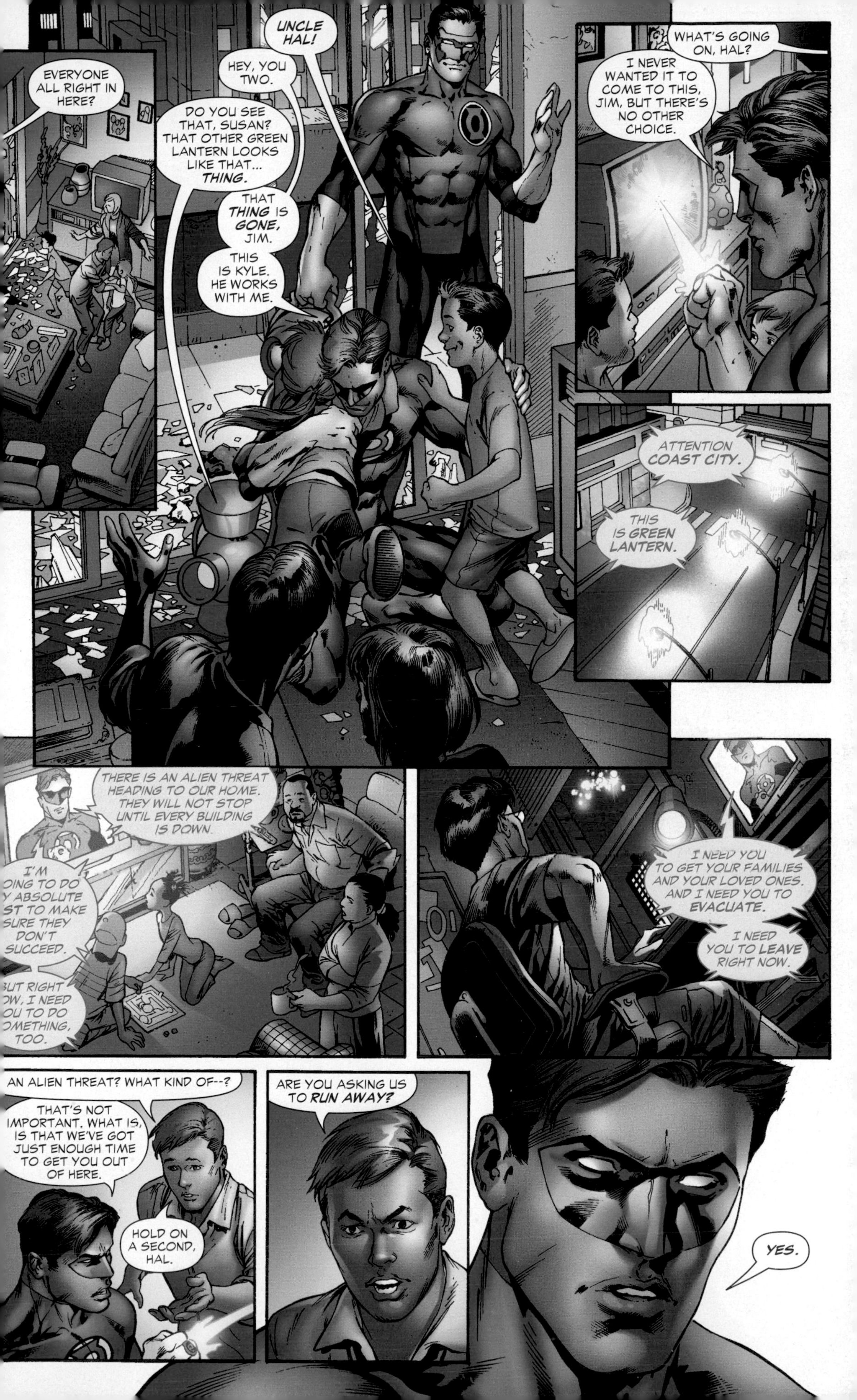
EVERYONE ALL RIGHT IN HERE?
UNCLE HAL!
HEY, YOU TWO.
DO YOU SEE THAT, SUSAN? THAT OTHER GREEN LANTERN LOOKS LIKE THAT... THING.
THAT THING IS GONE, JIM.
THIS IS KYLE. HE WORKS WITH ME.
WHAT'S GOING ON, HAL?
I NEVER WANTED IT TO COME TO THIS, JIM, BUT THERE'S NO OTHER CHOICE.
ATTENTION COAST CITY.
THIS IS GREEN LANTERN.
THERE IS AN ALIEN THREAT HEADING TO OUR HOME. THEY WILL NOT STOP UNTIL EVERY BUILDING IS DOWN.
I'M OING TO DO Y ABSOLUTE ST TO MAKE SURE THEY DON'T SUCCEED.
BUT RIGHT OW, I NEED OU TO DO OMETHING, TOO.
I NEED YOU TO GET YOUR FAMILIES AND YOUR LOVED ONES. AND I NEED YOU TO EVACUATE.
I NEED YOU TO LEAVE RIGHT NOW.
AN ALIEN THREAT? WHAT KIND OF--?
THAT'S NOT IMPORTANT. WHAT IS, IS THAT WE'VE GOT JUST ENOUGH TIME TO GET YOU OUT OF HERE.
HOLD ON A SECOND, HAL.
ARE YOU ASKING US TO RUN AWAY?
YES.

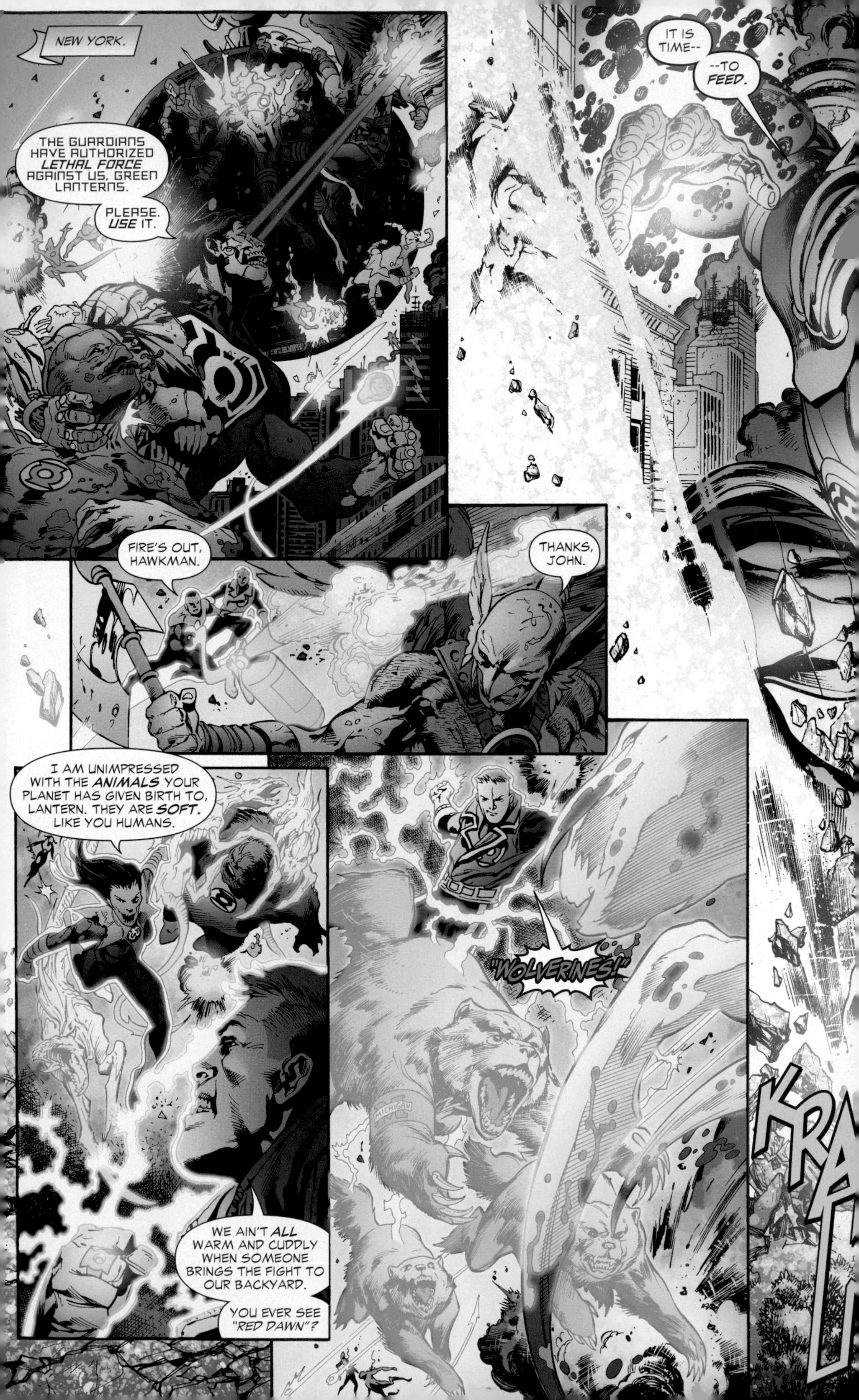
NEW YORK.
THE GUARDIANS HAVE AUTHORIZED LETHAL FORCE AGAINST US, GREEN LANTERNS.
PLEASE. USE IT.
IT IS TIME--
--TO FEED.
FIRE'S OUT, HAWKMAN.
THANKS, JOHN.
I AM UNIMPRESSED WITH THE ANIMALS YOUR PLANET HAS GIVEN BIRTH TO, LANTERN. THEY ARE SOFT. LIKE YOU HUMANS.
"WOLVERINES!"
MICHIGAN
WE AIN'T ALL WARM AND CUDDLY WHEN SOMEONE BRINGS THE FIGHT TO OUR BACKYARD.
YOU EVER SEE "RED DAWN"?

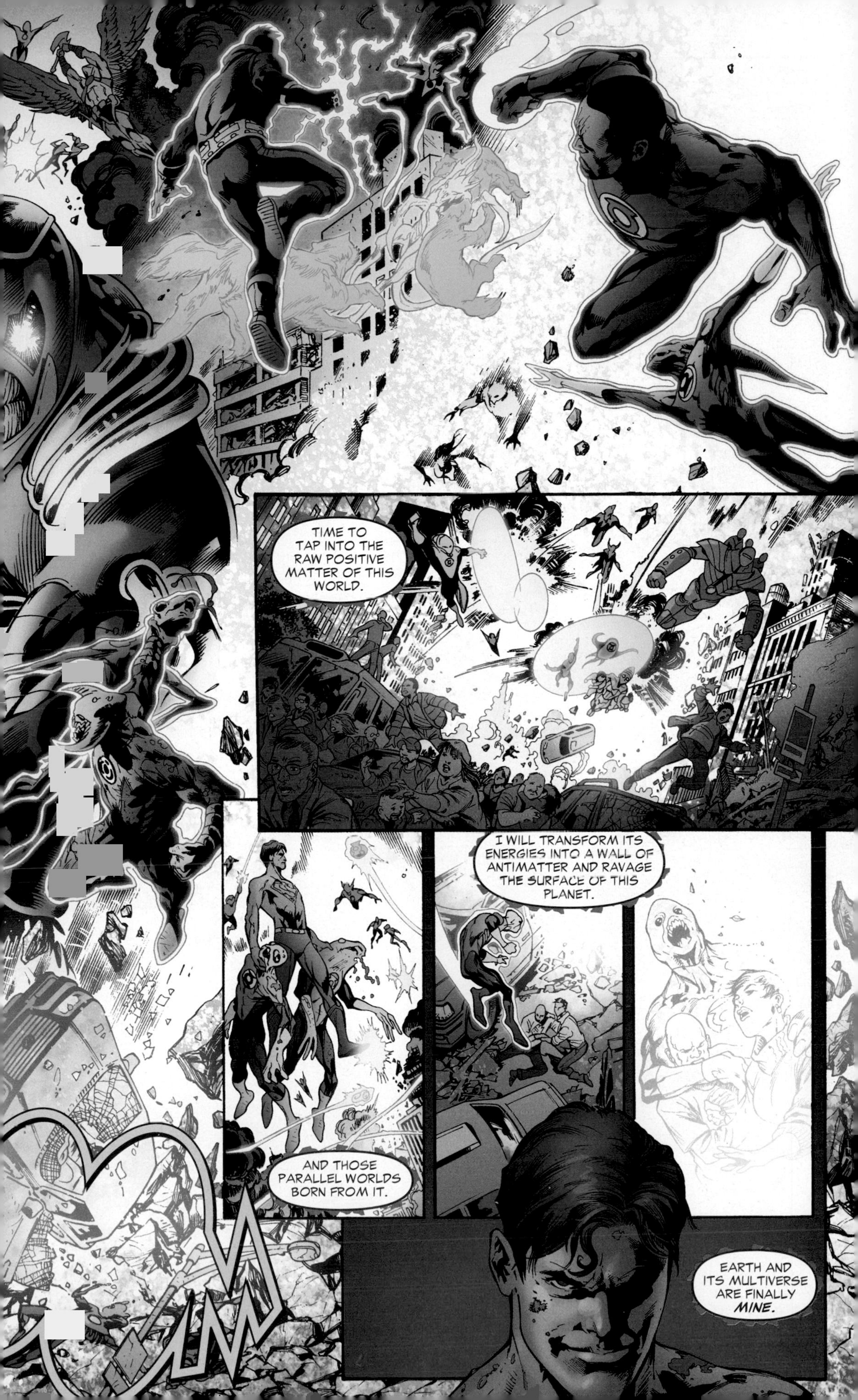

TIME TO TAP INTO THE RAW POSITIVE MATTER OF THIS WORLD.
AND THOSE PARALLEL WORLDS BORN FROM IT.
I WILL TRANSFORM ITS ENERGIES INTO A WALL OF ANTIMATTER AND RAVAGE THE SURFACE OF THIS PLANET.
EARTH AND ITS MULTIVERSE ARE FINALLY *MINE.*

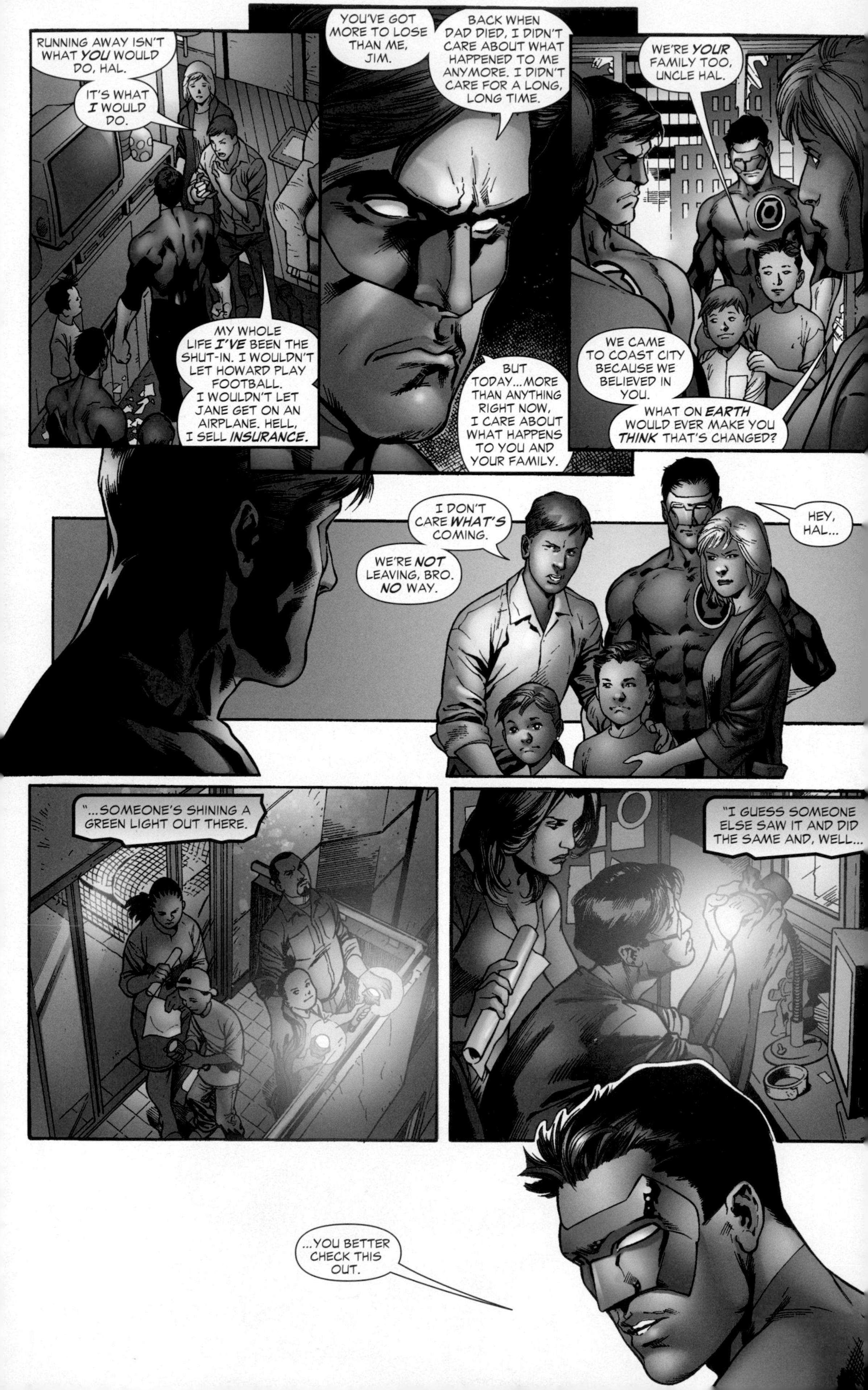
RUNNING AWAY ISN'T WHAT YOU WOULD DO, HAL.
IT'S WHAT I WOULD DO.
MY WHOLE LIFE I'VE BEEN THE SHUT-IN. I WOULDN'T LET HOWARD PLAY FOOTBALL. I WOULDN'T LET JANE GET ON AN AIRPLANE. HELL, I SELL INSURANCE.
YOU'VE GOT MORE TO LOSE THAN ME, JIM.
BACK WHEN DAD DIED, I DIDN'T CARE ABOUT WHAT HAPPENED TO ME ANYMORE. I DIDN'T CARE FOR A LONG, LONG TIME.
BUT TODAY...MORE THAN ANYTHING RIGHT NOW, I CARE ABOUT WHAT HAPPENS TO YOU AND YOUR FAMILY.
WE'RE YOUR FAMILY TOO, UNCLE HAL.
WE CAME TO COAST CITY BECAUSE WE BELIEVED IN YOU.
WHAT ON EARTH WOULD EVER MAKE YOU THINK THAT'S CHANGED?
I DON'T CARE WHAT'S COMING.
WE'RE NOT LEAVING, BRO. NO WAY.
HEY, HAL...
"...SOMEONE'S SHINING A GREEN LIGHT OUT THERE.
"I GUESS SOMEONE ELSE SAW IT AND DID THE SAME AND, WELL...
...YOU BETTER CHECK THIS OUT.

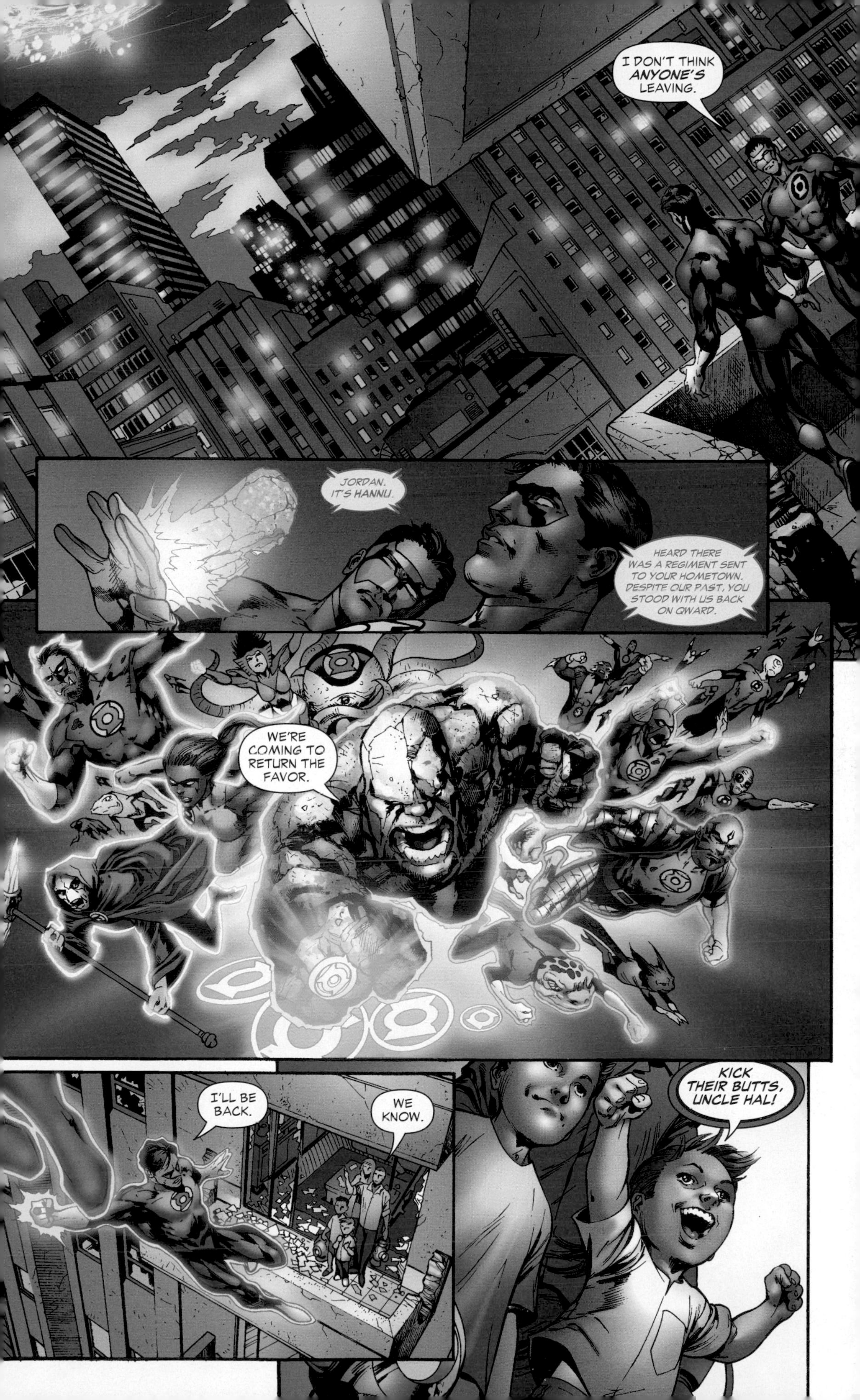
I DON'T THINK ANYONE'S LEAVING.
JORDAN. IT'S HANNU.
HEARD THERE WAS A REGIMENT SENT TO YOUR HOMETOWN. DESPITE OUR PAST, YOU STOOD WITH US BACK ON QWARD.
WE'RE COMING TO RETURN THE FAVOR.
I'LL BE BACK.
WE KNOW.
KICK THEIR BUTTS, UNCLE HAL!

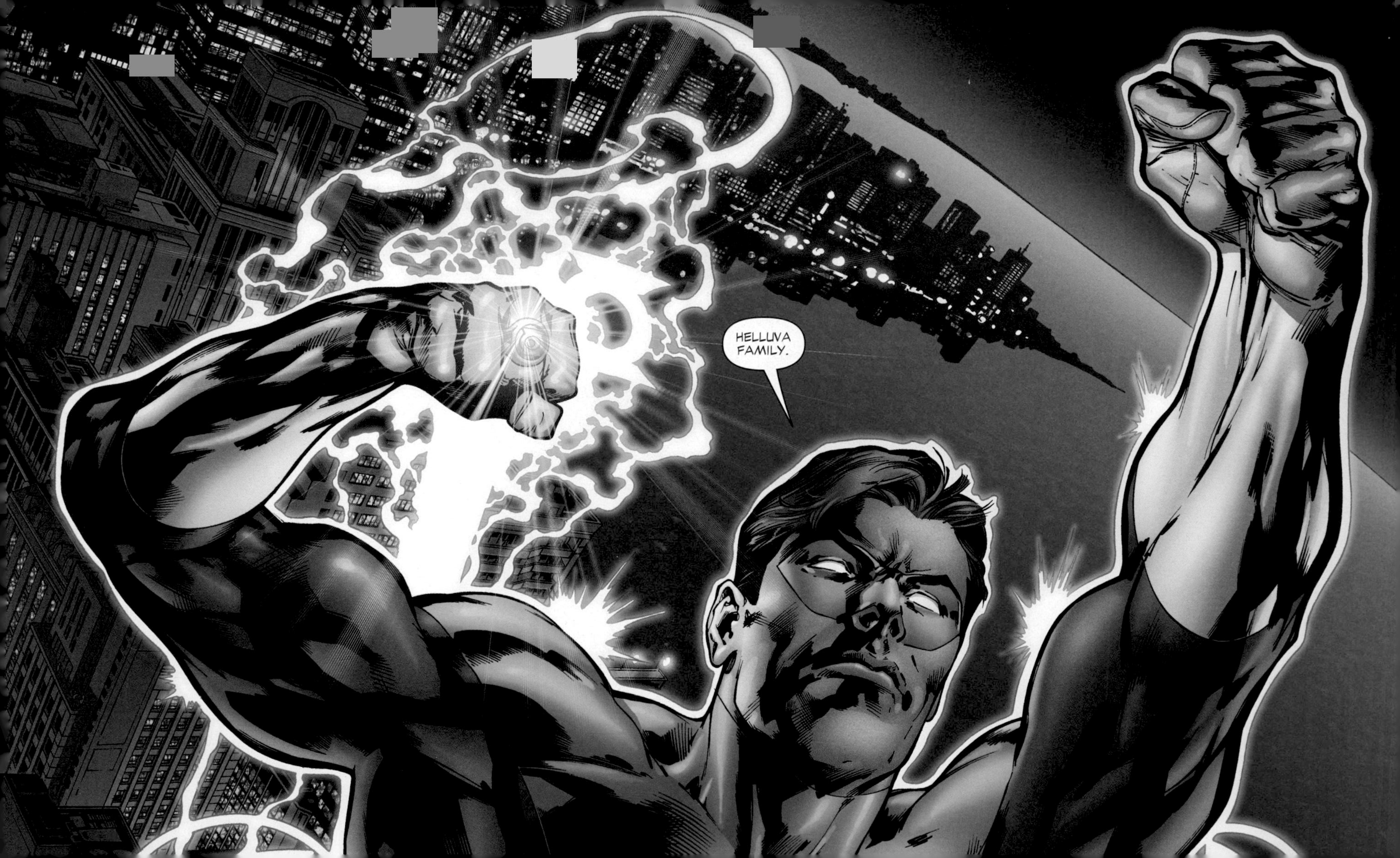
HELLUVA FAMILY.

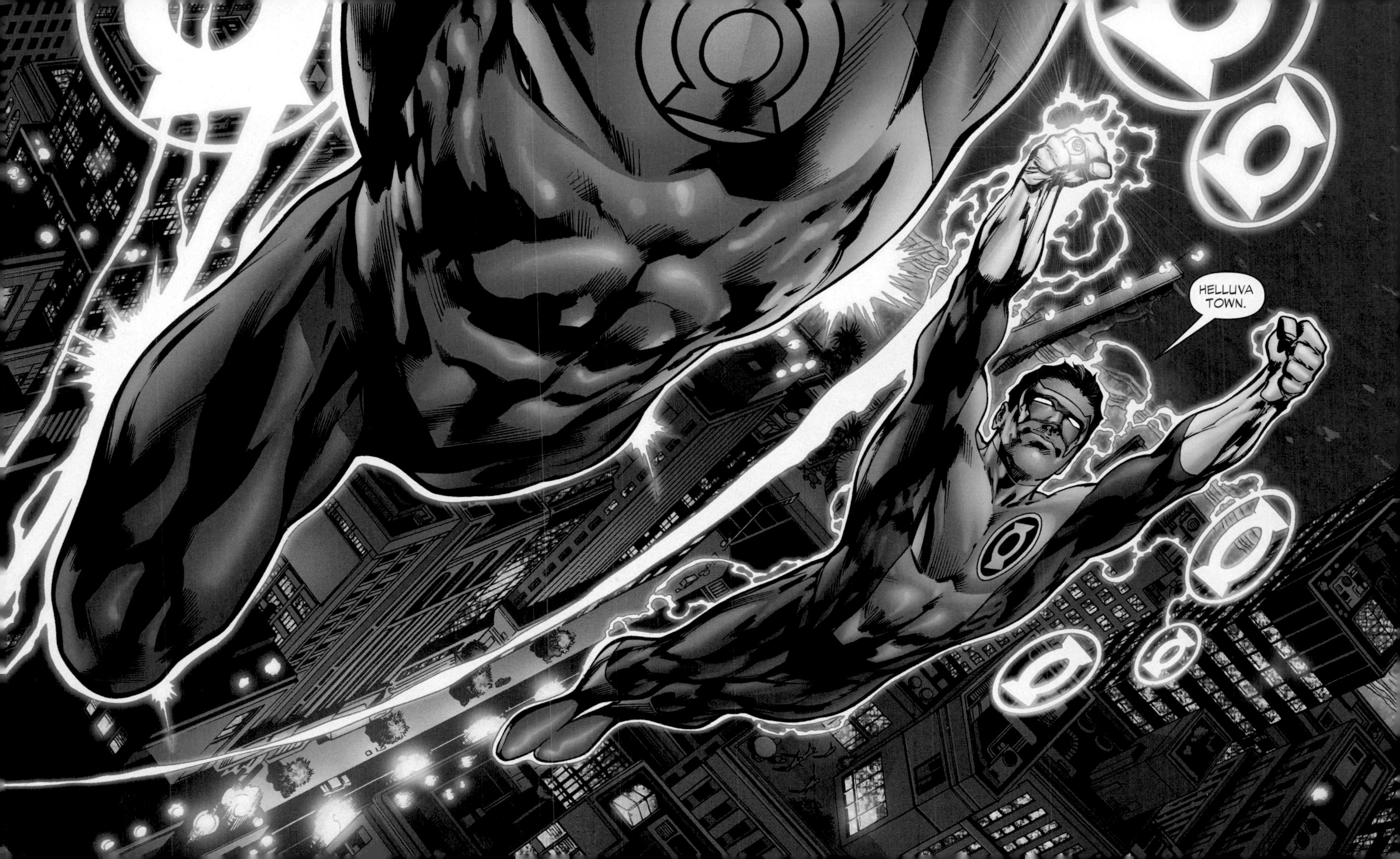
HELLUVA TOWN.

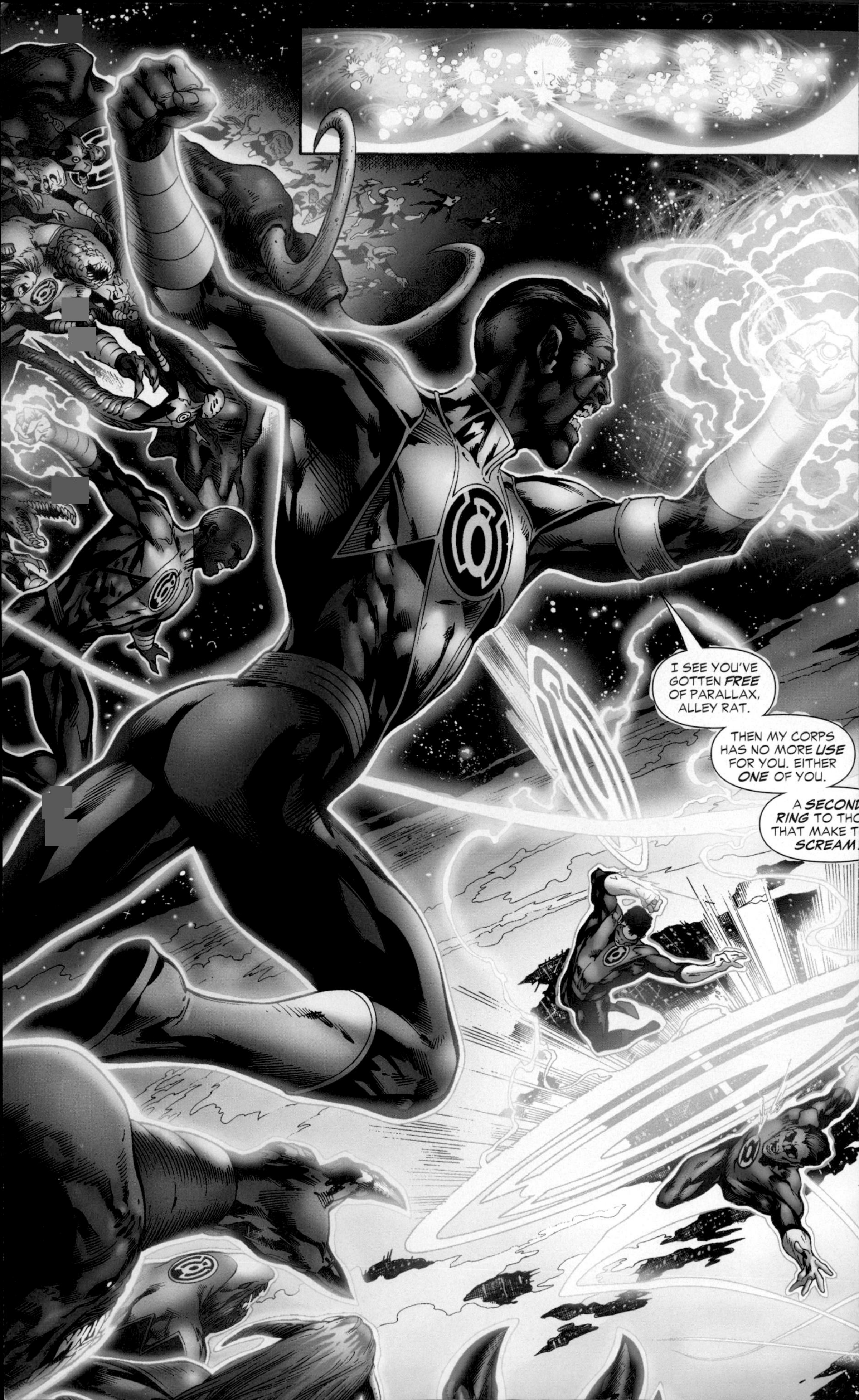
I SEE YOU'VE GOTTEN *FREE* OF PARALLAX, ALLEY RAT.
THEN MY CORPS HAS NO MORE *USE* FOR YOU. EITHER *ONE* OF YOU.
A *SECOND RING* TO THO THAT MAKE T *SCREAM!*

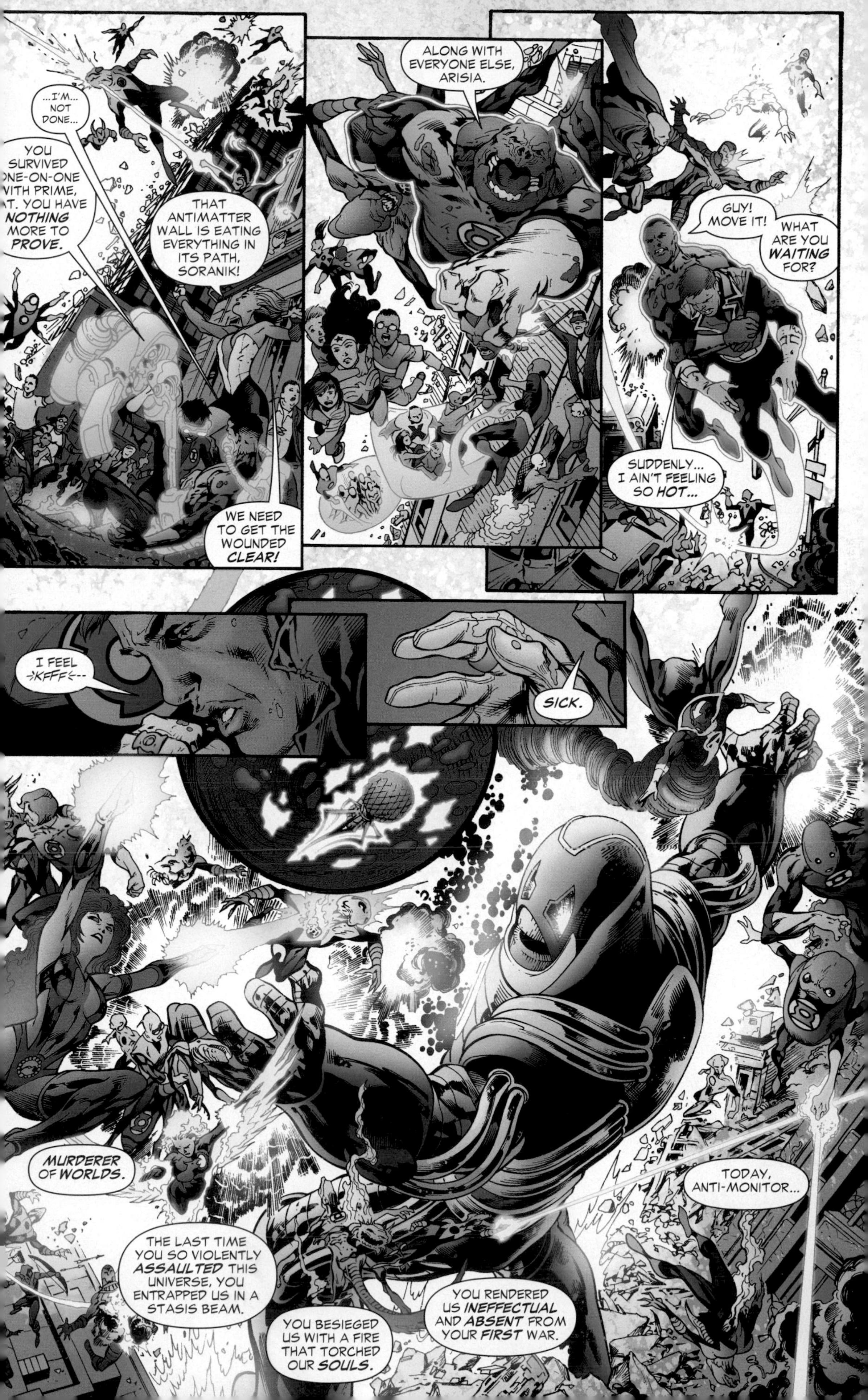
...I'M... NOT DONE...
YOU SURVIVED ONE-ON-ONE WITH PRIME, KT. YOU HAVE NOTHING MORE TO PROVE.
THAT ANTIMATTER WALL IS EATING EVERYTHING IN ITS PATH, SORANIK!
WE NEED TO GET THE WOUNDED CLEAR!
ALONG WITH EVERYONE ELSE, ARISIA.
GUY! MOVE IT!
WHAT ARE YOU WAITING FOR?
SUDDENLY... I AIN'T FEELING SO HOT...
I FEEL -KFFF--
SICK.
MURDERER OF WORLDS.
TODAY, ANTI-MONITOR...
THE LAST TIME YOU SO VIOLENTLY ASSAULTED THIS UNIVERSE, YOU ENTRAPPED US IN A STASIS BEAM.
YOU BESIEGED US WITH A FIRE THAT TORCHED OUR SOULS.
YOU RENDERED US INEFFECTUAL AND ABSENT FROM YOUR FIRST WAR.

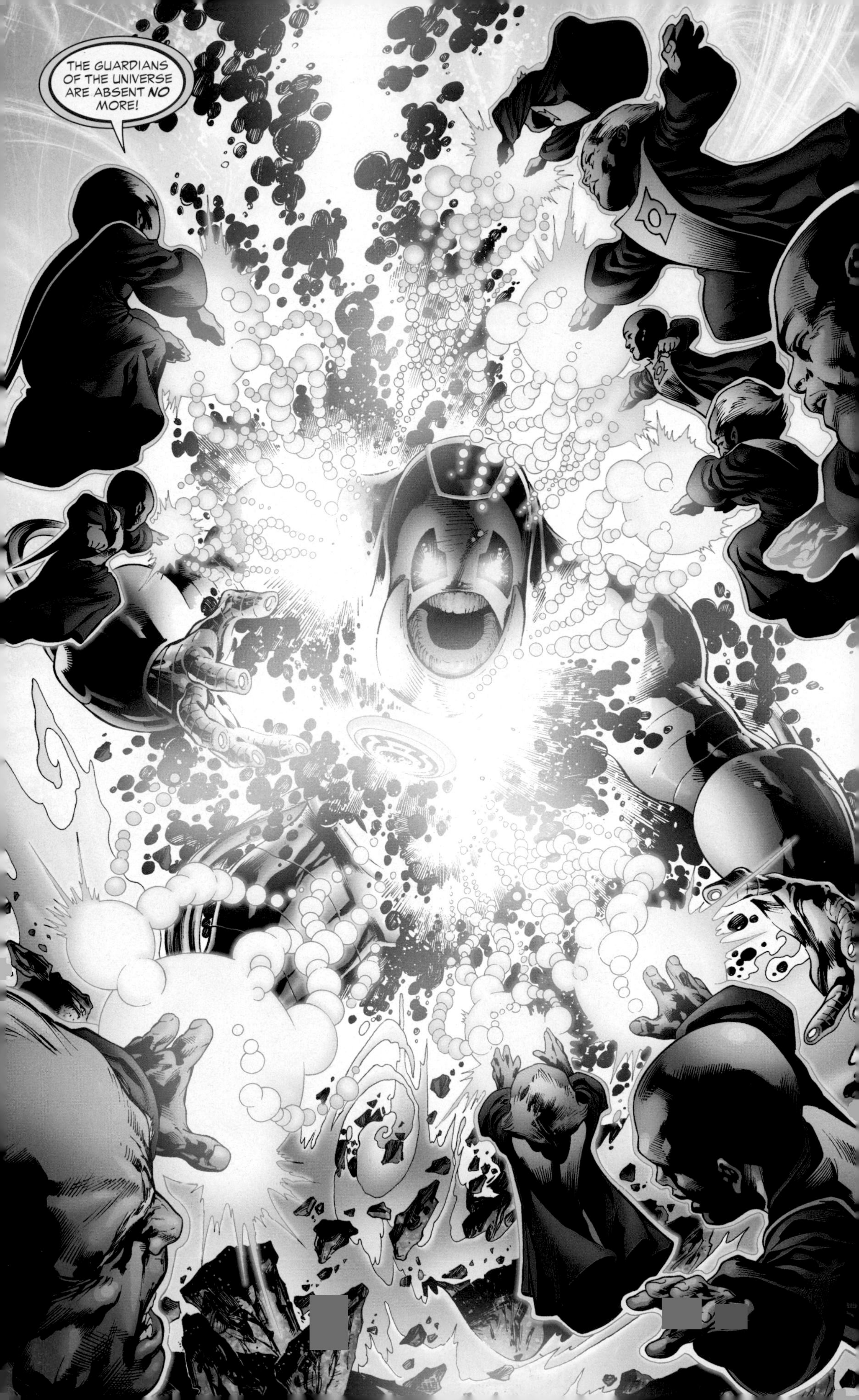
THE GUARDIANS OF THE UNIVERSE ARE ABSENT NO MORE!

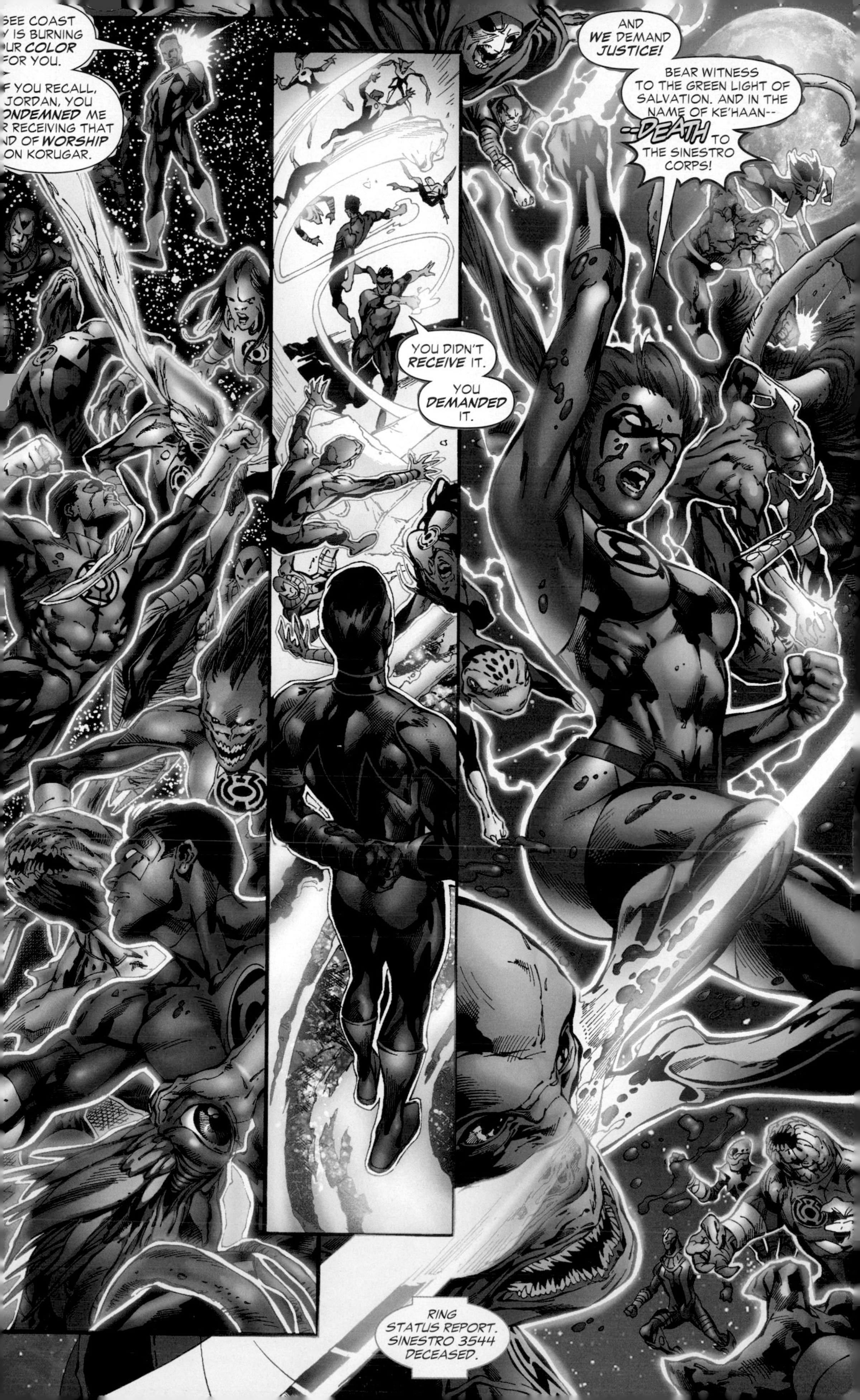
SEE COAST Y IS BURNING UR COLOR FOR YOU.
F YOU RECALL, JORDAN, YOU ONDEMNED ME R RECEIVING THAT ND OF WORSHIP ON KORUGAR.
YOU DIDN'T RECEIVE IT.
YOU DEMANDED IT.
AND WE DEMAND JUSTICE!
BEAR WITNESS TO THE GREEN LIGHT OF SALVATION. AND IN THE NAME OF KE'HAAN--
--DEATH TO THE SINESTRO CORPS!
RING STATUS REPORT. SINESTRO 3544 DECEASED.

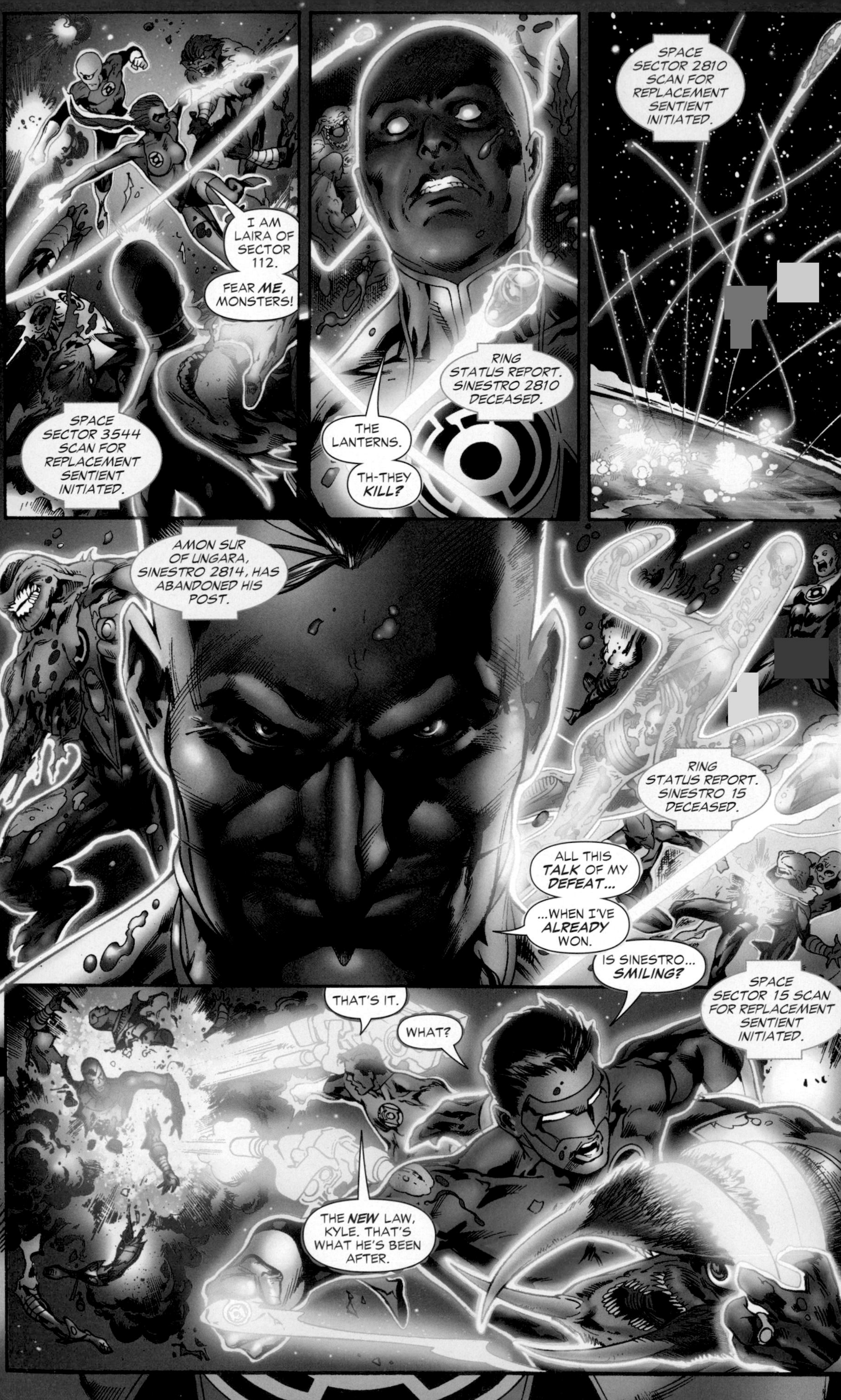
I AM LAIRA OF SECTOR 112.
FEAR ME, MONSTERS!
SPACE SECTOR 3544 SCAN FOR REPLACEMENT SENTIENT INITIATED.
RING STATUS REPORT. SINESTRO 2810 DECEASED.
THE LANTERNS.
TH-THEY KILL?
SPACE SECTOR 2810 SCAN FOR REPLACEMENT SENTIENT INITIATED.
AMON SUR OF UNGARA, SINESTRO 2814, HAS ABANDONED HIS POST.
RING STATUS REPORT. SINESTRO 15 DECEASED.
ALL THIS TALK OF MY DEFEAT...
...WHEN I'VE ALREADY WON.
IS SINESTRO... SMILING?
THAT'S IT.
WHAT?
SPACE SECTOR 15 SCAN FOR REPLACEMENT SENTIENT INITIATED.
THE NEW LAW, KYLE. THAT'S WHAT HE'S BEEN AFTER.

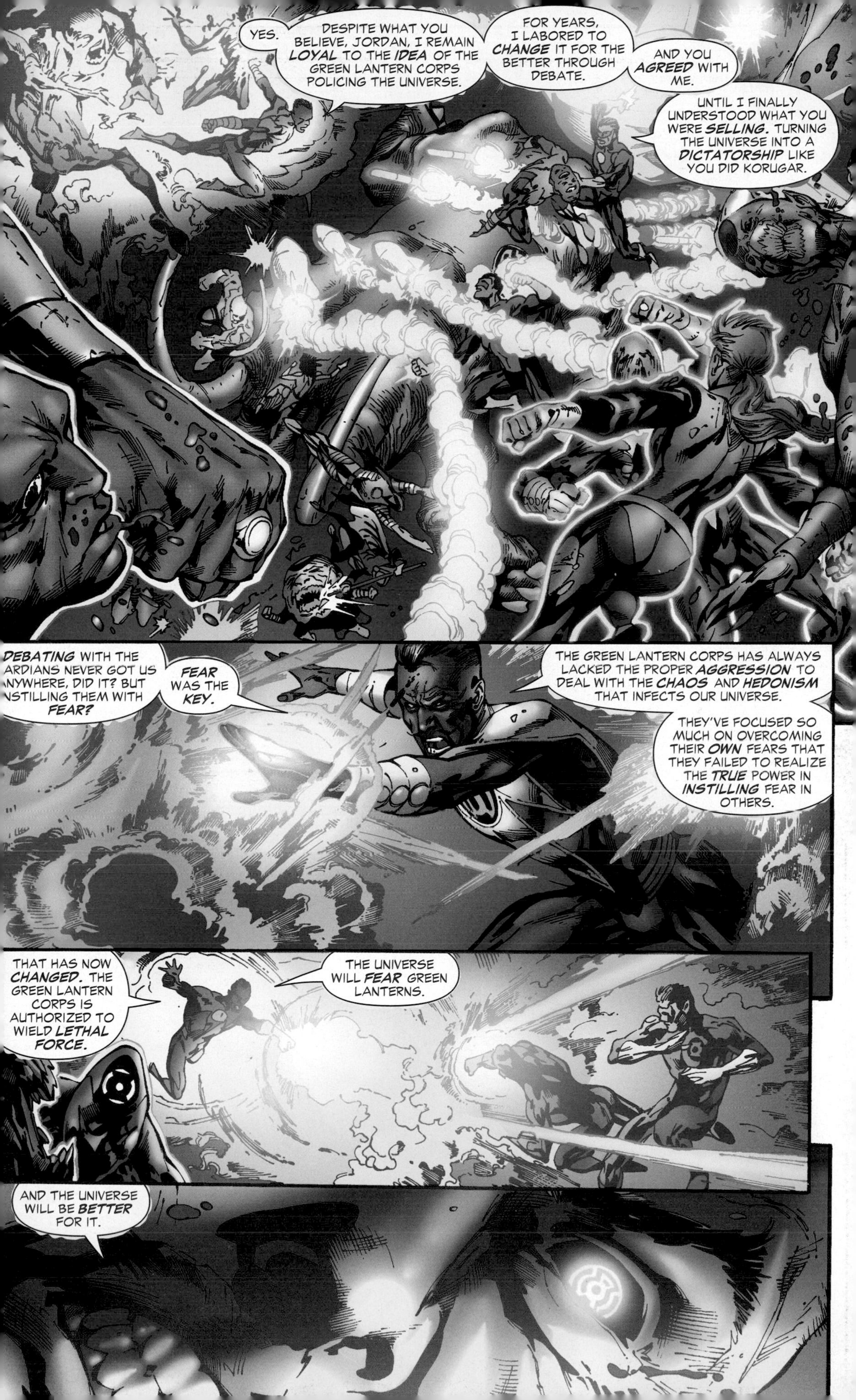
YES.
DESPITE WHAT YOU BELIEVE, JORDAN, I REMAIN LOYAL TO THE IDEA OF THE GREEN LANTERN CORPS POLICING THE UNIVERSE.
FOR YEARS, I LABORED TO CHANGE IT FOR THE BETTER THROUGH DEBATE.
AND YOU AGREED WITH ME.
UNTIL I FINALLY UNDERSTOOD WHAT YOU WERE SELLING. TURNING THE UNIVERSE INTO A DICTATORSHIP LIKE YOU DID KORUGAR.
DEBATING WITH THE ARDIANS NEVER GOT US ANYWHERE, DID IT? BUT NSTILLING THEM WITH FEAR?
FEAR WAS THE KEY.
THE GREEN LANTERN CORPS HAS ALWAYS LACKED THE PROPER AGGRESSION TO DEAL WITH THE CHAOS AND HEDONISM THAT INFECTS OUR UNIVERSE.
THEY'VE FOCUSED SO MUCH ON OVERCOMING THEIR OWN FEARS THAT THEY FAILED TO REALIZE THE TRUE POWER IN INSTILLING FEAR IN OTHERS.
THAT HAS NOW CHANGED. THE GREEN LANTERN CORPS IS AUTHORIZED TO WIELD LETHAL FORCE.
THE UNIVERSE WILL FEAR GREEN LANTERNS.
AND THE UNIVERSE WILL BE BETTER FOR IT.

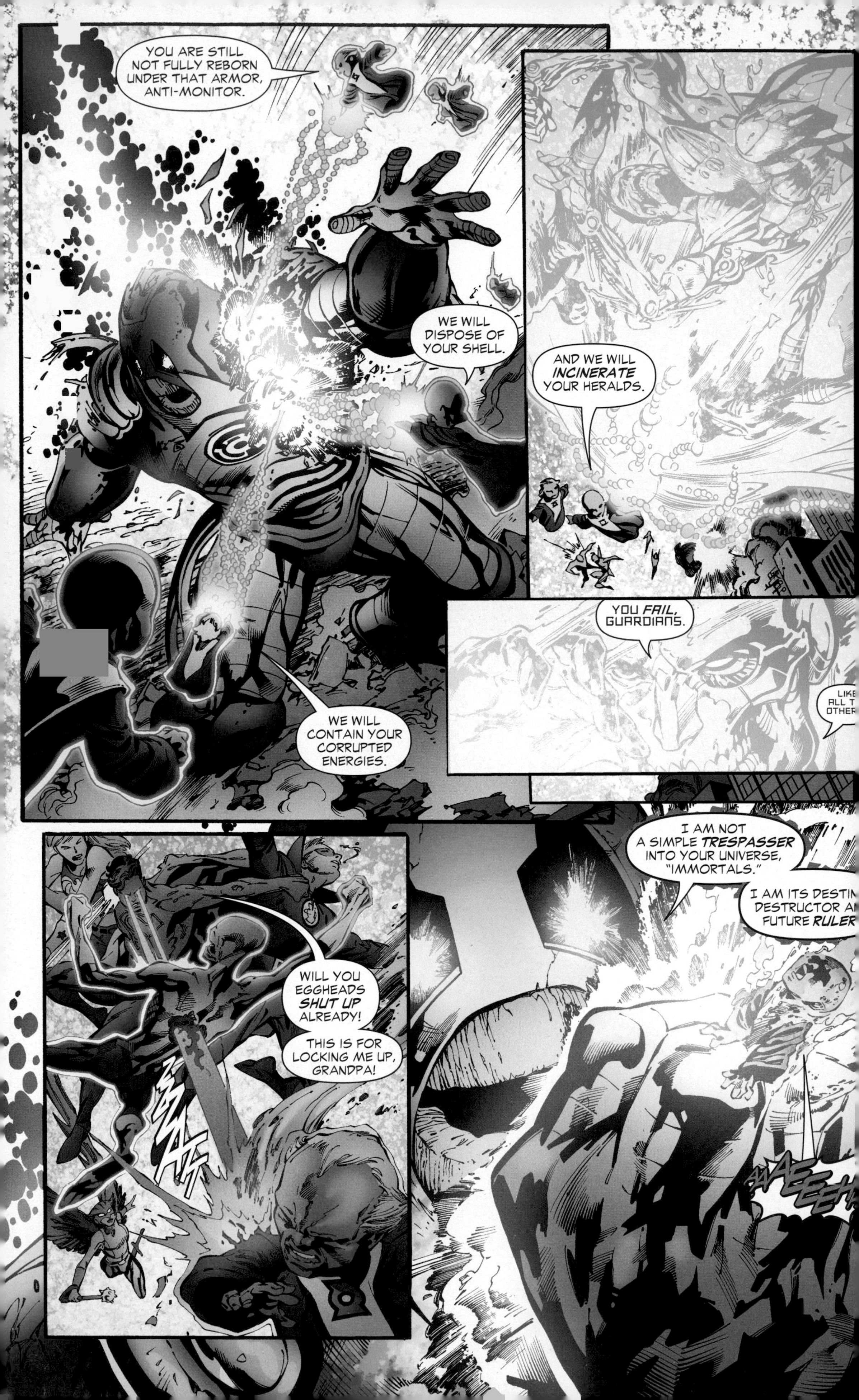

YOU ARE STILL NOT FULLY REBORN UNDER THAT ARMOR, ANTI-MONITOR.
WE WILL DISPOSE OF YOUR SHELL.
WE WILL CONTAIN YOUR CORRUPTED ENERGIES.
AND WE WILL *INCINERATE* YOUR HERALDS.
YOU *FAIL*, GUARDIANS.
LIKE ALL T OTHER
WILL YOU EGGHEADS *SHUT UP* ALREADY!
THIS IS FOR LOCKING ME UP, GRANDPA!
I AM NOT A SIMPLE *TRESPASSER* INTO YOUR UNIVERSE, "IMMORTALS."
I AM ITS DESTIN DESTRUCTOR A FUTURE *RULER*
AAAEEEH

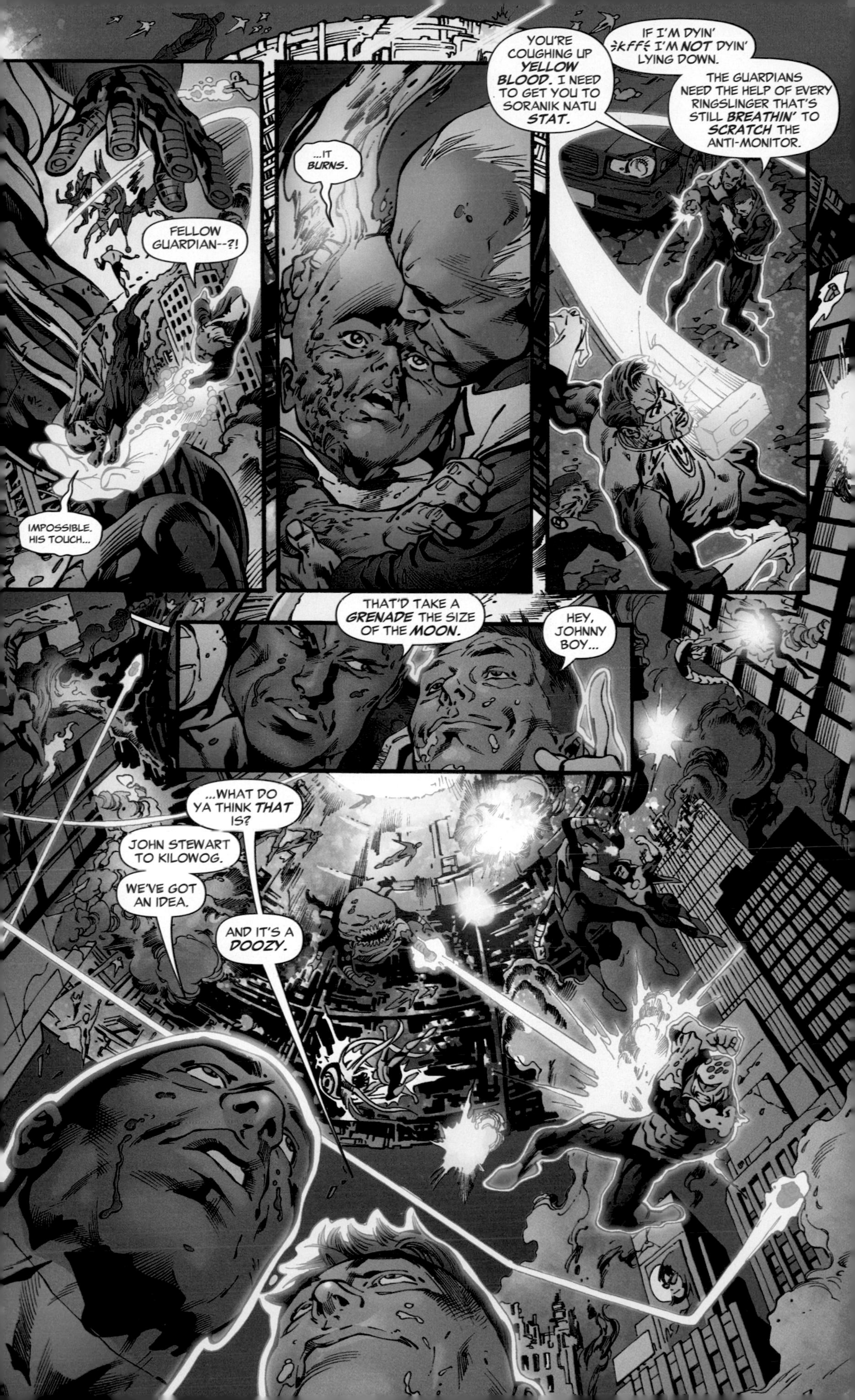
FELLOW GUARDIAN--?!
IMPOSSIBLE. HIS TOUCH...
...IT BURNS.
YOU'RE COUGHING UP YELLOW BLOOD. I NEED TO GET YOU TO SORANIK NATU STAT.
IF I'M DYIN' *KFF* I'M NOT DYIN' LYING DOWN.
THE GUARDIANS NEED THE HELP OF EVERY RINGSLINGER THAT'S STILL BREATHIN' TO SCRATCH THE ANTI-MONITOR.
THAT'D TAKE A GRENADE THE SIZE OF THE MOON.
HEY, JOHNNY BOY...
...WHAT DO YA THINK THAT IS?
JOHN STEWART TO KILOWOG.
WE'VE GOT AN IDEA.
AND IT'S A DOOZY.

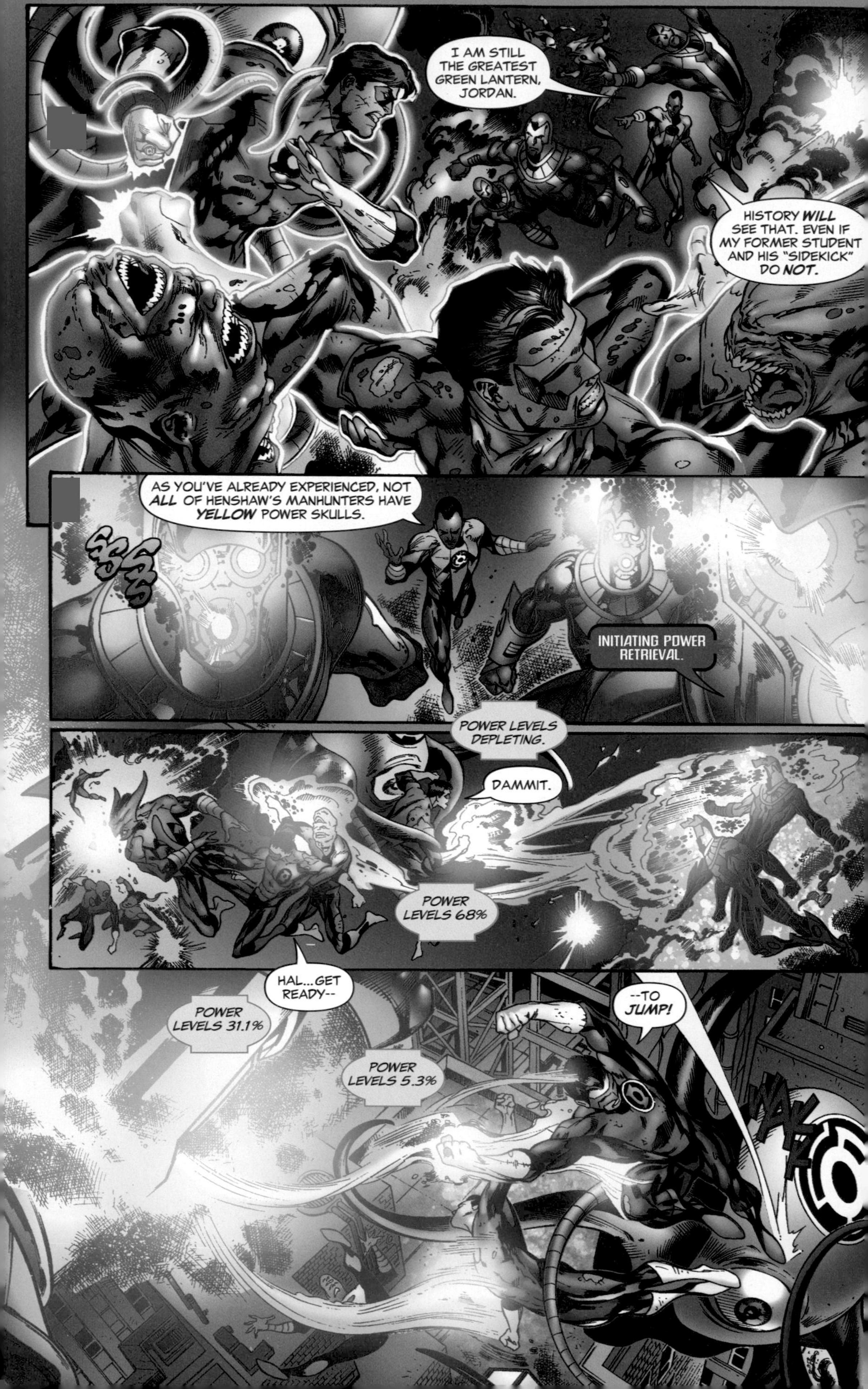
I AM STILL THE GREATEST GREEN LANTERN, JORDAN.
HISTORY WILL SEE THAT. EVEN IF MY FORMER STUDENT AND HIS "SIDEKICK" DO NOT.
AS YOU'VE ALREADY EXPERIENCED, NOT ALL OF HENSHAW'S MANHUNTERS HAVE YELLOW POWER SKULLS.
INITIATING POWER RETRIEVAL.
POWER LEVELS DEPLETING.
DAMMIT.
POWER LEVELS 68%
HAL...GET READY--
POWER LEVELS 31.1%
--TO JUMP!
POWER LEVELS 5.3%

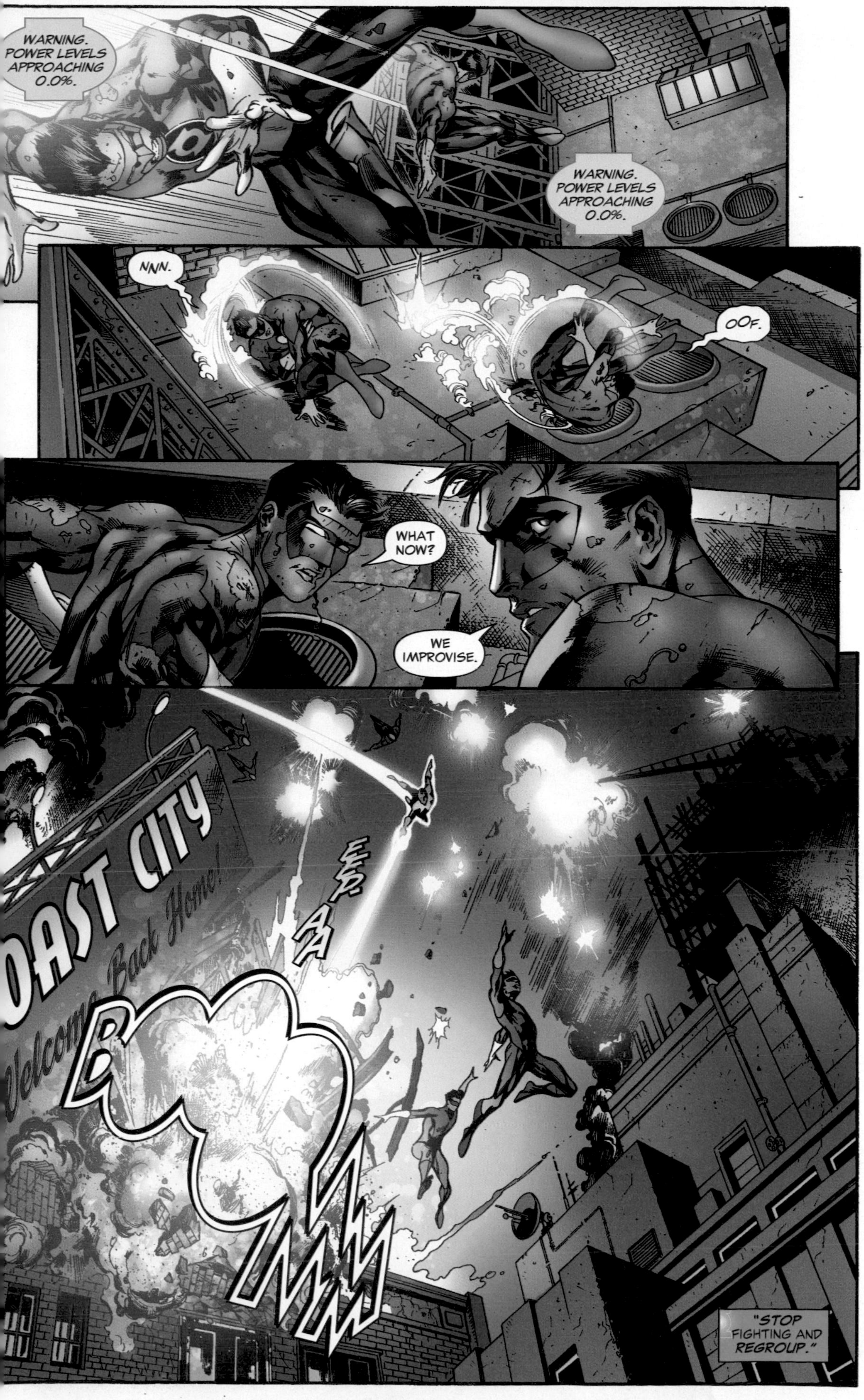
WARNING. POWER LEVELS APPROACHING 0.0%.
WARNING. POWER LEVELS APPROACHING 0.0%.
NNN.
OOF.
WHAT NOW?
WE IMPROVISE.
OAST CITY
Welcome Back Home!
EESPAA
BOOM
"STOP FIGHTING AND REGROUP."

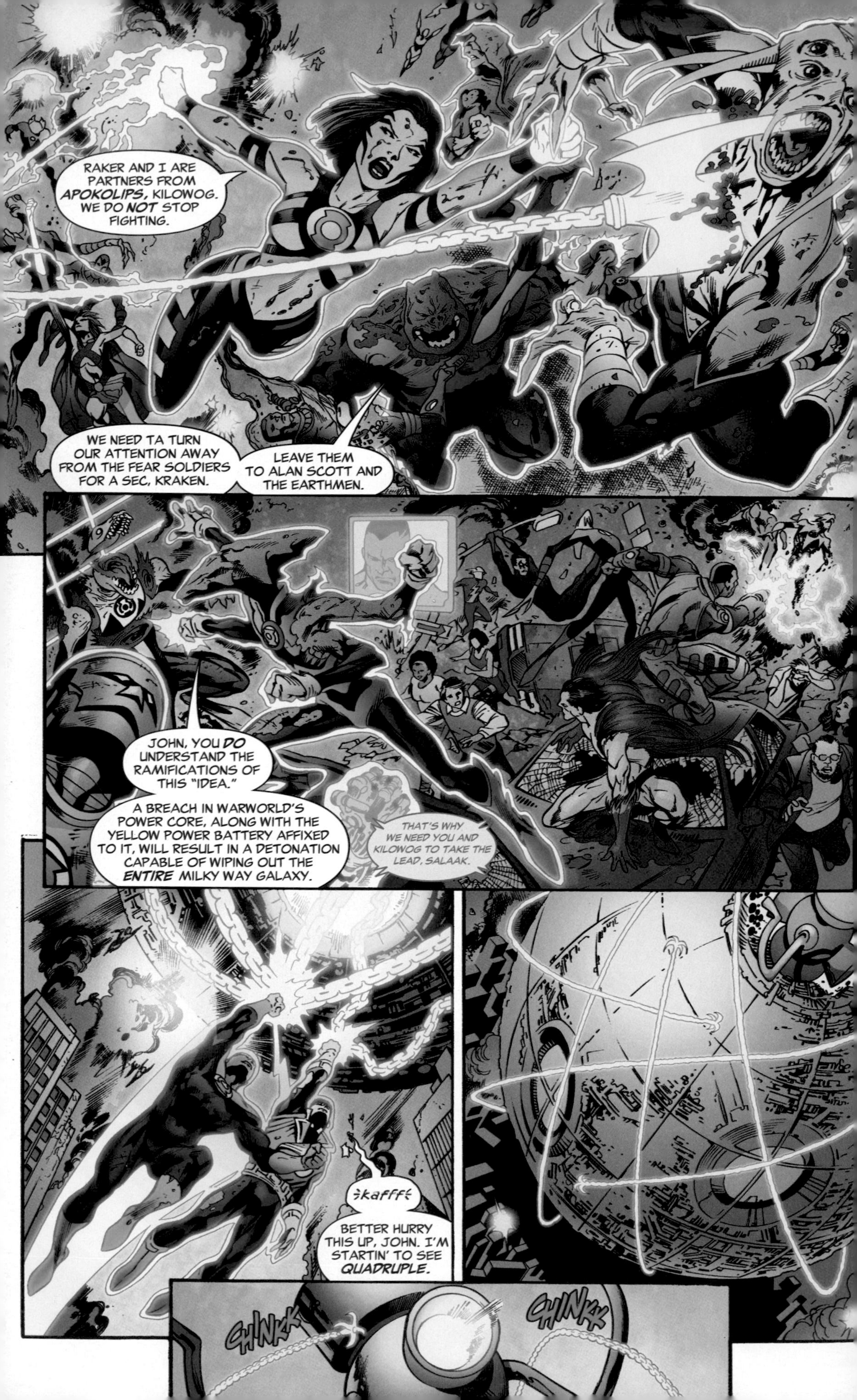
RAKER AND I ARE PARTNERS FROM APOKOLIPS, KILOWOG. WE DO NOT STOP FIGHTING.
WE NEED TA TURN OUR ATTENTION AWAY FROM THE FEAR SOLDIERS FOR A SEC, KRAKEN.
LEAVE THEM TO ALAN SCOTT AND THE EARTHMEN.
JOHN, YOU DO UNDERSTAND THE RAMIFICATIONS OF THIS "IDEA."
A BREACH IN WARWORLD'S POWER CORE, ALONG WITH THE YELLOW POWER BATTERY AFFIXED TO IT, WILL RESULT IN A DETONATION CAPABLE OF WIPING OUT THE ENTIRE MILKY WAY GALAXY.
THAT'S WHY WE NEED YOU AND KILOWOG TO TAKE THE LEAD, SALAAK.
kafff
BETTER HURRY THIS UP, JOHN. I'M STARTIN' TO SEE QUADRUPLE.
CHINKK
CHINKK

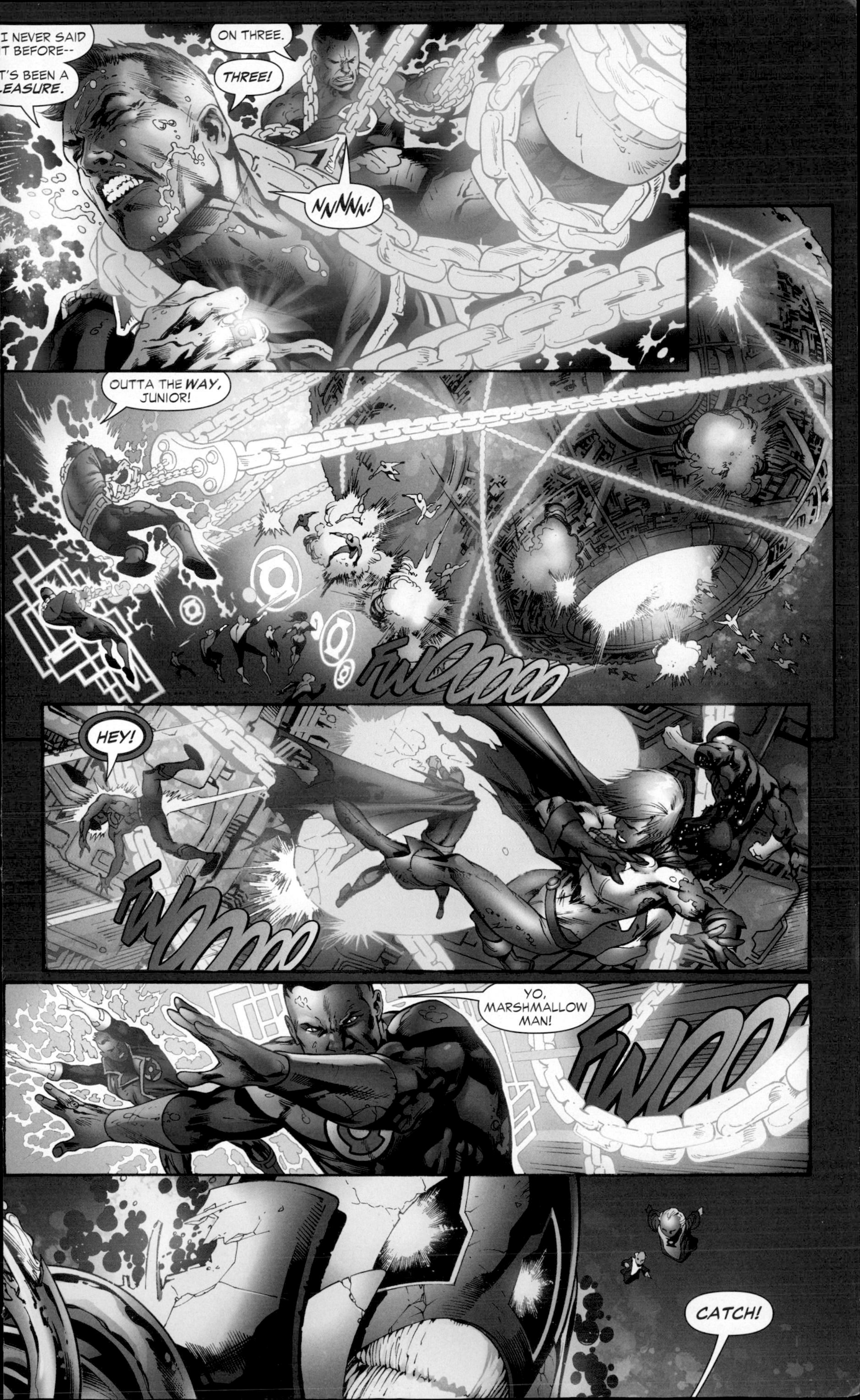
I NEVER SAID
IT BEFORE--
IT'S BEEN A
PLEASURE.
ON THREE.
THREE!
NNNNN!
OUTTA THE WAY, JUNIOR!
FWOOOOO
HEY!
FWOOOOO
YO, MARSHMALLOW MAN!
FWOOO
CATCH!

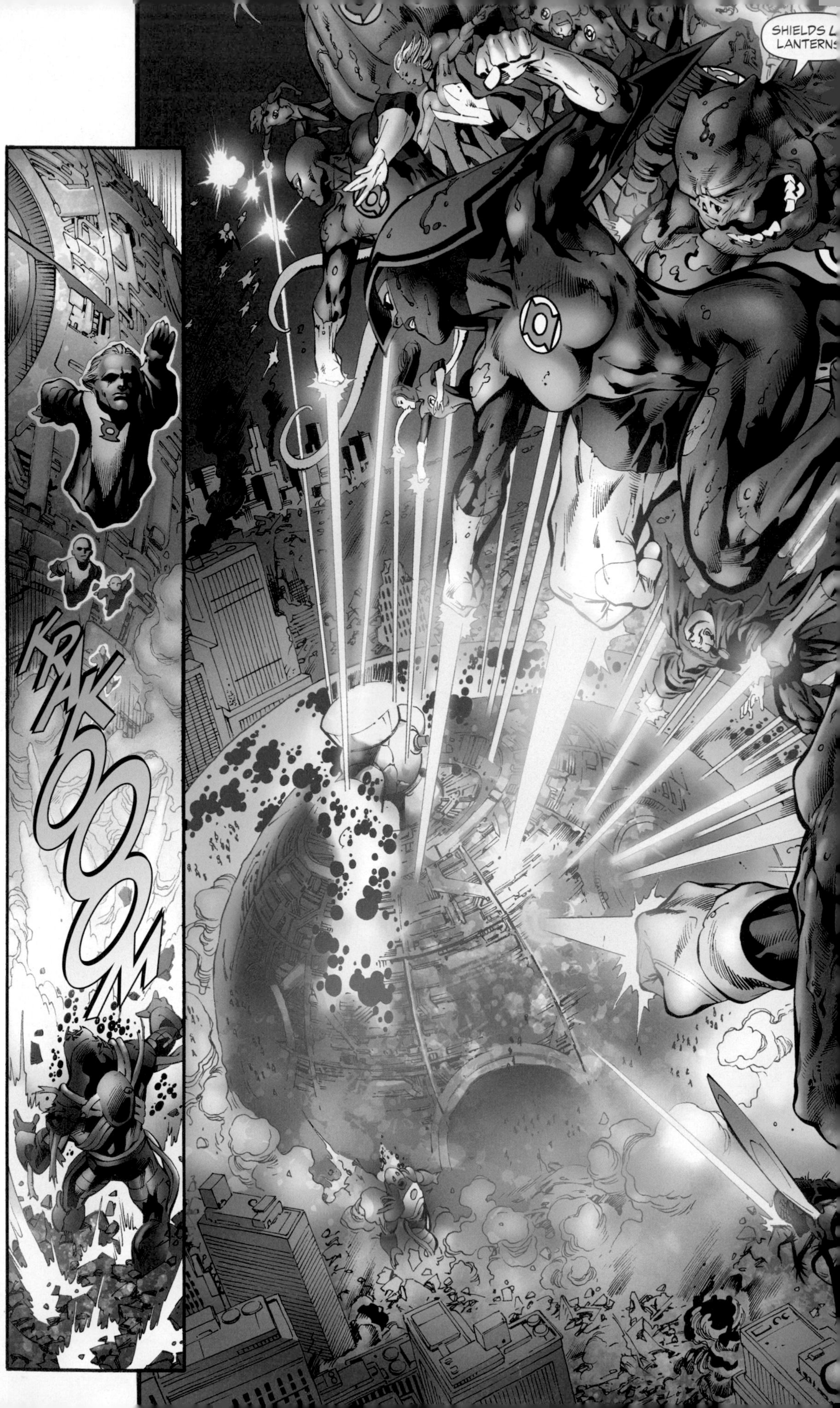
SHIELDS L
LANTERNS
KRAKBOOOM

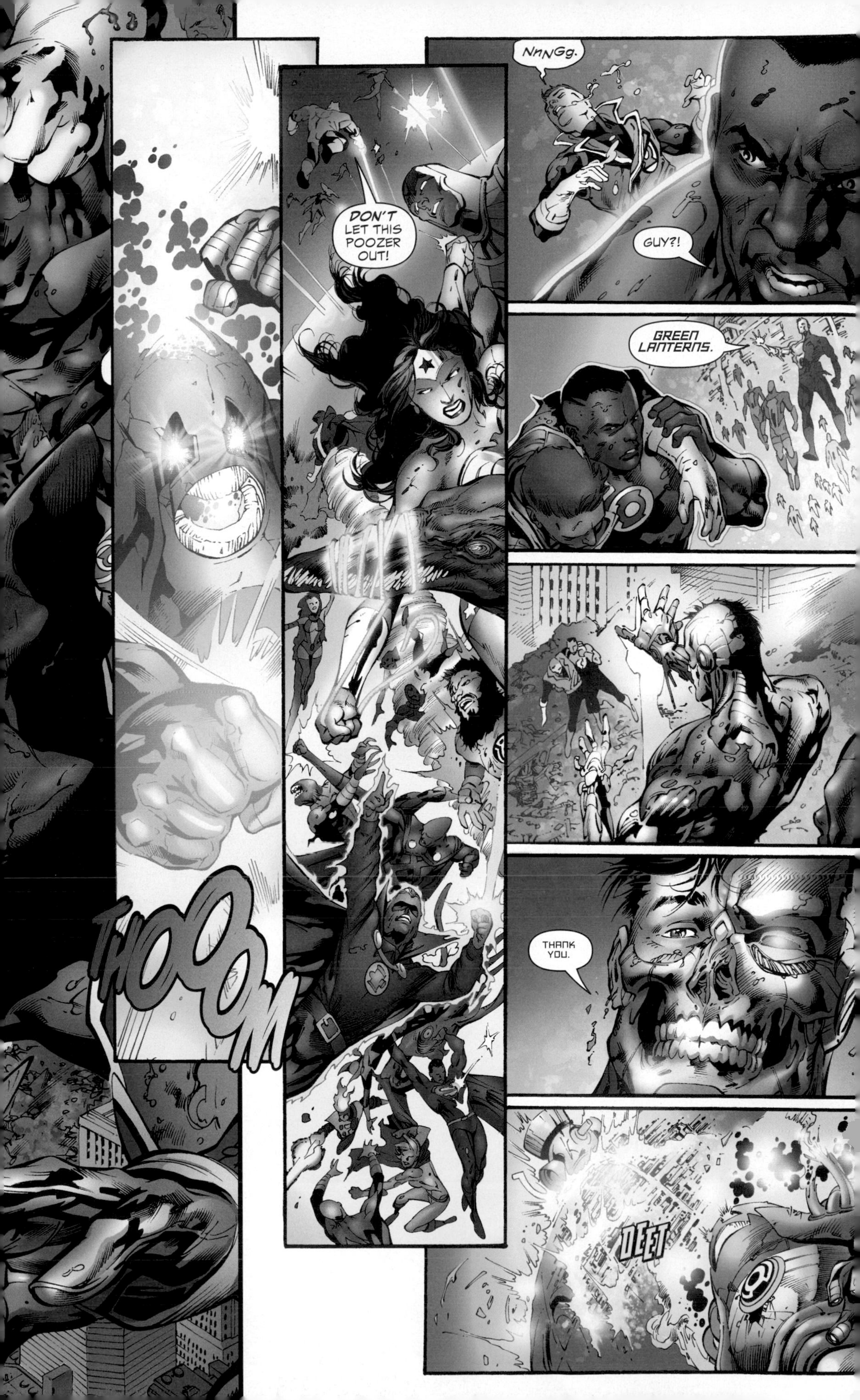
THOOOM
DON'T LET THIS POOZER OUT!
NnNGg.
GUY?!
GREEN LANTERNS.
THANK YOU.
DEET

BAAZZAAT

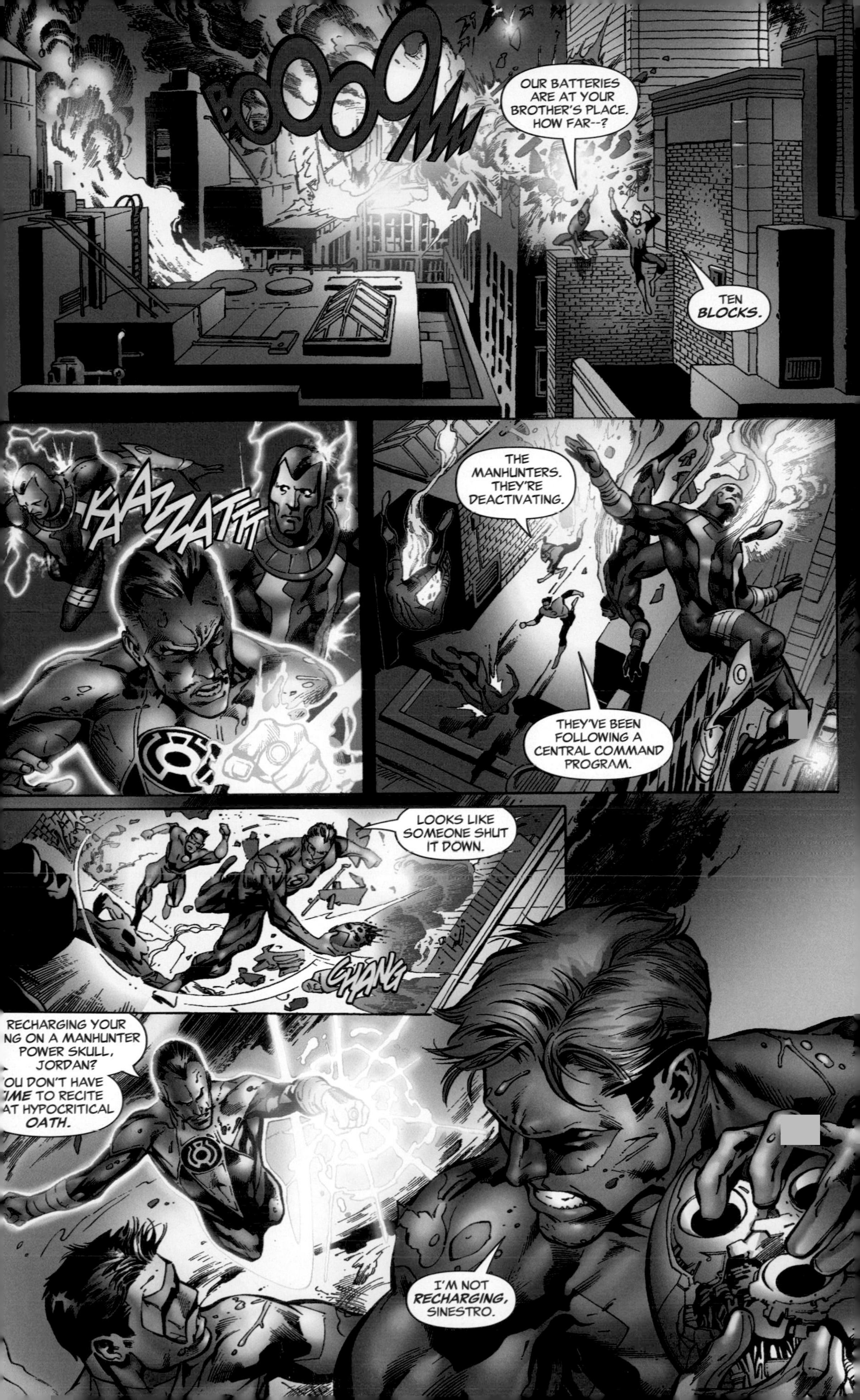
BOOOOMM
OUR BATTERIES ARE AT YOUR BROTHER'S PLACE. HOW FAR--?
TEN BLOCKS.
KAAZZATTT
THE MANHUNTERS. THEY'RE DEACTIVATING.
THEY'VE BEEN FOLLOWING A CENTRAL COMMAND PROGRAM.
LOOKS LIKE SOMEONE SHUT IT DOWN.
CHANG
RECHARGING YOUR NG ON A MANHUNTER POWER SKULL, JORDAN?
OU DON'T HAVE TIME TO RECITE AT HYPOCRITICAL OATH.
I'M NOT RECHARGING, SINESTRO.

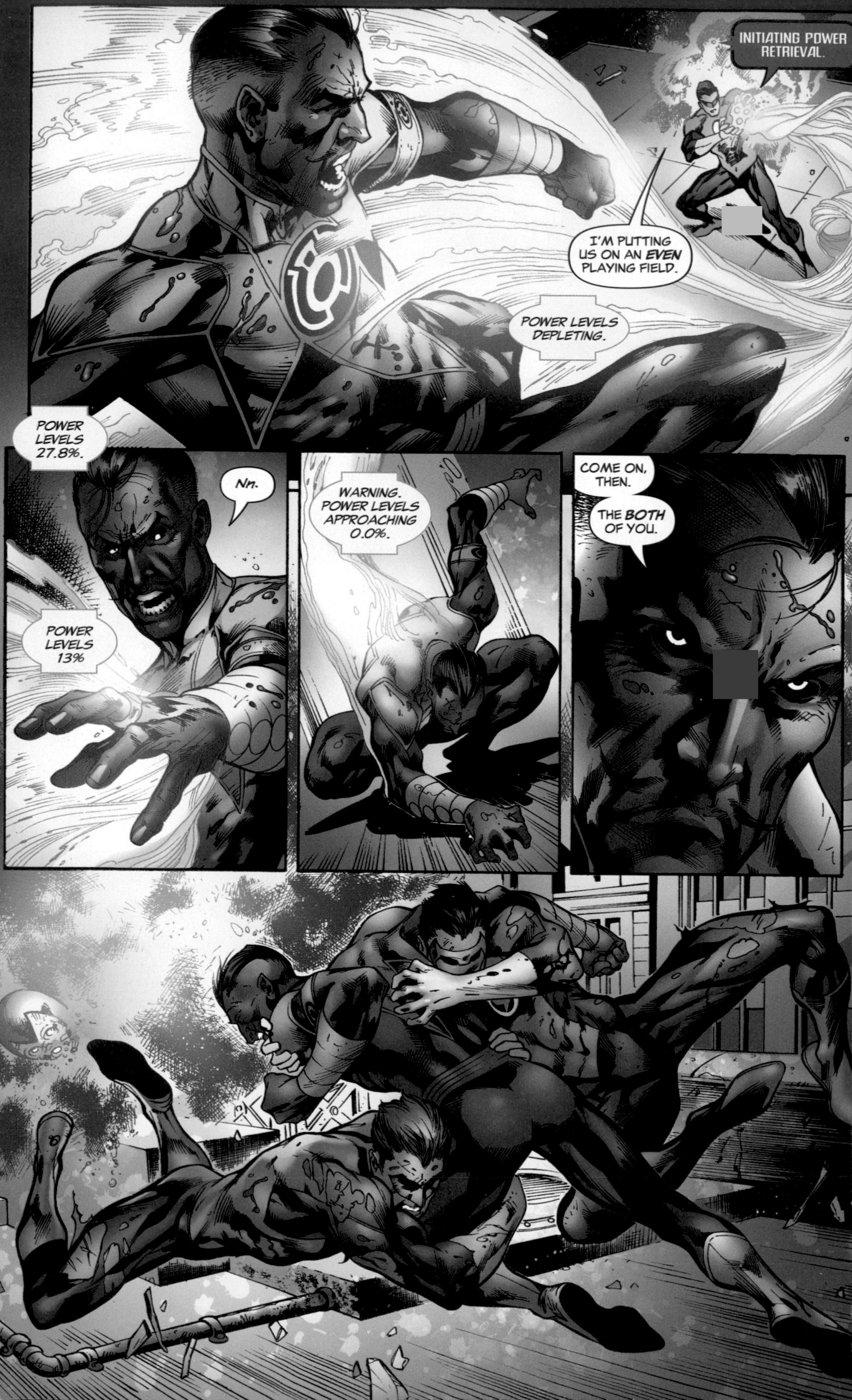
INITIATING POWER RETRIEVAL.
I'M PUTTING US ON AN *EVEN* PLAYING FIELD.
POWER LEVELS DEPLETING.
POWER LEVELS 27.8%.
Nn.
POWER LEVELS 13%
WARNING. POWER LEVELS APPROACHING 0.0%.
COME ON, THEN.
THE *BOTH* OF YOU.

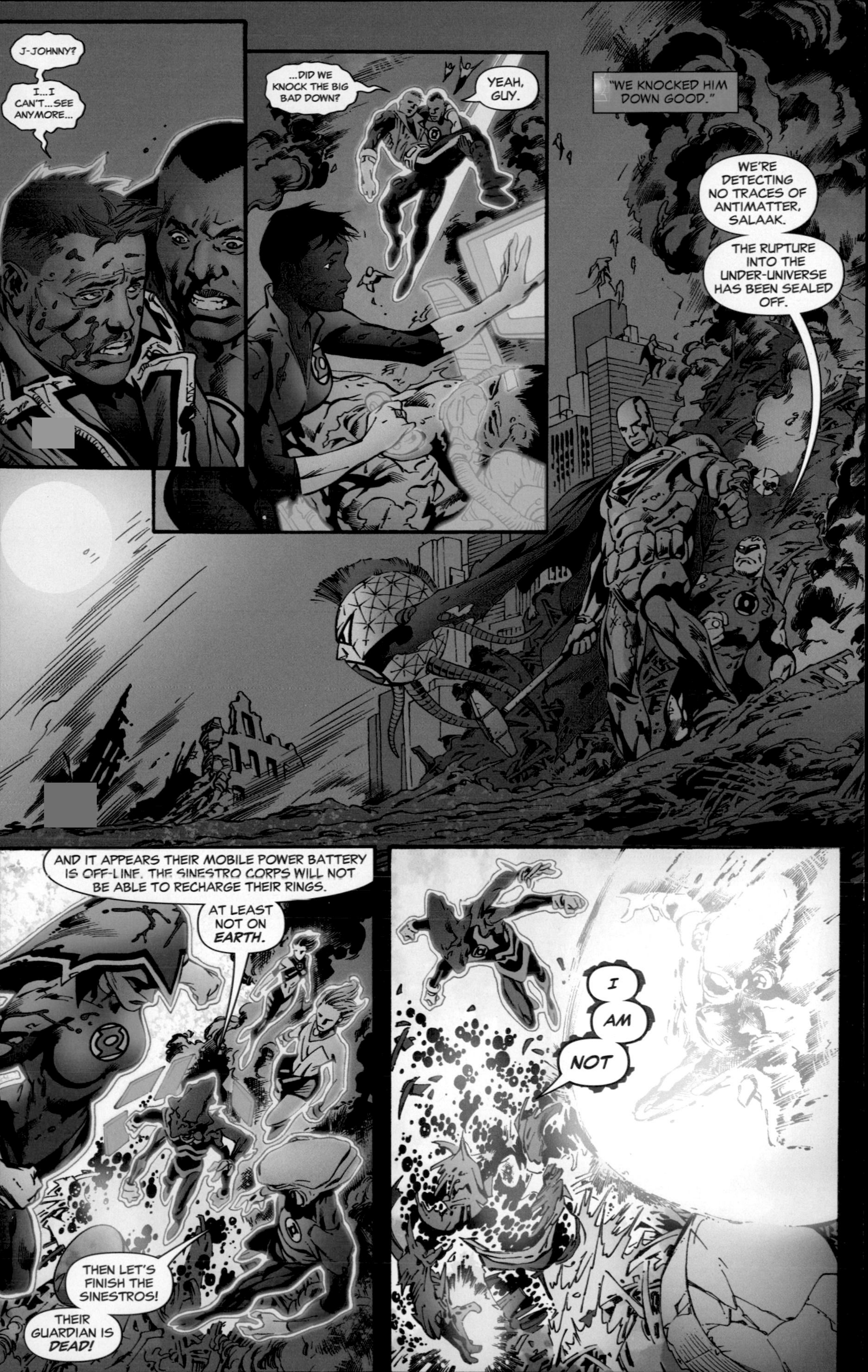
J-JOHNNY?
I...I CAN'T...SEE ANYMORE...
...DID WE KNOCK THE BIG BAD DOWN?
YEAH, GUY.
"WE KNOCKED HIM DOWN GOOD."
WE'RE DETECTING NO TRACES OF ANTIMATTER, SALAAK.
THE RUPTURE INTO THE UNDER-UNIVERSE HAS BEEN SEALED OFF.
AND IT APPEARS THEIR MOBILE POWER BATTERY IS OFF-LINE. THE SINESTRO CORPS WILL NOT BE ABLE TO RECHARGE THEIR RINGS.
AT LEAST NOT ON EARTH.
THEN LET'S FINISH THE SINESTROS!
THEIR GUARDIAN IS DEAD!
I
AM
NOT

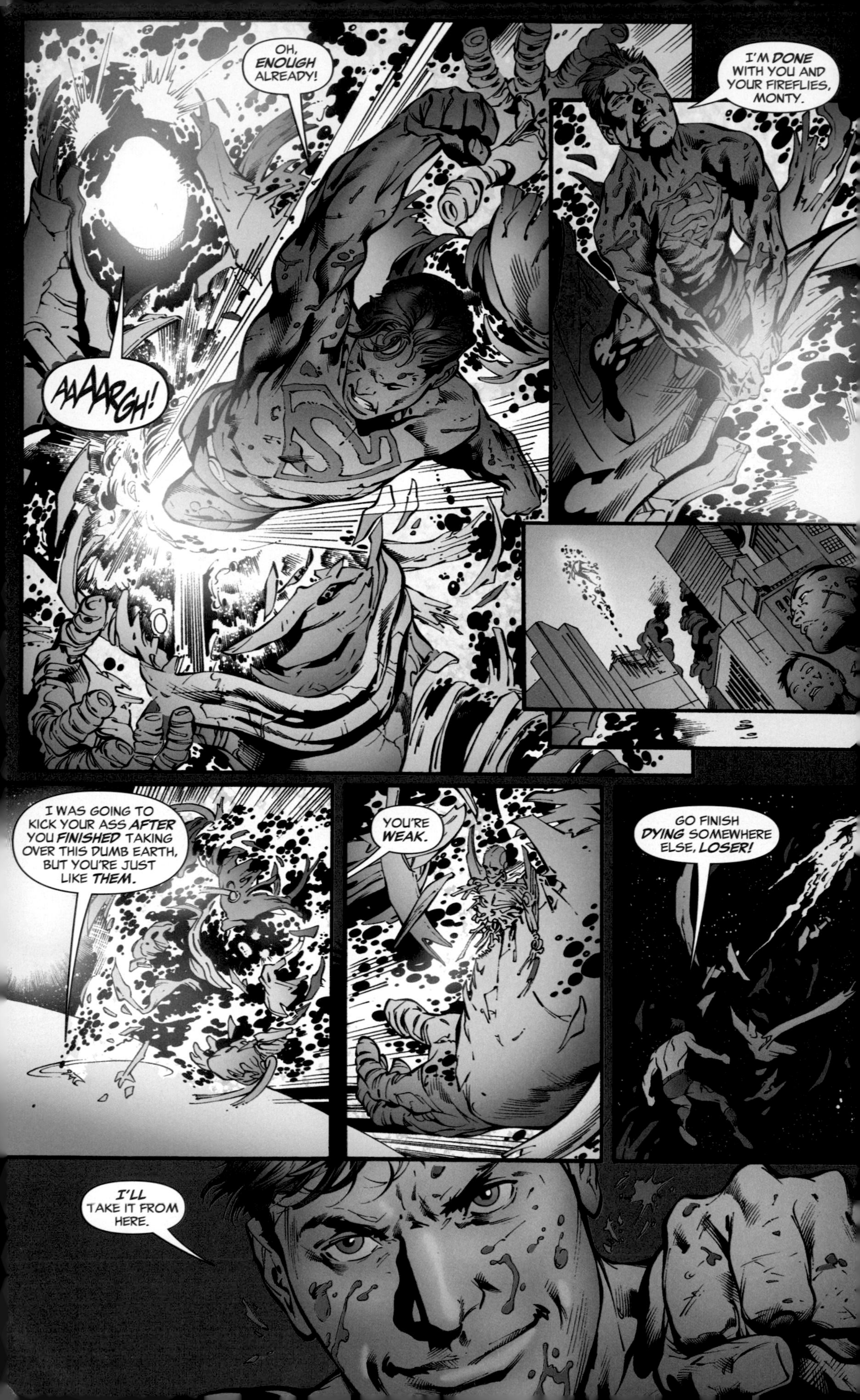
OH, ENOUGH ALREADY!
AAAARGH!
I'M DONE WITH YOU AND YOUR FIREFLIES, MONTY.
I WAS GOING TO KICK YOUR ASS AFTER YOU FINISHED TAKING OVER THIS DUMB EARTH, BUT YOU'RE JUST LIKE THEM.
YOU'RE WEAK.
GO FINISH DYING SOMEWHERE ELSE, LOSER!
I'LL TAKE IT FROM HERE.

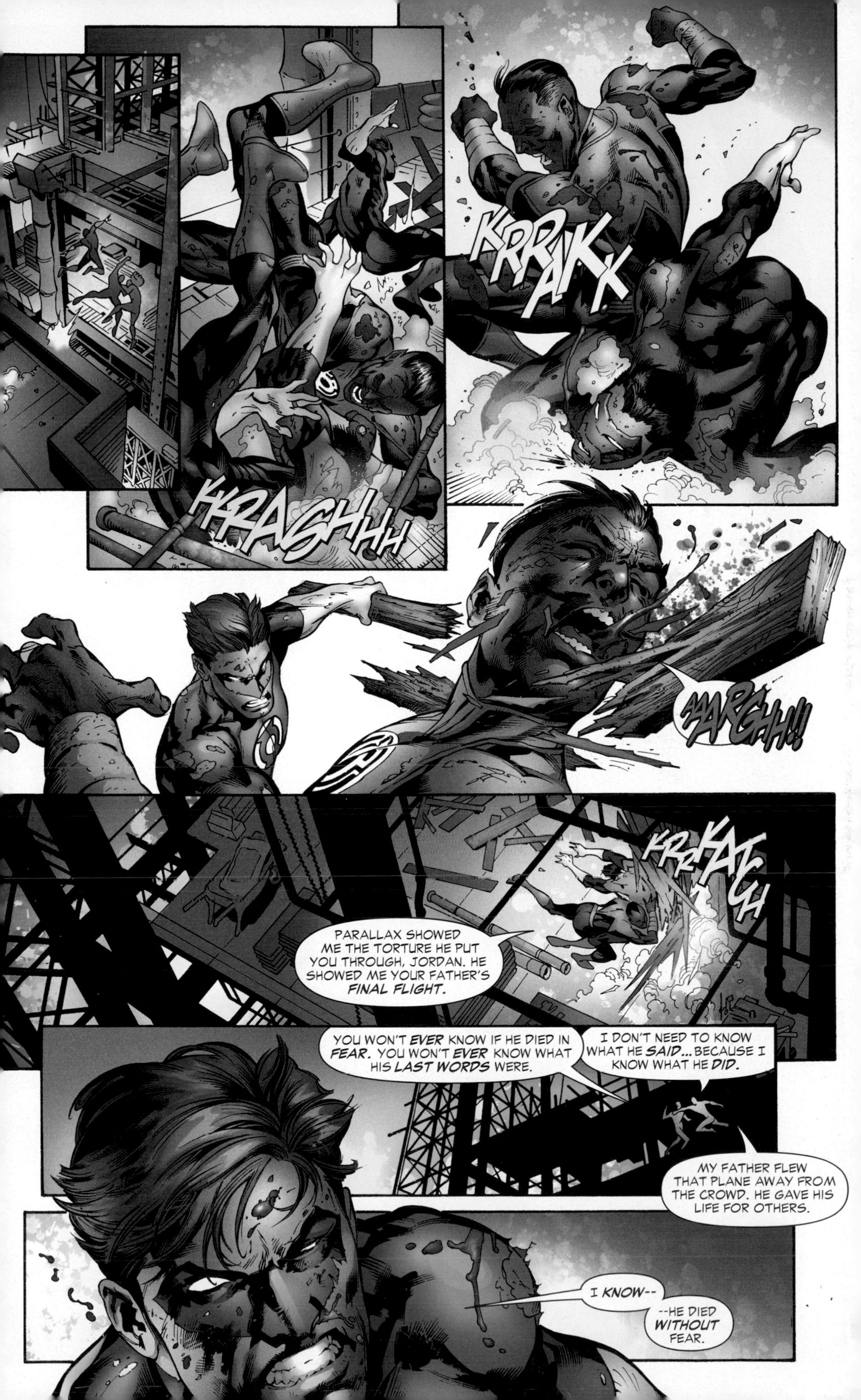
KRRAKK
KKRASHHH
AAARGHH!!
KRRKATCH
PARALLAX SHOWED ME THE TORTURE HE PUT YOU THROUGH, JORDAN. HE SHOWED ME YOUR FATHER'S FINAL FLIGHT.
YOU WON'T EVER KNOW IF HE DIED IN FEAR. YOU WON'T EVER KNOW WHAT HIS LAST WORDS WERE.
I DON'T NEED TO KNOW WHAT HE SAID... BECAUSE I KNOW WHAT HE DID.
MY FATHER FLEW THAT PLANE AWAY FROM THE CROWD. HE GAVE HIS LIFE FOR OTHERS.
I KNOW--
--HE DIED WITHOUT FEAR.

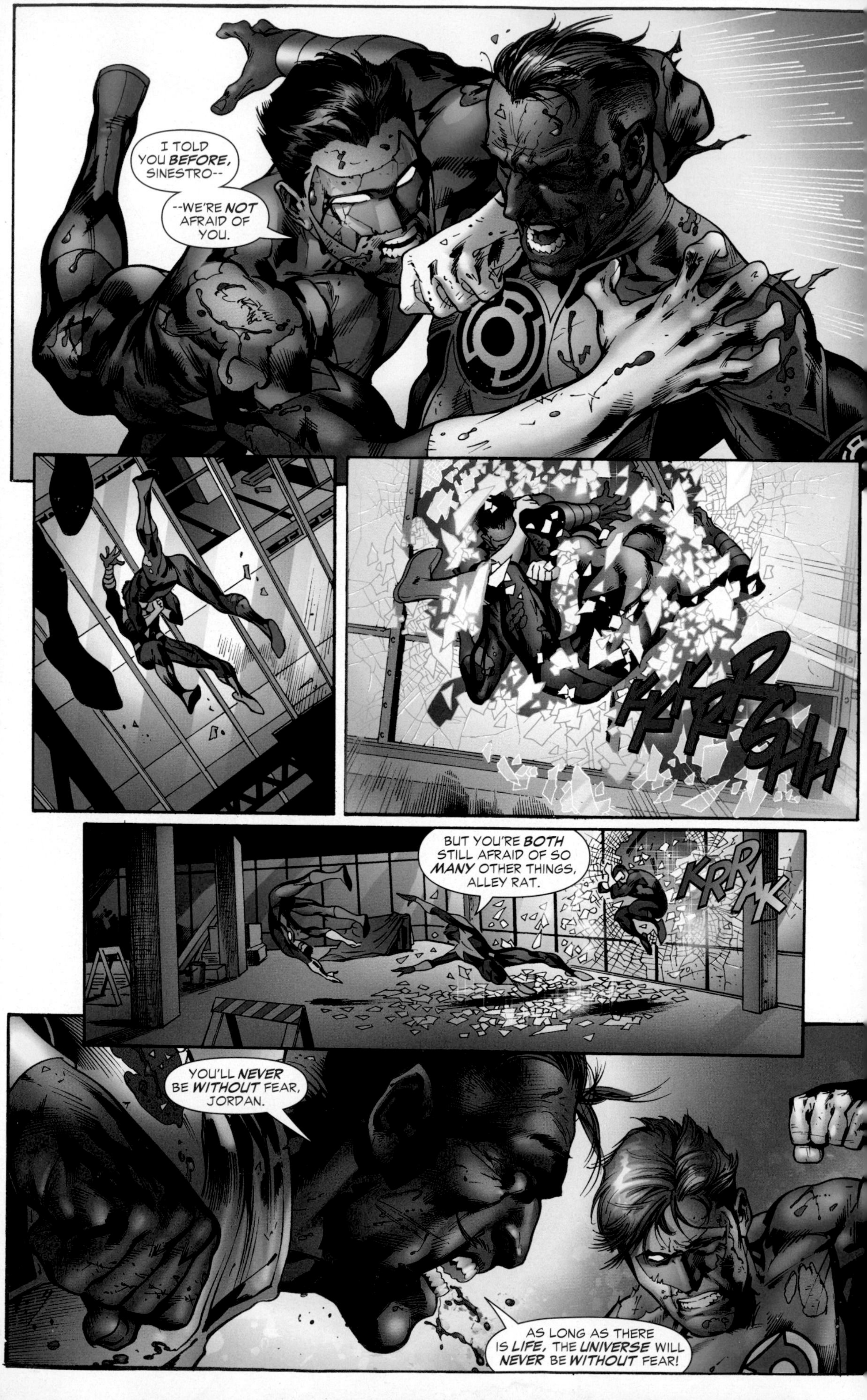
I TOLD YOU BEFORE, SINESTRO--
--WE'RE NOT AFRAID OF YOU.
KKKRSHH
BUT YOU'RE BOTH STILL AFRAID OF SO MANY OTHER THINGS, ALLEY RAT.
KRRRAK
YOU'LL NEVER BE WITHOUT FEAR, JORDAN.
AS LONG AS THERE IS LIFE, THE UNIVERSE WILL NEVER BE WITHOUT FEAR!

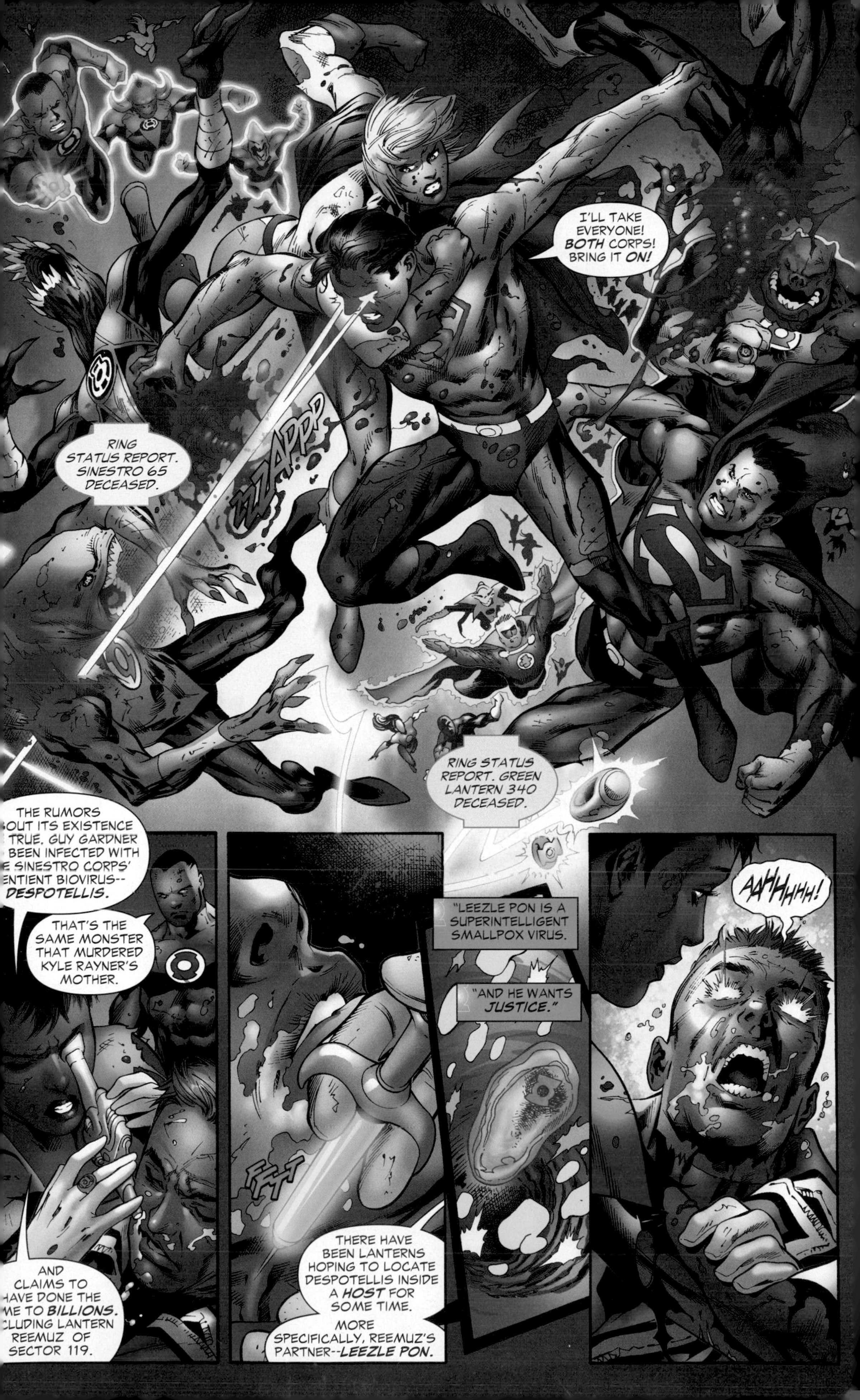
I'LL TAKE EVERYONE! BOTH CORPS! BRING IT ON!
RING STATUS REPORT. SINESTRO 65 DECEASED.
RING STATUS REPORT. GREEN LANTERN 340 DECEASED.
THE RUMORS BOUT ITS EXISTENCE TRUE. GUY GARDNER BEEN INFECTED WITH E SINESTRO CORPS' ENTIENT BIOVIRUS-- DESPOTELLIS.
THAT'S THE SAME MONSTER THAT MURDERED KYLE RAYNER'S MOTHER.
AND CLAIMS TO HAVE DONE THE ME TO BILLIONS. CLUDING LANTERN REEMUZ OF SECTOR 119.
THERE HAVE BEEN LANTERNS HOPING TO LOCATE DESPOTELLIS INSIDE A HOST FOR SOME TIME.
MORE SPECIFICALLY, REEMUZ'S PARTNER--LEEZLE PON.
"LEEZLE PON IS A SUPERINTELLIGENT SMALLPOX VIRUS.
"AND HE WANTS JUSTICE."
AAHHHHH!

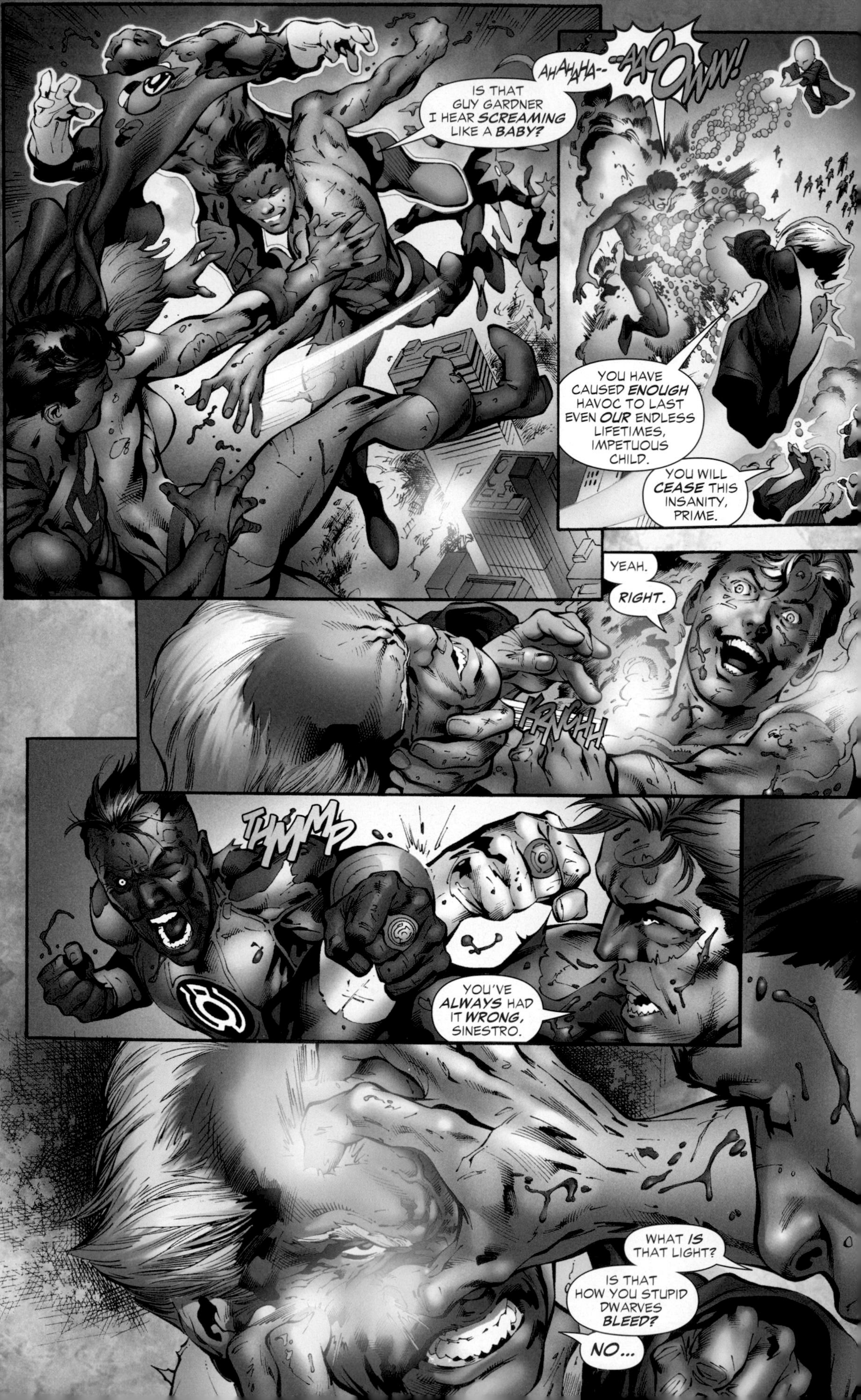

IS THAT GUY GARDNER I HEAR SCREAMING LIKE A BABY?
AHAHAHA--AAOOWW!
YOU HAVE CAUSED ENOUGH HAVOC TO LAST EVEN OUR ENDLESS LIFETIMES, IMPETUOUS CHILD.
YOU WILL CEASE THIS INSANITY, PRIME.
YEAH.
RIGHT.
KRNCHH
THMMP
YOU'VE ALWAYS HAD IT WRONG, SINESTRO.
WHAT IS THAT LIGHT?
IS THAT HOW YOU STUPID DWARVES BLEED?
NO...

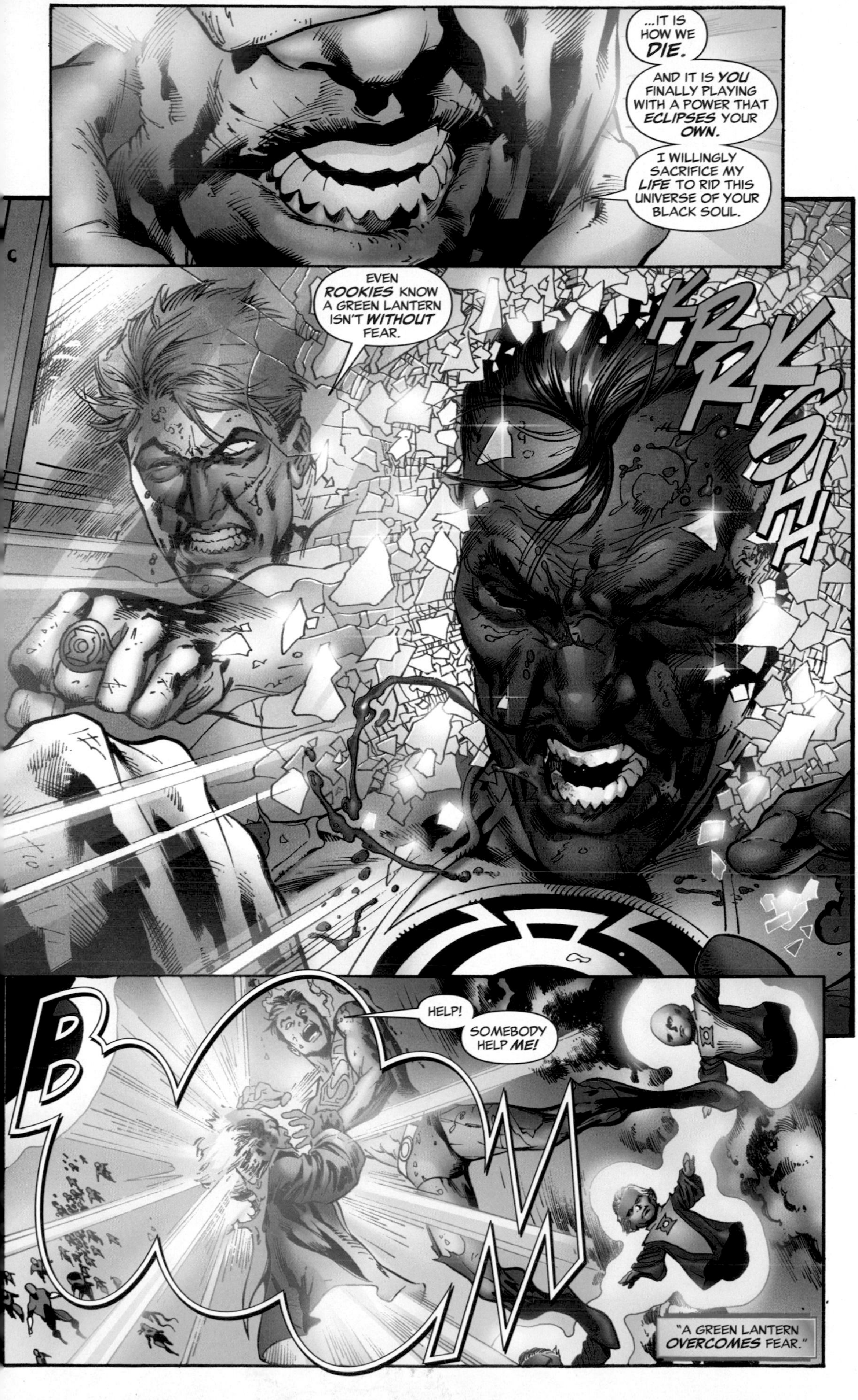

...IT IS HOW WE DIE.
AND IT IS YOU FINALLY PLAYING WITH A POWER THAT ECLIPSES YOUR OWN.
I WILLINGLY SACRIFICE MY LIFE TO RID THIS UNIVERSE OF YOUR BLACK SOUL.
EVEN ROOKIES KNOW A GREEN LANTERN ISN'T WITHOUT FEAR.
HELP!
SOMEBODY HELP ME!
"A GREEN LANTERN OVERCOMES FEAR."

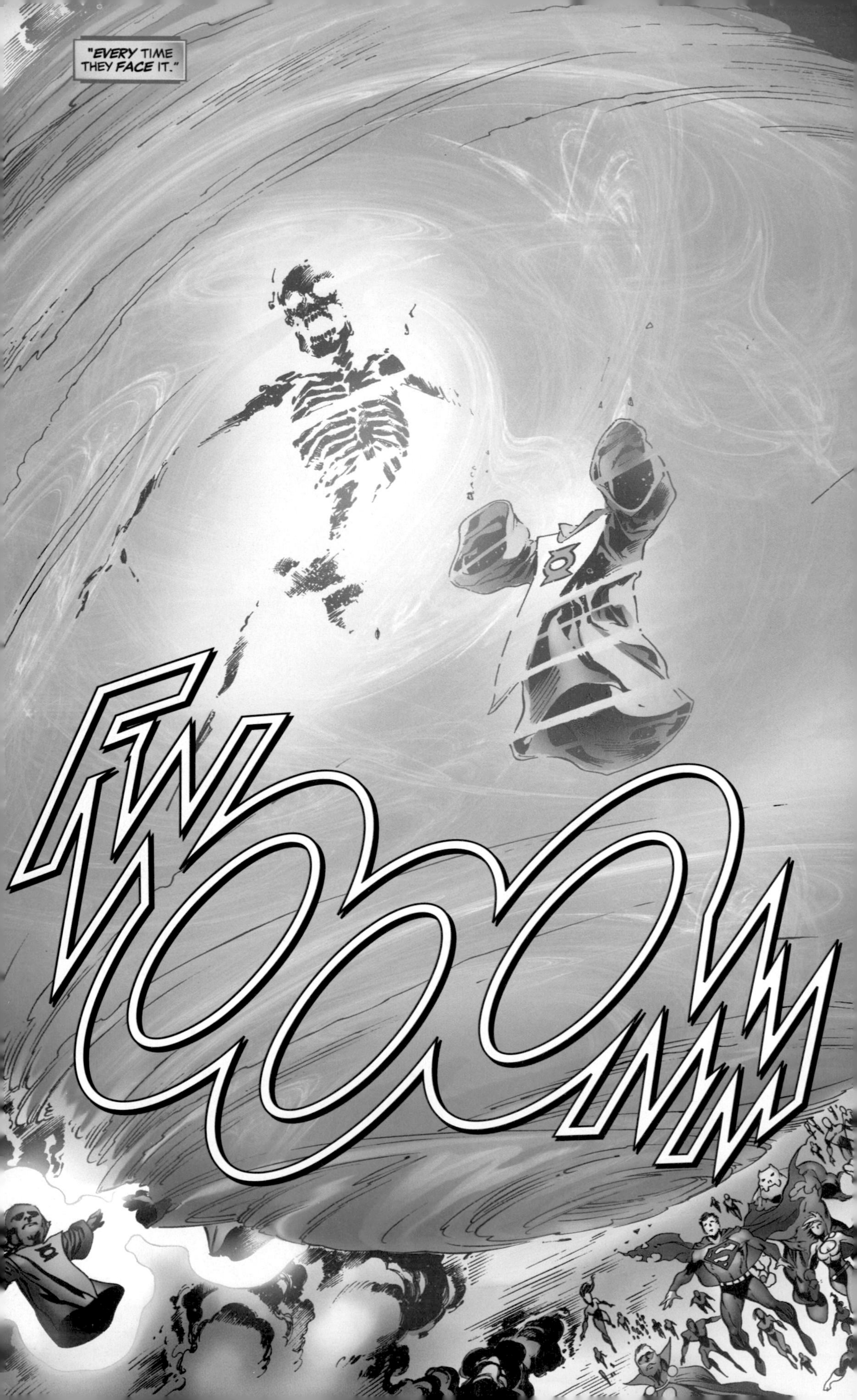
"EVERY TIME THEY FACE IT."
FWOOOMM

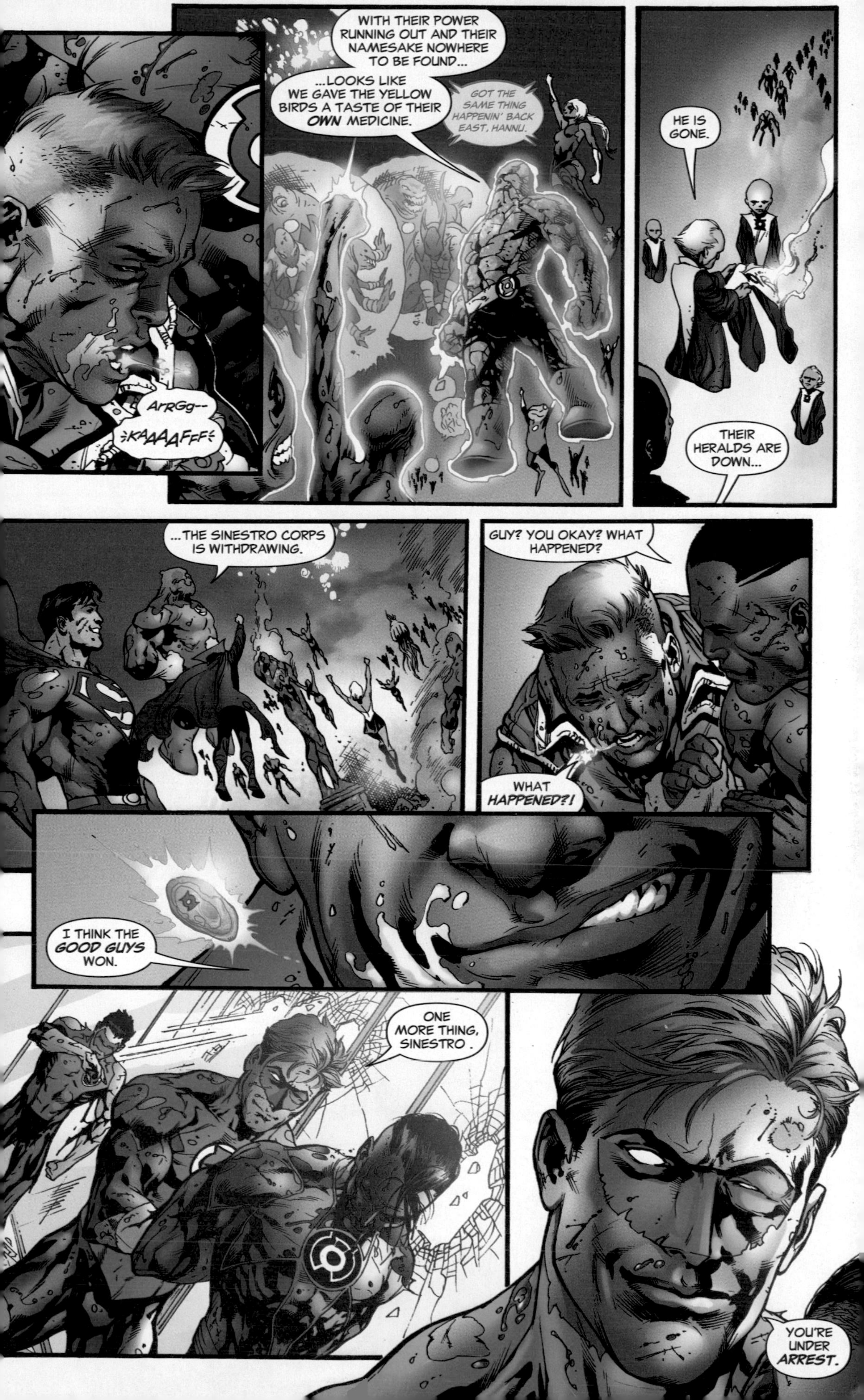
ArrGg--
KAAAAFFF
WITH THEIR POWER RUNNING OUT AND THEIR NAMESAKE NOWHERE TO BE FOUND...
...LOOKS LIKE WE GAVE THE YELLOW BIRDS A TASTE OF THEIR OWN MEDICINE.
GOT THE SAME THING HAPPENIN' BACK EAST, HANNU.
HE IS GONE.
THEIR HERALDS ARE DOWN...
...THE SINESTRO CORPS IS WITHDRAWING.
GUY? YOU OKAY? WHAT HAPPENED?
WHAT HAPPENED?!
I THINK THE GOOD GUYS WON.
ONE MORE THING, SINESTRO.
YOU'RE UNDER ARREST.

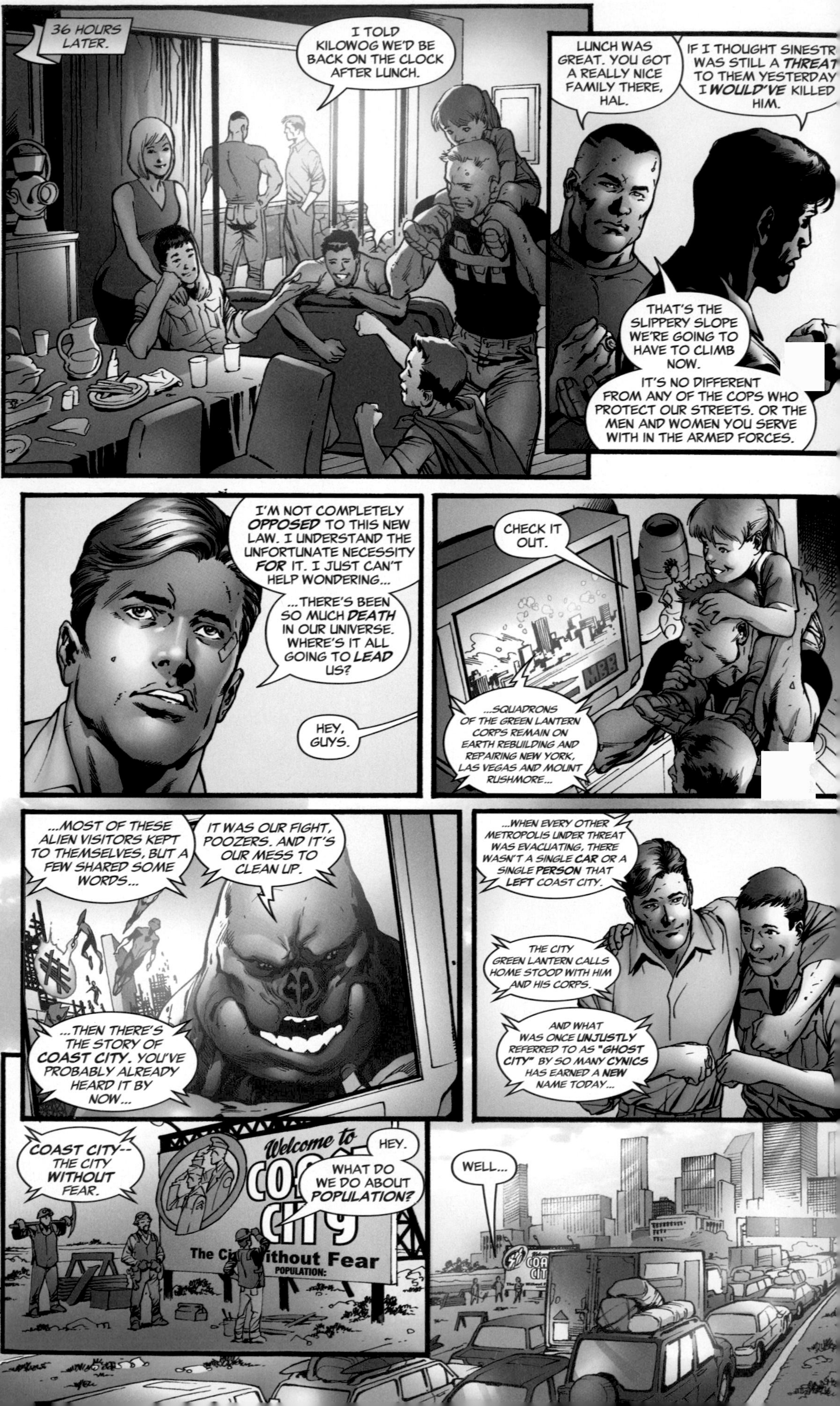
36 HOURS LATER.
I TOLD KILOWOG WE'D BE BACK ON THE CLOCK AFTER LUNCH.
LUNCH WAS GREAT. YOU GOT A REALLY NICE FAMILY THERE, HAL.
IF I THOUGHT SINESTR WAS STILL A THREAT TO THEM YESTERDAY I WOULD'VE KILLED HIM.
THAT'S THE SLIPPERY SLOPE WE'RE GOING TO HAVE TO CLIMB NOW.
IT'S NO DIFFERENT FROM ANY OF THE COPS WHO PROTECT OUR STREETS. OR THE MEN AND WOMEN YOU SERVE WITH IN THE ARMED FORCES.
I'M NOT COMPLETELY OPPOSED TO THIS NEW LAW. I UNDERSTAND THE UNFORTUNATE NECESSITY FOR IT. I JUST CAN'T HELP WONDERING...
...THERE'S BEEN SO MUCH DEATH IN OUR UNIVERSE. WHERE'S IT ALL GOING TO LEAD US?
HEY, GUYS.
CHECK IT OUT.
...SQUADRONS OF THE GREEN LANTERN CORPS REMAIN ON EARTH REBUILDING AND REPAIRING NEW YORK, LAS VEGAS AND MOUNT RUSHMORE...
...MOST OF THESE ALIEN VISITORS KEPT TO THEMSELVES, BUT A FEW SHARED SOME WORDS...
IT WAS OUR FIGHT, POOZERS. AND IT'S OUR MESS TO CLEAN UP.
...THEN THERE'S THE STORY OF COAST CITY. YOU'VE PROBABLY ALREADY HEARD IT BY NOW...
...WHEN EVERY OTHER METROPOLIS UNDER THREAT WAS EVACUATING, THERE WASN'T A SINGLE CAR OR A SINGLE PERSON THAT LEFT COAST CITY.
THE CITY GREEN LANTERN CALLS HOME STOOD WITH HIM AND HIS CORPS.
AND WHAT WAS ONCE UNJUSTLY REFERRED TO AS "GHOST CITY" BY SO MANY CYNICS HAS EARNED A NEW NAME TODAY...
COAST CITY-- THE CITY WITHOUT FEAR.
Welcome to
The Ci Without Fear
POPULATION:
HEY.
WHAT DO WE DO ABOUT POPULATION?
WELL...

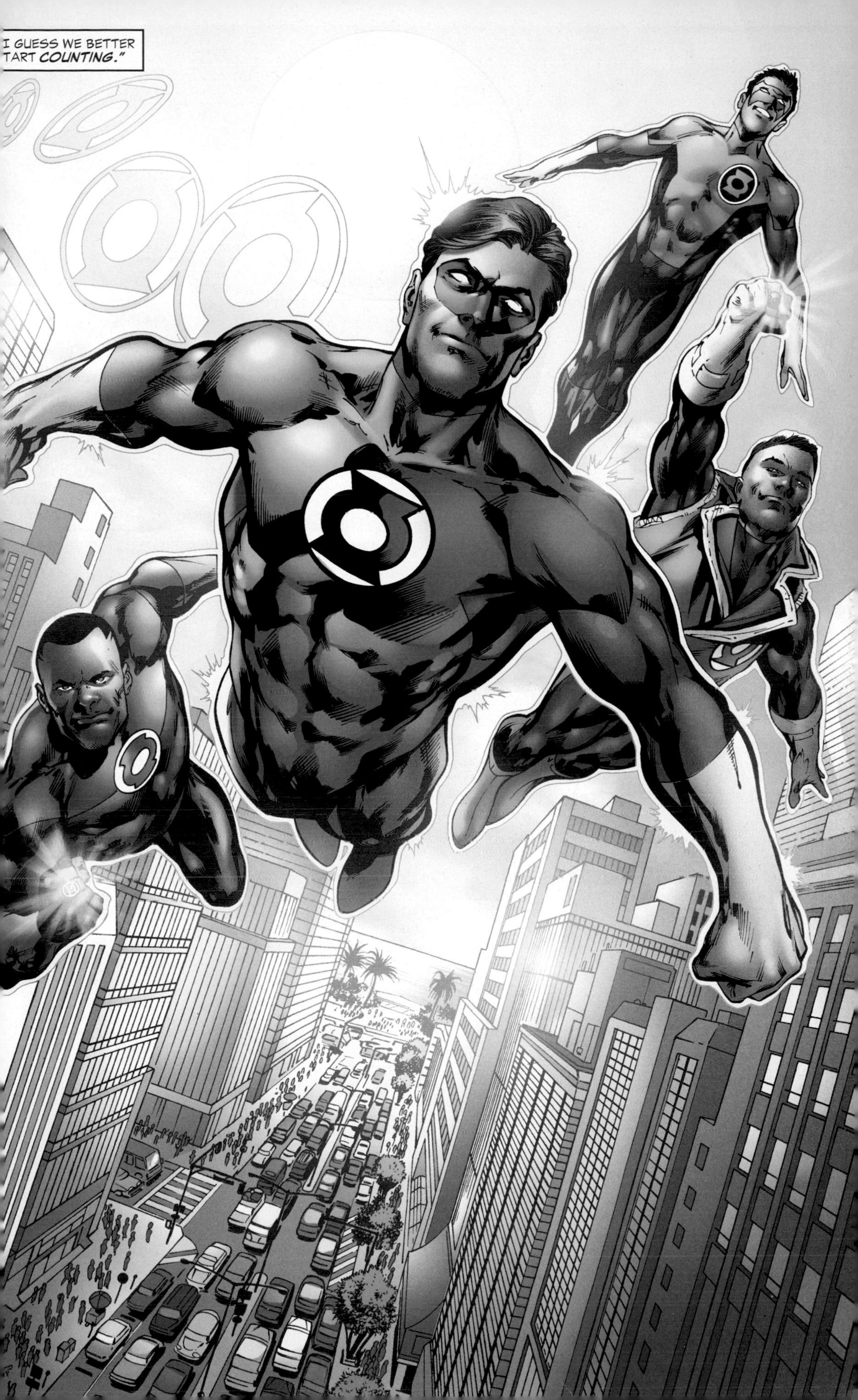
I GUESS WE BETTER
TART COUNTING."

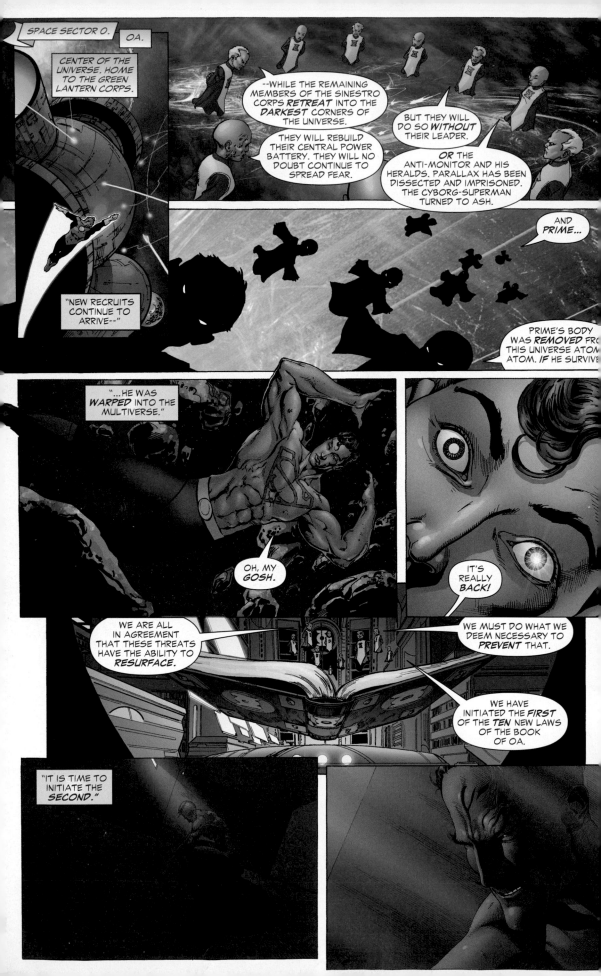

SPACE SECTOR O. OA.

CENTER OF THE UNIVERSE. HOME TO THE GREEN LANTERN CORPS.

--WHILE THE REMAINING MEMBERS OF THE SINESTRO CORPS *RETREAT* INTO THE *DARKEST* CORNERS OF THE UNIVERSE.

THEY WILL REBUILD THEIR CENTRAL POWER BATTERY. THEY WILL NO DOUBT CONTINUE TO SPREAD FEAR.

BUT THEY WILL DO SO *WITHOUT* THEIR LEADER.

OR THE ANTI-MONITOR AND HIS HERALDS. PARALLAX HAS BEEN DISSECTED AND IMPRISONED. THE CYBORG-SUPERMAN TURNED TO ASH.

"NEW RECRUITS CONTINUE TO ARRIVE--"

AND *PRIME*...

PRIME'S BODY WAS *REMOVED* FRO[M] THIS UNIVERSE ATOM[...] ATOM. *IF* HE SURVIVE[D...]

"...HE WAS *WARPED* INTO THE MULTIVERSE."

OH, MY *GOSH*.

IT'S REALLY *BACK*!

WE ARE ALL IN AGREEMENT THAT THESE THREATS HAVE THE ABILITY TO *RESURFACE*.

WE MUST DO WHAT WE DEEM NECESSARY TO *PREVENT* THAT.

WE HAVE INITIATED THE *FIRST* OF THE *TEN* NEW LAWS OF THE BOOK OF OA.

"IT IS TIME TO INITIATE THE *SECOND*."

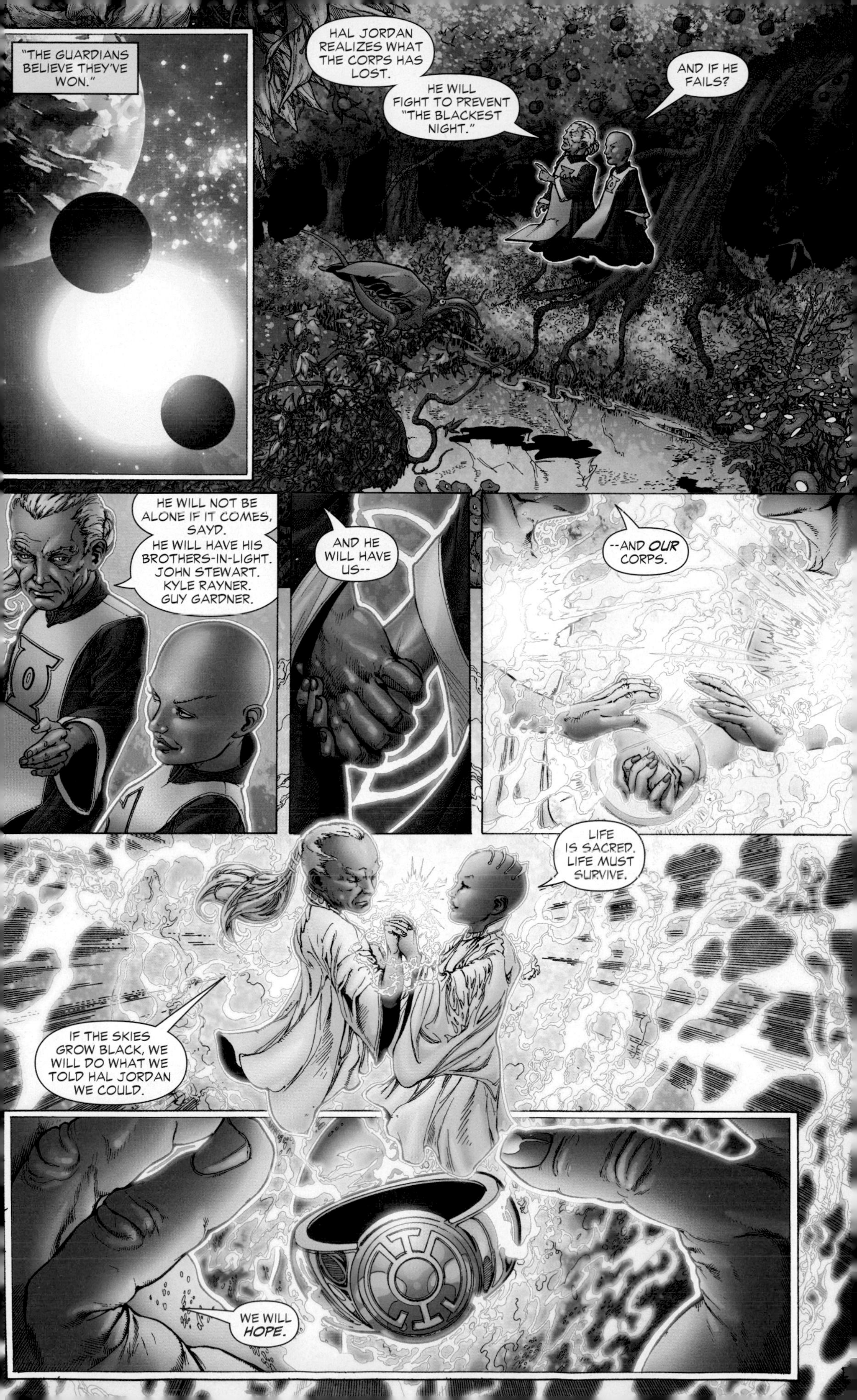
"THE GUARDIANS BELIEVE THEY'VE WON."
HAL JORDAN REALIZES WHAT THE CORPS HAS LOST.
HE WILL FIGHT TO PREVENT "THE BLACKEST NIGHT."
AND IF HE FAILS?
HE WILL NOT BE ALONE IF IT COMES, SAYD. HE WILL HAVE HIS BROTHERS-IN-LIGHT. JOHN STEWART. KYLE RAYNER. GUY GARDNER.
AND HE WILL HAVE US--
--AND *OUR* CORPS.
LIFE IS SACRED. LIFE MUST SURVIVE.
IF THE SKIES GROW BLACK, WE WILL DO WHAT WE TOLD HAL JORDAN WE COULD.
WE WILL *HOPE*.

GRANDMASTER LOCATED.

LIFE READINGS-- *NEGATIVE*.

LEADERSHIP PROGRAMMING REQUIRED.

GRANDMAS... REQUIRED

VZZT

VZZT

VZZT

KAZZAT

LIFE READINGS--

--*POSITIVE*.

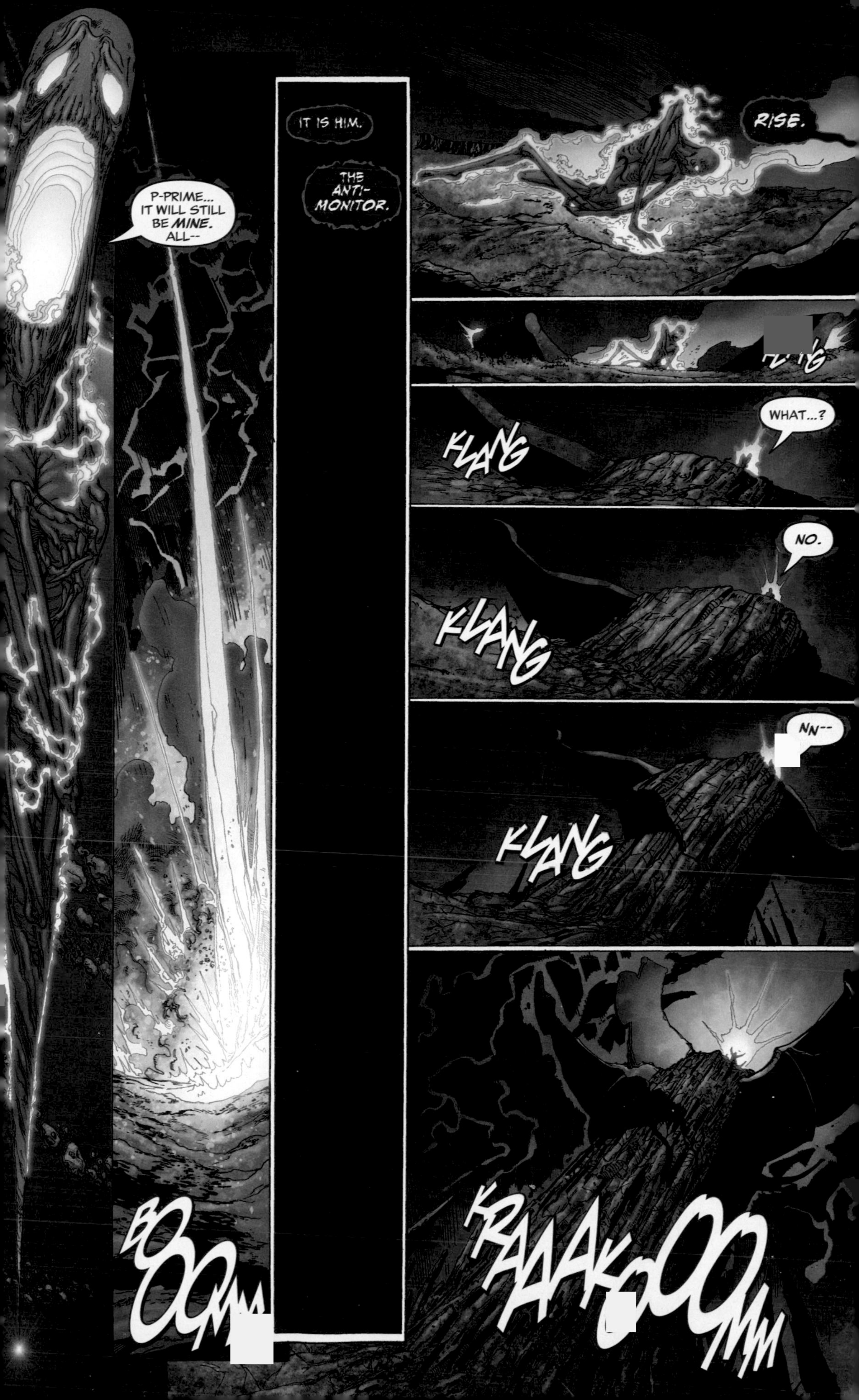

P-PRIME... IT WILL STILL BE MINE. ALL--
BOOOM
IT IS HIM.
THE ANTI-MONITOR.
RISE.
WHAT...?
KLANG
NO.
KLANG
NN--
KLANG
KRAAAKOOOMM

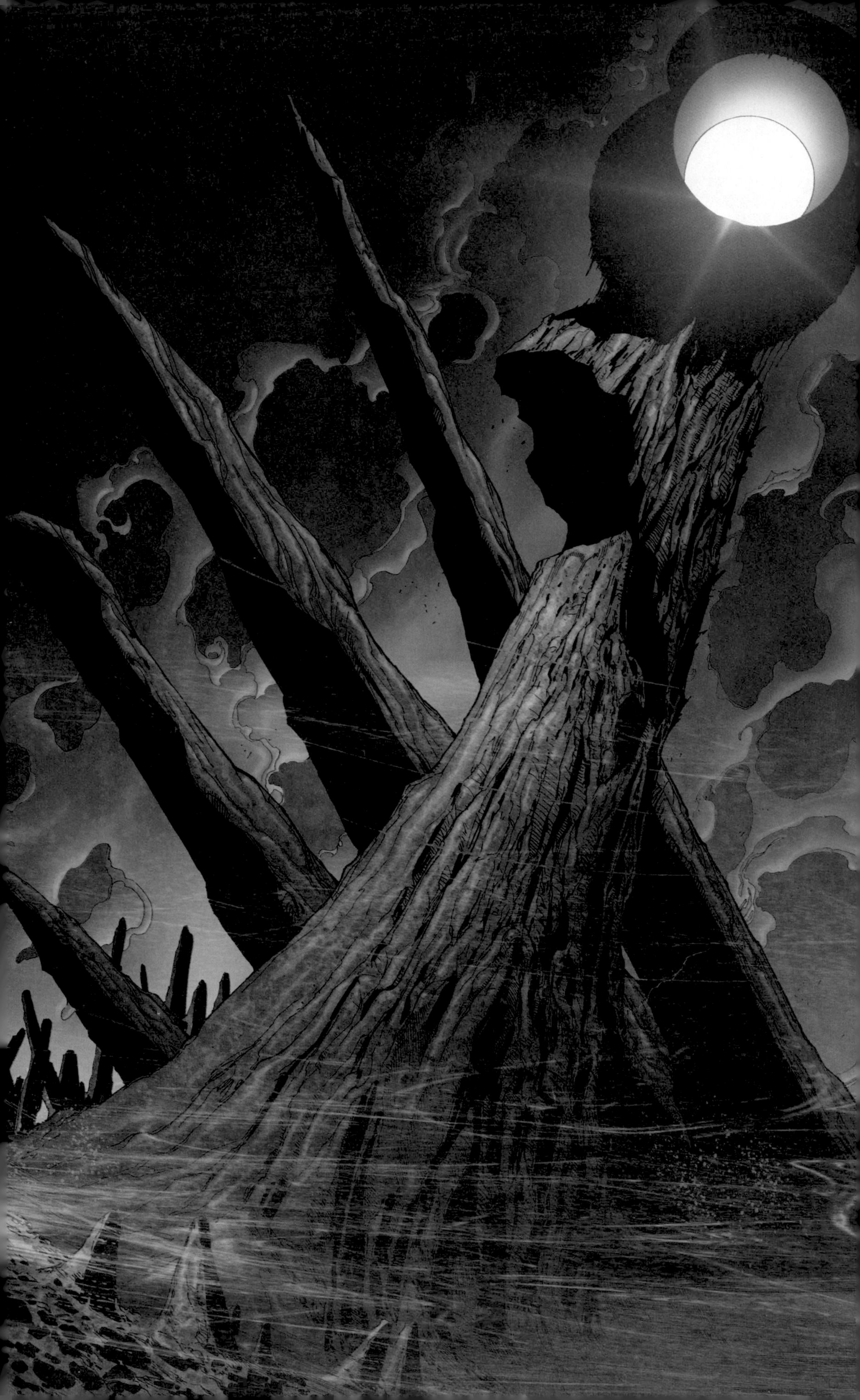

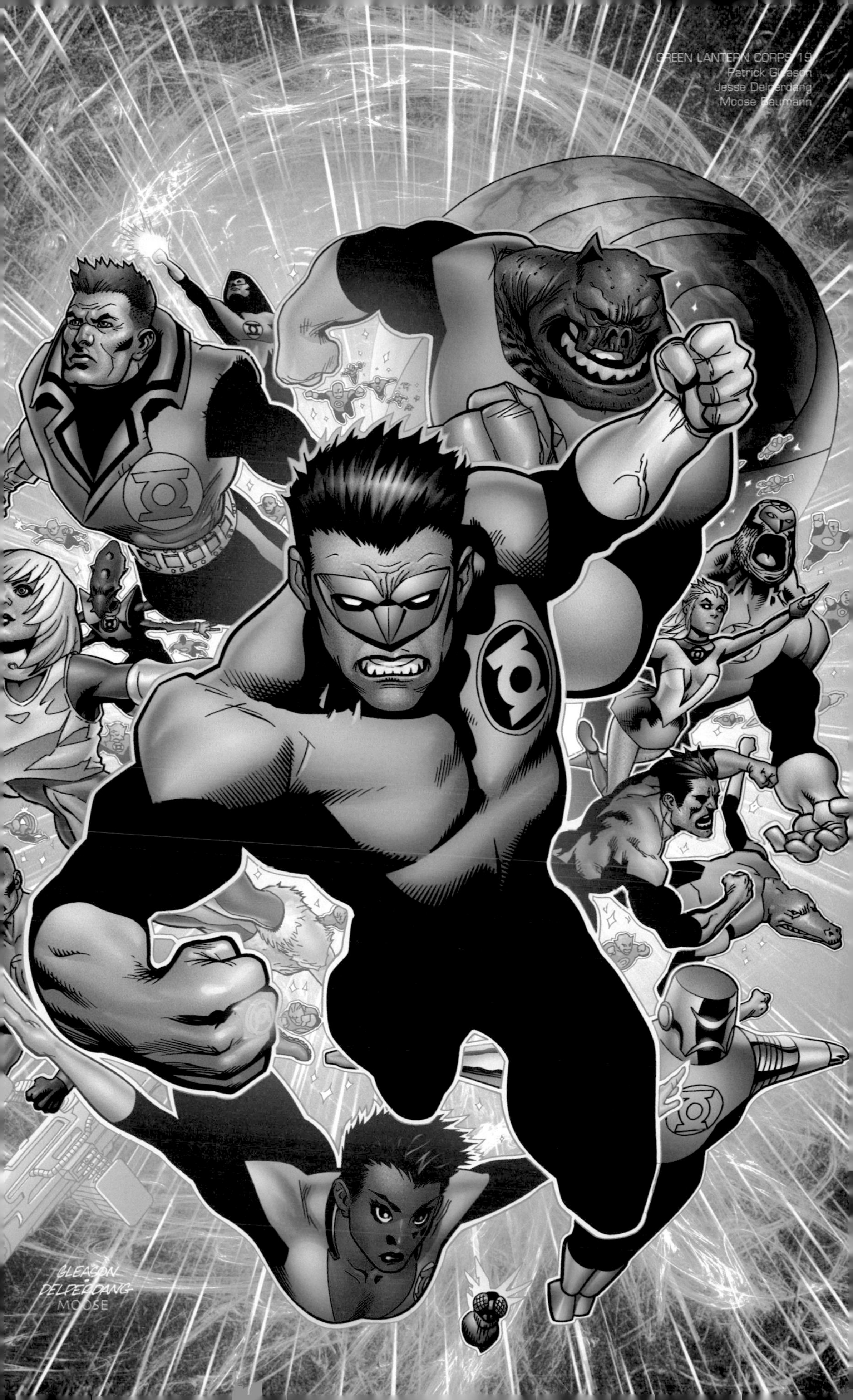
GLEASON
DELPERDANG
MOOSE

GREEN LANTERN CORPS 19
Patrick Gleason
Jesse Delperdang
Moose Baumann

THE SINESTRO CORPS WAR
Epilogue
... LIBERTY'S LIGHT!
Writer: **Peter J. Tomasi**
Penciller: **Patrick Gleason**
Inkers: **Prentis Rollins, Derek Fridolfs, Tom Nguyen, Drew Geraci, Dan Davis** and **Rebecca Buchman**
Colorists: **David Curiel, JD Smith** and **Guy Major**

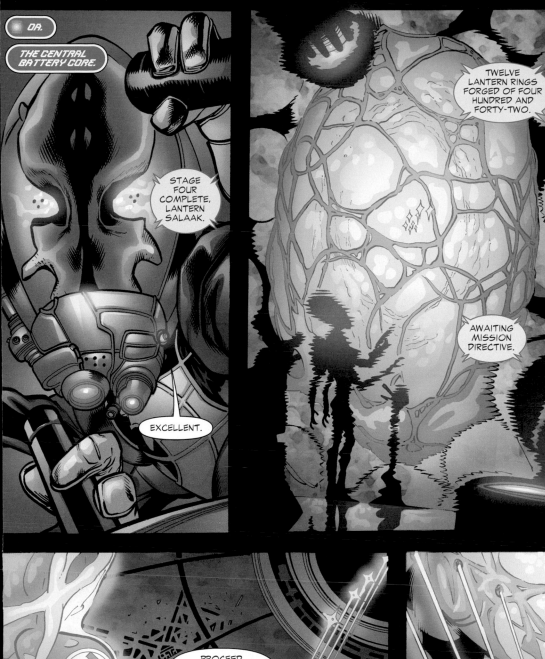

OA.

THE CENTRAL BATTERY CORE.

STAGE FOUR COMPLETE, LANTERN SALAAK.

EXCELLENT.

TWELVE LANTERN RINGS FORGED OF FOUR HUNDRED AND FORTY-TWO.

AWAITING MISSION DIRECTIVE.

PROCEED TO MOGO FOR LANTERN ENCRYPTION SIGNATURE.

TOO MANY OF US THIS TIME.

FAR TOO MANY.

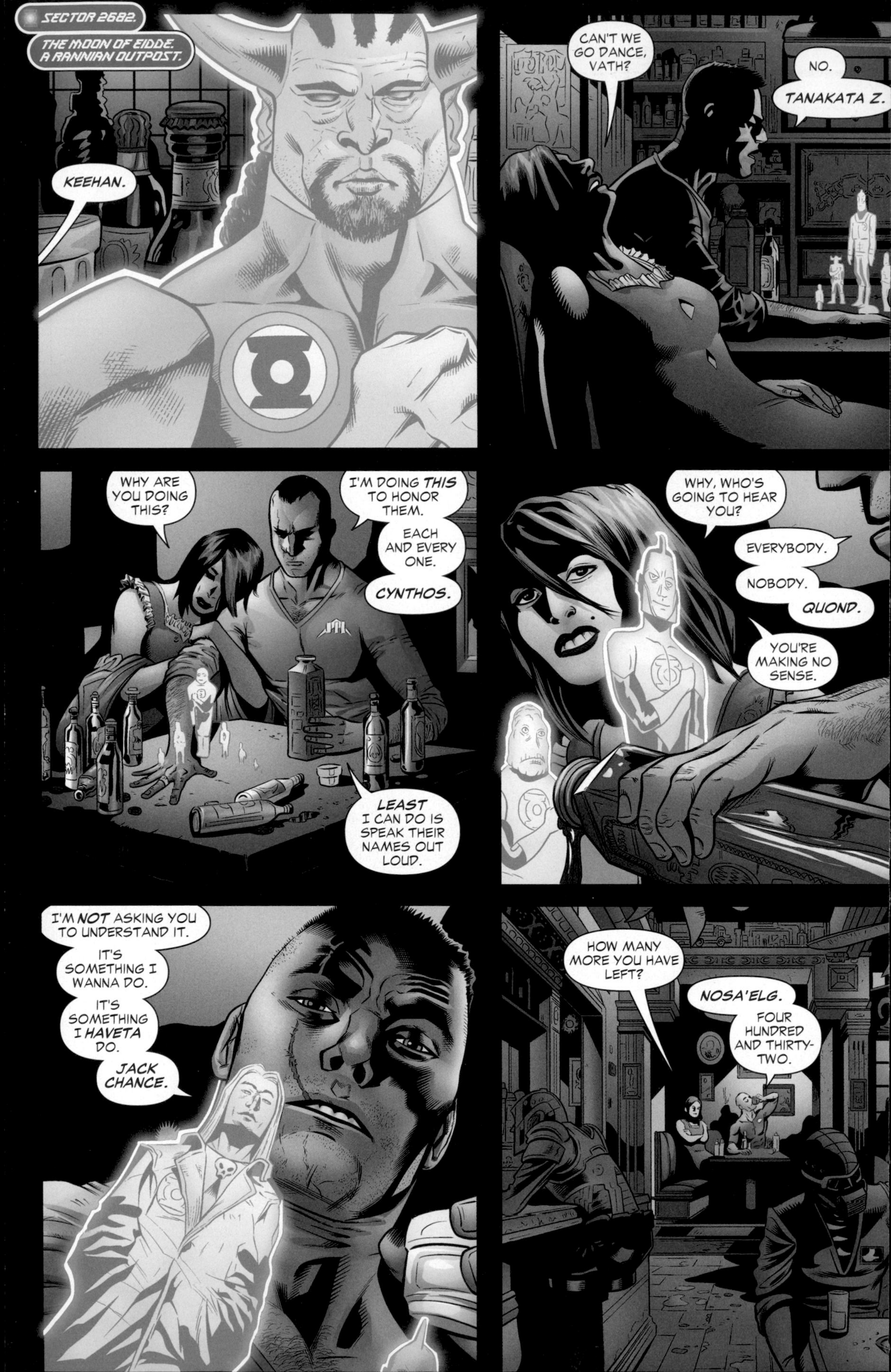
SECTOR 2682.
THE MOON OF EIDDE. A RANNIAN OUTPOST.
KEEHAN.
CAN'T WE GO DANCE, VATH?
NO.
TANAKATA Z.
WHY ARE YOU DOING THIS?
I'M DOING THIS TO HONOR THEM.
EACH AND EVERY ONE.
CYNTHOS.
LEAST I CAN DO IS SPEAK THEIR NAMES OUT LOUD.
WHY, WHO'S GOING TO HEAR YOU?
EVERYBODY.
NOBODY.
QUOND.
YOU'RE MAKING NO SENSE.
I'M NOT ASKING YOU TO UNDERSTAND IT.
IT'S SOMETHING I WANNA DO.
IT'S SOMETHING I HAVETA DO.
JACK CHANCE.
HOW MANY MORE YOU HAVE LEFT?
NOSA'ELG.
FOUR HUNDRED AND THIRTY-TWO.

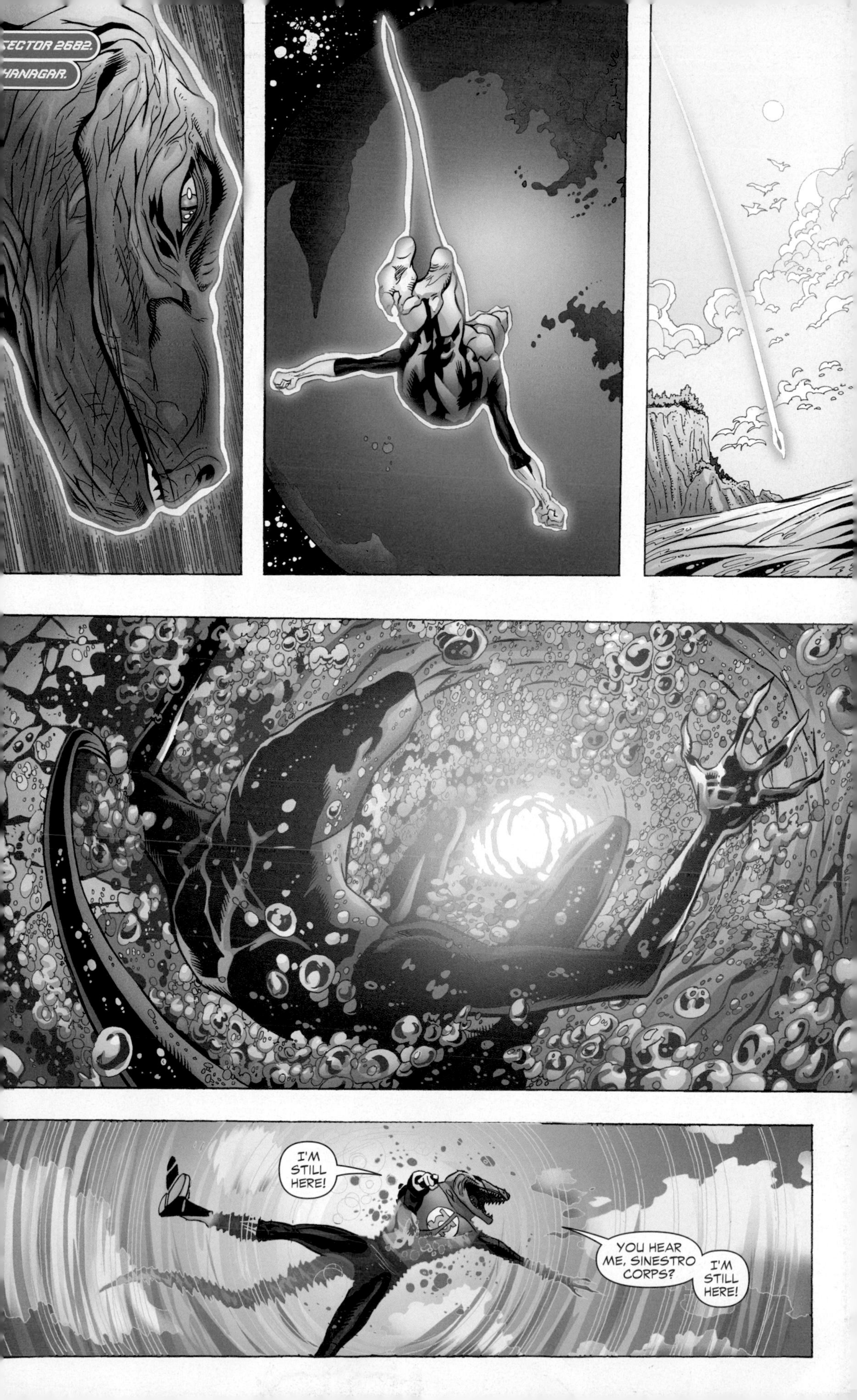

ECTOR 2682.
HANAGAR.
I'M STILL HERE!
YOU HEAR ME, SINESTRO CORPS?
I'M STILL HERE!

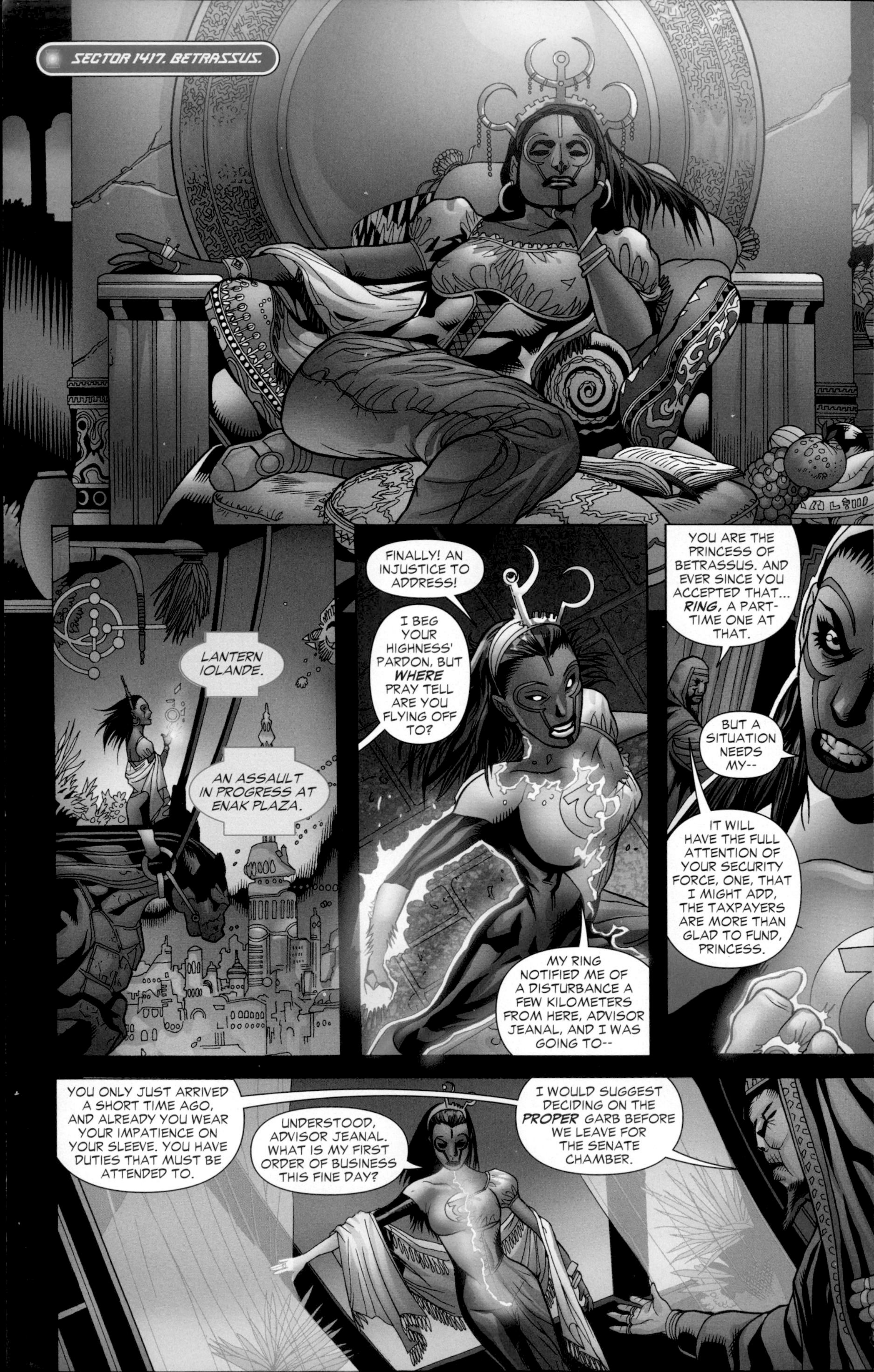
SECTOR 1417. BETRASSUS.
LANTERN IOLANDE.
AN ASSAULT IN PROGRESS AT ENAK PLAZA.
FINALLY! AN INJUSTICE TO ADDRESS!
I BEG YOUR HIGHNESS' PARDON, BUT WHERE PRAY TELL ARE YOU FLYING OFF TO?
MY RING NOTIFIED ME OF A DISTURBANCE A FEW KILOMETERS FROM HERE, ADVISOR JEANAL, AND I WAS GOING TO--
YOU ARE THE PRINCESS OF BETRASSUS. AND EVER SINCE YOU ACCEPTED THAT... RING, A PART-TIME ONE AT THAT.
BUT A SITUATION NEEDS MY--
IT WILL HAVE THE FULL ATTENTION OF YOUR SECURITY FORCE, ONE, THAT I MIGHT ADD, THE TAXPAYERS ARE MORE THAN GLAD TO FUND, PRINCESS.
YOU ONLY JUST ARRIVED A SHORT TIME AGO, AND ALREADY YOU WEAR YOUR IMPATIENCE ON YOUR SLEEVE. YOU HAVE DUTIES THAT MUST BE ATTENDED TO.
UNDERSTOOD, ADVISOR JEANAL. WHAT IS MY FIRST ORDER OF BUSINESS THIS FINE DAY?
I WOULD SUGGEST DECIDING ON THE PROPER GARB BEFORE WE LEAVE FOR THE SENATE CHAMBER.

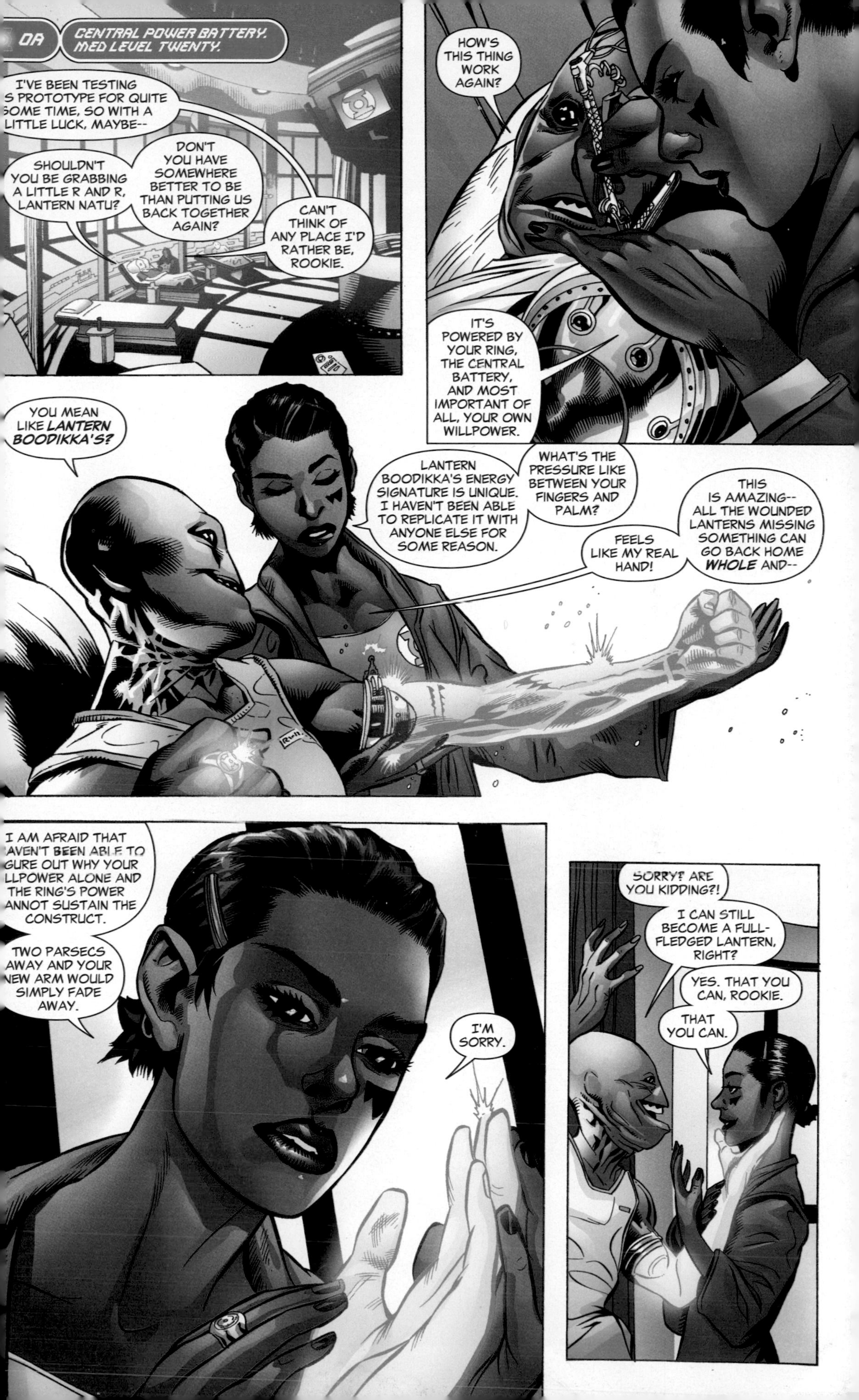
OA
CENTRAL POWER BATTERY. MED LEVEL TWENTY.
I'VE BEEN TESTING S PROTOTYPE FOR QUITE SOME TIME, SO WITH A LITTLE LUCK, MAYBE--
SHOULDN'T YOU BE GRABBING A LITTLE R AND R, LANTERN NATU?
DON'T YOU HAVE SOMEWHERE BETTER TO BE THAN PUTTING US BACK TOGETHER AGAIN?
CAN'T THINK OF ANY PLACE I'D RATHER BE, ROOKIE.
HOW'S THIS THING WORK AGAIN?
IT'S POWERED BY YOUR RING, THE CENTRAL BATTERY, AND MOST IMPORTANT OF ALL, YOUR OWN WILLPOWER.
YOU MEAN LIKE LANTERN BOODIKKA'S?
LANTERN BOODIKKA'S ENERGY SIGNATURE IS UNIQUE. I HAVEN'T BEEN ABLE TO REPLICATE IT WITH ANYONE ELSE FOR SOME REASON.
WHAT'S THE PRESSURE LIKE BETWEEN YOUR FINGERS AND PALM?
FEELS LIKE MY REAL HAND!
THIS IS AMAZING-- ALL THE WOUNDED LANTERNS MISSING SOMETHING CAN GO BACK HOME WHOLE AND--
I AM AFRAID THAT AVEN'T BEEN ABLE TO GURE OUT WHY YOUR LLPOWER ALONE AND THE RING'S POWER ANNOT SUSTAIN THE CONSTRUCT.
TWO PARSECS AWAY AND YOUR NEW ARM WOULD SIMPLY FADE AWAY.
I'M SORRY.
SORRY? ARE YOU KIDDING?!
I CAN STILL BECOME A FULL-FLEDGED LANTERN, RIGHT?
YES. THAT YOU CAN, ROOKIE.
THAT YOU CAN.

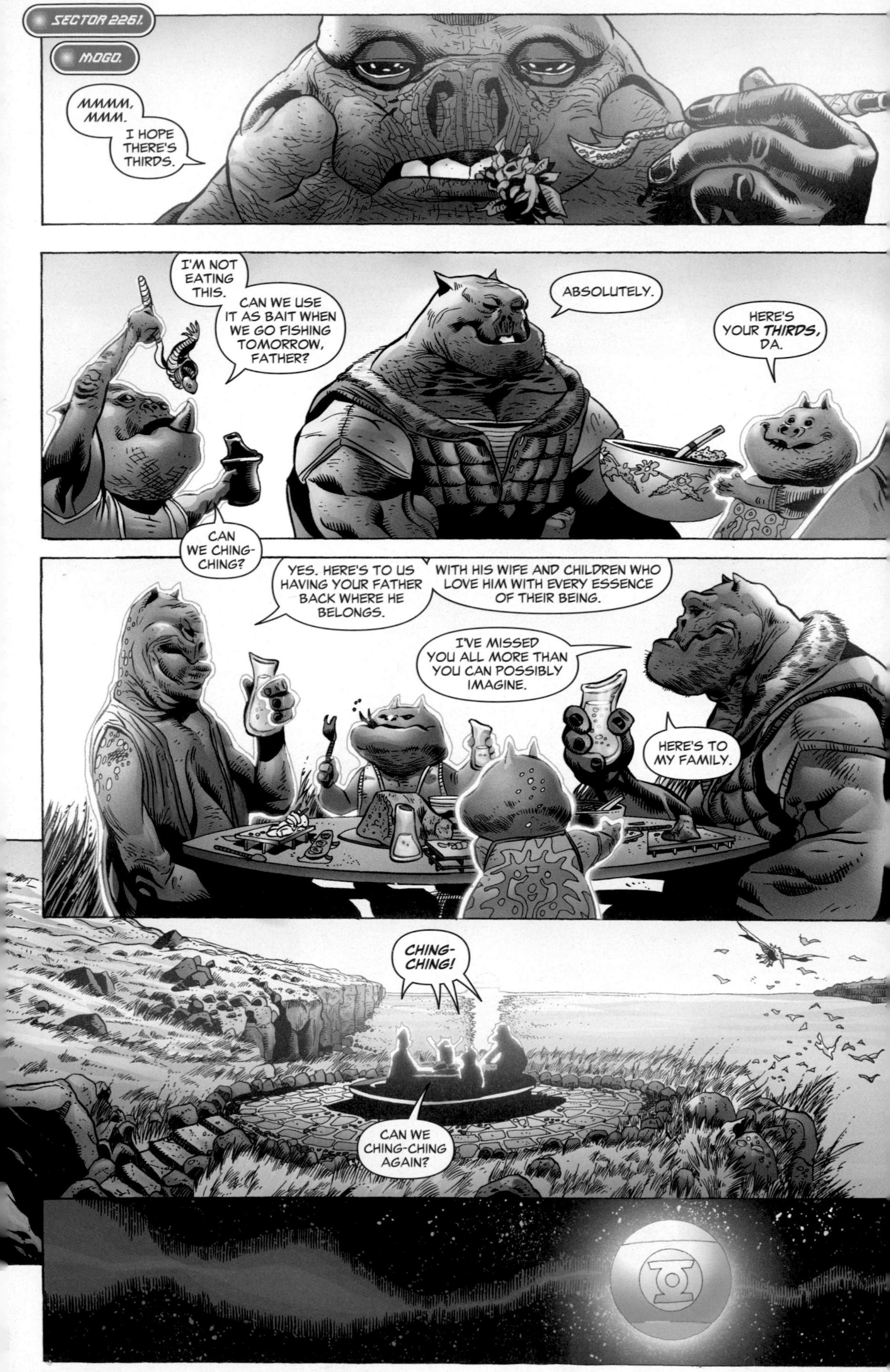
SECTOR 2261.
MOGO.
MMMM, MMM.
I HOPE THERE'S THIRDS.
I'M NOT EATING THIS.
CAN WE USE IT AS BAIT WHEN WE GO FISHING TOMORROW, FATHER?
ABSOLUTELY.
HERE'S YOUR THIRDS, DA.
CAN WE CHING-CHING?
YES. HERE'S TO US HAVING YOUR FATHER BACK WHERE HE BELONGS.
WITH HIS WIFE AND CHILDREN WHO LOVE HIM WITH EVERY ESSENCE OF THEIR BEING.
I'VE MISSED YOU ALL MORE THAN YOU CAN POSSIBLY IMAGINE.
HERE'S TO MY FAMILY.
CHING-CHING!
CAN WE CHING-CHING AGAIN?

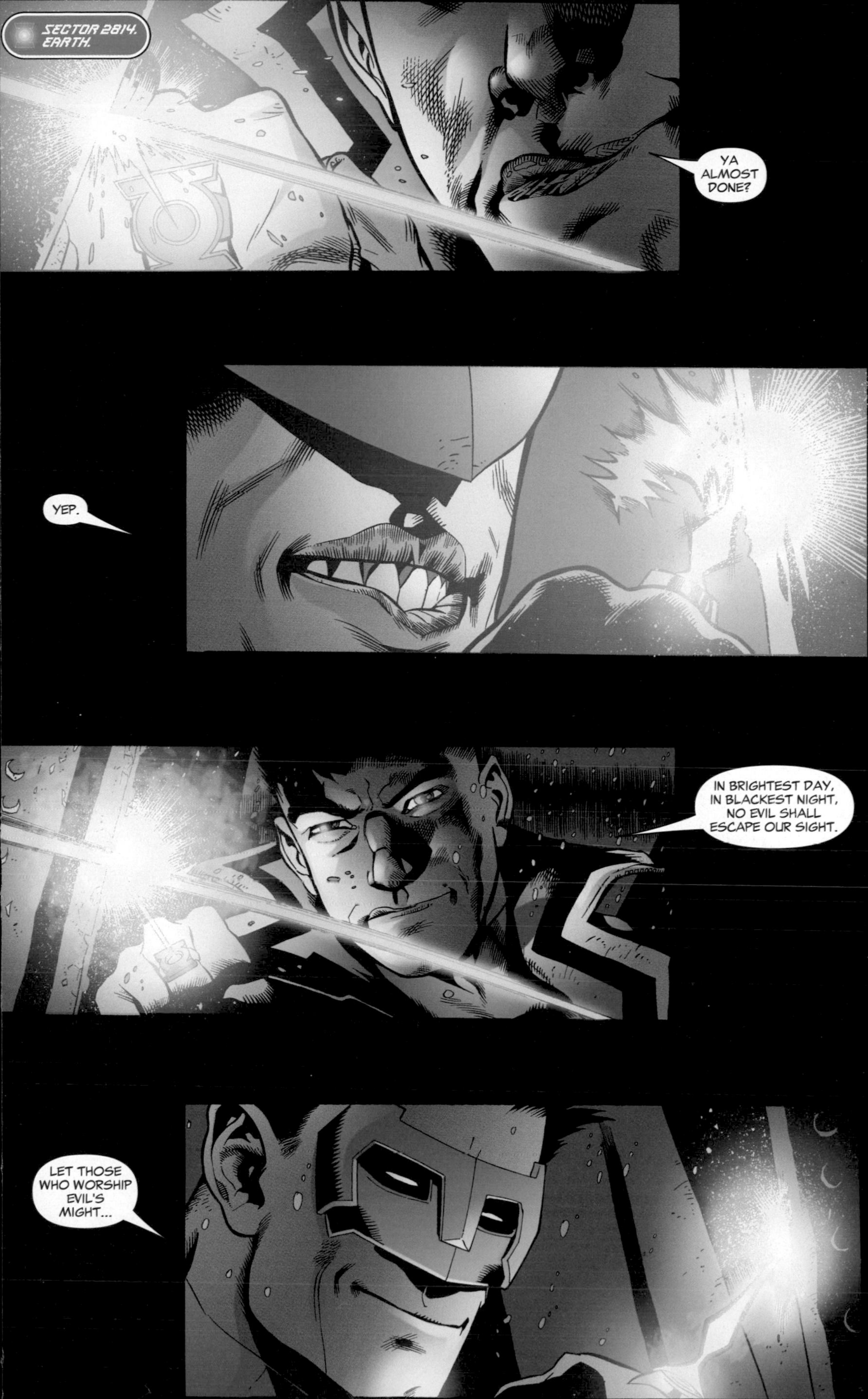
SECTOR 2814. EARTH.
YA ALMOST DONE?
YEP.
IN BRIGHTEST DAY, IN BLACKEST NIGHT, NO EVIL SHALL ESCAPE OUR SIGHT.
LET THOSE WHO WORSHIP EVIL'S MIGHT...

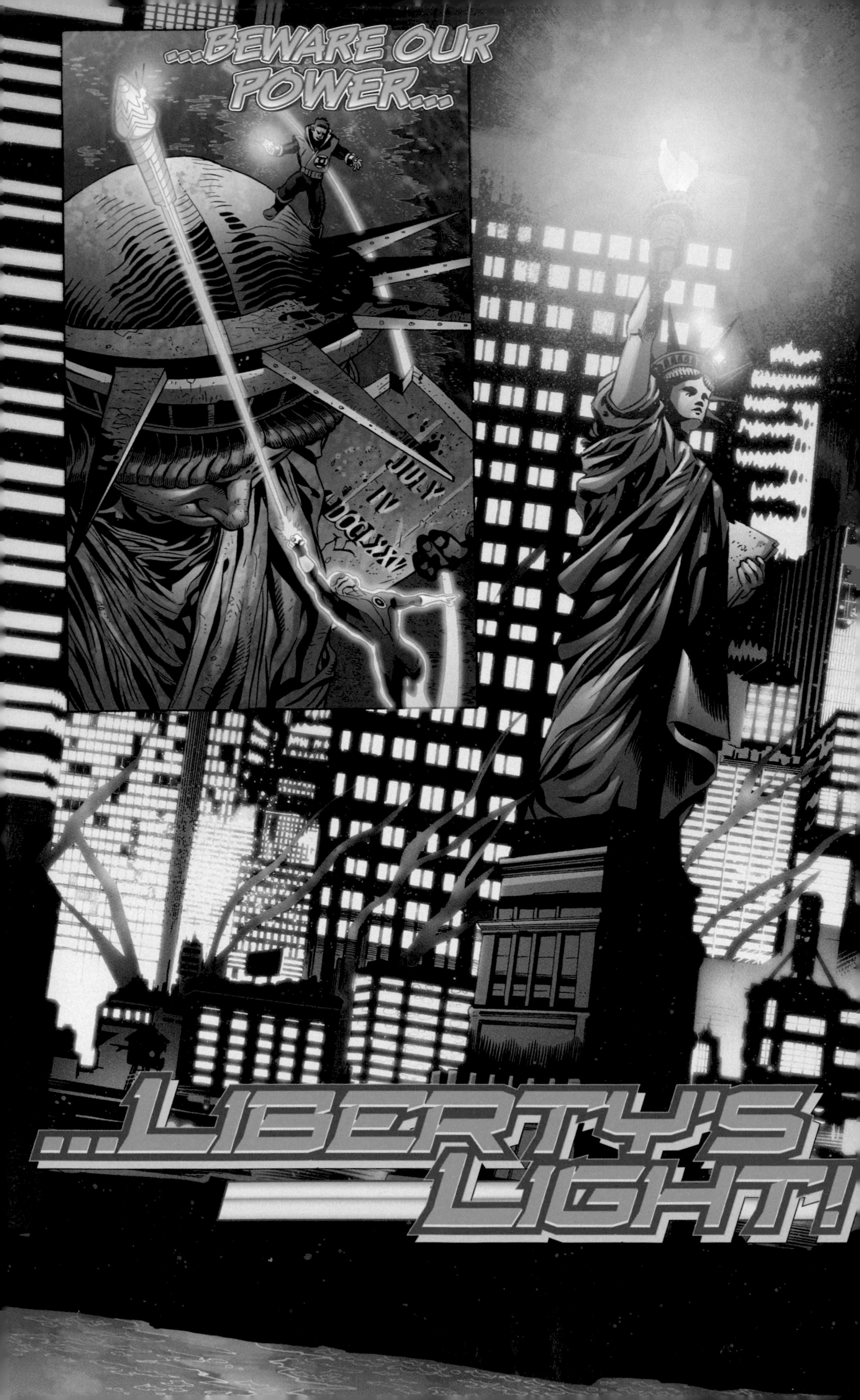
...BEWARE OUR POWER...
JULY IV MDCCLXXVI
...LIBERTY'S LIGHT!

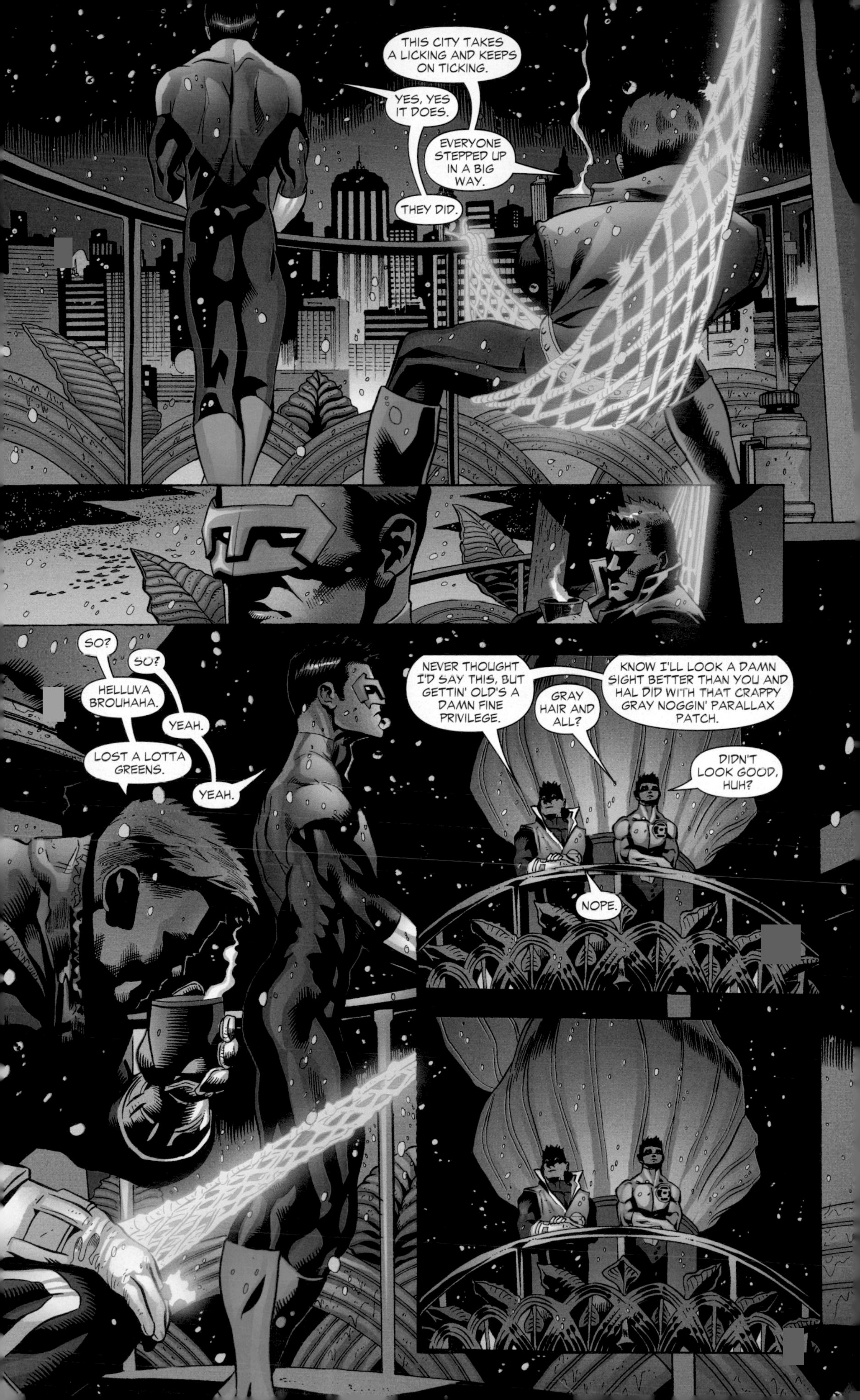
THIS CITY TAKES A LICKING AND KEEPS ON TICKING.
YES, YES IT DOES.
EVERYONE STEPPED UP IN A BIG WAY.
THEY DID.
SO?
SO?
HELLUVA BROUHAHA.
YEAH.
LOST A LOTTA GREENS.
YEAH.
NEVER THOUGHT I'D SAY THIS, BUT GETTIN' OLD'S A DAMN FINE PRIVILEGE.
GRAY HAIR AND ALL?
KNOW I'LL LOOK A DAMN SIGHT BETTER THAN YOU AND HAL DID WITH THAT CRAPPY GRAY NOGGIN' PARALLAX PATCH.
DIDN'T LOOK GOOD, HUH?
NOPE.

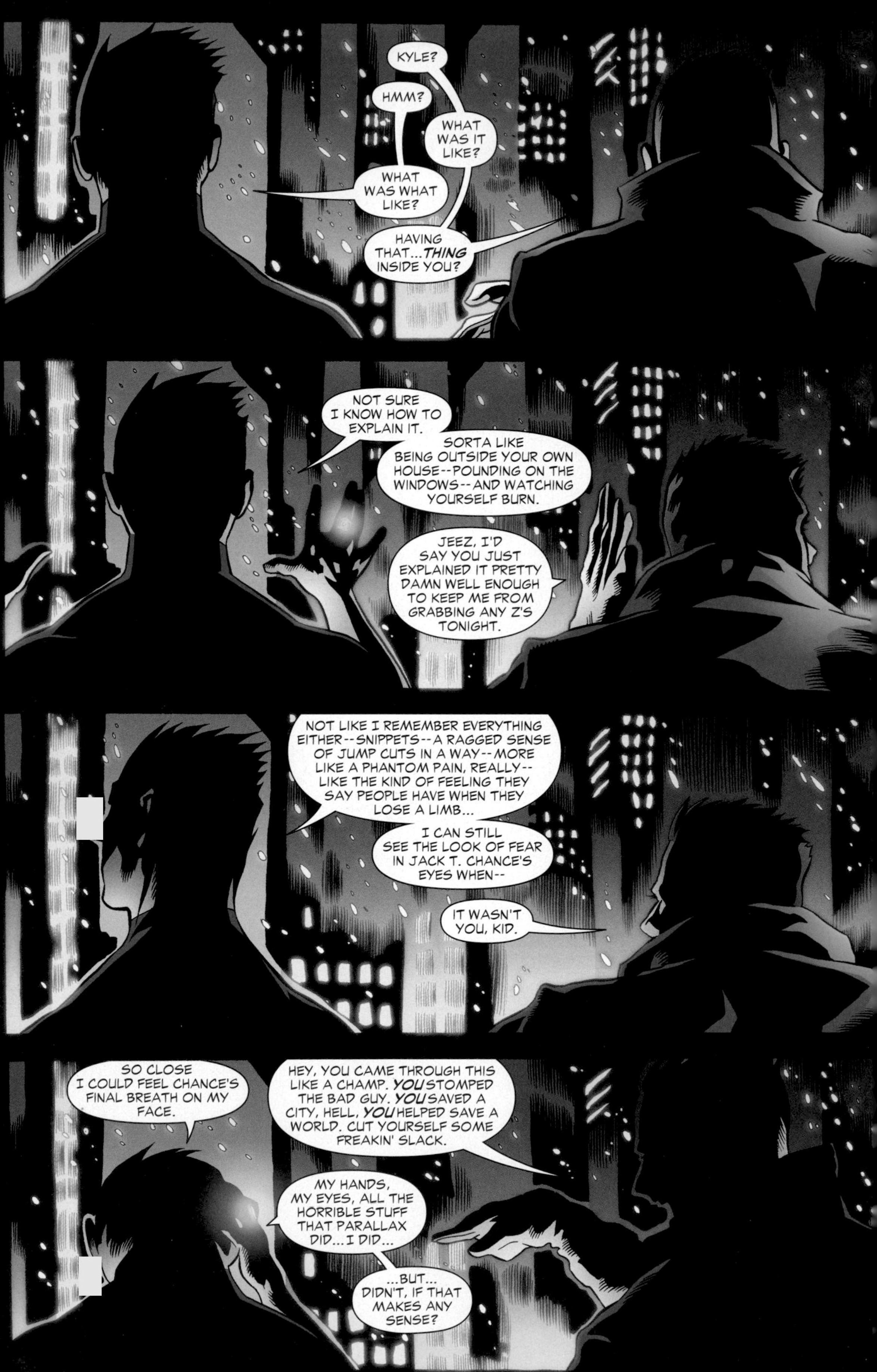
KYLE?
HMM?
WHAT WAS IT LIKE?
WHAT WAS WHAT LIKE?
HAVING THAT...*THING* INSIDE YOU?
NOT SURE I KNOW HOW TO EXPLAIN IT.
SORTA LIKE BEING OUTSIDE YOUR OWN HOUSE--POUNDING ON THE WINDOWS--AND WATCHING YOURSELF BURN.
JEEZ, I'D SAY YOU JUST EXPLAINED IT PRETTY DAMN WELL ENOUGH TO KEEP ME FROM GRABBING ANY Z'S TONIGHT.
NOT LIKE I REMEMBER EVERYTHING EITHER--SNIPPETS--A RAGGED SENSE OF JUMP CUTS IN A WAY--MORE LIKE A PHANTOM PAIN, REALLY--LIKE THE KIND OF FEELING THEY SAY PEOPLE HAVE WHEN THEY LOSE A LIMB...
I CAN STILL SEE THE LOOK OF FEAR IN JACK T. CHANCE'S EYES WHEN--
IT WASN'T YOU, KID.
SO CLOSE I COULD FEEL CHANCE'S FINAL BREATH ON MY FACE.
HEY, YOU CAME THROUGH THIS LIKE A CHAMP. *YOU* STOMPED THE BAD GUY. *YOU* SAVED A CITY, HELL, *YOU* HELPED SAVE A WORLD. CUT YOURSELF SOME FREAKIN' SLACK.
MY HANDS, MY EYES, ALL THE HORRIBLE STUFF THAT PARALLAX DID...I DID...
...BUT... DIDN'T, IF THAT MAKES ANY SENSE?

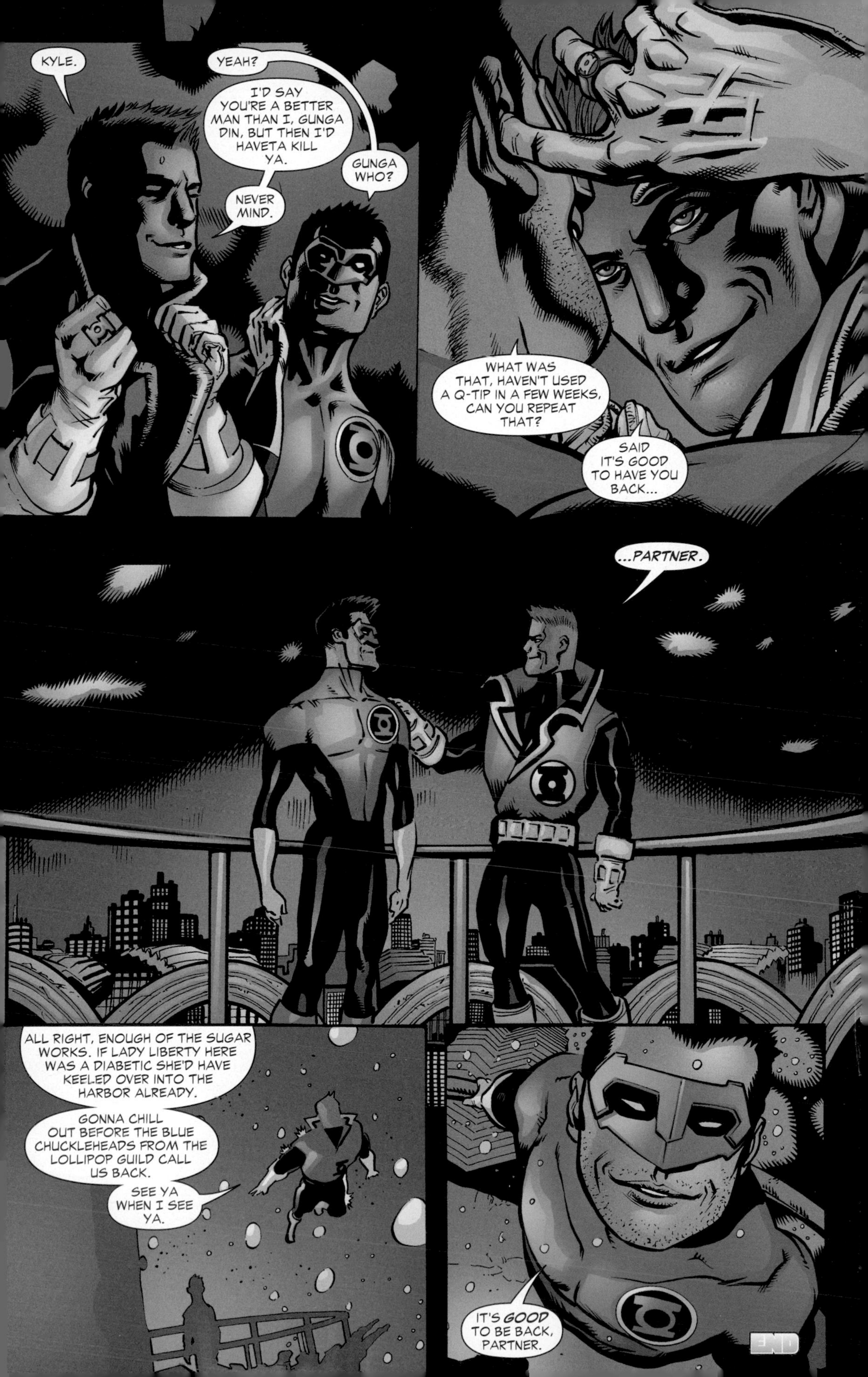
KYLE.
YEAH?
I'D SAY YOU'RE A BETTER MAN THAN I, GUNGA DIN, BUT THEN I'D HAVETA KILL YA.
GUNGA WHO?
NEVER MIND.
WHAT WAS THAT, HAVEN'T USED A Q-TIP IN A FEW WEEKS, CAN YOU REPEAT THAT?
SAID IT'S GOOD TO HAVE YOU BACK...
...PARTNER.
ALL RIGHT, ENOUGH OF THE SUGAR WORKS. IF LADY LIBERTY HERE WAS A DIABETIC SHE'D HAVE KEELED OVER INTO THE HARBOR ALREADY.
GONNA CHILL OUT BEFORE THE BLUE CHUCKLEHEADS FROM THE LOLLIPOP GUILD CALL US BACK.
SEE YA WHEN I SEE YA.
IT'S GOOD TO BE BACK, PARTNER.
END

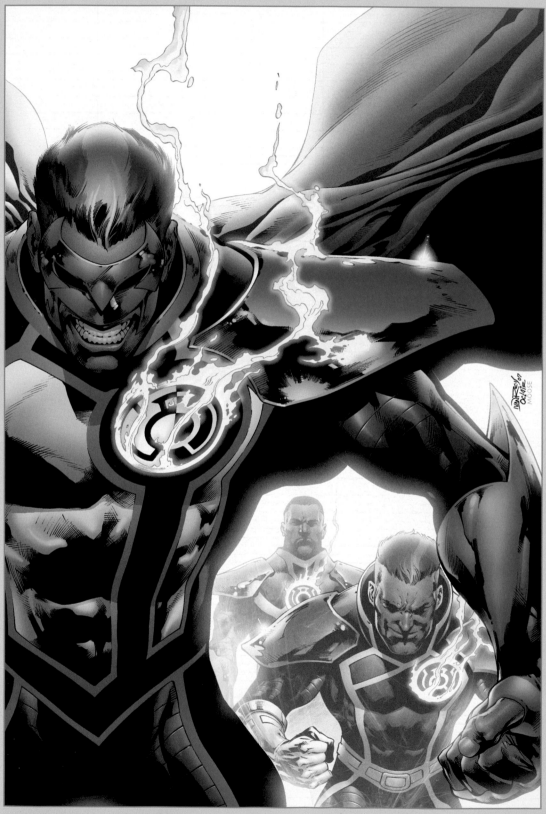

Once upon a time, John and Guy also joined Kyle as Parallax.
Art: Ivan Reis/Oclair Albert

Geoff Johns, Dave Gibbons, Ethan Van Sciver, Ivan Reis, Pat Gleason and the original editors of the series, Peter Tomasi, Adam Schlagman and Eddie Berganza, recall what went into the making of one of the greatest battles the Green Lantern Corps has ever fought.

EDDIE: I wasn't even the editor on the book when Geoff told me his battle plans. As a Green Lantern fan I was excited about hearing all about it, especially the notion of Kyle Rayner becoming a new Parallax. So, how did the War begin? It's been said to be the most obvious idea, yet no one had ever done it. What made you think of it?

PETER: I believe it simply initiated from the idea of wanting to do something big, something to really push the scope of the GL mythos into a whole other strato-sphere — that would not only get us excited, but also garner reader and retailer interest.

GEOFF: I'd already come up with and introduced the emotional electromagnetic spectrum – the idea that emotions can be harnessed as power — in GREEN LANTERN: REBIRTH with Parallax and the yellow impurity being absolute fear. I wanted to expand on that, and my goal had been to build to the return of Sinestro. And I came up with the idea that Sinestro would be forming his own Corps. That the reader would see it build slowly like lighting a fuse to a bomb. I went on to name it the "Sinestro" Corps because that's exactly what Sinestro would call it. He's really driven by his perception of justice, ego and revenge. In another life, his sense of right might've been strong enough to overpower the taint of his arrogance and vengeance, but not this one.

EDDIE: Why did you open with the JLA, who Hal refuses help from and then later needs?

From a design by Ivan Reis, Ethan Van Sciver was eager to try his hand at Kilowog's opposite number, Arkillo.
Art: Ethan Van Sciver

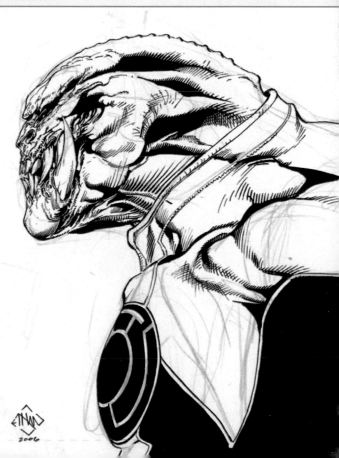

GEOFF: For several reasons. One was to put Hal Jordan and the Green Lanterns in context with the rest of the DC Universe. I wanted Hal to fly off and say, "This is Green Lantern business now. We'll handle it." And throw the reader off the trail that the war was all going to point back to Earth. I wanted the readers to get comfortable, as much as they could, with the idea that we were going to be bat-tling it out in space. Then when we returned to Earth it was a shock.

EDDIE: Ethan, what was your inspiration for some of the Sinestro Corps members like Arkillo?

ETHAN: Whoa whoa whoa! Arkillo was one of the first Sinestro Corps members, and he was an Ivan Reis design! Ivan gets the nod for creating the perfect anti-Kilowog with Geoff.

EDDIE: Right in issue #10 as a barbarian, so Ivan, how did you and Geoff come up with him?

IVAN: We needed someone as big as Kilowog, so I did a mirror image of Kilowog. Arkillo has

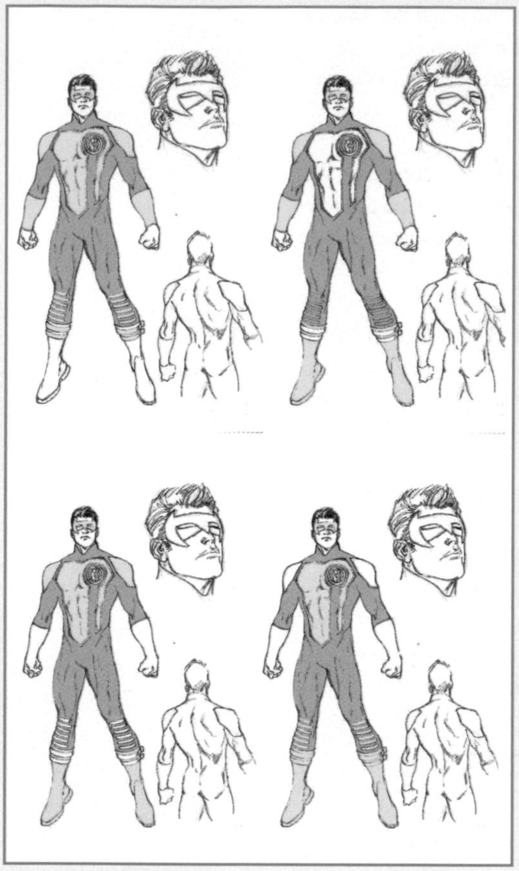

Variations of Kyle's costume.
Art: Ivan Reis

three fingers like Kilowog, his teeth work as Kilowog's mouth. He's really the anti-Kilowog. Arkillo is just more savage, and behaves like a dangerous and violent animal.

EDDIE: He could have had a dog head. Right?

IVAN: I thought that was a secret!

EDDIE: Well, Ivan, explain how in the big splash of Sinestro and his Corps, you draw a dog as a Sinestro Corps member?

IVAN: It was fixed in the finished book…but actually that was a dog I know. It is a really dangerous and crazy dog!

EDDIE: Or Karu-Sil, who is really disturbing?

GEOFF: Karu-Sil was all Ethan in design. I added the twisted "Jungle Book" backstory to her later on, but she's Ethan's nasty child.

ETHAN: Karu-Sil was another one of these ideas that comes from a nightmare I had, or just a little visual cue that appears out of nowhere. And they're always sort of embarrassing to have to describe. I'm always worried that Geoff or my editor won't see it the way I do, which is why it's a good thing I can draw!

I was thinking about a strange, ghostly woman in white

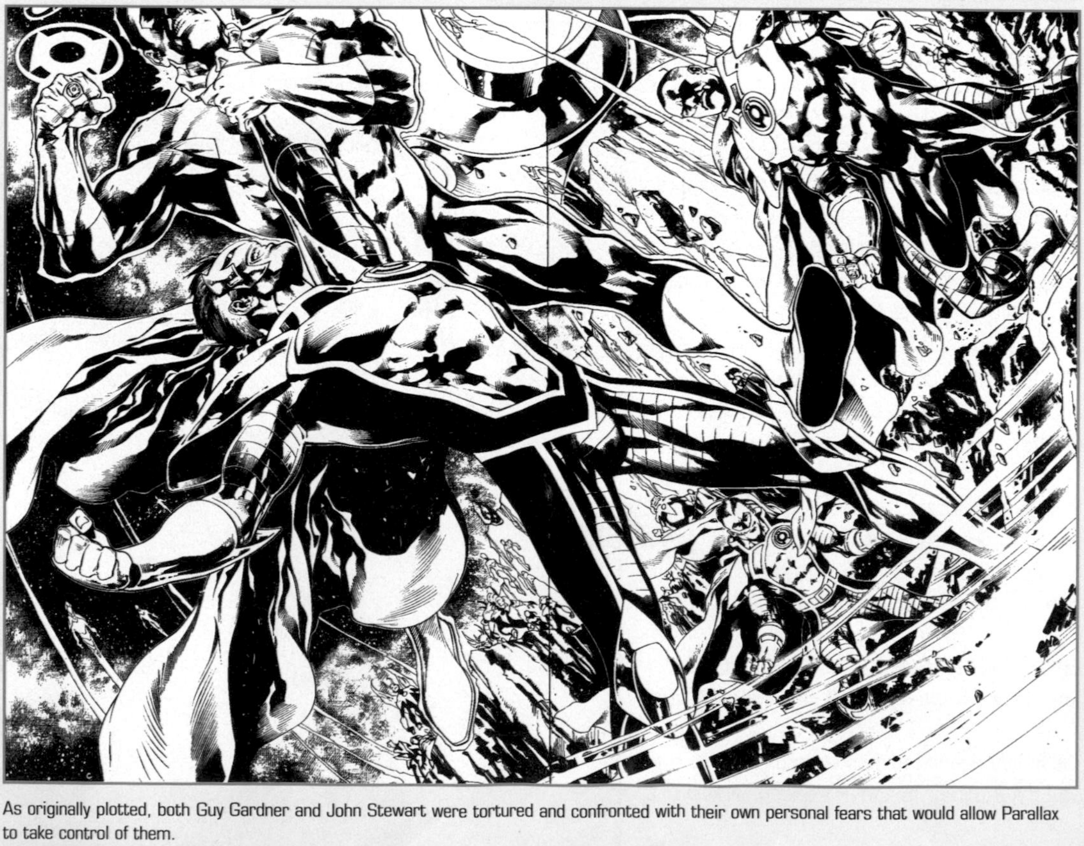

As originally plotted, both Guy Gardner and John Stewart were tortured and confronted with their own personal fears that would allow Parallax to take control of them.
Art: Reis/Albert

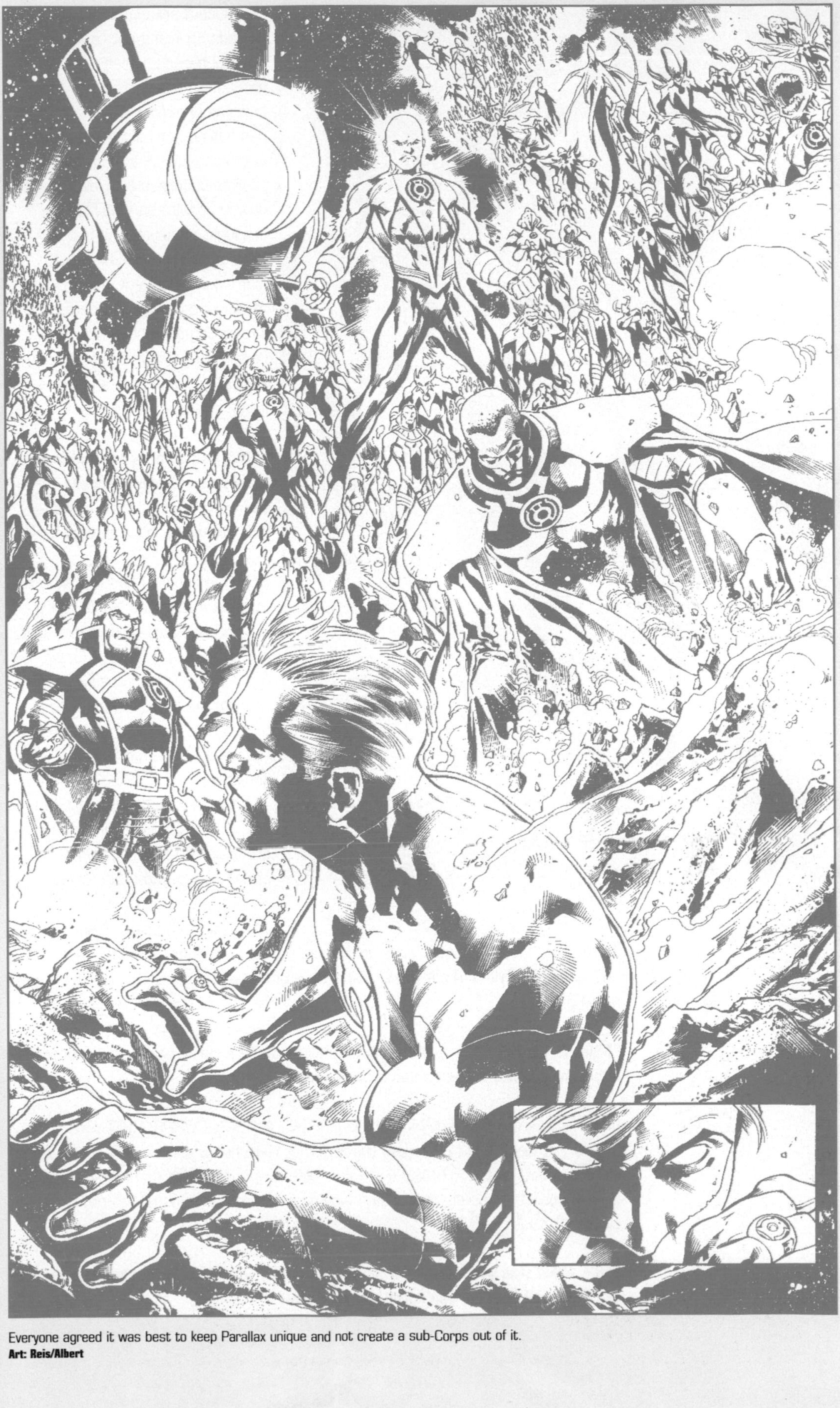

Everyone agreed it was best to keep Parallax unique and not create a sub-Corps out of it.
Art: Reis/Albert

The pencils from this page in the war reveal one of Ivan Reis's fears.
Art: Ivan Reis

translucent silk clothing with long threads stringing out to three skeletal horses, which danced around her like a maypole. Her face would almost always be hidden behind her hair, except for an occasional glimpse of something terrible underneath. Now.... what do you do with an idea like that? I thought about making her a Batman "villain," but even that didn't quite work. A few modifications, and she became an interesting alien character that certainly was capable of inducing fear. I told Geoff that she was a living carousel.

EDDIE: And then my first editorial input was reversing Guy and John becoming infected by Parallax — that changed a lot of things!

GEOFF: Originally I had the idea that Parallax inside Kyle would reach out and temporarily take over Guy and John. But it was too much. It made Parallax less special. When Parallax takes over someone, it should be a big deal. Yes, Eddie, you were finally right about something.

IVAN: I thought Guy and John were great visually for the story, but after hearing Eddie's thoughts about the changes, I realized it was really important to keep Kyle as the only one. It was just stronger to see Parallax as a unique entity taking possession of Kyle and not have it be a case of our waiting to see who will be the next Parallax.

EDDIE: GL Soranik Natu really grew in this arc, and the curse of her ring was really interesting. When did you come up with that?

DAVE: Right from the beginning of the GREEN LANTERN CORPS: RECHARGE miniseries, Geoff and I played on the fact that Natu had a dislike of the Ring. After all, it had been the ring of the archvillain Sinestro, and Katma Tui had died wearing it. This superstitious distrust was a nice contrast to Natu's usual scientific, clinical attitude.

EDDIE: What was your take on Natu and how did it feel to finally get to draw the big bad Sinestro? How did you make him your own?

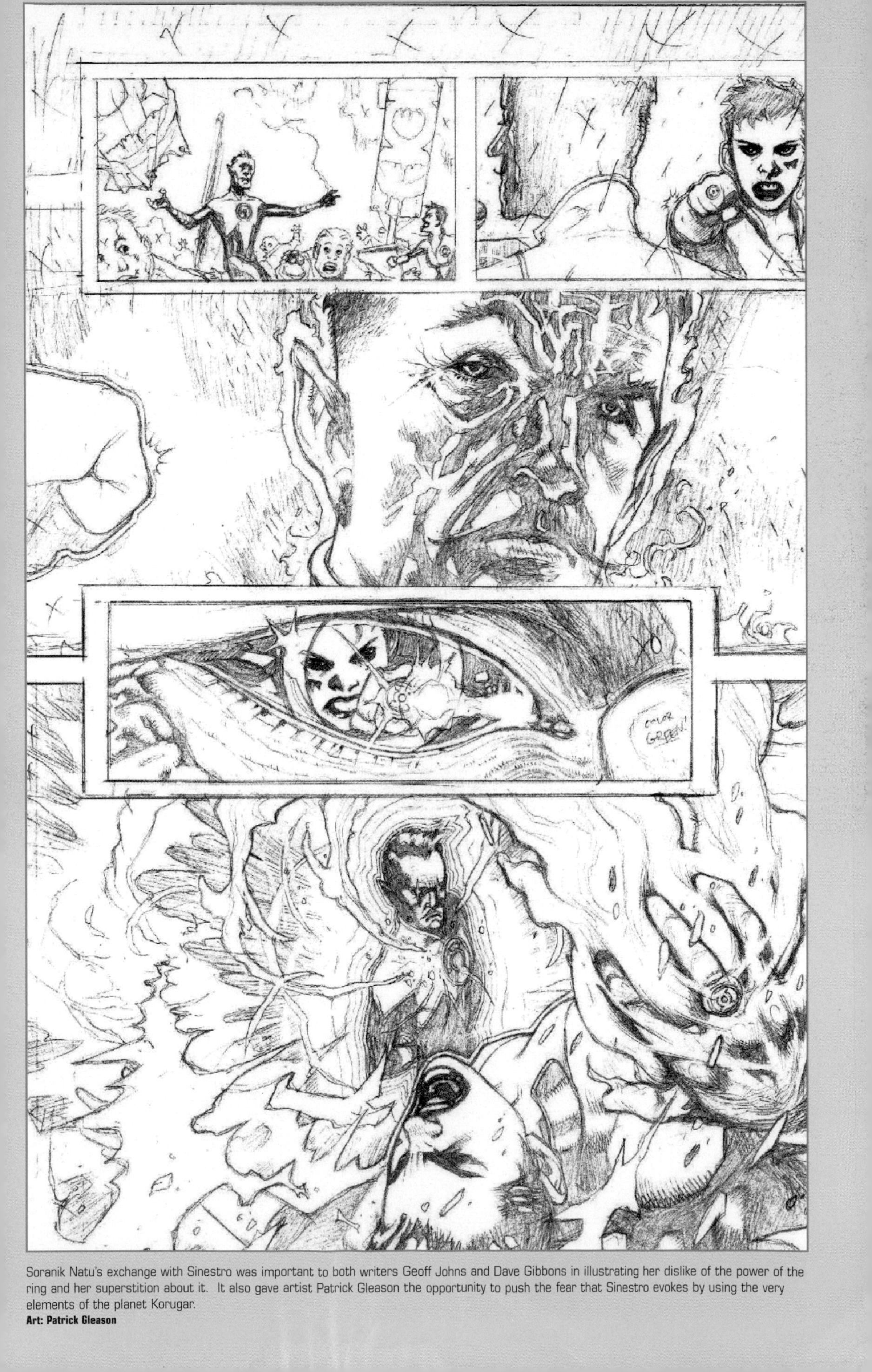
COLOR GREEN!

Soranik Natu's exchange with Sinestro was important to both writers Geoff Johns and Dave Gibbons in illustrating her dislike of the power of the ring and her superstition about it. It also gave artist Patrick Gleason the opportunity to push the fear that Sinestro evokes by using the very elements of the planet Korugar.

Art: Patrick Gleason

PAT: The exchange between Sinestro and Soranik in issue 14 was such an important moment in the war. I really felt these two had to reflect an extreme discomfort in a very intimate way. My take was to just make sure we all felt the weight and horror of what Natu was going through whenever Sinestro opened his mouth or waved his ring around. I remember when I finished the cover to 14, I had Sinestro smiling fiendishly. Pete liked it but he made sure to tell me when I started on the pages, "Don't make him smile, he's not the Joker," which was great direction. Plus, the look that Ethan gave him was just perfect. I just took all of that and set out to depict him as frighteningly as I could. I focused mainly on Sinestro's presence. So I relied heavily on the atmosphere of Korugar with the lightning and rain to set the mood in portraying him more as an icon of tyrannical power and will.

EDDIE: Why did you pick Prime to be part of this?

GEOFF: He was going to be a part from the beginning. Prime tore through the Green Lanterns and the DC Universe in INFINITE CRISIS and then was imprisoned on Oa. Another bomb waiting to go off. And I wanted to stack the deck totally against the Green Lantern Corps. I wanted them to face the most powerful cadre of villains they had in history. So I went as far as I felt I could.

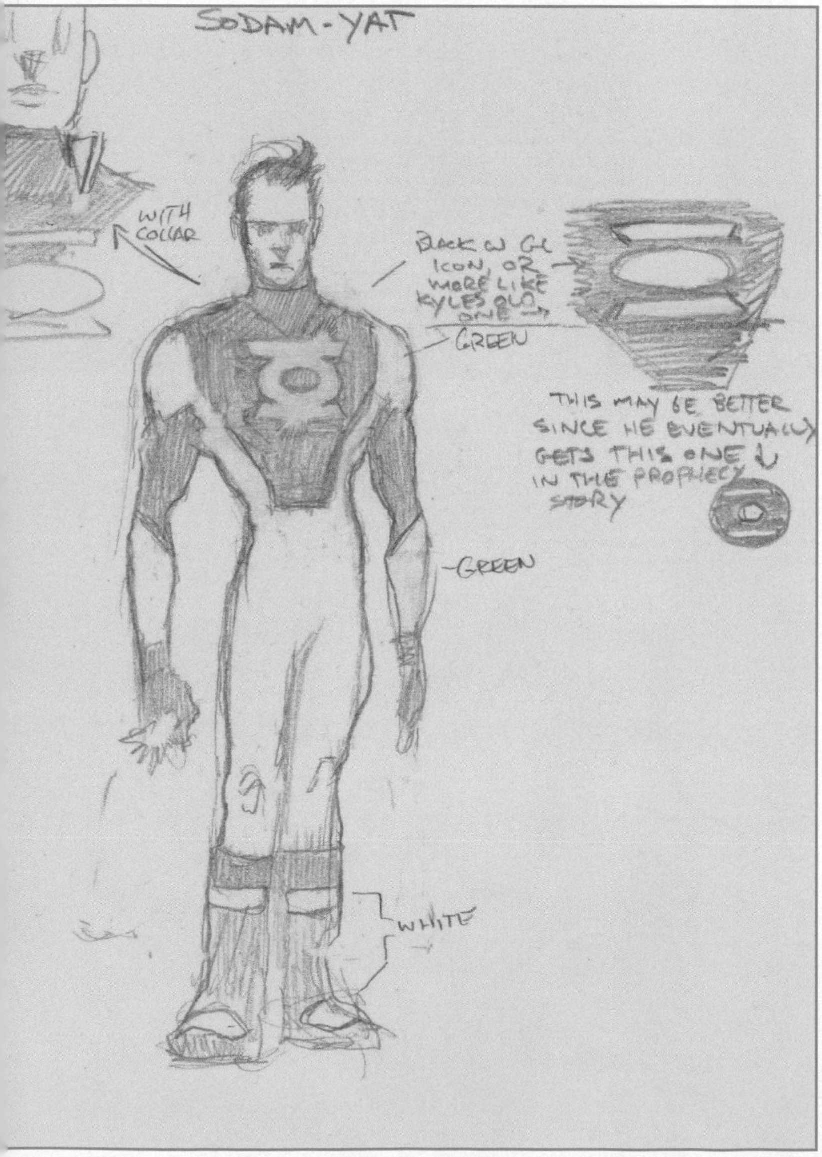
SODAM-YAT
WITH COLLAR
BLACK W GL ICON, OR MORE LIKE KYLES OLD ONE
GREEN
THIS MAY BE BETTER SINCE HE EVENTUALLY GETS THIS ONE IN THE PROPHECY STORY
GREEN
WHITE

Sodam Yat became another important piece of the war as writer Alan Moore had prophesied long ago.
Art: Patrick Gleason

EDDIE: Why did you pick Jack T. Chance to die? And then Ke'haan?

GEOFF: I felt it was important for both Kyle as Parallax and the Anti-Monitor to hit the Corps where it hurts. Although there are many casualties, these mean something. For Kyle, he now has the experience Hal did when he lost control and someone died. I wanted to continue to build that brotherly bond between Hal and Kyle. I believe the friendship and relationship between those two is vital to the Green Lantern Corps in spirit. Jack T. Chance was chosen because, quite honestly, he was Guy Gardner-lite. He had the same attitude as Lobo and a lot of those other '90s characters. I felt he was one that we could lose and be all right about. Ke'haan was a whole other thing. I loved Ke'haan as the leader of the Lost Lanterns. A former trainer like Kilowog. I'd spent a lot of time building him up from his one-panel appearance in EMERALD TWILIGHT and I knew if the leader of the Lost Lanterns went, they'd be directionless. And with the plans coming up after this storyline, pulling them apart would be a lot easier with their leader gone. But seeing them come back together will be worth it.

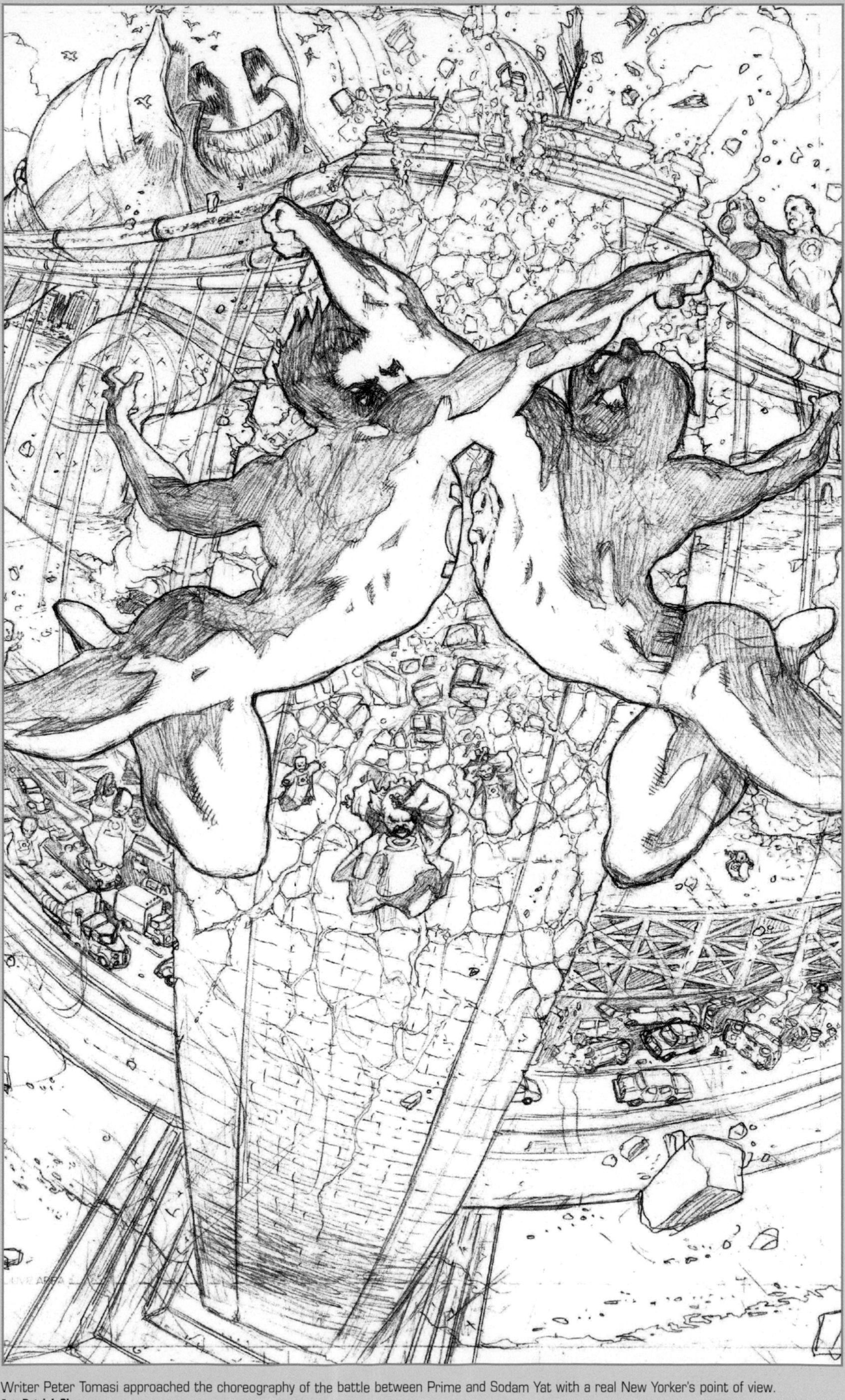

Writer Peter Tomasi approached the choreography of the battle between Prime and Sodam Yat with a real New Yorker's point of view.
Art: Patrick Gleason

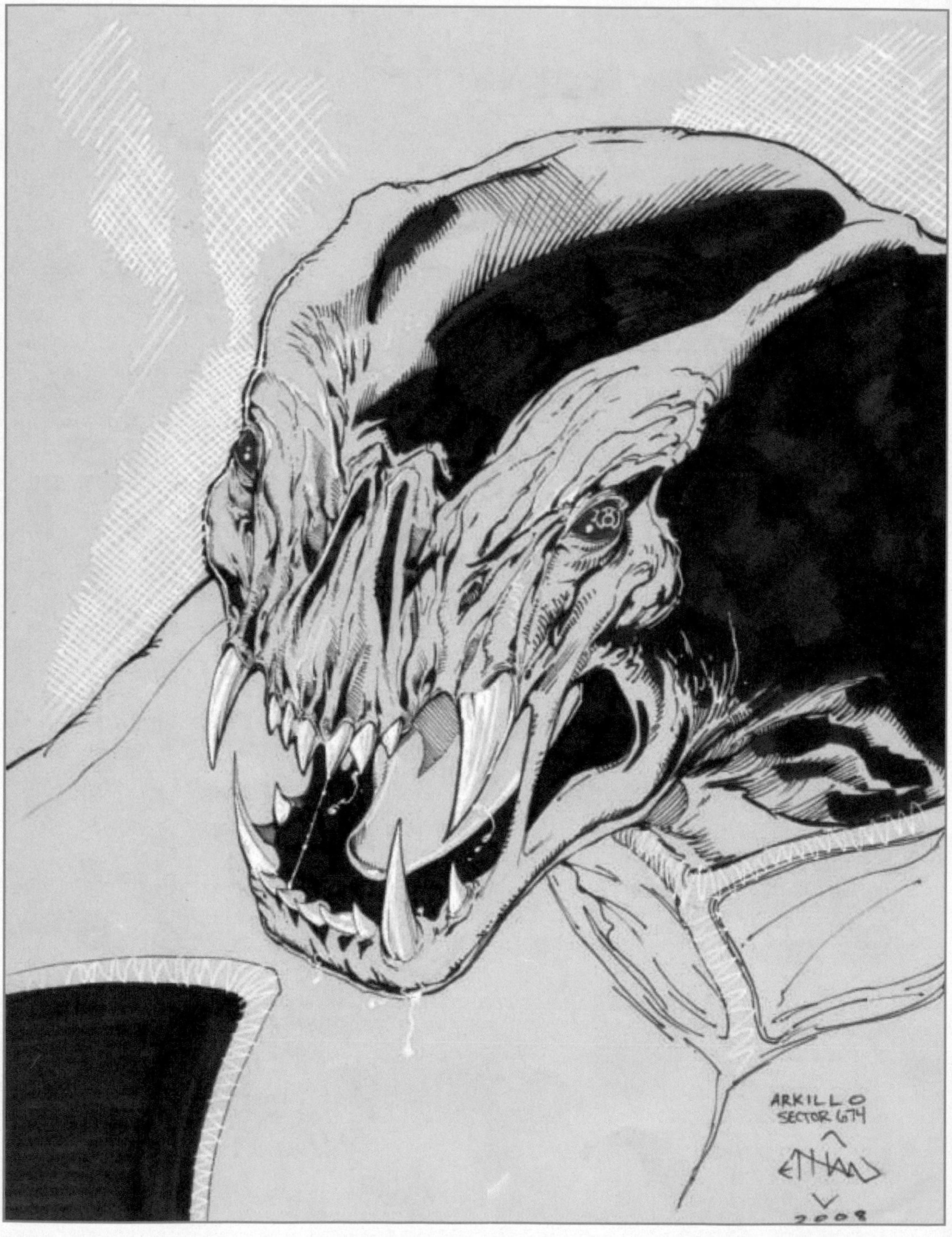
ARKILLO
SECTOR 674
ETHAN
2008

Arkillo is the distorted image of Kilowog (opposite page, top right) and would test the Green Lantern Corps members' submission to the newly enabled Lethal Force law.
Art: Ethan Van Sciver

EDDIE: How did Sodam Yat become such a big part of this? Explain the prophecy.

DAVE: I always loved the Tales of the Green Lantern Corps story where Alan Moore laid out the prophecy that Abin Sur was given, leading to his self-doubt and death and resulting in Hal getting the ring. It seemed something so central to the whole Green Lantern mythos, I felt it deserved investigating further. Sodam Yat, said to be the greatest Green Lantern of all, had presumably been inducted into the Corps like all the others, and I wanted to show how he came to be the greatest.

Kilowog
Art: Ethan Van Sciver

EDDIE: You really like Mogo. Why?

DAVE: Again, it's all Alan Moore's fault! We had great fun doing the original Mogo story together and, at the size of a planet, Mogo certainly stands out as a Green Lantern. Geoff suggested that he might have a spiritual significance for the rest of the Corps, and this really opened up many possibilities.

GEOFF: I wanted Mogo to be like Yoda and Dagobah combined. A place where the trees would part and the landscape would change according to the emotional state of the Lantern making pilgrimage there. I wanted Mogo to be one of the most important elements in the Green Lantern mythos. And that's where the idea of making him the compass for the rings selecting their bearers came from as well.

EDDIE: You like Mogo as well, right, Pat? Why?

PAT: Three words: Easy. To. Draw. Seriously though, I really liked the challenge of depicting him in a scenic way. I tried to do that in a transition starting on the last page of GLC #13. Natu gives Mogo a clean bill of health from the spores that infected him, and there is this beautiful clear bright sky that Moose colored. Then I transitioned to the exact same shot on the third page of issue 15 to lead into the Sinestro invasion. Same sky, only now with Ranx dominating it and a million yellow sparks descending on Stel and Green Man. That kind of thing was fun to try to pull off. ...Did I mention he was easy to draw?

EDDIE: What brought you to the act of creating a Lethal Law?

GEOFF: They're cops. Soldiers. And in reality, lethal force is sometimes the only option. I wanted to put that burden on the Green Lanterns. Give them that power and that right. And treat it a little more seriously. I mean, how many Stormtroopers did Han Solo kill? He shot first! I thought exploring the delicate balance of whether to kill or not would be a great topic for debate. And "death" vs. "life" is really what the core of this epic is to me. From Rebirth to Sinestro Corps to The Blackest Night.

EDDIE: What kept you from using lethal force with every character, Dave?

DAVE: Every Lantern would have a different reaction to being empowered to kill. Kilowog, for instance, was hugely reluctant whereas someone like Isamot, a soldier to his core, welcomed the directive.

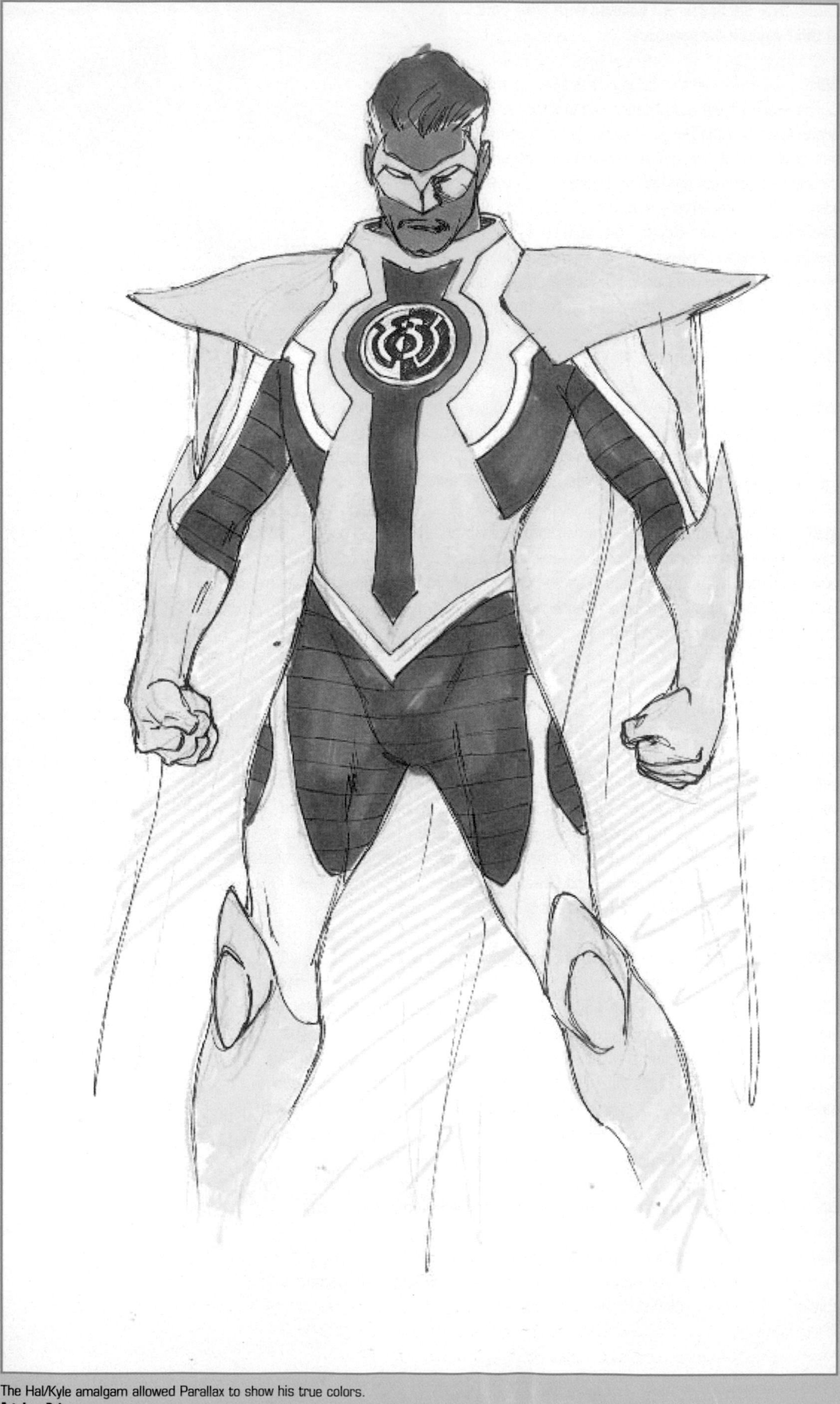

The Hal/Kyle amalgam allowed Parallax to show his true colors.
Art: Ivan Reis

EDDIE: In your art, you went more for the "R" rating when it went for the kills, no? Anything you didn't get to do?

PAT: I just tried to make it ruthlessly clear that this was WAR. Things were forever going to be different in the Corps; I think the violence was supposed to divide the readers just as much as it did the Lanterns. In all honesty, I may have crossed the line a bit in the violence department; I wasn't very subtle. But it is hard to keep yourself in check when it's just some alien getting hacked and blown to pieces. I did try to balance the heavy with the silly. I mean, I filleted a fish lantern for Pete's sake! I had a fly mow down some bad guys with a train! That's just comedy to me.

EDDIE: I liked the fact that we finally got around to giving Parallax a yellow costume.

GEOFF: Yeah, that actually came from a scene in GREEN LANTERN #8 where Hal is caught in a Black Mercy plant and sees a vision of himself fighting with the Corps alongside Sinestro against Parallax. Carlos Pacheco drew Hal as Parallax rather than the "bug." But colored yellow it looked really cool. And, of course, it made sense. Parallax only took the green appearance to mask himself from others. In reality, he was yellow inside. You can see his blood in REBIRTH and SINESTRO CORPS, and it's a deep yellow.

Ivan Reis proves he could conjure up frightening images with his renditions of Parallax.
Art: Ivan Reis

EDDIE: The double-page spread of all the Corps is insane! How did you come up with those designs? What do the different symbols represent?

ETHAN: More subconscious horrible little notions. I thank God for my nightmares. The responsibility for designing the symbols for the new Corps weighed heavily on me. I have to assume that we'll be seeing a lot of them in the future, and they needed to be natural. They needed to seem as though they were always there, and I've only uncovered them after eons of their having been hidden away. Primitive symbols for universal emotions and motivations.

I took from whatever was already there wherever I could, and had to fill in some blanks in other places. What do they mean? Wait and see!

EDDIE: The green lights in all the windows of Coast City was genius. What made you come up with that?

GEOFF: That, to me, was a symbol of Hal finally realizing how contagious bravery can be. When he first came back to Coast City, it was a ghost town. Everyone was afraid. And it was at that moment, when Hal's family and specifically his brother Jim who was everything his mom was — obsessed with safety and living a life according to fear — who almost was too afraid to move back to Coast City — when Jim and his wife stood there and said they believed in Hal and they weren't leaving. No matter what the threat, they weren't leaving. And that carried over to the city. It spread as the lights were lit. It is the single most important

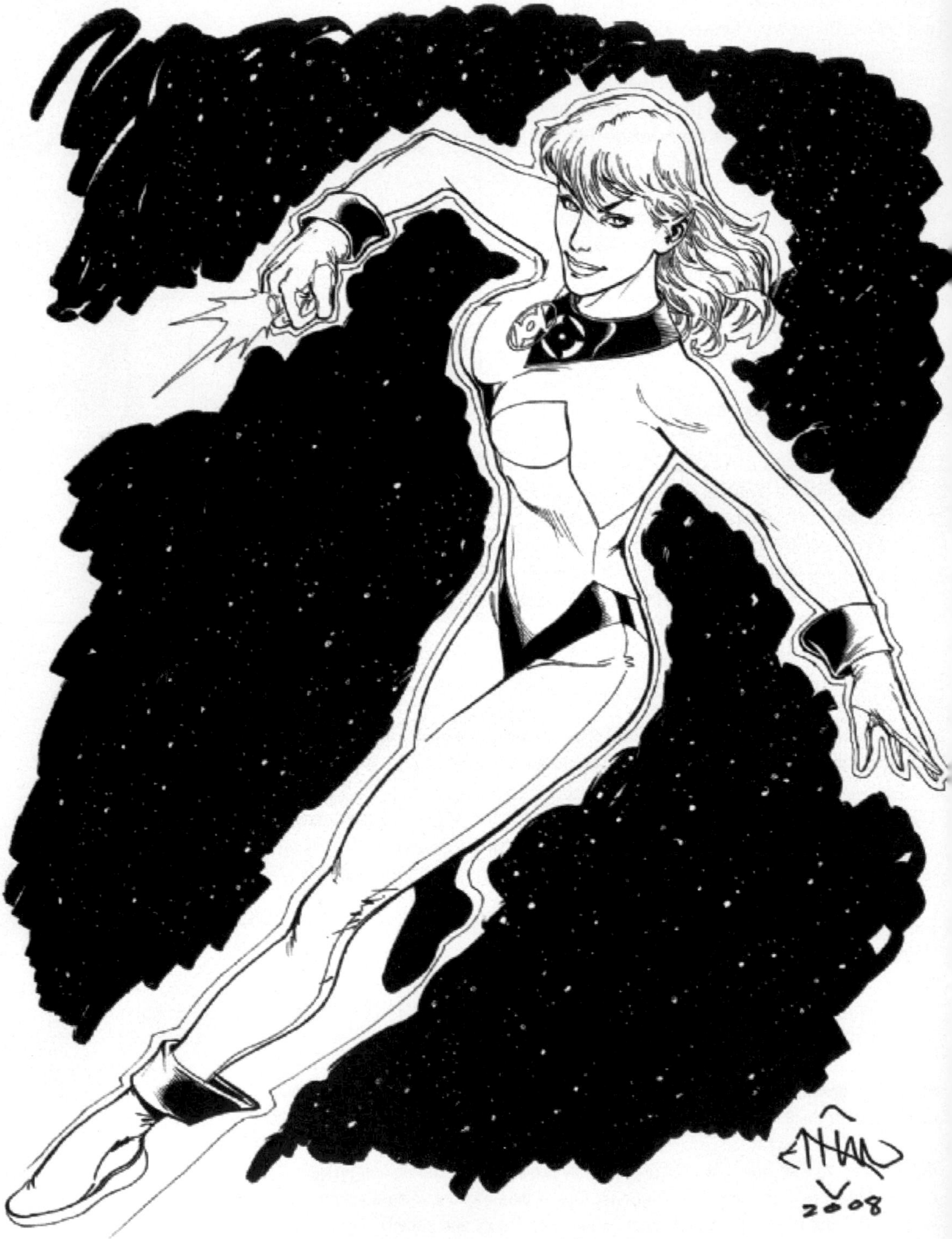

Corps member Arisia's future remains to be determined.
Art: Ethan Van Sciver

moment in this entire storyline to me and to Hal Jordan. In that moment, Coast City became the City Without Fear. And that city and its citizens did what Hal had done for them — they inspired the Green Lantern to believe in victory and to fight on.

EDDIE: There's a very special sound effect that we have when Hal and Kyle confront Sinestro on the rooftops of Coast City that we owe to the Simpsons. Can you explain, Geoff?

GEOFF: That came from the Simpsons Movie, and it was a special request from Dan DiDio. We're both massive Simpsons fans, so when the Comic Book Guy said in the film, "This is the sound of Sinestro battling the Green Lantern!" or something to that effect, Dan was like, "You gotta use it!" So we did.

EDDIE: Prime and Sodam really got to go at it in your first issue, Pete. What was your thinking behind the fight, and why did you pick the places you did for the super-slugfest?

PETER: I thought instead of cutting around to other story elements or characters involved in the War, the best way to do this fight was to keep it focused and centered on the combatants and the combatants alone. No other distractions. Then I realized that even during the course of my editing tenure we had never fleshed out Sodam Yat as a character — there was no real backstory. There was a possible endpoint for the character, of course, in regard to the Alan Moore story, but no

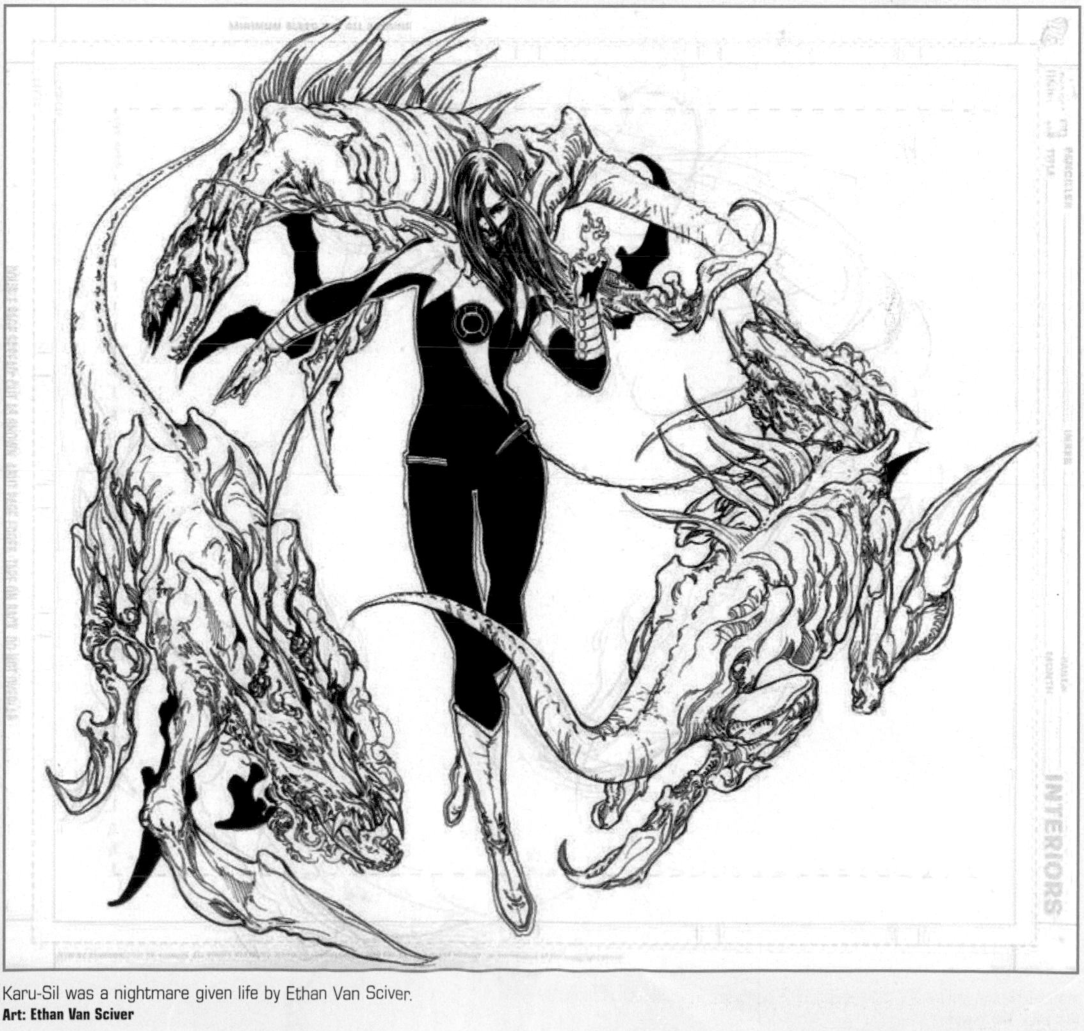
INTERIORS

Karu-Sil was a nightmare given life by Ethan Van Sciver.
Art: Ethan Van Sciver

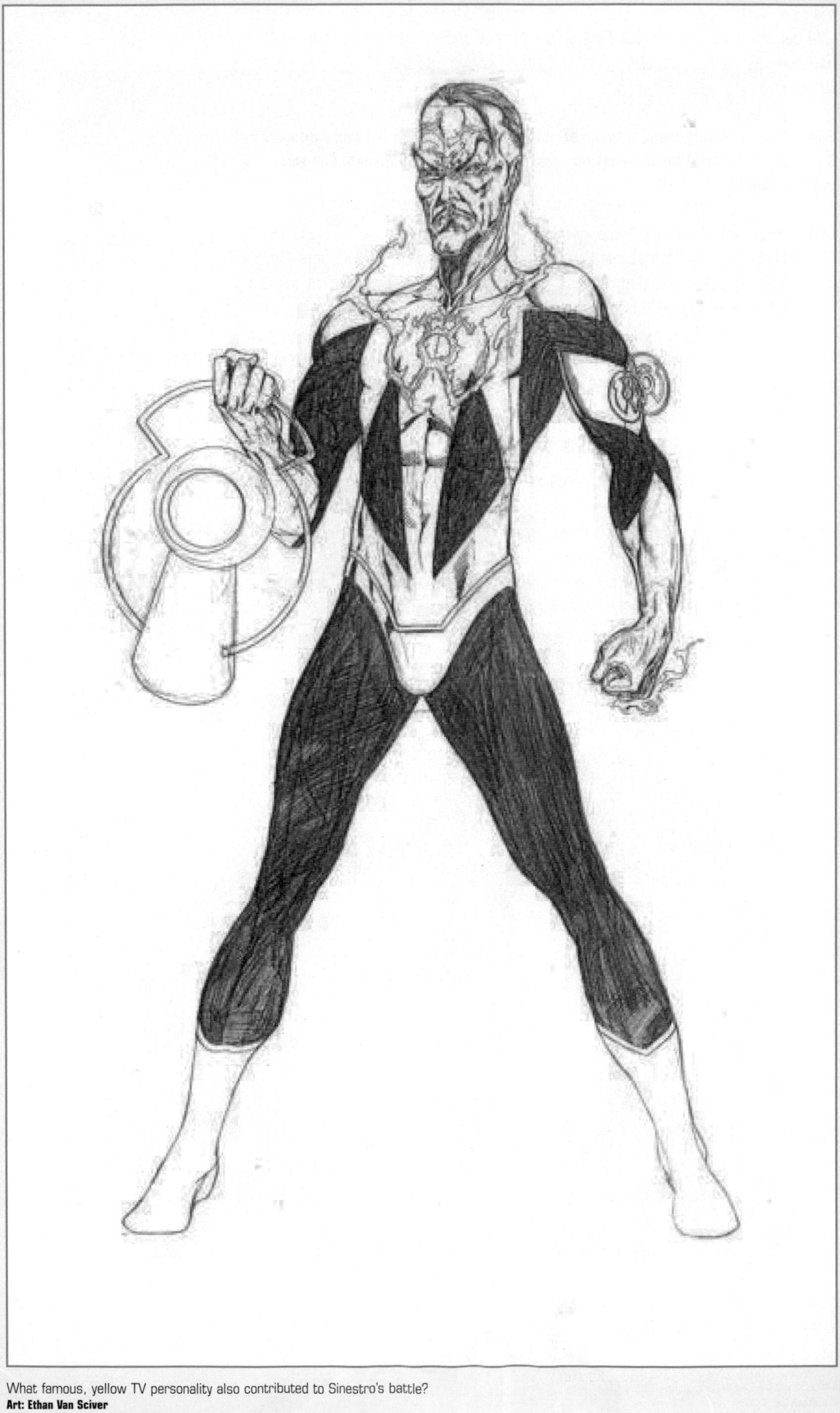

What famous, yellow TV personality also contributed to Sinestro's battle?
Art: Ethan Van Sciver

true beginning for him, so I thought the fight would mean something — have more emotional value — if we cared for Sodam and knew a little more about what made him tick since Superman-Prime had a fully fleshed-out character. So in other words, I thought we should know the good guy as well as the bad guy. And in regard to the fight locales, I approached it from a New Yorker's point of view. One of the things that drives me crazy in comics, movies, and TV shows is when they screw around with location continuity, like having someone appear in downtown Manhattan and then when they turn the corner they're suddenly on 96th Street or even in Brooklyn. And don't get me started about when they substitute Toronto for New York City. So being the crazy nut that I am, I imagined what the strength of the punches would be and plotted out trajectory points as to where they could realistically land that would be interesting as a set piece for the fight.

ADAM: Funny how that issue came about. GREEN LANTERN CORPS #18 was originally scheduled to be the epilogue, but things change and wars grow bigger and better. Geoff was on the phone with me and, he's like 54 pages isn't enough for #25. We need more room to give the Sodam Yat vs. Superman-Prime fight its due. The easy solution we came up with was to showcase the fight in GREEN LANTERN CORPS #18 and have #19 be the epilogue. Geoff, what were you going to do if we couldn't get #18 in as the fight?

GEOFF: Asked you for 80 pages! But honestly, I thought Pete did a tremendous job with Sodam Yat. That backstory, the issue itself, was really an amazing issue.

ADAM: I remember when Ivan sent in the pages 4-5 spread from GL #25 and freaking out. It was incredible. I started running up and down the hallway showing it to everyone. Ivan, how'd you fit so many characters on one page and still make the page so dynamic?

IVAN: Good question! It was a crazy spread to work on. First, I thought that the scene couldn't be a mess. You need to understand what's happening even without color, so I tried to do the scene in a logical way that the eye could follow. I put the spotlight on Prime and on the superheroes, but I did the battle like a "necklace" all around Anti-Monitor's neck, so that the fight could be seen without hiding him too much....it is always hard to explain it...OK, when I see a blank area in the spread I add more and more characters. It's easy...blank area?... more characters LOL!

Thanks for running up and down and showing it to everyone. I think you liked it.

GEOFF: I was blown away every time Ivan turned those pages in. I knew this was only getting bigger. He drew this massive spread of Green Lanterns attacking

One of the Blue Lanterns, a peek by Ethan Van Sciver of what is still to come in the Green Lantern saga as we head to the final chapter in the trilogy with Blackest Night.
Art: Ethan Van Sciver

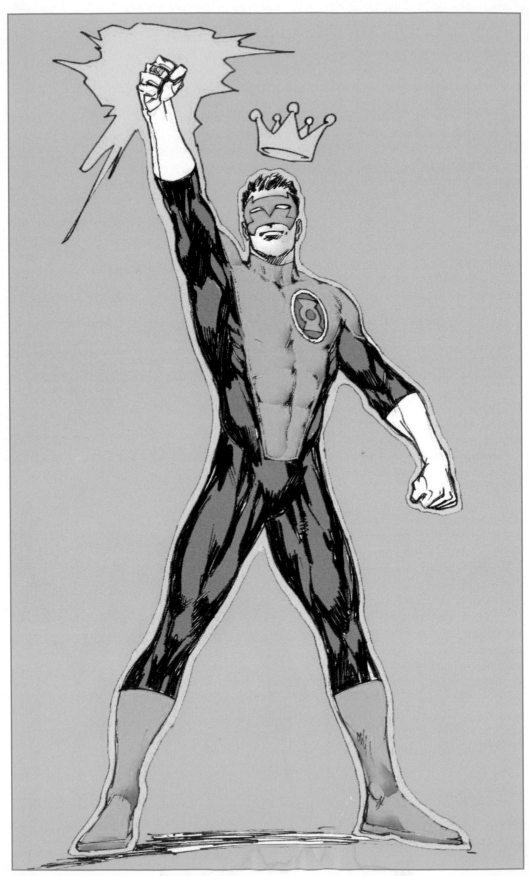

One of the consequences of the War is Kyle Rayner's return to being a Green Lantern with a costume design by Ivan Reis which Geoff Johns wanted to have the feel of his original GL uniform.
Art: Ivan Reis

Sinestro Corps members on Qward early on. Then he drew Superboy-Prime leading an army. Then Hannu leading the Corps. Then it got bigger and bigger until issue #25. Only Ivan could do it, and he knocked it out of the park and into space.

EDDIE: Looking back, what are your favorite moments? For me there are two. One was actually just reading the script to the Special. It was great seeing how Geoff had constructed the lore of the Green Lanterns into this second part of what will become an epic trilogy, that and the Star Wars references that just evoke amazing special effects in space, which all come to an explosive conclusion in #25. The other was seeing Dave and Pat mobilize the Corps into this amazing armada as he had Mogo and Ranx battling. Two planets fighting; you don't get bigger than that!

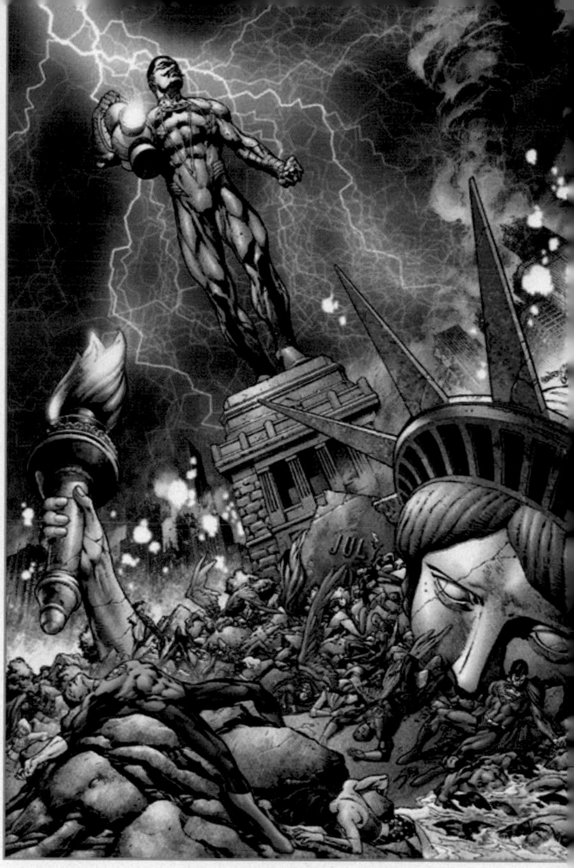
A more electrifying take on the cover to Green Lantern #24. It was deemed too busy with everything else going on.
Art: Ivan Reis/Moose Baumann

GEOFF: There are too many to list. Dave and Pat introducing Ranx on that insane splash page, Soranik Natu confronting Sinestro on Korugar, Coast City standing up for its hero, Hal and Kyle diving from unfinished building to unfinished building against Sinestro. There're so many moments. It all came together. It came together exactly as I'd hoped, and that's because all the people working on it are passionate and talented and part of this Green Lantern Corps of artists and writers. It's a story I'm extremely proud of and one I hope people read for years to come.

DAVE: Although Geoff and I had talked over the general gameplay, it was always a thrill to see how his part of the War was playing out, like a communiqué from another battle-front. And, as always, I loved what Pat brought to the table. His visualization of my scripts has always delighted me, and here he surpassed himself.

PETER: Honestly, the best part for me was simply talking to Geoff about it as it grew and grew, and has now turned into — without a doubt — the best epic story in the GL mythos to date (soon to be surpassed by Blackest Night, I'm

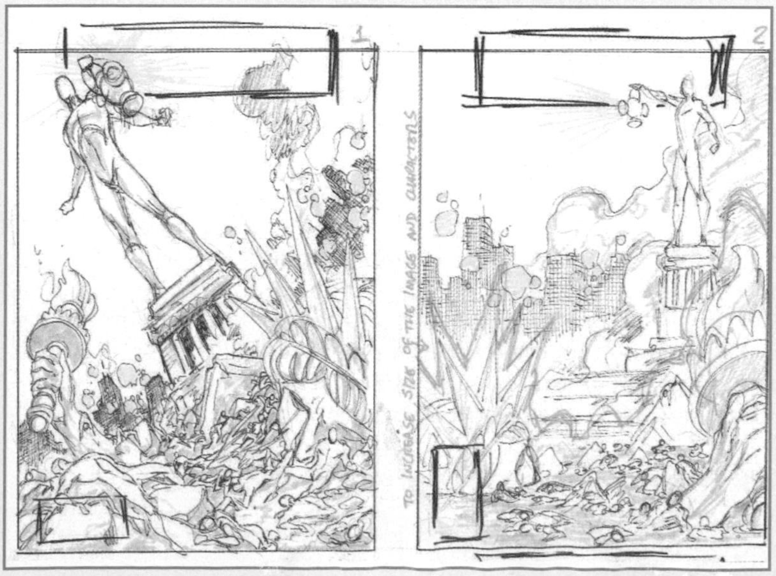
1
2
TO INCREASE SIZE OF THE IMAGE AND CHARACTERS
Making of a War cover: Here are Ivan's initial ideas for the cover of GREEN LANTERN #24.
Art: Ivan Reis

sure). I feel privileged to have been a part of it, and though I was excited to begin the writing phase of my career, it was incredibly tough to hand the editing reins over to Eddie Berganza. I really wanted to see it to the end. But at least I was lucky to participate in the final chapters from the writing end, which took the sting out. And the other best part was also seeing the amazing original art come into the office from Ethan, Ivan and Patrick. To watch them visualize Geoff's scripts for this story was a pure pleasure.

ETHAN: There are moments when you just get a buzz, "This whole thing is going to WORK." The center of the whole affair was Sinestro, and if we couldn't sell Sinestro as an icy cold fascist, I'm not sure it would have happened as easily. He needed to become one of DC's A-villains, and countless discussions with Geoff and Pete helped to find that path. Drawing him, in his new uniform, his new outlook, his new demeanor was overwhelming. It clicked, I knew people would like it, and I felt like something wonderful would come of this. I'm proud of this series. I'm proud of everyone who worked their brains out to make it something special. Everyone built on the work of everyone else, and it was a purely creative collaboration between people who understand and love these characters. The best part is, we're going to do it again.

IVAN: My favorite was when I got the first Sinestro Special's pages by Ethan with no colors...one of the pages was Kyle as Parallax, so I knew in that moment how big this epic would be, and another moment was when I got the fight between Prime and the new Ion by Pat. The pages were not inked...man, that fight was unbelievable. I remember, I talked with Joe Prado about those pages (Ethan and Pat's pages) for a month!

Finally, I read the last few pages of GL #25... and I hate Geoff for making me wait a whole year to find out what happens next. LOL

PAT: My favorite moments from the War started when I saw the first four colored pages of the Sinestro Special. Knowing that I was going to have a part in this war, I quite literally had goosebumps. It reminds me of the same nervous excitement I had the time my boss (at the local comic shop) handed me the keys to his Camaro. With a wink and a grin he told me to take her out and go run an errand for him. Ooh baby. My other moment really was when I read the last few pages of GL #25. The goosebumps returned. I thought, I have truly worked with the best people in the business. This is going to be great. Man oh man, I cannot wait to take this baby for a spin in '09.

ADAM: I remember getting a phone call at midnight one night from Geoff who was ecstatic, yelling "I'm done!" He had just finished writing issue #25. I read the entire issue right then and there, and now just as you wait for Blackest Night, so must I.

EDDIE: And the battle is won, but the War continues, right?

GEOFF: The Black Lanterns are around the corner. Along with the rest of the emotional spectrum. I'm just getting under way on the outlines and plans for Blackest Night. We've been through one war together, Eddie, in the trenches, tossing grenades, taking out snipers, struggling to win the battle. Ready for another?

EDDIE: Yes! I know readers will be. So get ready to be recruited...

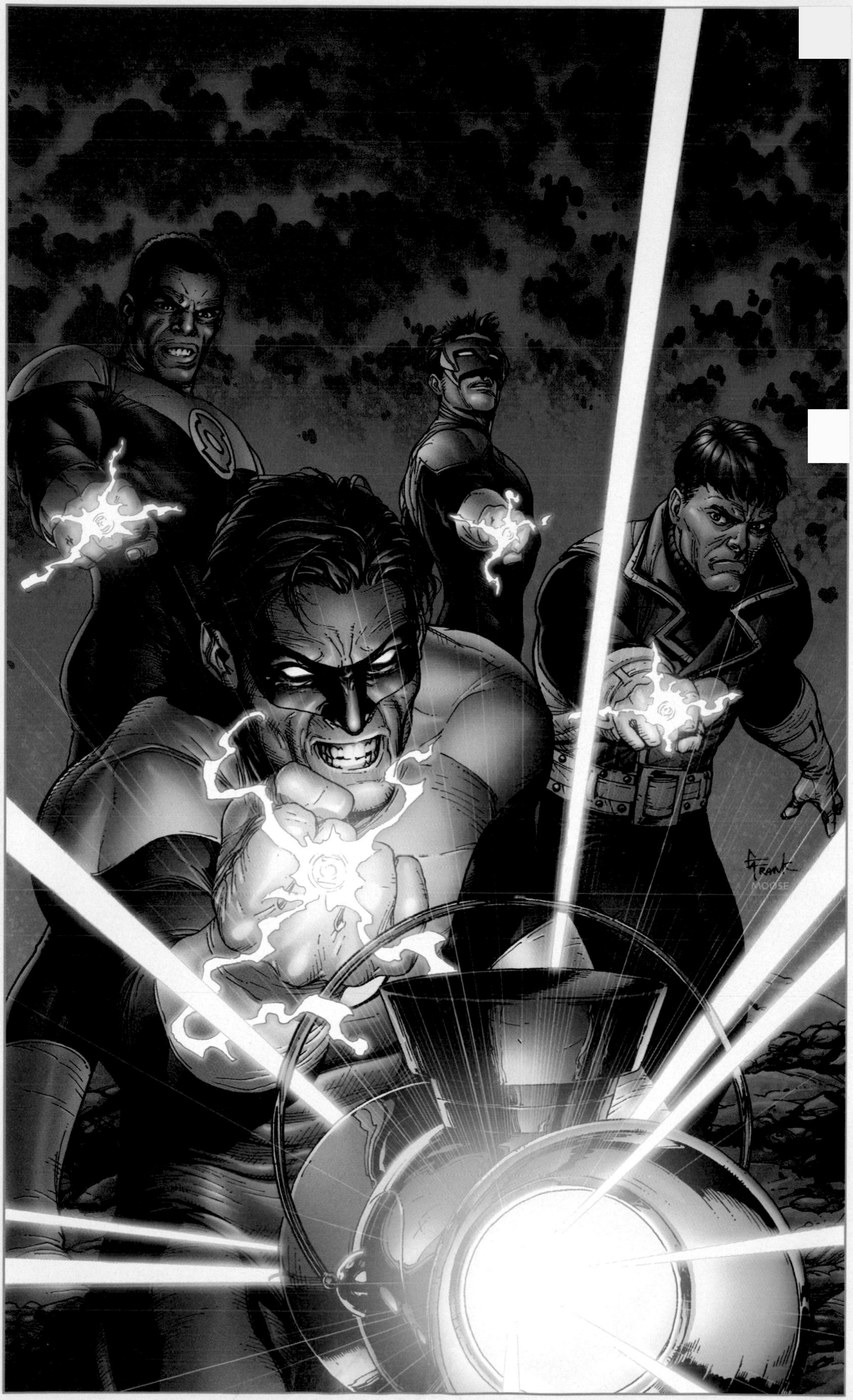
MOOSE

Green Lantern #25 alternate cover.
Art: Gary Frank/Moose Baumann

FROM THE WRITER OF
THE FLASH AND JSA

GEOFF JOHNS

"Consistently entertaining..."
– NEWSARAMA.COM

"Johns is the master of streamlining the GL mythos and distilling the cool essence of the character."
– BOOKLIST

"Define[s] DC's heroes for a new generation of readers."
– WIZARDUNIVERSE.COM

"Everything Geoff Johns has done with (Green Lantern) has been fantastic."
– SILVERBULLET.COM

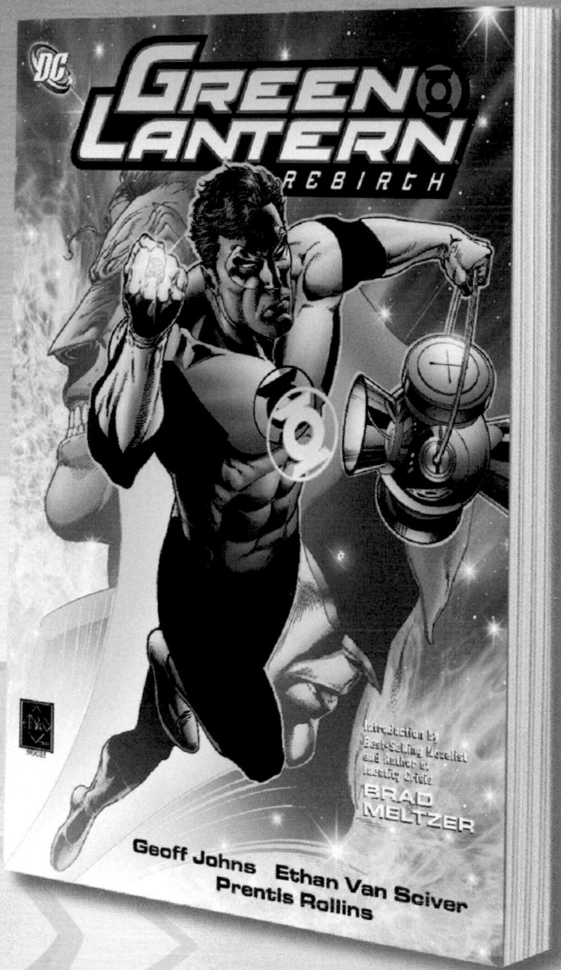
GREEN LANTERN
REBIRTH
BRAD MELTZER
Geoff Johns
Ethan Van Sciver
Prentis Rollins

GREEN LANTERN:
NO FEAR

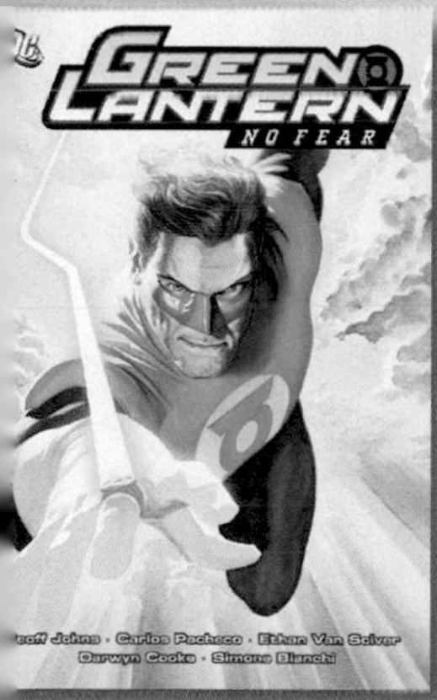
GREEN LANTERN
NO FEAR

with
CARLOS PACHECO & OTHERS

GREEN LANTERN:
REVENGE OF
THE GREEN LANTERNS

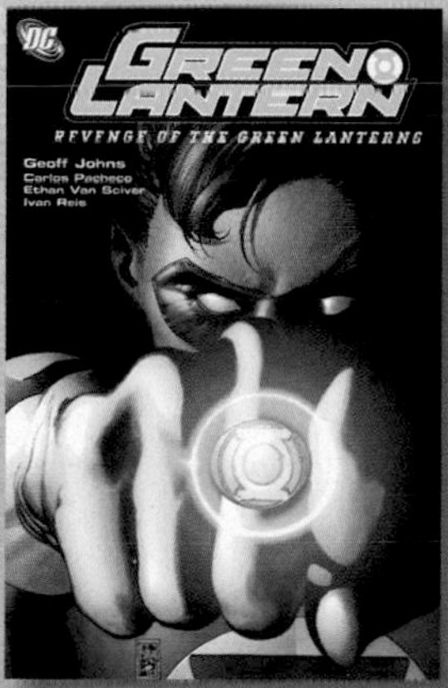
GREEN LANTERN
REVENGE OF THE GREEN LANTERNS
Geoff Johns
Carlos Pacheco
Ethan Van Sciver
Ivan Reis

with
CARLOS PACHECO
ETHAN VAN SCIVER
IVAN REIS

GREEN LANTERN:
WANTED –
HAL JORDAN

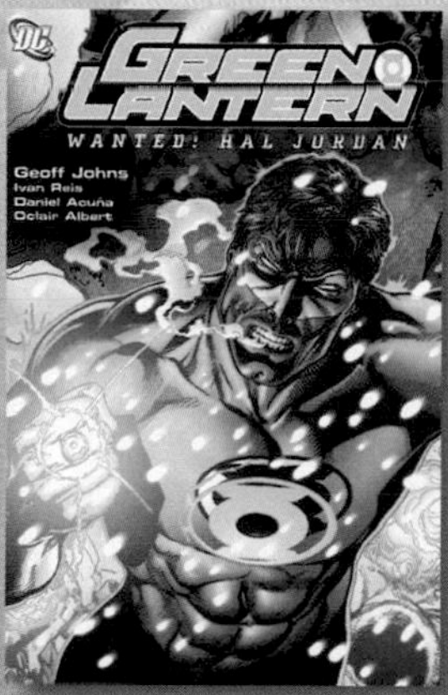
GREEN LANTERN
WANTED: HAL JORDAN
Geoff Johns
Ivan Reis
Daniel Acuña
Oclair Albert

with
IVAN REIS & OTHERS

GREEN LANTERN:
THE SINESTRO CORPS
WAR VOL. 1

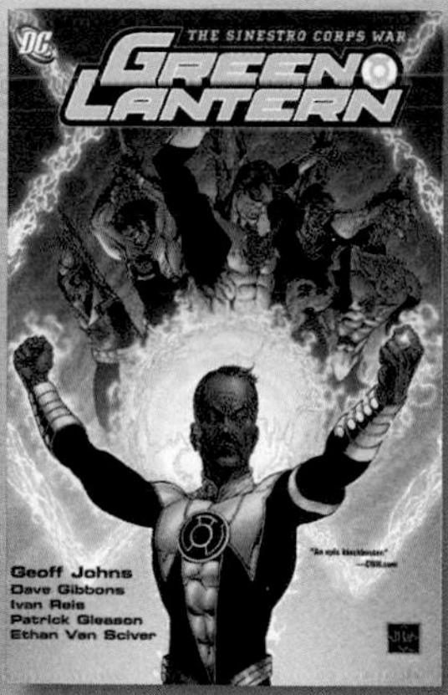
THE SINESTRO CORPS WAR
GREEN LANTERN
Geoff Johns
Dave Gibbons
Ivan Reis
Patrick Gleason
Ethan Van Sciver

with
IVAN REIS
ETHAN VAN SCIVER
& OTHERS

SEARCH THE GRAPHIC NOVELS SECTION OF
DCCOMICS.COM
FOR ART AND INFORMATION ON ALL OF OUR BOOKS!

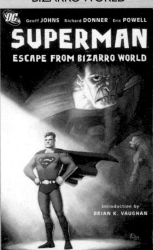